TAYLORED FOR JAZZ

Published in the United States by
Beckham Publications Group, Inc.

ISBN 0-931761-94-8
10 9 8 7 6 5 4 3 2 1

Library of Congress Cataloging-in-publication data: : 2007941651

TAYLORED FOR JAZZ

The Life and Music Of Billy Taylor

AN ORAL HISTORY

William F. Lee III, Ph.D., Mus.D.

THE Beckham
PUBLICATIONS GROUP, INC.
Silver Spring

CONTENTS

WHAT THEY SAY... i

OVERTURE xi

I.   HOW IT STARTED 1

II.   NEW YORK 12

III. 52nd STREET 33

IV.   THE BILLY TAYLOR TRIO 48

V.   BROADCASTING – THE JAZZMOBILE –
      THE DAVID FROST SHOW 66

VI.   DR. TAYLOR! – NATIONAL PUBLIC
      RADIO – MEDIA RECOGNITION, AWARDS 94

VII. CBS SUNDAY MORNING – AUTHOR –
      MORE MEDIA RECOGNITION, AWARDS 115

ALL PHOTOGRAPHS COURTESY OF THE LIBRARY
      OF CONGRESS AND DR. BILLY TAYLOR 149

VIII. EDUCATION – THE KENNEDY CENTER
      INTERNATIONAL ASSOCIATION FOR JAZZ
      EDUCATION 157

N O T E S 207

BILLY TAYLOR TRIO-QUARTET-QUINTET BASS
      PLAYERS AND DRUMMERS 210

THE MUSIC OF BILLY TAYLOR 211

DISCOGRAPHY 220

BIBLIOGRAPHY 240

INDEX 247

WHAT THEY SAY . . . . .

KIM TAYLOR THOMPSON (daughter): "We (my brother Duane and I) had wonderful childhoods. My father (BILLY) used to take us to see jazz events where we met big stars. We didn't realize our father's standing in jazz then."

RUDOLPH (RUDY) TAYLOR (brother): "He is a very inspirational big brother. We have always had a good relationship. He set a high standard for trying to make accomplishments. The only way I would have been in many of the places where he's played, e.g., the White House, State Department, Library of Congress, Supreme Court, etc., would have been by waiting tables."

JOYCE TAYLOR HYNES (half-sister): "BILLY was great to me when I was growing up. I was always "little sister". I remember going to the David Frost Show and meeting all the famous people."

MUSICIANS

LALO SCHIFRIN: "He was one of the reasons why I decided to embrace jazz with passion and conviction and one of the reasons why I came to this country. BILLY TAYLOR represents the essence of the whole history of jazz and I have no words to express my admiration and respect for his work as a performer and as an educator."

GEORGE SHEARING: "He is a great educator, brilliant mind, and a great player. I like his playing. He's probably the best person to do any form of lectures. He is a wonderful pianist."

HORACE SILVER: "I've always admired his mastery of the instrument and always liked his compositions. He's a fine pianist and also a fine composer. He's been an ambassador for our music throughout the world for many years."

LONNIE LISTON SMITH: "When I was in high school they always talked about BILLY TAYLOR. When I heard him he did something that set me back. He played "I Remember April" with just his left hand. That just threw me. I took it personally. I took stock of it and said 'wow'!! Out of all the jazz educators BILLY TAYLOR is the best because no one else has the background he has – experience all the way back to Art Tatum and anyone else you want to name."

DAVE BRUBECK: "BILLY TAYLOR is one of the greatest jazz pianists who has ever performed, and he continues to play in top form today. He has reached many thousands, bringing a variety of jazz artists to the attention of the general public. I respect his insistence that jazz be elevated; to be recognized as America's truest art form."

HILTON RUIZ: "I had his records first – I was one of his fans. He's kept his style up to date. He can play any style – he's one of the originals. He's got his chops together. I respect BILLY and I believe he's one of the greatest piano players that I've ever heard and a super nice person. He's stayed on top of it, he's got all the tools."

CHIP JACKSON – "I've been with BILLY since the fall of '93. BILLY is really a pianist. He's got total command of the instrument. He's got so much going on. He has a wonderful historic background. Of all the bandleaders I've ever played for he's, by far, the finest human being."

LARRY RIDLEY – "I've played with so many great piano players through the years, and been blessed with that in my experience, and BILLY'S right up there with the greatest of them and his music never suffers."

ED THIGPEN – "Oh, BILLY'S special. He's very special. I learned a great deal about a lot of things from BILLY. He was brought up in a time when virtue was a plus. My working with him was what got me interested in getting more involved in jazz education because he was at the forefront in a lot of this stuff."

WALTER PERKINS: "It was very enjoyable working with BILLY. We did an album called "Impromptu". BILLY is a beautiful pianist."

MUNDELL LOWE: "BILLY is one of the nicest people in this so-called business. I worked with BILLY in the 1950's and the 60's. We worked Birdland and some other places around New York City."

SHELLY BERG: "I always think of BILLY TAYLOR as a way of listening to the whole history of the piano. You are listening to a two-handed piano player who understands what's going on now but has lineage all the way back to Tatum. There are very few individuals who are so brilliantly extemporaneous as BILLY is, and it makes him a fabulous ambassador for jazz music."

JIMMY OWENS: " BILLY TAYLOR influenced a whole crop of younger musicians, who didn't ever know they were influenced by BILLY TAYLOR. I was always an activist and BILLY TAYLOR helped me in the kind of direction that was going to be important for jazz. Just being around him, I learned."

CLEM DEROSA: "He's spent a lot of time working in education. He was one of the few that saw the opportunities for young people in education. He's always had a young attitude. I've always admired him and I've always been glad that he's in our corner."

DICK HYMAN: "Although we've developed different specialties, we come from the same Art Tatum-to-bebop background, and I think I can always identify his playing. I very much admire BILLY for his playing, his career as a performer and educator, and because he stands up for what he believes."

DR. FRED TILLIS: "He is an administrator, a world-class pianist, one of the greats. He is an effective administrator. He's done broadcasting, everything. I think he's a major person; a real ambassador for the music."

DAVE CAVANAUGH: "BILLY TAYLOR is truly a man who knows jazz inside out. He is not only one of the most melodic of the top jazz pianists, but is also a musician whose flowing style fits in with almost any school of jazz."

JOANNE BRACKEEN: "BILLY TAYLOR is incredible, amazing! He is the essence of the kind of swing that we had in the 20's, 30's, and 40's that hardly anybody carries through today, as well as maintaining modern, too. I don't know how old he is but he acts likes he's 17 or 18 all the time with all that energy and inspiration. He is absolutely amazing!"

WARREN CHIASSON: "He's really helped a lot of people and has always had a positive viewpoint. I marvel at his technique. He covers the whole piano and that makes a big impression on me. He's been a model for us where the music business is so brutal."

RAMSEY LEWIS: "I've always admired him and he was one of the pianists whose records I bought early on. His technique, his sense of melodic lines and harmony, and his piano tone – he has one of those good piano tones."

DAVID BAILEY: "BILLY TAYLOR has probably been the most influential man, in terms of the recognition of jazz as America's classical music – that is his mantra, Jazz-America's Classical Music. I think he has made a believer out of most of the people who are in the sanity of their minds. He's a giant. He's been a giant and will always be a giant. He's probably the most respected jazz musician in the world! My hat's off to him."

EARL MAY: "When I go back and look at my musical life I would say that playing with BILLY was the happiest time for me. BILLY has accomplished so many things in his life it's astounding; when they introduce him and start rattling off his credits it's about twenty minutes before they are finished. He's my main man!!"

RAY MOSCA: "BILLY was great! We had a good time together. I had a wonderful time. We had a nice trio. We used to be able to play for a whole week without repeating a tune."

WAYNE ANDRE: "BILLY was one of the most pleasant, respecting the musicians, conductors whose baton I have performed under. BILLY had a good sense of humor and always had a smile. He was a great integrationist of musicians."

GRADY TATE: "If you're around him often enough as I was and that just begins to rub off on you, the niceness and the gentility. It's just something you have to see. I can't describe it, adequately."

BOBBY THOMAS: "When we played ballads, the voicing he would use would just be superb. He has that way with chords. And when it came to the up tempo things, he would dazzle you so it was always enjoyable playing with him."

JON FADDIS: "BILLY'S very, very knowledgeable and intelligent when it comes to jazz and politics and education because he's been doing that for years. I don't know of a better spokesperson for jazz. He's right in there and knows what he's talking about."

JANE IRA BLOOM: "He's just a completely open and embracing musician. I don't even think about age with BILLY, he's young in mind and heart, that's how I look at him. It's his complete sincerity and it's a very rare and wonderful thing in the jazz world."

DAVID BAKER: "BILLY is one of the giants. He is so unselfish in sharing all the things that he does. He's amazing. I think BILLY is one of the great piano players."

JIMMY COBB: "BILLY is a very brilliant man, he's good for music and he's done a whole lot for music. He's made a very large contribution. He's explained the music to a lot of people."

WINARD HARPER: "BILLY is a walking history of jazz – he's very important in that way, to the music and to all of us. He's been around and played with a lot of the cats – he passes that history on."

EDDIE BERT: "He's been an orchestra leader, he's been a pianist, he's been an educator, he has been a speaker on the television interviewing people, etc. so he's in a lot of bags. He's good for jazz!"

JOHN DUFFY: "I see BILLY as one of the outstanding leaders of his generation – the most articulate in terms of public presence in government in Washington, D.C. but also as a person whose artistry and ideas and technique are so commanding that he can just soar with music."

PERCY BRICE "Playing with BILLY was very enjoyable. I think BILLY'S a big-time player. He treated everybody well – he's that kind of a guy."

AARON BELL: "Playing with BILLY was very enjoyable; he's a perfect gentleman. BILLY is an excellent pianist. There were just three guys in my career who were articulate, spoke well, dressed well and conducted themselves well: BILLY TAYLOR, Teddy Wilson and Andy Kirk."

KETER BETTS: "What can you say about a man who has done as much for jazz as BILLY? There are people who come into this world and they just play and they make the people happy that they play for. BILLY is on another step and introduced people who really didn't know much about jazz – like the whole series at the Kennedy Center – and helping people to become knowledgeable about jazz."

JIMMY HEATH: "BILLY'S music is always impeccable. He is a consummate professional. Every time he comes to play. It's always flawless. He's amazing in his consistency. He is an overall nice guy. He's one of the nicest guys you could meet."

CLARK TERRY: "There's a whole slue of things BILLY has done. It's a good part of the American repertoire. He's made a couple of major contributions and I'm sure he's going to do some more. He's my man!!"

MICHAEL ABENE: "He's always got a good musical situation going. When you listen to him you can always tell his sound. He's got a kind of a really warm sound, no matter what tempo it is he always has this nice sound, not a jarring sound, it just flows."

LOREN SCHOENBERG: "BILLY and his wife, Teddi, are the most wonderful neighbors you could have, outside the fact that he's a world famous jazz person. He's just a great human being."

NANCY WILSON: "They don't come any nicer than BILLY. There's not a finer gentleman in the business. Talent, wonderful teacher, and a gentleman – put it all together and it spells one fantastic man. He's just a delight."

FRANK WESS: "BILLY'S a beautiful person. He's done a whole lot for a lot of people and for the music. He's been playing all this time. He was playing in 1935 and he wasn't playing like a kid then! He was before bebop – we both were."

NNENNA FREELON: "He's an excellent teacher, but he's a human being. He's very unusual. He's warm, always has time for you. He can make a phone call or make a suggestion and things can happen in your career that couldn't happen otherwise; he's done that for me time and time again."

OTHER PROFESSIONALS

DAN MORGENSTERN (Head, Jazz Studies, Rutgers University): "BILLY is a marvelous player – he was great when I first heard him and he's even greater now! He's an extraordinary person, somebody who has done so many things for jazz and continues to do that."

GEORGE WEIN (Producer, Impresario) "BILLY has made a contribution to Jazz and American music in the way that John Lewis and Duke Ellington had. They have shown that the playing of jazz is an art form that need not be distorted by drugs and the difficult lifestyle available to jazz musicians."

HILDE LIMONDJIAN (General Manager, Concerts and Lectures, Metropolitan Museum of Art, NY): "BILLY TAYLOR is a person of immense musical talent, a giant in jazz, but blessed with the ability to translate this to an audience not only through music alone, but also through his thoughts and verbal communication."

ROBIN BELL STEVENS (Jazzmobile): "I adore him. I admire him. I respect him. He grew up in a very difficult time in terms of trying to make your mark in the world and in order to make a living just playing and writing your music."

PHIL SCHAAP (Broadcaster, Author): "BILLY has contributed a way of understanding quality in jazz, a whole system, from performance to classroom. He is both congenial and thorough in terms of broadcasting and, as a first generation jazzer, there's nobody he didn't know."

REVEREND DALE LIND (Minister): "I'm not only fond of him personally, but I have the greatest respect for him as a musician, he keeps growing. He is a tower of energy. I'd say I have as much or more respect for BILLY as anybody I've ever met."

NAT HENTOFF (Writer, Jazz Critic): " As a musician, as a leader of groups, and an extraordinary educator through the years, I think he's probably done more than any single person, who knows, you can't quantify these things, but I would expect hundreds of thousands of people may have been introduced, or at least accelerated in their interest in the music through just hearing him introduce people on television, in live performances, etc."

COBI NARITA (Director, Universal Jazz Coalition): "I think he is absolutely one of the main people who is perpetuating this music called jazz. I wish he would get more recognition. I know he's received a lot of honors but I think he deserves more. I love him dearly."

PHOEBE JACOBS (Executive VP, Louis Armstrong Educational Foundation, Inc.): "BILLY TAYLOR is wonderful; a real credit to American music. He is an American icon. He was one of the first people to bring jazz an image of dignity and professionalism and a lot of style, a lot of style; and he was very popular."

CHARLES OSGOOD (CBS-TV Sunday Morning Host): "BILLY'S the nicest, sweetest man. I've been to several BILLY TAYLOR tributes and everybody says the same thing: that he's not just an expert in this, he's like a playing-manager. He knows what to do and also knows everybody. In dealing with him you would not ever want to deal with a nicer man."

OSSIE DAVIS (Actor): "Ssh . . . here he comes now . . . hold on to my hand, and also to your ears, they'll never believe what they're about to hear!"

BILL MCFARLIN (Executive Director, IAJE): "BILLY TAYLOR is the ultimate jazz and renaissance man! As an artist (first and foremost), producer, broadcaster, composer, conductor, and educator, BILLY is a passionate advocate for jazz on all fronts. From the living rooms of America to the White House, BILLY has become the national spokesperson for jazz and continues to be a passionate advocate for its preservation and promotion."

BRUCE LUNDVALL (President, Blue Note Records): "He's wonderful. He's extraordinary. He's one of the nicest, friendliest men and lives his life for this music and dedicates his life to it. He's just one of those guys we're all fortunate to have among us as a musician and as a spokesman for the music."

HERB WONG (Educator, Producer, Past Pres. IAJE): "BILLY is very generous as a player – ego less, in the sense of his playing. He's very generous in sharing space and time for improvised solos – very deep humanism in him. He is always available to lend you a hand or give you an idea or tell you about somebody else, never forcing anything, just a beautiful way of sharing."

TIM OWENS (Executive Producer, NPR Jazz): "He was really instrumental and probably the most instrumental person in giving me an historical point of view. He really opened my ears and opened my head up to the history, what better teacher? He's warm, he's friendly, he's knowledgeable, he's authoritative, he's enthused; you put together all these ingredients and that really makes him absolutely special."

MARQUITA POOL ECKERT (Senior Producer, CBS Sunday Morning): "BILLY knows everyone in the music business, certainly in jazz. If you think you're coming up with something new, forget it. He already knows almost what you're going to say."

DEREK GORDON (Vice President for Education, Kennedy Center): "He is a very generous gentleman and, as I have met other artists, artists I meet are so respectful of BILLY and so grateful for something that BILLY has done for them at one point or another. He continues to be that way and to have that impact."

CHRIS ANDERSON (Sound Reinforcement Technician): "I've always thought he's a great guy. He's very generous. He's always interested in what's going on. Every time I see him he says: "How's your family – how's your mom?" He's always been just as much a person as an artist."

JIM ANDERSON (Recording Engineer): "I'm so happy that I know BILLY. If I hadn't gotten to know him I know I would have certainly listened to his music. He's a lovely man; a true gentleman of jazz."

KENNY WASHINGTON (Broadcaster-Drummer): "He was so hip on the radio, not one of those slick talkers but you could tell he definitely knew about the music. He had a very friendly type voice and later on, as I got to know him, I realized that his voice is actually like he really is, a very together person."

ALAN BERGMAN (Attorney): "BILLY is a jewel. He's made a great contribution to music in terms of having stayed with the trio format – he's discovered so many great players – he's a great composer – he's also made a contribution to race relations in America."

IRA SABIN (Jazz Times Founder): "I've known Billy for quite a number of years and I've always been amazed at the fact that he can do so many things at one time and still do them all well. One time I asked him how he did it and he said: 'Well, you do something, you give it all you've got, then you finish it and go on to the next thing.'"

DAVID FROST (Commentator, TV Personality): "The very swinging, very crucial ingredient of the David Frost Show was the BILLY TAYLOR ORCHESTRA. BILLY, known to jazz buffs for years through his fantastic piano playing with his trio got a much wider audience with his performances on the show. Every guest I had on the show raved about BILLY TAYLOR and his Orchestra."

FRAN RICHARD (Vice President, ASCAP): "I think of BILLY as a performer, as an improviser, as an artist, as a composer, as an educator, in all the areas, and certainly also as a host and recognizable spokesperson for jazz, an advocate; as people in the last few years have gotten to know him on CBS Sunday Morning and other places, he has, I think, an enormous place in American Music."

JOHNNY GARRY (Manager): "I wish there were more BILLYS! He's a great, clean, piano player. BILLY is in the top ten of all jazz players in America. Tatum, Garner, Powell, Peterson; BILLY'S right there in the top ten. Not only that. BILLY did so much for the music."

MEDIA

KEN DRYDEN (ALL MUSIC GUIDE): "Jazz has been very fortunate to have BILLY TAYLOR in its midst for so long; this very talented composer and educator, who has shared his love of jazz in so many ways for so many decades."

OWEN MCNALLY (HARTFORD COURANT): "BILLY TAYLOR is indeed, the jazz world's urban griot, bearer of the good news alive and well in the music."

SCOTT YANOW (LA JAZZ WEEKLY): "BILLY TAYLOR is still very much in his musical prime. He swings hard with his trio and shows that even after all of the years, he is still a modern jazz master."

JAZZTIMES MAGAZINE: "I'll be damned if TAYLOR isn't hiding a third hand inside one of his shirt sleeves."

MARK HOLSTON (JAZZIZ): "Technique is uncommonly clean, his playing relaxed and assured, his improvisations inventive and logical, and a sense of the blues is present. The pianist and his trio have created a time capsule that documents BILLY TAYLOR'S stature as a musician of uncommon taste and stylistic depth."

PHILIP BOOTH (ST. PETERSBURG TIMES): "If jazz were a religion, BILLY TAYLOR might be thought of as its greatest and most effective living preacher, a tireless, listener-friendly evangelist for the cause."

JACK FRANCIS (SESAC MUSIC): "BILLY TAYLOR is truly one of the present-day 'Prophets of Jazz'."

CHRISTIAN RENNINGER (RADIO FREE JAZZ): "The drive, the desire, the interest, the spirit and the excitement of this incredible man who, at this stage of a remarkable career, just may be the greatest friend jazz has."

PETER BAILEY (BLACK STARS): "An indefatigable composer-pianist – one of the most active, determined and persistent fighters for jazz."

CANDACE WOMBLE (ENCORE): "A man dedicated to his music and his community."

MARK RIBOWSKY (SEPIA): "BILLY TAYLOR – "The force who keeps jazz alive!!"

LISA GREIM (GREELEY TRIBUNE): "Jazz pianist BILLY TAYLOR hasn't stopped learning and doesn't plan to. He's a teacher, composer, arranger, conductor, author and activist on behalf of jazz."

JIM ROBERTS (DOWN BEAT): "BILLY TAYLOR is a great jazz musician. His style is strong and deeply rooted, but even the most powerful passages are marked by the unmistakable elegance of the TAYLOR touch."

JOHN MCDONOUGH (DOWN BEAT): "BILLY TAYLOR – pianist, educator, composer, and probably the most articulate performer/spokesperson jazz has ever had."

DAN MORGENSTERN (DOWN BEAT): "BILLY TAYLOR – a man with impeccable jazz credentials."

JOE BLUM (JAZZ TIMES): "I'm not going to say that BILLY TAYLOR is solely responsible for the vast changes that have occurred in academia over the past two decades, but he certainly has had an awful lot to do with them."

SCOTT GUTTERMAN (ESSENCE): "BILLY TAYLOR is America's unofficial 'Ambassador of Jazz,' playing and speaking on behalf of the music in schools and concert halls from the Soviet Union to South America."

TED DYER (SATELLIT ORBIT): "There is little in the unassuming manner of DR. BILLY TAYLOR to suggest that he is the premier spokesman for jazz today."

LEONARD FEATHER (LOS ANGELES TIMES): "It is doubtful that any individual now active has had a greater impact on the appreciation of jazz than the genial protean pianist and educator BILLY TAYLOR."

OWEN CORDLE (DOWN BEAT): "The good doctor does his neatly swinging trio thing exactly as usual here. The trim, tastefully decorated lines, the smooth reharmonizations, and the ability to swing with a sense of decorum are part of it (DR. T, GRP GRD-9692)."

KEN FRANCKLING (JAZZ TIMES): "It is clear that the youthful TAYLOR, in spite of his 72 years, has not slowed down in his multi-pronged role as a jazz ambassador – through playing, writing, teaching and broadcasting."

JOE MIDDLETON (GALLERY OF SOUND GAZETTE): "To me, DR. BILLY TAYLOR is a genius. The simplicity with which he explains jazz to the audience is unique. Forget book learning, this man was there when the history was being written."

JEFF LEVENSON (ARTISTS & MUSIC-BILLBOARD): "He is the most honored jazz man in academic history or the most honored academic in jazz history."

LAWRENCE J. WILBURN, KENNEDY CENTER PRESIDENT (AMERICAN WEEKLY): "His fame as a jazz educator has grown out of his prodigious knowledge."

JONATHAN LESSER (DAILY OPTIONS – THE VAIL TRAIL): "When the doctor is in, you get much more than wonderful jazz performed by one of the world's top trios: you get a jazz education from a man who knows best."

STEPHEN HOLDEN (THE NEW YORK TIMES): "A musical extrovert who is naturally and fluently melodic, he writes music that is bright, blunt and friendly and that rarely pauses to reflect. Mr. TAYLOR displayed a vivacious stage personality that matched his music."

BOB BERNOTAS (JAZZ PLAYER): "TAYLOR is one of jazz's most visible and eloquent advocates, a tireless jazz propagandist with a single, overriding goal: to develop and expand the audience for this great music."

BRET PRIMACK (JAZZ TIMES): "BILLY TAYLOR has touched the lives of many during his half century plus in jazz as pianist, composer, author, activist, teacher, lecturer and actor, as well as radio and television personality."

OVERTURE

Dr. BILLY TAYLOR is an anomaly. He possesses the scholarly, well-mannered, articulate traits of a university professor and the practical knowledge and humanity of a man who has moved through life with the wealthy and the destitute spreading the word of America's classical music, jazz. He is not a jazz piano player. He is a jazz pianist, a title that can only be associated with players of the caliber of Art Tatum, Oscar Peterson, and very few others. Born the son of a dentist in North Carolina, TAYLOR is a formally educated artist who graduated from Virginia State University at the beginning of World War II, moved to New York and was privileged to have moved into the ranks at the forefront of the bebop revolution. He worked with the finest musicians at the time including Ben Webster, Stuff Smith, Dizzy Gillespie, Eddie South, Slam Stewart, Billie Holiday, among others. His career has taken him to radio, television, dozens of universities and colleges and to the artistic advisor and spokesman on jazz for the JOHN F. KENNEDY CENTER FOR THE PERFORMING ARTS IN Washington, D.C. BILLY has performed worldwide for millions of jazz lovers. He played at state dinners for Presidents Nixon, Ford and Clinton and before royalty in many countries. Thousands of jazz musicians and teachers have heard him perform throughout the world and as he has performed and introduced the annual awardees of the National Endowment for the Arts at the annual conferences of the International Association for Jazz Education. Millions have seen him on the CBS SUNDAY MORNING television program introducing music guests and commenting on their talents. His excellent book, JAZZ PIANO, is the bible for students and professionals in that field.

A cursory look at his chronology gives you an insight into how he arrived.

1921 – July 24. Born in Greenville, North Carolina to a musical family. His father was a dentist who sang, played piano, various brass instruments, and was a choir director

1926 – Moved to Washington, D.C. and entered Lucretia B. Mott elementary school

1928 - Studied saxophone, guitar and drums; began piano lessons

1932 – Entered Shaw Junior High school – uncle played recordings of FATS WALLER and ART TATUM

1934 - Earned $1 playing first gig at age 13 – Billy attended Dunbar High School – studied classical piano with Elmira Streets and Henry Grant

1938 – Graduated from high school – enrolled in Virginia State University – studied piano with Professor Undine Moore who also served as his advisor

1942 – Received the Bachelor of Science degree from Virginia State University

1943 – Moved to New York City – studied piano with Richard McClanahan

1944 – Played with Ben Webster at the Three Deuces – appeared in the Broadway Musical "Seven Lively Arts" – played with Billie Holiday, Stuff Smith, Eddie South, Dizzy Gillespie and Foots Thomas

1946 – Played with Machito, Slam Stewart at the Three Deuces – married Teddi Castion in New York City – toured Europe with the Don Redman Band

1947 – Freelanced in Paris, France

1948 – Played in a duo with organist Bob Wyatt

1949 – Formed own quartet; which Artie Shaw fronted

1950 – Wrote articles for Down Beat magazine, Saturday Review, Esquire and others

1951 – Continued as house pianist at Birdland working with Charlie Parker, Dizzy Gillespie, Georgie Auld, Roy Eldridge, Slim Gaillard, Terry Gibbs, Gerry Mulligan, Howard McGhee, Lee Konitz, Oscar Pettiford, Kai Winding, and others

1952 – Led own trio which included Earl May, bass and Charlie Smith, drums

1953 – Won the New Star Award from Down Beat magazine

1955 – Began own music publishing company, Duane Music, Inc.

1958 – Began "disc jockey" career on WLIB in New York City – was Music Director for the NBC TV Series "The Subject Is Jazz"

1961 – Began long tenure as pianist at the Hickory House in New York City

1962 – As "disc jockey", switched to station WNEW – began doing concerts in schools

1964 – Returned to station WLIB – initiated workshop series for George Wein at the Newport Jazz Festival and Hunter College – appointed to the advisory board on Jazz for Lincoln Center in New York City – appointed to an officers position with the National Academy of Arts and Sciences (NARAS)

1965 – Co-founder of the Jazzmobile in Harlem – lectured at Yale and the Music Educators National Conference (MENC)

1966 – Hosted Jazz TV show on channel 47 in New York City

1969 – Began four-year tenure as Music Director for the David Frost Television Show – awarded an honorary doctorate from Fairfield University

1970 – Co-Founder and Officer of Black Communications Corporation that purchased radio station WGOK in Savannah, Georgia – awarded an honorary doctorate from Virginia State University

1972 – Appointed to a six-year term to the National Council On The Arts by President Richard Nixon

1973 – Formed new trio with Larry Ridley, bass and Bobby Thomas, drums – founded BILLY TAYLOR Productions

1974 – Led band for the New York Repertory Company – played at the White House State Dinner for President Nixon

1975 – Received the doctoral (DME) degree from the University of Massachusetts; the doctoral dissertation was "The History And Development Of Jazz Piano: A New Perspective For Educators" – replaced Harold Arlen on the ASCAP (American Society of Composers, Authors, and Publishers) Board Of Directors – began a lecture series at Howard University – played at the White House State Dinner for President Gerald Ford

1977 – Began directing the Jazz Alive program for National Public Radio

1981 – Received the honorary degree, Doctor of Music, from the Berklee College of Music in Boston

1982 – TAYLOR'S book, "Jazz Piano" (from his 1975 doctoral dissertation), was published by Wm C. Brown Co. BILLY TAYLOR was named art correspondent for the television program "CBS Sunday Morning"

1986 – Received the honorary degree, Doctor of Fine Arts, from the University of Massachusetts

1987 – Received the honorary degree, Doctor of Music, from St. John's University, New York

1988 – Named an Arts American Jazz Master by the National Endowment For The Arts. Received the honorary degree, Doctor of Humane Letters, from Carleton College, Minnesota

1989 – Received an honorary doctorate from Clark College

1990 – Received the honorary degree, Doctor of Arts, from Long Island University, New York

1991 – Received the Tiffany Award from the International Society of Performing Arts Administrators (ISPAA) and the Award of Merit from the Association of Arts Presenters (APAP). Received the honorary Doctor of Music Degree from the State University College of New York at Fredonia

1992 – Began to serve annually as Master of Ceremonies for the Jazz Masters awards by the National Endowment For The Arts at the annual IAJE conference. President George Bush presented Dr. Taylor with the National Medal of Arts, the nation's highest award for accomplishment in the arts. Received the honorary degree, Doctor of Humane Letters, from the University of North Florida, Jacksonville

1993 – Named Artistic Advisor and Spokesman on Jazz for the John F. Kennedy Center For The Performing Arts in Washington, D.C. Received the honorary degree, Doctor of Music, from Temple University, Philadelphia

1994 – Received the honorary Doctor of Musical Arts Degree from the University of Illinois. Received the George Peabody Award from Johns Hopkins University. Received the honorary degree of Doctor of Fine Arts from Rutgers University, New Jersey

1995 – The Kennedy Center commissioned BILLY TAYLOR to compose a work for jazz and symphony orchestra. The work, "Theme and Variations for Jazz Trio and Symphony Orchestra" premiered at the Kennedy Center on April 23, 1995 with the BILLY TAYLOR TRIO and the National Symphony Orchestra, conducted by Leonard Slatkin

1997 – Florida Memorial College in Miami, Florida awarded BILLY with an honorary doctorate

1998 – Two distinguished institutions, The University of Florida and The University of Delaware awarded honorary doctorates to BILLY

2000 – Honorary doctorates were awarded to BILLY from Bard College and The Pennsylvania State University

2001 – Received an honorary doctorate from The University of North Carolina

2003 - Received honorary doctorates from the University of Michigan at Flint and George Washington University

***

BILLY TAYLOR grew up musically at a time when the depression was waning in the US. Many jazz pianists had to play solo at rent parties or sporting houses in order to survive. This solo playing, sans bass and/or drums, forced the keyboardists to create rhythm with their left hands, resulting in stride playing. This, of course, preceded early bebop pianists who grew up with the left hand "claw" style of playing. BILLY experienced both styles and, as a result, developed a much more functional left hand technique than many of his contemporaries. One only needs to hear his left-hand-only version of "Body and Soul" to appreciate this competency. Ergo the complete jazz pianist.

As an international ambassador for jazz, Dr. TAYLOR performed during the Third International Music Festival in Leningrad and visited the Soviet Union as a member of the International Commission of Distinguished American composers and Educators formed by the American Council of Learned Societies and the Union of Composers of the USSR. At the music conservatories of Shanghai and Beijing, China, he was a guest of the Chinese Cultural Commission as a lecturer and performer. In addition, he opened the International Arts Festival in Hungary, toured seven Middle Eastern countries and was the artistic consultant to the American delegation to UNESCO in Mexico. Taylor's trio represented the U.S. at the international gala in Hungary for the thirty-three signatory countries of the Helsinki Agreement. As on-air correspondent for CBS-TV's "Sunday Morning" where he recently celebrated his 20th anniversary with the show, Dr. TAYLOR has profiled such jazz artists as Ella Fitzgerald, Quincy Jones, Sarah Vaughan and Peggy Lee. On BRAVO TV, Dr. TAYLOR hosted the series "Jazz Counterpoint." And his radio series "Taylor Made Jazz" on National Public Radio was winner of the Peabody Award.

Dr. TAYLOR was the recipient of two Peabody awards, a Tiffany Award, an Association of Arts Presenters Award of Merit, an Emmy, twenty-three honorary doctoral degrees and the National Endowment for the Arts Masters Fellowship Award. He was the recipient of the first Certificate of Recognition given by the U.S. Congressional Arts Caucus.

Dr. TAYLOR was a Presidential appointee to the National Council on the Arts (one of only three jazz musicians to be so honored) and has been a guest artist at the White House on five occasions. He acts as consultant and advisor to music schools, civic and cultural groups and serves as mentor to jazz organizations across the United States.

He has been artist-in-residence at the University of Massachusetts (where he holds the prestigious Wilmer D. Barrett Chair), the University of California at Berkeley, Notre Dame, and Vassar, and has given an annual series of sold-out lectures at the Detroit Montreaux Jazz Festival and is Jazz Consultant of the Tampa Bay Performing Arts Center as well as serving on numerous boards and commissions. His experience as a performer and an educator has inspired him to create a number of innovative programs that strengthen the bonds of both students and teachers in the music that they share.

BILLY'S passion for jazz has never diminished during his more than six decades of productive participation. His role as performer/teacher will continue to expand as he discovers more and more ways to bring America's classical music to the fore.

William F. Lee III, Ph.D., Mus.D.
2007, New Smyrna Beach, Florida

THANK YOU!!!

My gratitude to those who were so helpful in providing materials, granting interviews, and assisting in seeing this biography to reality.

Michael Abene, Chris Anderson, Jim Anderson, Wayne Andre, David Bailey, David Baker, Aaron Bell, Shelley Berg, Alan Bergman, Eddie Bert, Keter Betts, Jane Ira Bloom. Joanne Brackeen, Lynda Bramble, Percy Brice, Dave Brubeck, Dave Cavanaugh, Warren Chiasson, Jimmy Cobb, Ossie Davis, Clem DeRosa, John Duffy, Marquita Pool Eckert, Jon Faddis, Nnenna Freelon, David Frost, Derek Gordon, Winard Harper, Jimmy Heath, Nat Hentoff, Dick Hyman, Joyce Taylor Hynes, Chip Jackson, Phoebe Jacobs, Ramsey Lewis, Hilde Limondjian, Rev. Dale Lind, Mundell Lowe, Bruce Lundvall, Don Lucoff, Bill McFarlin, Earl May, Dan Morgenstern, Ray Mosca, Cobi Narita, Sandy Nelson, Charles Osgood, Jimmy Owens, Tim Owens, Walter Perkins, Lloyd Pinchback, Fran Richard, Larry Ridley, Hilton Ruiz, Ira Sabin, Phil Schaap, Lalo Schifrin, Loren Schoenberg, George Shearing, Horace Silver, Lonnie Liston Smith, Robin Bell Stevens, Grady Tate, Randy Taylor, Rudolph (Rudy) Taylor, Clark Terry, Ed Thigpen, Bobby Thomas, Kim Taylor Thompson, Dr. Fred Tillis, Kenny Washington, George Wein, Frank Wess, Nancy Wilson, Herb Wong.

I

HOW IT STARTED

Early in my life I found myself wanting to learn everything I could about jazz: where it came from, how it developed, and, most important of all, how I could better express myself through it. – BILLY TAYLOR

WILLIAM EDWARD TAYLOR, Jr. was born at his home in Greenville, North Carolina, next to a church on July 24, 1921. His father, William Edward Taylor, born in North Carolina, was a dentist who sang, played piano, some brass instruments, and directed a choir. His mother Antoinette Bacon Taylor was born in Washington, D.C. BILLY has one younger brother, Rudolph (Rudy), born in 1926 in Washington, D.C. and one younger sister, Joyce born in 1949. BILLY was very interested in music and music instruments and played with drums, guitar, and tenor saxophone before settling on piano.

BILLY TAYLOR: I have vague memories of having the measles and going to kindergarten in Raleigh, North Carolina. We lived in Raleigh for about a year, just prior to coming back to Washington, D.C. in 1926. I remember my dad decided to move probably because of the school. So he started his office there and then he moved to D.C. I lived three blocks from the school.

BILLY started first grade at the Lucrecia B. Mott School at the age of five in 1926. He was always interested in music. There was a piano at his home in Washington, D.C.; his father played piano.

RUDOLPH (RUDY) TAYLOR: We always had a good relationship. I remember him learning to play the piano and finding girls. That's how we separated. Once he found out the piano brought the girls, then he didn't have need for a younger brother. We were very tight up to that point.

When we used to leave the church, we would go to my aunt's house that was within walking distance (in those days we walked everywhere) right off 1st Street to 2nd and Florida Avenue. My aunt would give us rolls that were like soft balls. We'd fill up with those and go from there over to 4th Street; which was where my grandmother lived. There we would fill up with pound cake. When we got home we didn't want any dinner that my mother had fixed and she would be pretty upset.

After grade school BILLY attended Shaw Jr. High School. At that time he was playing music and played in school, at school concerts and the like. His first teacher was Elmira Streets but he didn't consider himself a very good student because he wanted to play jazz. He was very bored. He wanted to play like his uncle, Bob Taylor, who played like Willie "The Lion" Smith (William Henry Joseph Bonaparte Bertholoff). Willie "The Lion" Smith, born in 1887 in Goshen, NY, was one of the outstanding jazz pianists, songwriters during the 20's and 30's.

BILLY TAYLOR: I was given the usual classical training, but I found that very boring and was upset because my music lessons did not help me master the music that I heard on the radio and on records. My first influence was Fats Waller. My uncle, Bob Taylor, my father's middle brother, was the one who started me listening to Fats. Everybody else in my family played classical music except for Uncle Bob and my Uncle Clint who became the head of the art department at North Carolina A & T University in Greensboro. My Uncle Bob was considered the maverick in the family. He became a newspaperman and assistant to the mayor in Washington, D.C. All of the other members of the family were playing Bach and Mozart; Uncle Bob was playing jazz in a very energetic style. I asked my uncle to show me how to do the things he was doing. He said: "Taught myself. You teach yourself." He gave me my first Fats Waller record, "Ain't Misbehavin" featuring Fats playing and singing. I heard him live in the theaters a lot; I also heard Earl Hines but I wasn't as impressed with Hines because he had a big band and you couldn't hear the piano as well. My ears weren't that well developed. My uncle said; "If you really want to hear Fats Waller listen to this!" He gave me a record of Art Tatum's 'The Shout'! At that time you could buy sheet music by Art Tatum and Teddy Wilson. I subsequently got into Billy Kyle, Nat Cole and local musicians like Claude Hopkins, Harold Francis, Toby Walker, and Norma Shepherd.

BILLY'S uncle, Bob Taylor, was self-taught and was BILLY'S father's middle brother. There were five brothers in BILLY'S father's family. BILLY'S father was the eldest.

RUDOLPH (RUDY) TAYLOR: Our father was the choral director for our grandfather's church, Florida Avenue Baptist Church. Out grandfather was the pastor there. Our dad was quite a character. He inspired us both in several directions. His stepsister was the organist and his brother also played organ. My dad was a dentist who was inclined to be interested in music and athletics. So he was a very good athlete. BILLY followed the musical side and I the athletic side. I was interested in sports and BILLY was interested in music, so BILLY followed the musical side and I was inspired by the athletic situation. In the early 30's my dad played tennis on clay courts and taught me how to play volleyball, baseball, etc. The thing that BILLY always got away from was the sport side and got to the music side. The sport side was the thing that always interested me and I had more activities with dad in that respect as opposed to music. I didn't realize the awful problem, to my father, was BILLY'S inclination to jazz. My father's brother was the one that inspired him to become interested in playing jazz. The musical side of the family was my father's side. They had a quartet in which all five of the brothers participated. I never had the occasion to hear them sing.

While attending Shaw Jr. High School there were several student colleagues who played jazz and BILLY was really stuck on jazz by that time. He had played guitar and had done a lot of things that really got him interested in music. He met a fellow student, Cooper Gibson who was a neighbor to one of his aunts who was a guitarist. BILLY won an amateur prize playing with Cooper. BILLY played chords while Gibson improvised and played the melody. He thinks they played "Honeysuckle Rose" during the competition.

In 1932, at age eleven BILLY attended Shaw Jr. High School. His uncle played some records of Art Tatum and Fats Waller and BILLY fell in love with jazz. Soon after, his family moved to Washington, D.C., to Fairmont Street NW, near Howard University, where he attended Dunbar High School, a segregated school. BILLY had the opportunity to hear great big bands fronted by Duke Ellington, Count Basie, Chick Webb, and Jimmie Lunceford. During high school BILLY also played saxophone but in his words: "I played saxophone very badly." One of his close friends, Billy White, played alto saxophone. BILLY considered himself a dilettante when it came to music. He wanted to play but he didn't take it very seriously. He played a lot of things by ear and when he came under the tutorage of Henry Grant he began to be serious about playing scales and practicing and really doing things that were musical, things that were helping him to play better. Henry Grant was himself a pianist.

BILLY TAYLOR: In high school I was very involved in music. I didn't have the jazz band but I played in it. We didn't have a formal jazz band but we got together at lunchtime and played. There was no faculty leader for jazz. Henry Grant was the music teacher when we were in high school and he was not only a very wonderful musician but he was very liberal in terms of allowing us to play jazz during that period. I'm not sure that many of the other teachers were that enthusiastic about it. I was blessed when I was growing up. Because of segregation, I had overqualified teachers. I had five teachers with doctorates who were teaching at the high school level. And they were excellent teachers. We were exposed to all kinds of life-changing experiences in school. 1

Before I got really interested in jazz I was involved in athletics, I ran, etc. I wasn't a serious athlete but I liked it. I played ball and all the kid's games. Where I lived in Washington there was a lot of social activity, dances, etc. One of the things we did was to go to the Howard Theater; almost every week or whenever we could afford it, borrow 15 cents or a quarter, whatever it cost. I graduated from high school in 1938.

RUDOLPH (RUDY) TAYLOR: Our neighbor was Henry Grant and Henry had three students. When I was in high school I used to ride to school with him where I played (alto saxophone) in the Dunbar High School Band. He had BILLY as a harmony student and another guy from Washington named Duke Ellington. Two out of three weren't bad! I just happened to be the third one!!

One thing Rudy Taylor remembered was the clothes that BILLY grew out of became his. Their grandmother was a seamstress. She could sew anything; take the shoulder pads out or whatever. Rudy never got any new clothes except on special occasions, e.g., Easter, Christmas, graduation, etc. "BILLY always had an affinity for clothes; he always had good taste. Once he started playing piano and found out about girls he really started to get nice clothes."

JIMMY OWENS: BILLY and Frank Wess went to high school in Washington, D.C. BILLY tells the story about how he (BILLY) was a good saxophonist supposedly until he heard Frank Wess play. That's when he decided to give up the saxophone and stick with the piano, so Frank Wess is somebody who is very, very important in BILLY'S life. They have come up all these years together. (Frank Wess was 80 on January 4, 2002 – BILLY, of course, was 81 on July 24, 2002).

In 1934 when BILLY was thirteen he played his first gig and earned $1. While attending Dunbar High School he continued to study classical piano with Elmira Streets and Henry Grant.

RUDOLPH (RUDY) TAYLOR: BILLY and I attended the same school, Dunbar High School, but never at the same time. BILLY would upset everybody in the auditorium by playing jazz and my mother would have to go down and get him back in the school.

FRANK WESS: In 1935 in high school I first met BILLY TAYLOR. I came from Oklahoma. I was born in Kansas City. I started out playing alto saxophone when I was ten years old in Sapulpa, Oklahoma. We went to school and we played. BILLY was phenomenal. He had a saxophone but he didn't play too much – he was a piano player. He and Billy White were working at a nightclub at night while they were in high school. I wasn't playing at first because I had stopped playing for a while. I was playing concert music so I stopped playing for a year and came to Washington, D.C. and heard BILLY and all the cats in the orchestra room jamming at noontime. So I got my horn back out and got interested again.

BILLY didn't get to New York too often when he was in high school although he had relatives living there. He recalled riding the train to New York with his mother and while in his teens BILLY made occasional trips to Harlem in New York where he became acquainted with pianists Art Tatum, Clarence Profit, and Thelonious Monk.

BILLY TAYLOR: When I was living in Washington, D.C., Charlie Parker and Dizzy were with Earl Hines, and little Benny Harris, who had lived in Washington, came through with the band, and he was telling everybody about these two guys that were coming out with what really were extensions of Roy, and other people that we were familiar with; and at the particular time that he was saying these things he was playing some lines himself that were really quite different from the Roy Eldridge, Louis Armstrong, or Shad Collins, and those kinds of things, quite different, very attractive things, funny little twists in them and really demanding a much clearer knowledge of harmony to make the proper kind of phrasing and so Benny Harris was for me one of the first people who pointed a finger at this. I was aware of changes myself, just as a pianist, because Tatum, the kinds of things he did were basically, well, Tatum on the piano, Hawk on the tenor saxophone, Ellington with the orchestra were doing the things that later became really formalized in the bebop context, in terms of harmonic extensions and melodic extensions, and really the kinds of rhythms that were first found in the Ellington band. So between late 1936 and 1941, there is a period that I call pre-bop, 'cause it's not really swing, nor was it bebop, but it had all of the ingredients being kind of formalized by various people, like Clyde Hart, Sid Catlett, Jo Jones, and other people. When I first really embraced bop, it was, of course, becoming aware of Parker and Gillespie, prior to coming to New York, but I was very much into Tatum and that kind of thing. In 1944 I had some knockdown, drag-out arguments with Bud Powell, because I'd run into him frequently at Minton's and other places.

As for the beginnings of bebop Billy felt "there were other contingents in various cities and all of these guys played some extension of swing. I mean it was their transition period where they were beyond the heavy 4/4 and the other stuff. Whether they listened to Charlie Christian, or whether they listened to Django Reinhard, who was a big influence on many on the concepts. Not just guitar but Django had these long lines, long lyrical lines that he did, and that became part of the guy's consciousness, too. So, there were a lot of different influences that led into guys approaching bebop. It's easy to say that out of Lester (Young) this came, out of Hawk (Coleman Hawkins) this came, and you can certainly document that, but it wasn't that clear cut."

FRANK WESS: I used to go up to his house and we would play in his basement. He played a lot of records for me while we were in high school and later. He had stacks of 78's. He was a disc jockey at home. He had all kinds of records. His mother was a teacher and his father was a dentist and they supported his interest in music.

Upon graduation BILLY applied to Virginia State University where he was accepted and began to study in 1936. His classical piano teacher at Virginia State was Undine Moore.

BILLY TAYLOR: I chose Virginia State because it was my father's alma mater. He did his undergraduate work there. He was quite an athlete. He had hoped that maybe I would play football. I did too, of course. My father and my uncle both went to Virginia State. Virginia State didn't have a music reputation at that time. They had a good music department but it wasn't outstanding. I had fallen in love with the school when I was very young. I went there to visit the campus from Raleigh, NC on a trip with my father who was playing tennis and I went up and ran around; kicked some balls and did what kids did but I remembered it throughout the years, because I loved it. It was in Petersburg, Virginia, about a half hour from Richmond. I don't remember if I had to audition in music to be admitted – I just remember I got in. I'm sure my dad and a lot of friends helped me get in. At the time I went to college, not everybody went to college. When I was in Dunbar High School it was settled that I was going to college. Since I was the oldest I was going to college, my mother being a teacher and my father being a professional man. So it was a given. I had to measure up and make my folks proud of me.

BILLY'S freshman year was a lot of fun, he had a lot more freedom living in a dormitory and pledging a fraternity, Kappa Alpha Psi, at the end of his freshman year. As an undergraduate student BILLY played in the university dance band and led the jazz band. At one point during his academic pursuit he told his music teacher/mentor, Undine Moore, that he was pursuing a degree in sociology because his father told him it was difficult to make a living as a musician. Dr. Moore advised BILLY to change his major to music, which he did. He played a solo recital in his senior year. He was a big fan of Debussy. He loved his music and when he had an opportunity to play something he chose something from that era – the late 19th century. He picked that up from one of his teachers, Henry Grant, who started him with Debussy and the Preludes. He was very turned on by those sounds.

BILLY TAYLOR: I most remember Undine S. Moore. She was a wonderful pianist and a wonderful teacher. She was the high influence of many in the music department. She was not only an excellent pianist but she knew so much about music. One of those persons who you could go up to and show her something off the wall and she would say: "Well, that's interesting, but have you thought about this!" She really made more sense than I made out of what I was trying to make out of it. She was an excellent teacher and she used anything that made me, as a student, really want to learn. She was really a role model. One of the reasons I taught was because I had the energies of these people who were really excellent teachers. She was a relatively young woman when I studied with her. She had just gotten married when I was a student there and she wanted to be, in addition to being a music teacher, she wanted to be a wife, mother, and so forth. She played in church. She was an organist but was known as a pianist. In many of the things she did, she used the kind of literature that I was talking about, just wonderful; the music of Debussy or Beethoven, or whatever it was. It was something that I found delightful.

During one of BILLY'S occasional trips to New York he recalled an incident that made an indelible impression on him; a trip he never forgot:

BILLY TAYLOR: I heard Clarence Profit* play solo, I met him in a strange way. I had come to New York to a place called Jock's. Now, it used to be called the Yeah Man Club, and a friend of my father's was the manager. We were talking: and he said, 'Your father tells me you're a piano player,' and I said, 'Yeah,' and he said, 'Why don't you come in the back and play something. I got a trio back here." That was kind of nice so I went back there and I didn't

---

* Clarence Profit was considered a child prodigy. He was born in New York City on June 26, 1912 and began playing piano at age three; did broadcasts with his friend Edgar Sampson while still a teenager. After leading his own ten-piece band, he played with Teddy Bunn's Washboard Serenaders during 1930 and 1931and then traveled to the West Indies where he spent six years. He returned to the United States in 1937 and led a trio at various clubs in Boston and New York City. Profit died in New York City on October 22, 1944.

know any of the guys by sight. This was in 1938. I was just visiting. I knew who Clarence Profit was, but I had never seen him, and so my father's friend introduced me. In fact he didn't even give me the guys' names. He just said, "Fellers, I got a young player here, the son of a friend of mine, and I'd like for him to play a little bit." and the guys said, "Sure, come on." And I sat down and of all the pieces I could of picked up, I picked 'Lullaby in Rhythm' (written by Clarence Profit) because it was my favorite song at the time, and I played it. I shot my best shot. I'm playing for New York musicians, so the piano player had the damnedest left hand I ever heard in my life. I ended 'Liza,' and all of them played 'Liza" after me, and it was quite an experience. I really don't remember all of the guys now but I do remember Gibby (as it turned out three of the other players were Stephen Henderson, nicknamed The Beetle, Marlow Morris, and Thelonious Monk). These were older pianists, but they really could play in that post-ragtime style.

It wasn't swing as played by Teddy Wilson or guys like that, but it was the extension of the Harlem stride thing that James P. and Fats did, because harmonically they were more into more current Art Tatum. But the style was stride. That's what I was trying to play, for them, which was a big mistake, but I got to know several of them after when I came to New York later and I met and listened to Donald Lambert and several of the other guys. But everybody had his 'crip,' everybody had his particular thing.

Donald Lambert would play, for example, a classical piece like 'Anitra's Dance', or something like that, and he'd swing it; he'd play it in the jazz style, and other guys had particular things they'd do. Clarence Profit was just a master of substitutions as far as harmonies are concerned. You just wondered, "What is the logic of going from there to here?" But it all made sense, and I really wish someone had recorded him. I've listened to some of the re-releases on Columbia and other things, which we now associate with Tatum, and some with Monk, because he used a lot of tonal things that Monk used, and I'm sure Monk was aware of his playing because he was one of the guys that was around in Harlem. 3

BILLY'S grades at Virginia State were about average. He didn't do as well as he would have had he been able to attend under different circumstances. He felt that his father's trying to teach him how hard it was going to be (majoring in music) did him a little disservice. BILLY felt that if he hadn't had to earn his own living while studying music he would have done better at school. He would have gotten more rest and that would have helped him to become better prepared. He felt he had achieved something, however, by finishing and graduating with his class. He was really behind in his studies due to the heavy schedule of required courses that he had to take in order to get music as a major. On the whole, however, he felt very fortunate. As his degree was in music education, he was offered a job teaching as soon as he graduated. The money he was offered was far short of the money he was making playing with bands on weekends. He thought, "Wow, there must be something wrong with this picture!" He wanted to go to New York and he also wanted to save some money so, upon graduation, he returned home and took a government job for a short time.

BILLY graduated from Virginia State University in 1942 and received the Bachelor of Science degree in music.

BILLY had completed his education at Virginia State and was subject to be drafted (WW II). He was called up and given a 4-F on his physical test. He was in very bad shape physically. He had changed his major to music in his junior year in college. His father disapproved and informed BILLY that if he wanted to be a musician he would have to do it on his own time. His father didn't believe music was a good investment. So he discontinued BILLY'S allowance and BILLY was forced to pay for the remainder of his schooling playing nightly in two local bands, one in Petersburg and one in Richmond. There were a lot of dances during the 1941-1945 period due to World War II. Inasmuch as BILLY had no automobile he spent a lot of time commuting to the various dances, and he studied for his classes while riding the bus from dance to dance. By the time he was ready to take the draft test he was getting two hours of sleep a night. While he was young and able to make his classes, etc., his health deterioted at an alarming rate. The draft board told him: "Go back and get your health together and come back in another year." By the time he had regained his health the war was practically over. His family was concerned.

BILLY TAYLOR: I was in such bad shape that I had to get my health together. I went to the doctor and put on some weight and all that stuff. I had tuberculosis. It was easy to get in that period, especially doing what I was doing because I was not eating properly. It was a wonder I didn't die. I went home, had ex-rays, etc. I got a lot of rest. I was lucky in D.C. I lived two blocks from Howard University. Every good doctor was a neighbor of mine. I had really excellent care.

BILLY was indeed fortunate. Many of the young, great musicians fell ill with tuberculosis and perished during that period including bassist Jimmy Blanton who died in 1943 at age 23, guitarist and early bebop exponent Charlie Christian who died in 1942 at age 25 and trumpet player Fats Navarro who passed on in 1950 at age 26.

This writer also had a narrow escape with the traitorous tuberculosis disease:

WILLIAM F. LEE III: The year was 1947. I was a trumpet player at North Texas State Teachers College (now the University of North Texas). After testing positive in a mobile x-ray unit on campus I was forced to withdraw immediately from school, return home, and receive medical attention. I had a large lesion in the upper lobe of my left lung. At that time there was no medication for tuberculosis. The first shot of penicillin ever given in the world was in 1941 and had no effect on tuberculosis. The TB germ killer streptomycin was neither discovered nor available until the early 50's so I turned to 24-hour bed rest and all kinds of fattening foods, creams, steaks, ice cream, vitamins, etc. After a years rest I was back at school. I had gained 75 pounds, had discontinued wearing my glasses full-time (my eyesight had improved), and I was now a fast bebop piano player. At any rate, there I was, all 208 pounds of me. I saw a girl there that I had known prior to leaving school in 1947, got up from the piano and gave her a hug and a kiss. She immediately slapped me – she didn't recognize me at all. 4

BILLY had a lot of professional people in his family. The uncle who was a dentist, his father, and a lot of people in D.C. who were part of his family. At the time he was growing up Washington, D.C. was really a very small town. The black community was like a small Southern town and you didn't have to go very far to get any information you needed. Living two blocks from Howard University, BILLY used their library for sources of information. He opted not to go to Howard University although his father would have liked it much better if he had stayed at home and gone to Howard. He thought it was the better of the two schools. His dad settled because BILLY attended his alma mater. When BILLY was growing up there were several concerts in the D.C. area; some on the Howard University campus and others at churches in the neighborhood. This gave BILLY an opportunity to hear all kinds of classical music. He saw many plays.

Washington, D.C. was really a cultural oasis in terms of people active in music. James Reese Europe got his start in D.C. and many of the people who worked with him in various groups were from D.C. They were incredibly well trained as violinists, chamber players, choral directors, etc. and very active as composers and players. In Duke Ellington's biography he is quoted as saying about one of his mentors who was a concert violinist who was so good that when he gave his concert at Carnegie Hall in New York, and the New York Times reviewed it, he was insulted because they said he was "the best Negro player in the country". He said: "No, I'm the best!" He was quite adamant about it. That's the thing about black history that's really a lost chapter as far as music is concerned.

BILLY TAYLOR: There were people at Howard and at other places who had gone to Europe to study and really brought all of that back to this community. It's remarkable that some of the people did what they did; incredibly talented people who were in New York, D.C., and Philadelphia, musicians of international repute.

So many of the people who wrote for Broadway shows, so many of the people who were neighbors of mine or my parents, all from the same community, they sang together, played together; quite an honor. I had no idea what I was turning my back on when I decided to go into jazz. I don't regret it. I wasn't aware of the quality of what people were doing.

Although Washington, D.C. has never been considered a "hot bed" in the birth and development of serious jazz musicians, it has certainly fostered some of the famous and soon-to-be famous talents of our times. This stream began with music statesmen like Will Marion Cook (composer-conductor, 1869-1944), Andy Razaf (songwriter, 1895-1973), Edward Kennedy "Duke" Ellington (pianist-composer, 1899-1974), Otto (Toby) Hardwicke (alto, soprano saxophones, 1904-1970) and Billy Taylor* (bass, 1906-1986). Washington, D.C. musicians born in the teens and twenties include Mercer Kennedy Ellington (trumpet-composer, 1919-1996), Osie Johnson 1923-1966 (drums, 1923-), 1923-1986 Markowitz (trumpet, 1923-), Charlie Rouse (tenor saxophone, 1924-1988), Leo Parker (baritone saxophone, 1925-1962), Rob Swope (trombone, 1926-1967) and Jimmy Cobb (drums, 1929-). During the thirties the following were born in D.C.: Jack Nimitz (baritone saxophone, 1930-), Ira Sullivan (trumpet-saxophones-flute, 1931-), 1934-2005 Horn (piano-voice, 1934-), John Livingston Eaton (piano, 1934-), Marshall Hawkins (bass-piano-drums, 1939-) and Butch Warren (bass, 1939-).

The younger talents born during the 40's, 50's and 60's include Billy Hart (drums, 1940-), Andrew White (woodwinds-piano-composer, 1942-), Frank Tate (bass, 1943), Ken Archer (piano, 1944-), Carter Johnson (tenor-soprano saxophones, 1945-); Gil Goldstein (piano-composer, 1950-), Ron Holloway (tenor saxophone, 1953-), Stephanie Nakasian (voice, 1954-), Jay Hoggard (vibes-composer, 1954-), Ed Howard (bass, 1960-), Laurent DeWilde (piano-composer, 1960-), Harry Adams Allen (tenor saxophone, 1966-), Marc Anthony Cary (piano-composer, 1967-) and Herb Harris (tenor-soprano saxophones, 1968-).

BILLY had survived the difficult years of growing up. He had made the decision to study music and completed his undergraduate degree in music education at Virginia State. He had taken a year off, regained his health and escaped the threat of the dangerous disease, tuberculosis. As a result of his early piano lessons and music experiences during high school and while attending Virginia State, he was ready to take a bite out of the Big Apple, New York City.

---

* Bass man Billy Taylor had a son, Billy Taylor, Jr. who also played bass. BILLY TAYLOR, for whom this biography is written, played with both bass players, Billy Taylor, Sr. and Billy Taylor, Jr., at various times. Billy Taylor, Sr. (the bass player) played with Elmer Snowden, Charlie Johnson, Duke Ellington, McKinney's Cotton Pickers, Fats Waller and Fletcher Henderson. Little is known about the bass player Billy Taylor, Jr.

II

NEW YORK

The tempos were ungodly. – BILLY TAYLOR

BILLY decided to move from Washington, D.C. to New York City. He immediately found himself in the middle of the transition from swing to bebop and would be able to interact with the top musicians from both idioms. He would eventually study piano, concentrating on touch, with Richard McClanahan.

BILLY arrived in New York City on a Friday night in 1943. He dropped his bags at a friend's apartment and headed directly for Minton's on West 118th St. He knew about the nightly jam sessions and was aching to sit in. While he was trying to display his power over the keyboard, Ben Webster came and sat in. After they had jammed for a while, Webster leaned over, told BILLY he had a combo at the Three Deuces, that featured drummer Big Sid Catlett and bassist Charlie Drayton, and invited him to go down on Saturday, and BILLY knew he was excited about going near The Street. (52nd Street). On Sunday night he found 72 West, took a deep breath, and went into the Deuces. It was a long basement room, a few steps down from the sidewalk, with about three rows of tables on each side of a center aisle. At the end of the aisle, to the right, was the bandstand. As he started down the aisle a girl stopped him. Norma Shepherd was a pianist from his hometown, Washington, D.C. "BILLY, what are you doing in New York?" she asked. He told her he was auditioning for a job and said hello to the people to whom she introduced him at her table. He was just sitting down at the piano when the name of one of the men to whom he had nodded politely hit him. It came on in capital letters: TATUM. It was rather dark and smoky in the room, but he turned around and tried to spot him. He couldn't. But just the idea that it might be Tatum – and he was on the bill with Webster – paralyzed him. He didn't play well, and he often wondered why Ben didn't change his mind about hiring him. Later, when he got to know Art rather well, he told him that he played a lot of fast things. When he asked, 'Did it sound all right?' Tatum said, 'Not particularly.' That's the way things happened in those days. BILLY TAYLOR had arrived in New York City on Friday night, an unknown with a bachelor of music degree from Virginia State University, and by Sunday night he was part of Ben Webster's quartet. And the way the older musicians watched over BILLY! There were three of them that treated him like a younger brother. Art Tatum, drummers Jo Jones, and Big Sid Catlett all went out of their way to guide him. Generally, you hear about older musicians having a bad influence on younger musicians, leading innocent young guys into drinking or dope. He was fortunate to have had an entirely different type of experience. He'd be at the White Rose bar on Sixth and 52nd where you could get torn up pretty fast for very little. Drinks were twenty-five to thirty-five cents and good-sized.

He'd put away a few and begin feeling no pain when Jo would suddenly be at his side. 'See you later,' he'd say. He didn't need a second invitation to know that he wanted him to split. 1

BILLY TAYLOR: One thing I always remember about the Deuces. The kitchen was in the back of the club, behind the bar. It had a beat-up old upright piano. There were some raucous sessions on that old box. Usually, guys who played other instruments, like Jo Jones or Tiny Grimes or Roy Eldridge – all of them could play some piano – would be there banging away, actually trying to cut one another at the keyboard. Frequently, they would come up with some interesting chord progressions, and they'd be after all the piano players to listen to their 'discovery.' 2

BILLY TAYLOR: When I first came to New York, I was playing a four-note chord in my left hand, and an octave – either just a plain octave or a four-note chord made in octaves – with my right hand. Everybody but Ben Webster objected to this. They'd say, "You're in my way. I can't hear. You're in the wrong part of the piano. Play down in the bass like Basie or Ellington for accompaniment." That wasn't what I heard. I had been playing with guitars and other things. I was playing locked hands 'cause I like that, but I didn't want to sound like Milt Buckner, whom I admire tremendously, but this was another kind of approach to it, and I heard Ellington do something like this, and I liked it, and it worked, so I began to do that, and I found that it got me out of the way of the bass player. So instead of being down here where the bass player was then, I was up in the middle of the piano, and up in the treble and the bass player was very audible, and Ellington, I guess, was really the first one to zero in on it. Basie did it, but Ellington really put the bass out there; if you listen to even his early records, you've got a clear picture of the top and the bottom, of the melody and the bass line with all this other stuff filling in, very classical in terms of orientation. But Basie did a little differently with Jo Jones on drums 'cause Jo is a strong drummer, so he did a lot of things that accented what he was doing. But Sonny Greer, who had his own flair for doing things, colors and all, was also out of the way, so that all of the weight of the rhythm section, that really became formalized once again in bebop, was with Billy Taylor, the bass player, and Jimmy Blanton and Junior Raglin, also strong bass players; so they really came in with that concept, and they became another kind of thing. 3

It was not uncommon for musicians to sit in and play a set or two with any of the groups at that time. Billy recalled a particular night involving the great trumpet player Roy Eldridge:

BILLY TAYLOR: One night in particular comes to mind. Roy Eldridge had just come in from Chicago, and he hadn't played in a couple of days, so he came to sit in with Ben Webster, to just kind of get his chops together. I guess he was supposed to open either there or another club, and so he came in and was taking it very easy. I mean he hadn't played, and so he was just playing simple kinds of things. Well, Charlie Shavers was at the bar, and he hurried out to his car and got his trumpet and came in and challenged Roy very quickly, and you've never seen a guy's chops get together so quick. And then Webster, who was one of the principal instigators of things like that, was just cheering him on. I mean he would play an opening chorus and then get out of the way. And say, "Hey, you all got it." And they played fours and twos and everything. Stop time and whatever. And so that was a very exciting night because these were really two master trumpet players at the height of their powers. Other nights similar to that would be the kind of sparks that used to fly between Don Byas and Coleman Hawkins. Don would play unbelievable choruses on "Cherokee" or some fast tune, and you would wonder, "What is Hawk going to do behind this?" And he'd come up with something that was very well worth listening to behind that. And there was that kind of surprise where at any given period someone would be invited up, and he may just be astounding. I remember there was a pianist who worked with Jackie Paris named Derrick Sampson, (Sampson made some boogie-woogie records for the Beacon label in 1944 but he never recorded the way he was playing on 52nd Street in 1945 or 1946. He died shortly after that, very young. But he had made the transition and was accomplished in the new style) and he was a dynamite player, a kid, I mean he was nineteen or twenty years old or something like that.

Then there were people like the guys that were out of the big bands that would come in from time to time, like Jimmy Crawford had left the Lunceford band and really was kind of nervous – he didn't consider himself a small-band drummer. And it took a lot of cajoling and a lot of stuff from Ben to say, "Well, come on, man. You know I want you because you can do what I need." And he came in, and of course, he became dynamite small-band, big band, any other kind of drummer you want. It was just terrific. 4

While BILLY was playing at the Three Dueces with Ben Webster in 1943 Dizzy Gillespie opened at the Onyx with the first bop band downtown. Prior to that Ben Webster and Ike Quebec and others were playing a more modern style. Webster had spent a lot of time at Minton's, and so he knew – even though he didn't play bebop per se – he knew all the lines, and he played a lot of things, and a lot of his compositions reflected his awareness of what was happening. He was a very big booster of what the guys were doing, and then Jo Jones was so secure in his own style (having worked with Hawkins and guys like that) that he just didn't choose to make that abrupt a change over from what he was most comfortable doing and what other guys were doing; but Hawkins got not only Monk to play piano with him, but he had Don Byas in his front line for a long time at the Downbeat. It was really an eye-opener to hear Byas playing all of those things that really weren't bebop, but were an extension of what Coleman Hawkins had done which was, in the first analysis, closer to what Bird was doing than most musicians realized at the time. The lines were long. They were four bars, eight bars, depending on what he was doing, but really long lines in terms of melodic development and they were very harmonically oriented. The group that opened at The Onyx was pictured in the New York Amsterdam News on December 11, 1943. The band included Dizzy Gillespie, trumpet; Don Byas, tenor saxophone; Oscar Pettiford, bass; Max Roach, drums; and BILLY TAYLOR, piano. The story read: "The Onyx Club is scoring nightly with the new John (Dizzy) Gillespie Band, led by Gillespie, former trumpet star with Cab Calloway . . ." During the first few weeks the personnel fluctuated considerably. Entrepreneur Jimmy Butts listed Thelonious Monk as the pianist and Lester Young as the tenor player. BILLY TAYLOR made it clear that he was taking time off from his gig at the Three Dueces to play in the Gillespie quintet.

BILLY TAYLOR: It was never my gig. When they opened, they actually didn't have a piano player, because they wanted to get Bud Powell. So I sat in with Dizzy. I sat in a lot at the Onyx, during that December, and I kept getting back late to play my next set across the Street with Ben Webster, so Ben fired me. I got my job back a little later, but for a while there I was playing quite often at the Onyx, and Monk was doing the same, taking time off from his job with Hawk.

The first thing that impressed me was that the tempos were ungodly. I mean Oscar Pettiford and Max Roach were two of the strongest rhythm players I'd ever played with at that time, and Max still is. Oscar would get annoyed if we played 'bebop' – if we played in that tempo and didn't give him a solo – now, most bass players they'd say, "Well, look, man, I've been playing four behind you guys all these choruses. Let the drummer take it." But he said, "Look, you played on it, I'll play on it, too." Until he broke his arm, playing ball with Woody Herman, he really had just unbelievable strength in terms of playing tempos and playing tremendously fast passages on the bass violin. But everything he did, fast, slow, medium, whatever, had the extension of what Blanton did. Blanton had started this melodic approach, which was perhaps more closely related to Charlie Christian and earlier players, but Pettiford's work was plugged right into Dizzy and Bird. That's right where he was coming from; the same kind of drive, the same kind of melodic impetus that stemmed from that rhythmic security. 5

Don Byas was never considered a great bebopper but was a great tenor saxophone player with ability to cope with the new jazz. He rapidly changed bands at the Onyx to work with Dizzy and Oscar Pettiford. BILLY TAYLOR said: "He'd work with just about everybody, Erroll Garner and others up and down the Street. But Byas wasn't a big enough name to draw crowds on his own. In fact Budd Johnson, who eventually replaced him, was far better known to the general public because he'd been with some high-profile big bands, like Earl Hines, which had put him in the public eye more than Don." 6

BILLY TAYLOR: One of the most exciting things that happened to me was to be on the bandstand with, say Dizzy and Ben Webster, Ike Quebec, Jack the Bear (Parker), the drummer; the bass player, it could have been any number of bass players – Charlie Drayton, John Simmons, guys that played really personal styles on the bass. But, it was really exciting because you got such a wide variety in one session. You would hear a whole gamut of things. One guy is really playing on the changes, another guy is playing all these beautiful melodies. You know, Lester Young. And just floating rubato all over the rhythm is Charlie Christian. He's doing something else entirely. Just the combination of those kinds of things and the fact that guys encourage the rhythm section to do other things with changes. If you're going to play "I Got Rhythm", I mean we've played those changes already, do something else with those changes to extend that. And, so the rhythm section was making small or large – depending on whom you're playing for – differences in the harmonies. You get a guy with ears like Don Byas or Hawk (Coleman Hawkins) or somebody like that, you could go into another direction, and you'd end up instead of the B-flat, g-minor, c-minor, F7th change, you'd end up doing the cycle of fifths starting on F-sharp, B, E, A, D, G, C, F and then back to the B-flat, and just that kind of thing that had been done prior to this period but weren't really dealt with on the level they're being dealt with now. And I recall listening to Clarence Profit, who wrote "Lullaby in Rhythm" and some other pieces, and who was never considered by most people more than an imitator of Fats Waller. Yet he and Art Tatum would sit down and jam, and they would jam on by playing the melody over and over. And changing the harmony so instead of coming up with different melodies, they came up with different harmonies, and that became particularly interesting when they started off with something like "Body and Soul", which already has some changes. And harmonically this guy was just unreal and to my knowledge he never recorded in that way. 7

ALYN SHIPTON: The irascible Pettiford, whose temper was as volatile as Dizzy's and whose fondness for the bottle occasionally led him into violent confrontations, was less accommodating (than Dizzy). Pettiford would shout (according to Dizzy) when George Wallington missed a chord change. Dizzy had nevertheless made a wise choice of pianist, and we know from BILLY TAYLOR'S account that in the band's helter-skelter arrangements and aggressive ensembles the pianist would be dominated by the pounding bass of Pettiford and the swirling drums of the young Max Roach, making Wallington's understated approach ideal for the group. 8

Surely Dizzy's appearance at the Onyx made an indelible mark on the beginnings of bebop. His yet-to-be opening with Charlie Parker and their quintet would formalize this new art form. Although this new music movement is primarily credited to New York and the players who worked there, BILLY TAYLOR felt it was gradually being developed in other parts of the country as well.

BILLY TAYLOR: But there were a lot of other people who didn't live in New York who had a great deal of impact on Bird and Dizzy when they would go to different towns. There was a musician whose nickname was 'Georgetown.' I don't know his real name. John Malachi and some of the guys who've been in Washington since would know, but he was such a phenomenal trumpet player that whenever Roy Eldridge would be in town, he would look him up. He said: "That's the guy I'm looking for", and he played in this style. It wasn't swing. It was beyond swing, approaching bop. There were a couple of saxophonists in D.C. There was a piano player named Toby Walker who did this. There was another pianist who since died – Toby's dead, too – but this pianist was the accompanist for the Ink Spots. He came out of the Army, and he just couldn't get into the jazz scene so he took a job with the Ink Spots. He never really got back into the jazz thing. His name was Harold Francis, and when I was coming up, he and Toby Walker were the baddest piano players in town. Everybody aspired to do what they did and the only way I can describe it is that Harold had, on all levels, a much more aggressive approach to Teddy Wilson and Art Tatum. It had harmonies that I associate more with Tatum because they were further evolved but he had a touch kind of like Teddy, so he and Julius Pogue and a lot of other guys were influential. Frank Wess and the baritone player, Leo Parker, and Charlie Rouse – all of these guys came up aware of this Washington contingent, and all of the guys knew Benny Harris and liked these little things he was doing and did things based on those things. And so on the whole, during that entire period I was most aware of the Washington contingent, but there was a contingent in Detroit. 9

During those last weeks of 1943 Dizzy patiently taught BILLY TAYLOR the changes to several of the new compositions the band played. Although he had written down some of the sequences, Dizzy preferred to explain what he was after by demonstrating at the keyboard. TAYLOR related: Dizzy said, "I could write out the chords for you, but I want this voicing here, and that voicing there. When I write chord symbols, you have a choice, and that doesn't mean you'll play the voicing I'm after." Of all the people who were taking part in this bebop revolution, Dizzy was the one who really intellectualized it. I'd meet him when he was playing the Howard Theatre in Washington, where I grew up, when he came there with Earl Hines. I knew Benny Harris, who was in Earl's trumpet section and who was vital in spreading the word about the changes Diz and Bird were making, and it was Benny who introduced us. And so I already knew Dizzy when I found myself sitting in with his band at the Onyx. In fact, even before Benny introduced us the word was out on Dizzy among musicians. "Here are some guys to watch in Earl's band: Dizzy and Charlie Parker." I think Dizzy was so keen to get his new concepts out there that that's why he started writing arrangements. Trying to get the widest group of people to buy in to what he was doing. Once he started teaching me those changes at the Onyx, he became a mentor to me, and I've never forgotten it." 10

BILLY'S involvement with the Onyx and the Dizzy Gillespie Quintet actually got him fired from his gig with Ben Webster at the Three Dueces. It was at the time that Coleman Hawkins was working with Billie Holiday at the Downbeat Club next door to the Dueces and Erroll Garner was playing for Billy Daniels at Tondelayo's down the street. Bud Powell was supposed to have played with Dizzy at the Onyx but was underage. His guardian was Cootie Williams who didn't allow Bud to play with Dizzy at that time. BILLY TAYLOR began sitting in and he was so excited about the new sounds that Dizzy had brought down from Minton's that he stayed longer and longer each night and would have to rush back to make his sets with Webster. He began getting dirty looks from the owners and managers of the Dueces, Irving Alexander and Sammy Kay, and finally when he really came late for a set Alexander fired him. BILLY understood the stand taken by Alexander, who was a former saxophone player, and didn't consider the move unfair.

ALYN SHIPTON: Characteristically, for a man, who, as BILLY TAYLOR recalled, had intellectualized the bop revolution, Dizzy was not prepared to deviate from his chosen path to emulate the sounds of the blues. "I am not the type to have followed the blues," he said. "I wasn't a blues follower. But Hot Lips Page and Charlie Parker had come from what was really a blues area, where the guys really did that. Now there was nobody playing anything in my hometown. I was listening to Roy Eldridge and Chu Berry and I was more inclined to that. I heard the blues all my life, so I knows it when I hears it – that's very bad grammar, but you see with the blues you have to say things like that. But anyway, Charlie Parker was really a blues player. Played a mean, low-down blues." 11

In 1944 BILLY played with Ben Webster at the Three Dueces, and played with Billie Holiday, Stuff Smith, Eddie South, Dizzy Gillespie and Foots Thomas.

BILLY'S first record date with his own trio occurred in New York City in 1944 and included Al Hall, bass, Jimmy Crawford, drums, and TAYLOR, piano. The recording, SAVOY XP8 095 included Mad Monk, Solace, Night and Day, and Alexander's Ragtime Band.

Bass man Al Hall (Alfred Wesley Hall) was born in Jacksonville, Florida on March 18, 1915. He was raised in Philadelphia and began his music career as a 'cello student. In 1932 he switched to bass and played with local bands in Philadelphia from 1933 to 1935. Moving to New York City he played with Billy Hicks, '36-'37, Skeets Tolbert, '37-'38, with the Teddy Wilson Orchestra in 1939 and Teddy's Sextet during 1940-'41. He began playing in trios led by Ellis Larkins and Mary Lou Williams during '42-'44, played with Kenny Clarke briefly in 1943, and did some staff work on CBS prior to making the 1944 record with BILLY TAYLOR.

Drummer Jimmy Crawford (James Strickland Crawford) was born in Memphis, Tennessee on January 14, 1910. He studied alto saxophone at an early age and was a self-taught drummer. Jimmie Lunceford was his high school physical education teacher in high school, which led to Crawford's recording with the LUNCEFORD CHICKASAW SYNCOPATORS in 1927. After touring with the Lunceford band from 1929 to 1942 Crawford worked in a defense plant until he began playing with Ben Webster on 52nd Street.

BILLY didn't feel that he knew any of the New York musicians very well with the exception of Jo Jones who he had met during the time Count Basie had traveled through Petersburg, Virginia. He felt they all had his best interest at heart, however, and kept their eyes out for him. They recommended him for a number of gigs although he was not aware of it at the time. Art Tatum, Sid Catlett and Ben Webster were particularly helpful in recommending BILLY. BILLY became Art Tatum's protégé and spent a lot of time listening to Art play at Tatum's home. He got a lot of confidence from Art Tatum just knowing that Tatum was interested in him. BILLY TAYLOR considered this time to be one the most exiting periods of his life.

BILLY did a record date on March 19, 1945 in New York City with drummer Cozy Cole. He had worked with Cozy on the stage for the Broadway Show, "Seven Lively Arts". With Cozy and BILLY were Don Byas, tenor saxophone, Tiny Grimes, guitar, Billy Taylor, bass (no relation), and singer June Hawkins who was appearing in "Seven Lively Arts". The tunes included Hallelujah, Stompin' At The Savoy, Dat's Love, and Through For The Night. The record was released on Classics 865.

In April another record date, with the same personnel with the exception of Sid Weiss who played bass rather than bassist Billy Taylor, was completed. On that date the Cole Band recorded Night Wind, Why Regret and Strictly Drums. The record was released on Classics 895.

> EDDIE BERT: The first time I met BILLY was in 1945. We played at Town Hall. That was all recorded. Jimmy Rosencrantz ran that thing. BILLY was with Stuff Smith and I was with Red Norvo. Shorty Rogers and I were in the army. We had to play in our uniforms. It was a drag – the war was on!

During the summer, on June 27, BILLY recorded with the Walter "Foots" Thomas All Stars on a date that featured Thomas, tenor saxophone, Hilton Jefferson, alto saxophone, Adolpus "Doc" Cheatham, trumpet, Buddy Saffer, baritone saxophone, Milt Hinton, bass, and others. Black Maria's Blues, Bird Brain, Dee-Tees and Back Talk were recorded.

> BILLY TAYLOR: During my young years I remember sitting in Billie Holiday's dressing room. Of course nobody knew me. I was just a kid. I was sitting there, trying to be unobtrusive. She was talking to guys like Sweets Edison, other guys on the Basie Band and others who came and went. She was very nice to me. I ultimately got to accompany her. She was already a star.

BILLY also played piano at a record date held during the later part of 1945 in New York that resulted in the release of a SUPER DISC (record) release of four tunes: Just A Riff, Before Long, What's Happenin' and Mop De Mop Mop. The group led by drummer Sid Catlett was labeled SID CATLETT and HIS ALL-STARS and included Catlett, TAYLOR, trumpeter Dick Vance, trombonist Tyree Glenn, alto saxophonist Hilton Jefferson, tenor saxophonist Coleman Hawkins, bassist Johnny Simmons and singer Matthew Merredith.

> BILLY TAYLOR: We were in California and I was playing in the Eddie South Trio opposite Sid Catlett. Zoot (Simms) was in the band, John Simmons and Mala Morris. Zoot was drafted while we were working that club and went

into the Army. He was the tenor of choice for Sid because he swung so hard. In those days there were not a lot of integrated groups.

BILLY TAYLOR: After the Deuces gig folded, I went on the road with Eddie South, a giant of a fiddler. When we hit California, I decided to stay put for a while. Art Tatum was living on the Coast at that time, and I remained for about six months until I felt I was getting into a rut musically, despite my daily sessions with him. 12

BILLY idolized Art Tatum. Tatum's musicality, technique, and mastery of the keyboard were a combination of things BILLY aspired to and worked toward obtaining.

BILLY TAYLOR: The first time Tatum came to New York he was exposed to the great stride pianists like James P. Johnson and Willie "The Lion" Smith and all the 'kings of the hill,' if you will, in that style. And they really wiped him out the first time. James P. Johnson just did him in. So he was nineteen – and worked on a lot of stuff. When he came back, he had his stuff together. One of the reasons he played a classical piece (Massenet's Elegie) is because there was a pianist named Donald Lambert whose gimmick was to play classical pieces in stride style. So this was his way of saying, "Okay. Try THIS one." And he played it about four times as fast as Lambert, and he played a lot more interesting harmonies, and he did all kinds of juxtapositions of melodic streams – playing a half-tone higher in his right hand than he was in his left-hand, things like that.

Tom Tilghman used to have Monday sessions with his piano players, and the attraction was that Tatum was a friend of his and Tatum would come up almost every Monday. And all of the piano players showed up, but Tatum wouldn't show up until after the gig or whatever. But all the piano players were there from about ten o'clock at night playing for one another. Marlow Morris, who was one of the closest in terms of style to Art in those days, never recorded like that on piano, and many people just knew him as an organist and had no concept that in feeling, in technique, he was perhaps the closest to Art, stylistically. He didn't play like that with any kind of rhythm section – he played another style. With Sid Catlett, for instance, he worked with Sid a lot, and he played very spare, almost like Monk, in some of the things he did. 13

Art Tatum usually sat around for quite a while before he'd feel ready to play. This was a situation that satisfied club owners who had enticed in other pianists worth hearing and didn't wish to have them put out before closing time. So it might have been seven or eight in the morning before Tatum started. As his fame increased, his procedure became more and more lofty and Olympian. He would visit the clubs with a protégé in tow, like some medieval monarch with a trusted knight at his elbow. In Los Angeles in the mid-forties, BILLY TAYLOR fulfilled this lieutenant's role. Tatum would seek out the top man in the region. He would know the guy's best number, and he'd ask BILLY to play it, to sort of bait the guy. BILLY didn't know what was going on, so he'd play it. If BILLY (or any of Art's students) were getting bested, Tatum would just step in and take over. Tatum encouraged BILLY to make deliberate mistakes to see how quickly he could recover.

The most obvious difference between Tatum and the other pianists was his unusual virtuosity. Despite his extremely limited vision in one eye (to the extent that he was judged legally blind), Tatum seemed to play everything twice as fast as his peers, while increasing the level of swing and harmonic variety. His influence on other pianists was profound, if not devastating. It is said that he intimidated many of them into taking up other instruments. But Tatumesque passages are evident in the music of many undaunted pianists who followed him, especially in the music of Bud Powell (in his ballads), Oscar Peterson, BILLY TAYLOR, and Hank Jones, to cite a few of the most obvious examples.

> BILLY TAYLOR: Returning to New York, I wound up – you guessed it – at the Three Deuces. Slam Stewart had the gig and Erroll Garner was working with him. But Erroll had just hit with his recording of 'Laura,' and he wanted to branch out. And so I replaced him with Slam; John Collins, who was part of my quartet in 1950-51, was on guitar, and Hal 'Doc' West on drums. 14

During that period with bassist Slam Stewart at the Three Deuces, BILLY had an interesting experience:

> BILLY TAYLOR: One evening I wandered into Tony's. It was directly across from the Three Deuces where I was then appearing with Slam Stewart. While I nursed a couple of drinks, the stage remained empty, except for a tall stool on which a pin spotlight shown. I was just about to leave when an elderly-looking lady, cabaret singer Mabel Mercer, came out, perched herself on the stool, and began to sing or recite. She had an absolutely unique style, not jazz but really beautiful. Her material was as personal as her approach. I used to come back whenever I could. She always had her audience spellbound. 15

While he was playing with Slam Stewart BILLY married Theodora (Teddi) Castion. They had met and dated during BILLY'S days at Virginia State University and sometime after he moved to New York, while he was playing with Slam Stewart, they fell in love and decided to get married which they did on June 22, 1946.

> BILLY TAYLOR: We got married and I lost my gig because Slam discovered a woman piano player, Beryl Booker, while I was on my honeymoon and hired her.

Prior to leaving for Paris, BILLY did a record date for HALO records with BUCK CLAYTON'S BIG EIGHT on July 24, 1946 in New York City. The personnel included Clayton, trumpet, Dickie Wells and Trummy Young, trombones, George Johnson, alto saxophone, Brick Feagle, guitar, Al McKibbon, bass and Jimmy Crawford, drums. The BIG EIGHT recorded Saratoga Special, Sentimental Summer, Harlem Cradle Song, My Good Man, Sam, and I Want A Little Girl.

> BILLY TAYLOR: Back in the mid-forties when I toured Europe with Don Redman and the first civilian jazz group to give concerts in Europe after WW II, I heard for myself the many fine pianists who had been influenced by the records and live performances of giants like Art Tatum and Fats Waller. These European pianists played well, but in a few short years, with records easier to obtain and with great jazz artists like Bud Powell, Kenny Clarke, Don Byas, and countless others living and working in Europe, the quality of jazz performances improved dramatically. Many more excellent European players began to emerge. 16

BILLY was heard on a recording in Paris on October 18, 1946. Don Byas and His Orchestra recorded two tunes for SWING records, Gloria and Mohawk Special. The personnel on that date included Byas, tenor saxophone, Peanuts Holland, trumpet, Tyree Glenn, trombone, Robert Rostaing, clarinet, Ted Sturgis, bass, Budford Oliver, drums and BILLY TAYLOR piano.

> BILLY TAYLOR: I love big bands and the only chance, the one time in my whole life that I really got to play with a big band, after I got out of school, was with Don Redman. I did a lot of things with this band and that band but Redman was my real experience. I remember the first time I heard Don Redman in person I went backstage to meet him. I talked to Tyree Glenn, one of the trombone players. I said: "I'd really like to meet Mr. Redman." He said: "Oh, sure, come on." He took me back and I was standing around thinking to say something intelligent. I saw this guy sitting down there and writing. I said: "I beg your pardon but what are you writing?" Redman said: "I didn't like something the reeds were playing behind the dancers so I want to have them play something different." I said: "Can I see it?" He said, "Sure." He showed

me he was actually writing individual parts like I write a letter, so I paid another admission of .25 or .30 so I could go back and hear what he had written and sure enough it worked.

After arriving in Europe the Don Redman Orchestra was broadcast and recorded for Geneva Records (1946 TCB 02112) The record featured Tyree Glenn, trombone and vibes; Don Byas, tenor saxophone; Peter Clark, clarinet; Peanuts Holland, trumpet; and BILLY TAYLOR, piano. The tunes recorded were My Melancholy Baby, Limehouse Blues, Laura, Carry Me Blues, I Got Rhythm, Alexander's Ragtime Band, Tea For Two, These Foolish Things and Stompin' At The Savoy.

DAN MORGENSTERN: I first saw BILLY in Denmark in the fall of 1946 when BILLY was part of the Don Redman Band, which was the first American band to come to Europe, to Scandinavia after World War II. It was a tremendous occasion because everybody was really starved for genuine American music. It was a wonderful band that had Don Byas, who was probably the star. BILLY was very young, about twenty-five, and he made an impression. Certainly he was one of the outstanding people in that band. He was well featured. There are a couple of recordings that came out, one in Denmark and one in Switzerland. I was too young to be in the service – that was before I came to the States. I came to the U.S. a little less than a year later. When BILLY was in Copenhagen I didn't get to meet him, I was just a sixteen-year-old kid.

In December 1946 English pianist, George Shearing traveled to the US to record for Savoy. He recalled hearing BILLY and remaining friends for many years.

GEORGE SHEARING: I've known BILLY for a number of years. He has a great education, brilliant mind, and is a great player. I like his playing. He's probably the only person to do any form of lectures. He is a wonderful pianist.

BILLY TAYLOR: During this time, because of my experiences in playing different styles of music, I began to see how important jazz was as a musical expression of what our culture is about. I became concerned because I realized that most of the written material about Afro-American musicians and their music was composed by jazz fans, not those qualified to make valid musical judgments. 17

On December 4, 1946 and while still in Paris, France, BILLY was the pianist in the Don Byas Quartet when they recorded I'm Beginning To See The Light, Rosetta,

Ain't Misbehavin', Body and Soul and Blue and Sentimental for SWING records. In addition to Billy, Don Byas played tenor saxophone, Jean Bouchety, bass, and Buford Oliver, drums.

> BILLY TAYLOR: As we were boarding the plane to leave for Europe Don Byas stated that he was never returning to the U.S. He said: "I'm going to Europe forever and never coming back to the States." For some unknown reason he was fed up with the States and he remained in Europe for most of the rest of his life. He returned to the States but only for a short time. Kenny "Klook" Clarke had told him about the life style he had enjoyed in France and throughout Europe. While in Europe he learned to speak French. Don drank too much but he was a nice guy. My wife, Teddi, was a great ping-pong player and she used to beat Byas regularly. I recall one time in Germany when they must have played for at least two hours. He kept trying to beat her but just couldn't.

Taylor made another record during his Paris tenure. He formed a trio that featured bassist Ted Sturgis and drummer Buford Oliver. The BILLY TAYLOR TRIO recorded the following for SWING records: The Very Thought of You and Stridin' Down Champs-Elysees. This record was also made on December 4, 1946.

The final recording that BILLY participated in during his 1946-47 stay in Paris was with Don Byas and His Orchestra on January 13, 1947. In addition to tenor saxophonist Don Byas and pianist BILLY TAYLOR, Peanuts Holland played trumpet, Tyree Glenn, trombone, Robert Rostaing, clarinet, Jean-Jacques Tilche, guitar, Jean Bouchety, bass and Oliver Buford, drums. They played Please Don't Talk About Me When I'm Gone and also recorded Walking Around, How High The Moon, Red Cross, Laura, Cement Mixer and Dynamo A without Glenn and Rostaing. Blue Star 27, 28, 29.

> BILLY TAYLOR: We went to Holland with this small group and some of these records were made in Hilversum. The ones on the French label, the October 1946 dates, were made when we first arrived in Paris. We went right from the airplane to the recording studio for the Hot Club of France. They just wanted to record a few musicians from the band. Peanuts Holland from the Charlie Barnet Band was there for a while. The December 1946 dates were made in Paris while we were working there. Ted Sturgis returned home to the USA so we used a French bass player, Jean Bouchety.

By 1947 BILLY'S father, William Edward Taylor had divorced BILLY'S mother and remarried. After some time had passed Mr. Taylor and his new wife welcomed their first child into the Taylor family. The girl, BILLY'S half-sister, is Joyce Taylor

Hynes. Joyce eventually graduated from Wheaton High School, in Washington, D.C., and Howard University where she majored in Education and minored in Science. By 2002 she had moved to California and was working for a consulting firm.

> JOYCE TAYLOR HYNES: I enjoyed growing up and having BILLY as one of my big brothers. I was always referred to as 'little sister'. BILLY'S contribution to American Music is one I would never be able to articulate. I remember going to the David Frost Show and meeting all of the famous people.

BILLY and Teddi thought about staying in Europe while BILLY was playing with the Don Redman Orchestra and with several jazz expatriates like Stuff Smith and Don Byas but made the decision to return to New York.

> BILLY TAYLOR: When I returned to New York after spending about eight months in some of my favorite European cities, bop was the new "in" thing. 52nd St. brought the music downtown, but the modern sounds were all over Broadway at the Royal Roost, where Monte Kay* served as midwife to the 'Birth of the Cool' with Miles Davis, and at Bop City, where they tried to serve a musical ragout of bop, pop, and rhythm-and-blues that did not quite make it with anybody. But both places showed a concern about bringing jazz to young people. They had bleachers where the Pepsi generation could come in for a low admission charge and soda fountains where they could satisfy their thirst. These innovations proved most successful at Birdland, where I was house pianist for nearly two years. Not only did teen-agers enjoy the jazz of that period, but they knew all the players and their records. 18

BILLY reformed his quartet replacing John Collins with Herman Mitchell on guitar but retaining John Levy on bass and Denzil Best on drums to record Mr. B. Bops, Restricted, Down The Champs Elysees and Mitch's Pinch for H.R.S. records on September 26, 1947 in New York City.

Jazz promoter *Monte Kay formed the New Jazz Foundation with Symphony Sid and Mal Braveman; he presented modern jazz concerts at Nick's in New York's Village and at Kelly's Stable on 52nd Street; he served as mid-wife to "Birth of The Cool" with Mike Davis; he established the Town Hall jazz concerts, managed Flip Wilson and the Modern Jazz Quartet and produced the Flip Wilson Show on television.

BILLY TAYLOR: I was looking for work. I had been away for a long time and the reputation that I had been able to establish was forgotten. I played a lot in Harlem, at Wells' restaurant and on the East Side in several places. I was hurting financially. I began putting together trios and quartets to find work; I was really hustling. It didn't matter that I had played in Europe for eight months.

KETER BETTS: When I first went to Washington, D.C. in 1947 I heard about BILLY (I got out of high school in 1946). I went to D.C. for four weeks and ended up playing there for thirteen weeks. BILLY had been gone by then.

In 1948 BILLY played piano and Bob Wyatt played organ in a piano-organ duo. This duo was mentioned in JOHN CHILTON'S book, BILLIE'S BLUES: "Billie Holiday had the option of going out again on tour (which she didn't feel ready for), or of taking theatre work in New York. A few weeks after the 'Welcome Home' concert she headed a 'Holiday on Broadway' presentation at the Manfield Theater, New York. The show, which featured Slam Stewart's Trio, Cozy Cole, and the organ-piano duo of Bob Wyatt and BILLY TAYLOR, received good reviews, but the unusual venue (the theatre had never before presented jazz) meant that the staging of the show was risky.

JOHNNY GARRY: I first met and got to know BILLY, at Café Society in the late 40's. When BILLY first came to New York in the early 40's he was just like he is now, same guy. He was playing at the 19th Hole. Sammy Price and Willie "The Lion" played there.

As early as December 29, 1948 BILLY was already recognized in the readers' poll of Down Beat magazine. BILLY followed well-known piano players including George Wellington, Tad Dameron, Bud Powell and Mel Powell.

DICK HYMAN: I met BILLY around the time I graduated from Columbia, got married, and began working at a club in Harlem, Wells Music Bar, all within the same two-month period in 1948. I'm pretty sure we heard each other at Wells, because BILLY played there as well at other times. From what I can remember, we were in and out of other venues as well and subbed for each other from time to time.

In 1949 Billy led the Artie Shaw Grammercy 5. Actually Billy formed his own quartet that Artie Shaw fronted.

BILLY TAYLOR: He had been in retirement and he had a little farm in upstate New York and for some reason or other he decided he wanted to play again so he shopped around and he wanted an organized group; he wanted to play his Grammercy Five book. He had some music that he had recorded, etc. He wanted a group that was perhaps a little more contemporary; he wanted to see what was going on; we were playing bebop. He came and heard us, liked us, and hired us as a group. We went over to his apartment and rehearsed; got many of the Grammercy Five pieces, learned those arrangements and played them and it was a lot of fun. We played one long engagement. We made a record that I guess never came out. We recorded with him; it wasn't with the Grammercy Five. It was in a larger context. I never heard the record so I guess it never came out.

It was felt that Artie probably had it salted away someplace. "He'll bring it out when he finds a label for it for his new band"; Dick Johnson who led the Shaw Ghost Band said: "They had a lot of stuff on wax but Artie hasn't settled on who he wanted to release it. Everyone felt his giving it up was a bad decision. Artie said that he never really learned to play the clarinet; it's hard to believe but that was a reason he gave."

BILLY TAYLOR: Well he's very careful and he's a man that I respect very much as a musician. When I played with him the musicianship that he displayed was very high level and his understanding that the tradition of jazz was better than most bandleaders of his time. I mean he really had a clear vision of the continuity of the music he was attempting to play. As a result, a lot of the music that he recorded was a lot more adventurous – when you think about those things he did with Mel Torme, Concerto for Clarinet, a lot of things were way ahead of their time. His standards were so high. I don't agree with him but I can understand his standards. His standards were so high he wanted to do something with the instrument that maybe for him just weren't possible. There's a guy now (1989), Eddie Daniels, really a virtuoso, who does all kinds of things with the clarinet. Many of those things are what Artie Shaw was attempting to do back in the 30's and 40's; which, for a variety of reasons may not have been possible at that time. 19

JOHN DUFFY: I met BILLY in the late 40s when he was playing with his trio at a bar around 46th St. – I think it was the Grand Piano or something like that. He was very young, of course, and he was a real nifty looking guy, real stylish. I was in awe of him. He wore those spread collars (Mr. B. collars – Billy Eckstein). I was always poking around to find a place where I could buy those and I found the place where BILLY bought them – a shirt place on Madison Avenue; they had BILLY'S photograph in the window.

On November 20, 1949 BILLY formed a quintet to record Take The A Train, Misty Blues, The Bug and Prelude To A Kiss for Savoy records. The group included

John Hardee, tenor saxophone, Milt Page Organ; John Simmons, bass, Joe Harris, drums, and BILLY TAYLOR, piano. The record label was Savoy XP8113.

In 1950 Billy continued writing articles for Down Beat Magazine, the Saturday Review, and Esquire Magazine.

ALYN SHIPTON: At the beginning of 1951, Dizzy's (Gillespie) small band played a season at Birdland, and surviving air shots reveal that it reverted to scaled down versions of the big band's best known numbers from the late 1940's. "Good Bait" was a popular feature, as was Dizzy's treatment of "I Can't Get Started." Milt Jackson settled back on vibes, alongside John Coltrane, who had by this time finally traded his alto for a tenor sax. BILLY TAYLOR appeared on piano on some broadcasts, and Jimmy Foreman on others, and the band had the benefit of Art Blakey on drums for almost two months. 20

BILLY TAYLOR: I had played a lot of solo jobs, accompanied a lot of singers and dancers, wrote my first piano instruction books, played the RKO in Boston, the Earle Theater in Philadelphia, the Royal Theater in Baltimore, the Howard Theater in Washington, D.C. and the Apollo Theater in New York.

Many jazz pianists influenced BILLY during his early days in New York City. His description of their musicality follows: 21

Bud Powell

Bud (Powell) was totally responsive to Charlie Parker. He wanted to make the piano sound like Charlie Parker, and he did. It really had that kind of rhythmic and almost tonal quality in his early work. I had great difficulty with that because I wanted to play pianistically and all of the things. Bud was influenced by Fats Waller and Art Tatum but he was most influenced by Charlie Parker. He began to work with Mary Lou Williams and became more interested in the sound of the piano. Mary Lou Williams took Monk and Bud up to her house and really worked with them because she's such a sensitive person that she said: "Look, I mean, you guys play too well not to make the piano sound any more pianistic than it does when you play." She made then both more aware of touch. And you could hear the difference in the early Powell records and the later Powell records in terms of just the touch. You can hear the same with Monk. When Monk was recording for Blue Note and labels like that it was one touch. And then later he began to record for other labels, it just wasn't the change in sound, he changed. And you could hear

a more pianistic approach. This was, in my opinion, a result of his close
association with Mary Lou. That was 1949, almost 1950.

Clyde Hart

Clyde Hart was very sensitive and he had a lot more technique than his
records would indicate. I remember one night up at Tom Tilghman's place,
the Hollywood Bar on 7th Avenue in Harlem. Art Tatum sat down and showed
about seven or eight piano players how to play a break that he had recorded
in "Battery Bounce," one of his early records. And somebody asked him,
"How did you do that?" And he said, "It's just this." And he played it. He
played it two or three times, and the only guy that got it the first time around
was Clyde Hart. And Clyde didn't use all that technique normally. You don't
hear it on the records. But he had tremendous facility, and he was a well-
rounded musician. He could play other styles. He could do a lot of things,
and I found out that time and on several other occasions where I heard him up
at Tom Tilghman's.

Mary Lou Williams

Mary Lou Williams is probably one of the best examples of someone
who made the transitions of style from ragtime – from early ragtime. She
played for Jelly Roll Morton, who put her down. She worked with and played
for James P. Johnson and Fats Waller. And she was, of course, influenced by
their work as well as Earl Hines. She not only composed and played in all of
the styles, boogie-woogie and all those things, but she is a walking
encyclopedia of what literally the styles were about. I heard the Scott Joplin
presentation at Lincoln Center, when they had Bill Bolcom and several other
pianists to play the Joplin works, and they all played them very well – they
read the music, and they gave it the kind of loving attention it should get –
but Mary Lou Williams was the only one, who improvised on it. She was so
secure with the music, she just said, "Yeah, it goes like this." And she went on
and wailed on it. The critics didn't understand that. They said she really
didn't learn the piece. She knew the piece from before and not only was
secure enough to improvise on it, but it became Mary Lou playing Scott
Joplin, which any jazz musician knows it's supposed to be. But she plays
authentic, stride, authentic boogie-woogie, absolutely authentic ragtime and,
of course, was in this pre-bop thing by – I think it was 1937 or '38 she wrote
the "Zodiac Suite" which had all of those intervals, and that whole number
that later became formalized in Dizzy's and Bird's work, but she had it all
because the piano was the obvious thing. I mean all that was in front of you

– the altered chords and the melodies that resulted from it. And, so she was quite a person in that regard.

Thelonious Monk

The first time I ever heard Monk, he was playing much more like Art than what he later became. When I heard him, with Hawk and other people, it was like another guy. I mean he was doing all those things before. And he was playing all these things, but I was accustomed to hearing him play tenths and others things – three-fingered runs like Tatum. I mean he didn't phrase it like Tatum, but you could tell that that was the influence. And the touch was so different. But there were so many pianists around that bridged that particular gap. Billy Kyle was primarily known for the Earl Hines kind of inspired style of his, yet Billy had a lot of those kinds of phrases that were like pre-bop. It was not quite bop yet. But in his style you could hear the phrase ending on the offbeat, and other kinds of things like that. And he had quite an influence on Bud Powell, too.

Hank Jones

When I first heard Hank (Hank Jones) he was working with Hot Lips Page, and he was playing what I have to call a pre-bop style because it was beyond swing harmonically and otherwise. And his touch was, even then, just gorgeous, and he had been playing with other kinds of bands. He had a really beautiful touch on the piano, and he reminded me in those days of Ellis Larkins, who had the same kind of harmonic approach. It wasn't bop, but many of the aspects of what he did were long flowing lines. And, because he was a pianist, there were other things he could do rhythmically. It was a very interesting style, and Hank just had a good feeling, was a great accompanist, and many of the things that he did with Lips Page and other bands were, to my ear, post-Teddy Wilson kinds of things, somewhere between Clyde and Teddy. He had memorized some Art Tatum things so he had that under his fingers and he was really quite a player, even then.

BILLY had worked hard and was fortunate to have been able to meet, work for, and record with some of the finest musicians in America. The trip to Europe and the various shows and recordings he made were adding enormously to his experience and notoriety as a professional musician. He had arrived in New York City at the beginning of the bebop explosion and worked with its creators. His apprenticeship with the master, Art Tatum, made an indelible impression on his piano style – one that would support his artistic endeavors throughout his career. The years during his touch studies with Richard McClanahan had also proven to be invaluable to his future prowess as one of America's outstanding jazz pianists. BILLY had the good fortune to work with the Ben Webster group at the Three Deuces when he arrived in New York City, at the Onyx Club with Dizzy Gillespie, complete his first record date with bassist Al Hall and drummer Jimmy Crawford, appear in the Broadway Musical "Seven Lively Arts" with drummer Cozy Cole, record with the Sid Catlett All-Stars, befriend and study with Art Tatum, play with Slam Stewart, court and marry Theodora (Teddi) Castion, tour Europe with the Don Redman Band and form the Artie Shaw Grammercy 5 band which Shaw fronted. He had an opportunity to observe and know the great jazz pianists of the day that included Tatum, Bud Powell, Clyde Hart, Mary Lou Williams, Thelonious Monk and Hank Jones among others.

The outstanding area of jazz achievement in the 40's was the musical development of 52nd Street in Manhattan. BILLY would continue to build his reputation playing at various venues on the 'Street' including the famous Birdland.

III

52ⁿᵈ STREET

Jazz is a very personal way of playing music. – BILLY TAYLOR

BILLY TAYLOR immediately plunged into the musical activity on 52ⁿᵈ Street and the jam sessions at Minton's. His early recordings show him mixing Tatum-like runs and accompaniments with bebop melodic figures. His comping behind the soloists placed him firmly in the bebop camp, however. In fact, he developed a distinctive comping style, using block chords in both hands.

> BILLY TAYLOR: In 1943, I remember The Deuces, the Downbeat, the Onyx, the Famous Door, Kelly's Stables and the Hickory House – Joe Marsala was still there. The three big draws on The Street were Art Tatum, Coleman Hawkins, and Billie Holiday. And things were flexible for musicians on The Street. Like Don Byas might have an engagement at the Three Deuces as a leader, and then he'd go next door to the Downbeat as a sideman with Coleman Hawkins. 1

The cutting sessions there were just fantastic. With all of the musicians regularly working on The Street and with all those sitting in, astonishing sessions were inevitable. There were nights with five trumpets on the stand and five saxophones. One night Leonard Feather had a session in the Three Deuces with four vibraphonists. The Three Deuces was a pretty narrow room, but every one of the musicians at a Monday session had his own instrument set up, and each one was out to outplay the other.

> BILLY TAYLOR: The thing that I really appreciated in those days on 52ⁿᵈ street was – there's a lot been said about specific musicians leading other musicians down the garden path in terms of drugs, in terms of other bad habits. I always looked back at Sid Catlett and Jo Jones and many other musicians who were the next generation – Art Tatum to me, who literally stopped me from going nuts. It wasn't due to tremendous strength on my

part in those days but those guys were self-appointed big brothers. On many occasions Jo Jones took me by the arm and led me out the White Rose and said, "You had enough. You have another set to play." And I'm trying to get closer to these guys who can belt 'em down all night and not feel it, and I'm trying to be one of the guys and everything, and he'd say "Get out of here – what are you trying to do?" There was more of camaraderie, for me, in those days. And I think people like Hank Jones and for many of the guys that came in on that. I know there was for Erroll Garner; there was for many of us who came to New York around that same time. The lack of feeling of competition – each guy was pretty secure – even the younger ones were pretty secure in what they did. First it was when Erroll Garner was going to leave Slam Stewart. He gave me the job. He said, "Look, I'm going to the Coast. The job's open." I talked to Slam and got the whole book that they were playing with Slam and Doc West – Erroll Garner's and Slam's tunes. I had to learn a lot of the things that he played. He said, "This cat can handle it", and, by the same token, on many occasions guys worked in different places on the Street; one guy would be the leader, and his name would be out front, and the same group would move down the street to another club and somebody else's name would appear, cause he got the gig. 2

The Street became more and more modern. Dizzy had the first all-modern group thing in 1943 – the first piano-less group. The group had Dizzy, Bird, Don Byas, Max Roach and Oscar Pettiford. Bud Powell was supposed to make it on piano, but Bud was in Cootie Williams' band and was under age. Cootie was his guardian and wouldn't let him go. So the band opened without a piano.

> BILLY TAYLOR: I was working on The Street with Ben Webster at the time, and used to go over between sets and sit in with Dizzy's band. I kept running back and forth like that until Alexander, the man, who ran The Deuces where I had a regular job, got sick of it and fired me. George Wallington finally got the regular piano job with Dizzy. 3

Bud Powell was supposed to be the pianist with Dizzy Gillespie, when he worked with Oscar Pettiford, but Bud was working with Cootie Williams at the time. Williams was the legal guardian for the underage Bud Powell and wouldn't let him go. Before George Wallington filled the piano spot, BILLY TAYLOR was doubling between his regular job with Ben Webster at the Three Deuces and Gillespie-Pettiford at the Onyx.

> BILLY TAYLOR: That's how I lost my job with Ben, but I played with Dizzy, and he taught me many of the early bebop tunes, like the tunes 'Bebop',

'Night in Tunisia', 'Round Midnight' - and some of those early ones. Dizzy sat down at the piano and said, "These are the changes" and some of the things he had written outlines on like 'Salt Peanuts' and things like that – the simpler things. But Dizzy preferred to show a piano player because he wanted certain voicings on the piano, and he said that if he wrote just C 6th, that may or may not have a ninth in it which he wanted in that particular case. And so, he would say, "This is the voicing that I like and that just does this". And much of it – much of his voicings, I'm sure – were influenced by Clyde Hart, who was out of the Tatum-Wilson school and who was a part of the newer thing coming in harmonically. 4

There was a lot of movement on The Street. Don Byas might have an engagement at the Three Deuces as a leader and, at the same time, be a sideman with Coleman Hawkins at the Downbeat next door.

BILLY TAYLOR: I've talked to a lot of people who came into jazz with the 52nd Street thing, and for them it has always been very democratic and the kind of music and social setting that really brought to the consciousness of a lot of people the contributions of the people who were from different backgrounds. Because its kind of stupid to go to a club and see Zoot Sims playing with Sid Catlett and say that he plays okay for a white guy. That's ridiculous. It became apparent that there were guys who were just tremendous players on whatever instrument, and it wasn't just that Dizzy Gillespie or whoever put the stamp of approval on them. They were there because they could play and they could do the job perhaps better than anybody else around for that particular occasion. I mean Al Haig and Zoot and Stan Getz and a whole bunch of other guys that were – Shelly Manne was in the Coast Guard, and he would come in, and Sid Catlett would say, "Hey man, come on play." Well, they didn't invite a whole lot of servicemen up to play. You better believe that. And for this guy to come around and be asked to play was, you know, he could play. And there were many other guys like that. 5

ARNOLD SHAW: As the 52d St. joints filled with men in khaki and Navy whites, black musicians suddenly found themselves facing nightly hazards. Many of the military were from the South. They were not accustomed to the easy mixing of colors among musicians and audiences. And they particularly resented the attention that white chicks showered on black performers. Dizzy Gillespie, BILLY TAYLOR, and many other musicians carry unforgettable memories of the dangers involved in going home after the clubs closed. They felt lucky if they could make the Sixth Avenue subway station without an encounter. 6

The club owners took advantage of the knowledge that a sideman could attract some business on his own if he were publicized. Eventually sitting-in got to be less and less frequent. For one thing, it got to the place where you had to protect your job. Jobs began to get scarce. Then a second factor: as modern jazz evolved, guys would rehearse groups and get things set musically. The patterns within a group got so involved that you couldn't sit-in unless you knew the group and what they were doing in their writing and arranging. In time, everybody began to work on getting something different in group sounds, so it got harder and harder for just anyone to sit-in. In some respects, this constriction of sitting in hurt because it was so wonderful to be able to exchange ideas with other musicians. Roy Eldridge and Chu Berry, for example, were famous for going into towns, sitting in on sessions, and cutting everyone in sight. But sitting in is always unpredictable. You never knew what ideas unknown musicians were developing. So there were always surprises.

BILLY TAYLOR: That sort of thing is good because it's stimulating. A man faced with the kind of challenge you get in a sitting-in session is not so prone to imitate. He's apt to concentrate on building better and more original solos. Because, if after the third chorus at a free session, a man is still imitating, the guys there who are playing original lines will make him sound pretty sad. So that was one of the very good things about The Street – one practice of sitting in all the time and the challenges that came out of it. Coleman Hawkins was THE saxophonist then, just as Pres was in the 50's. Each man playing an instrument had a certain standard, and for those who played tenor, it was Hawkins. You either had more or less tone than he did. Well, no one could have more, I guess, so I should say you had varying degrees of tone less than he did. 7

Coleman Hawkins was sympathetic to the newer musicians as The Street became more modern. Clyde Hart, the pianist, was another transitional figure who was important. Clyde was one of the first of the traditional musicians to understand and command the harmonic background to satisfy modern musicians like Dizzy and to play modern jazz piano well. He had a lot to do with what early success Dizzy had with the public when he played with Dizzy's band. He helped people cross the bridge. Sid Catlett, the drummer, was another of the traditional musicians who made the transition.

BILLY TAYLOR: Sid Catlett was a great soloist and a great showman. He was completely at home musically in whatever he was doing. I remember once on the Coast, when Buddy Rich, Dodo Marmarosa, and Buddy De Franco were all with Tommy Dorsey, they used to come into the clubs and cut everybody. Buddy was cutting all the drummers, but not Sid. It used to annoy Buddy so much. He'd play all over his head – play fantastically – and then Sid would gently get back on the stand, and play his simple, melodic lines – on drums – and he'd make his point. It was Sid who steadied Dizzy on some of the first modern jazz records, like those on Guild. Max Roach at that time hadn't gotten his style together, and he was playing those far-out rhythm things. But Sid could play both with Dizzy and with the Dixieland musicians. He was the first guy I was aware of who was THE complete drummer. He could play any style, and he could play equally well in a big band or in any kind of small band. Sid was also the first drummer I'd heard who would play regular choruses – like thirty-two or sixty-four bars, et cetera – the way a piano or a horn might. He thought very musically. And if he had two blues choruses, he would take just twenty-four bars, and if you didn't come in on the twenty-fifth bar, he'd say, 'What?' Another thing about Sid is that he had such a big heart. He was a wonderful person. And he was a really advanced drummer in his concern with a melodic approach to the drums. Even today, most drummers have the rhythmic approach with no attention to the melodic potentialities of percussion. 8

BILLY formed his own quartet with John Collins, guitar, John Levy, bass, and Denzil Best, drums to do an album for H.R.S. in New York City in June 1947. They recorded Well Taylored, Don't Ask Questions, So You Think You're Cute? and Twinkle Toes.

> BILLY TAYLOR: That was a group I always wanted to work with. Except for this recording, this is the only documentation I have. It was one of the best groups that I ever led because each guy was so perfectly suited for that time. John, the way he walked was just so special. The way Denzil played kicked off together with John, they just locked right up and John Collins had played with Tatum and everybody and he had this wonderful harmonic sense. I would play a chord with ten notes in it and he would find seven more.

John O. Levy was born in New Orleans, Louisiana on April 11, 1912. He was raised in Chicago, played violin at 8 and piano at 15. Ray Nance was one of his high school buddies. He began playing bass when he was 17 and played with Earl Hines, Tiny Parham and Red Saunders. In 1943 he joined the Stuff Smith trio with Jimmy Jones and traveled to New York with him in 1944. There he played with Ben Webster (where he met BILLY), Erroll Garner, Don Byas, Charlie Ventura, Phil Moore and others. Drummer Denzil Decosta Best was from New York City where he was born on April 27, 1917. Denzil's father was a tuba player. Denzil studied piano beginning at age 6 and took several years of trumpet lessons. He played with Chris Columbus in 1940 and sat in on several sessions at Minton's. He had a protracted lung disease (tuberculosis?) during 1940 and 1941 and played piano and bass. In 1943 he began to play drums and worked with Ben Webster for nine months during 1943-'44 where he met BILLY TAYLOR. In '44 and '45 he played with Coleman Hawkins and during 1946 with Illinois Jacquet.

BILLY TAYLOR: Everyone has his own style if he's good. Like Nat Cole was on The Street. Nat had that personal thing of his. Art Tatum could cut him up and down any way you go, but Nat had his own thing. I remember at a session he sat down after Art and without a rhythm section. Man, that's asking for it! Yet, Nat played his own way and played well. One thing about his style is that Nat was one of the greatest pianists for doing things with the blues. Nat had a trio on The Street in the early 40's, and other trios began to follow. The Stuff Smith Trio at the Onyx Club in 1944 was one of the greatest trios I ever heard. He had Jimmy Jones on piano; John Levy was on bass. Just three guys and no drums! It was one of the most rhythmic trios I ever heard. Their only records were made for Asch, but they didn't show what the trio could do. They had worked up some things for the session, but then Stuff goofed and played some other things instead, as he was likely to do. 9

ERROLL GARNER: While I was on The Street, I wrote some little tunes for Slam, things that he could bow on, 'Play, Piano, Play' was later buried in a time capsule in Paris the year (1957) I won the Grand Prix du Disque. When I left Slam, I got BILLY TAYLOR, who had just come back from Washington, to take my chair. And Billy turned the chair over to Beryl Booker 10

On September 26, 1947 BILLY returned to the recording studio in New York City with Herman Mitchell, guitar, John Levy, bass, and Denzil Best, drums, to do another quartet album for H.R.S. This time they recorded Mr. B Bops. Restricted, Down The Champs Elysees, and Mitch's Pitch.

BILLY TAYLOR: That was a working group. That was after Levy and those guys had left to go with Shearing and I was still trying to get that sound going because I love the sound of piano, bass, drums and guitar. Everything I needed was right there. I had another instrument playing melody and harmony.

BILLY TAYLOR: 52nd Street was a change because many black musicians, unless they were headliners, never worked 52nd Street, and when Dizzy and some of the other non-headliners for those days began – Ben Webster was not a headliner nor Sid Catlett or even Hawk, who was perhaps one of the best known. The Street really came alive if Billie Holiday or Art Tatum were there; on other occasions when they had the young Erroll Garner. The turnabout had been that 52nd Street had generally been a place where the guys who did studio, did other kinds of work, were pretty much the guys that played on the Street until things began to change during the war. Then during the war the black musicians began to play on 52nd Street, and by the time I got to New York the majority of people who supported the Street were blacks who were coming downtown in that regard to a midtown place because this was fun, and it was not the kinds of problems you had in some other places. If a black couple decided to go to the Blue Angel or one of the East Side clubs they may not feel as comfortable as in other places. 11

During the 1940s and early 1950s Taylor was a sideman for many different swing and bebop leaders, and led groups of his own. His favorite ensemble size has been the trio. Among his best have been those with Ben Tucker and Grady Tate (1967, Tower 5111) and especially with Victor Gaskin and Bobby Thomas (June 1988, Taylor-Made CD 1001). Although his mature style is clearly bebop-based, his activities as a world-renowned jazz educator led him to master earlier styles as well.

PHOEBE JACOBS: I first met BILLY in Kelly's Stable; Ralph Watkins establishment on 52nd Street. BILLY and he were good friends. Ralph was very friendly with most of the musicians that were more than just musicians; they represented something that Ralph admired like appearance and manners and style, which BILLY always had. BILLY was also a very sharp dresser. Ralph liked that too. I remember them both wearing suits with patched pockets and a belt in the back. It was a style that Billy Eckstein brought to America when he returned from London.

BILLY TAYLOR: Phoebe used to work with Ralph Watkins. She worked with everybody you can think of back in those days, the early 50's.

BILLY TAYLOR: So many musicians are immature in their approach to everything other than their music. Why? First: To become a good musician you have to spend so much time with your instrument. It doesn't necessarily follow, but it often happens that because so much time is spent on learning your instrument, you don't spend much time on the things that broaden you outside of music. So many, for example, have grown up musically and then have had to go back to catch up with the rest of their lives so far as maturity is concerned. Don't forget that time involved in studying is huge for a musician. There must be no less than four hours of practice a day, plus the times for lessons, plus a couple of hours for other studies connected with music. So figure eight to ten hours of music a day, added to eating and sleeping, and there isn't much time for other things that would broaden a person. Also, a musician's hours aren't conducive to social relationships. A guy gets married, say, but he plays nights, so when will he meet his wife's friends? Or his own?

The prognosis for modern jazz musicians is a very individual thing. It's hard to generalize on something as personal as this is. But you can say that if a musician is lucky enough to be able to go to school and get a general background as well as a specifically musical foundation, he can mature. One thing that would help is if the music magazines would minimize the hero worship that tends to cluster around the stars. Also, if the music magazines could spend time on young musicians – including teen-age musicians – in all sections of the country so these starting jazzmen can get some encouragement and moral support.

If an unknown youngster comes to New York, there's nothing for him to do. He has to get his work connections together, work out his union card, and sweat it out. If he's a strong person, he can withstand the temptation of falling into the habits of some of the men who have succumbed. He can hold himself back from conforming to the things he shouldn't conform to. But some youngsters can't. There should be guidance for these young musicians from out of town and in town too, for that matter. And that guidance could come from the union as a regular AFM service. All of these young guys have to have some help growing up. Now, I know a youngster who right now is much more mature in his PLAYING than many better-established musicians. But, EMOTIONALLY, he's still young. But he isn't known, and unless he's lucky, he'll fall by the wayside, not because he lacks the musical talent to make it but because there are other things in his way. By not working, by just being on the outside looking in, he can get discouraged enough to weaken.12

In New York City on November 20, 1949 BILLY TAYLOR took his quintet into the studio to do a record date for Savoy Records. The personnel included John Hardee, tenor saxophone, Milt Page, organ, John Simmons, bass and Joe Harris, drums. The tunes were Take The A Train, Misty Blues, The Bug, and Prelude To A Kiss.

BILLY TAYLOR: Teddy Reig was one of those guys that hung around jazz, managed jazz musicians, very hip and knew a lot about what was going on. He called me for this date. Milt Page was the organist at the Roxy Theater, in New York, and he used to come up to hear me play all the time. I had a piano and organ act. When Dick Hyman first met me, the place where he was working, Wells, was the place that always featured electric organ players and piano players. So Milt came up and heard me play with the guy I was working with then and then he wanted to play. He wasn't a jazz player but he wanted to play. And so he did pretty well on this record.

Bassist John Jacob Simmons was born on October 6, 1918 in Haskell, Oklahoma. He studied at the Chicago School of Music from 1945-'49 and in 1946 played with Clifford Jordan. During 1949 he formed his own trio prior to recording with BILLY TAYLOR.

Drummer Joe Harris (Joseph Allison Harris) was born in Pittsburgh, Pennsylvania on December 23, 1926. He began to study privately at age 15 and was introduced to bebop drumming by Art Blakey and Ray Brown. During 1946-'48 he played with Dizzy Gillespie (he was one of the featured players in the Parker-Gillespie concert at Carnegie Hall in 1947). In 1948-'49 he played with Arnett Cobb prior to the record date with BILLY TAYLOR in November '49.

In 1949 BILLY became the house pianist for Birdland. While there he played with Charlie Parker, Dizzy Gillespie, Georgie Auld, Roy Eldridge, Slim Gaillard, Terry Gibbs, Gerry Mulligan, Howard McGhee, Lee Konitz, Oscar Pettiford, Kai Winding, Miles Davis and many others.

BILLY got the job at Birdland because Al Haig decided to leave the music business and left suddenly. Bird (Charlie Parker) was preparing for his opening at Birdland with his Bird and Strings group the first time. At that time, Al Haig was Bird's regular piano player. Al called BILLY one afternoon and asked BILLY if he could cover for him (Al). BILLY, thinking Al meant for that evening, quickly agreed, went down to Birdland and played the opening evening. The following night BILLY didn't show up at Birdland and Monte Kay, who was the manager of Birdland at that time, called BILLY and said: "Where are you?" BILLY responded that he was at home. Kay retorted: "You're supposed to be here! Get down here!" BILLY explained that Al was supposed to be there – that he had agreed to sub for Al on the opening night. Monte Kay explained that Al was not there and was not coming. Al had apparently left town to become a gardener in nearby Connecticut but at that time nobody knew where he had gone.

BILLY TAYLOR: When I was playing with Bird (Charlie Parker) I was studying with Richard McClanahan at Steinway Hall on 57 Street playing Debussy, Bach and other classics. My lesson was always scheduled later in the evening so I usually practiced at the club before the gig. One time when I was practicing at the club Bird came in to get an advance on his pay. I was practicing on a piece by Debussy and sensed someone in the room. I looked up and saw that it was Bird. He said: "I really like that, man! That's Debussy, isn't it?" I answered: "Yes." He said: "I know that piece." He then took his horn out of the case and played the next section of the composition. It was the Debussy 'Arabesque'. I couldn't believe it!!

Joining Stan Getz and His Orchestra on a live date at the Apollo Theater, August 17, 1950, to do an album for Charlie Parker Records, BILLY played piano with Stan Fishelson, Al Porcino and Idrees Sulieman, trumpets, Johnny Mandel, bass trumpet; Don Lanphere, Zoot Sims, and Stan Getz, tenor saxophones, Gerry Mulligan, baritone saxophone, Tommy Potter, bass, Roy Haynes, drums, and Sarah Vaughan who sang on the vocal track "My Gentleman Friend." The other tunes on the album included Four Brothers and Early Autumn.

BILLY TAYLOR: Stan Getz put together a Four Brothers band. The record that came out of that was made at the Apollo Theater. I was playing both with him and Roy Haynes and Tommy Potter. We played for the Stan Getz Band and Charlie Parker with Strings.

On August 25, 1950 BILLY TAYLOR, piano, John Collins, guitar, Percy Heath, bass, and Art Blakey, drums joined tenor saxophonist Coleman Hawkins to do an album for Roost Records. They recorded You've Got Me Crying Again, Can Anyone Explain?, I Cross My Fingers and I'll Know.

BILLY worked with Miles Davis at Birdland, while house pianist, on several occasions and BILLY admired the new style Miles developed. BILLY felt that when Miles tried to play like Dizzy Gillespie he wasn't able to develop his own style and as a result was difficult to get along with personally. Miles loved the way BILLY played ballads and would often ask BILLY is he knew this tune or that tune. He would ask BILLY how he had learned all of the ballads that he played. BILLY told Miles he had learned them as a result of playing solo piano for such a long time. Miles was interested in a lot of show tunes as they gave him more interesting harmonies to work with. Miles particularly liked the ballad, "What Is There To Say" that was considered a hip show tune at the time.

DAVID BAILEY: BILLY and I have been friends since the early 50's. I wasn't playing with I first met him. I was producing concerts with Art Blakey and John Collins in New York; they were called "Three O'Clock High". They were held at the Audubon Ballroom and the Rockland Palace. BILLY was a good friend of John Collins. They lived in Riverton in the same apartment building. BILLY was playing solo piano at Birdland and he used to come and take tickets for us on Sunday afternoons; that's how I met BILLY.

BILLY'S Trio recorded the album PIANO PANARAMA in New York City in 1951. The personnel with BILLY were Earl May, bass and Ed Thigpen, drums. The tunes recorded were Wrap Your Troubles In Dreams, Good Groove, Thou Swell, Somebody Loves Me and All Ears.

TAYLOR reformed the BILLY TAYLOR Quartet, which consisted of TAYLOR, piano, John Collins, guitar, Al Hall, bass and Shadow Wilson, drums and recorded Good Groove, Wrap Your Troubles In Dreams, What Is There To Say?, Thou Swell, Willow Weep For Me, The Very Thought Of You, Somebody Loves Me, and If I Had You for Atlantic Records on February 20, 1951.

> BILLY TAYLOR: Al Hall was the bass player on the first record I ever made as a pro. Actually I'm on part of it and Clyde (Hart) is on the other part.

Shadow Rossiere Wilson was born in Yonkers, New York on September 25, 1919. He began playing professionally with Frankie Fairfax in 1938 and joined Lucky Millinder in 1939. After a short stint with Jimmy Mundy he played with Benny Carter, 1939, and Tiny Bradshaw in 1940. During the latter part of 1940 he joined Lionel Hampton and remained with him for about a year. From 1941 until 1943 he played with Georgie Auld and Louis Jordan prior to joining the Count Basie band in 1944. He played with Basie, on and off, through 1948 doing an interim stint with Illinois Jacquet in 1947. After a time with the Woody Herman Band in 1949 he recorded with BILLY TAYLOR.

On May 25, 1951 the BILLY TAYLOR Trio consisting of BILLY, Aaron Bell, bass and Kelly Martin, drums recorded several tunes for Brunswick Records in New York City including All Ears, Darn That Dream, My Heart Stood Still and Double Duty.

> BILLY TAYLOR: That album was recorded for Brunswick Records. One of the tunes was All Ears. That was a funny record. The guy who produced that wanted something different. He said: "You know, you play a lot of piano but what can you do that's different?" I said: "I don't know – I play it the way I play." He said: "Did you ever play any boogie-woogie?" I said: "Yeah." He said: "Is there any way you could combine that with the kind of thing you do?" So, I combined boogie-woogie and bebop – bebop with my right hand and boogie-woogie with my left hand. I don't know what happened with those records.

Bass player Aaron Samuel Bell was born in Muskogee, Oklahoma on April 24, 1922. He received the Bachelor of Arts degree from Xavier University in New Orleans in 1942 and a Master of Arts degree from New York University in 1951. He went on to receive a Ph.D. from Columbia University in New York City in 1971. Bell served in the US Navy during WW II and joined the Andy Kirk band in 1947. After that stint he returned to Muskogee and taught high school music. Returning to the road he worked with Ed Wilcox, Lucky Millinder, Herman Chittison, Teddy Wilson,

Lester Young, Eddie Heywood, Johnnie Smith, Dorothy Donegan and Mat Mathews. While attending NYU he made the records with BILLY TAYLOR.

AARON BELL: Playing with BILLY was very enjoyable – he's a perfect gentleman. He wants you to be on time. BILLY is an excellent pianist. He's a big help to jazz musicians, in general; by the way he carries himself. He gives respect and demands respect. He is very articulate, speaks well, dresses well and conducts himself on the job like a gentleman and obviously anybody who's working with him will do the same. There were three guys in my career who were like that: BILLY, Teddy Wilson and Andy Kirk. I was just a kid when I played with Andy Kirk. BILLY made people respect jazz and jazz musicians and educated a lot of people; he created a large audience for jazz.

ROBIN BELL STEVENS: I was first aware of BILLY in the womb. As my dad, Aaron Bell, is a bass player, played in BILLY'S trio years ago, so they were friends before I was even born. I first met him when I was a child and then started working with him professionally over twenty years ago (1980's) through the Jackie Robinson Foundation. He had been the Music Director of the Foundation's Afternoon Of Jazz Festival and I was brought on as the Executive Producer so we worked together for a lot of years. As a kid I first heard him play. My dad took me to many concerts. I was very young. I was a real little kid. My dad was really good that way. When we got older he would actually take us out on the road with him when he was with Duke Ellington's band. He really believed in taking his kids to work before it was really popular and fortunately for us it was music.

On September 29, 1951 BILLY joined with Mile Davis in a series of three tunes, The Squirrel, Move and Lady Bird that ended up in the album, MILES DAVIS: THE COMPLETE BIRDLAND RECORDINGS released by Definitive Records. The personnel including Miles and BILLY featuring Eddie "Lockjaw" Davis, tenor saxophone, Big Nick Nicholas, tenor saxophone, Charles Mingus, bass, and Art Blakey, drums.

In New York City on November 1, 1951 BILLY TAYLOR, piano, Zoot Sims, tenor saxophone/maracas, Mundell Lowe, guitar, Earl May, bass, Jo Jones, drums, and Frank Conion, congas, cut several tunes for Roost Records. The tunes were Cuban Caper, Cu-Blue, Squeeze Me and Feeling Frisky.

BILLY TAYLOR: I think Zoot just played maracas on that date. He just came to hang out – he was a friend.

MUNDELL LOWE: BILLY is one of the nicest people in this so-called business. I worked with BILLY in the 1950's and the 60's. We worked Birdland and some other places around New York City. Also, BILLY played piano on

"A Grand Night For Swinging" that I made for Riverside Records. In addition to that I believe we did some other recording together. In the quartet BILLY was using at the time was players like Charles Mingus, a drummer from Connecticut, etc. I will always consider BILLY a good friend. He befriended me with some (buddies) at a time when I needed it.

BILLY TAYLOR: He was cool. The thing I loved about Mundy was that when I did the show in '57, the first of the shows on jazz education, he was perfect, cool, just played his head off.

Earl May is a self-taught bass player who was born in New York City on September 17, 1927. He played with Gene Ammons, Miles Davis, Sonny Stitt and Mercer Ellington prior to joining the BILLY TAYLOR TRIO.

EARL MAY: I first met BILLY in 1950 or 1951 when we had a gig with Mercer Ellington. Mercer had a sextet and BILLY was in the rhythm section. BILLY thinks we met at a Lester Young gig that we had but we met before that.

BILLY TAYLOR: As I remember it, I had a call one night from a guy who asked if I was free to play a dance date with Lester Young at the Audubon Ballroom (the ballroom where Malcolm X was assassinated later on). I didn't drive at that time and took a subway or some other public transportation. After I arrived I sat backstage reading and a young fellow came up and spoke to me and we started a conversation. I thought he was just another fan, not a musician, so we continued talking until Prez arrived and then the young guy picked up a bass. I loved his playing and thought: "This guy's a swinging bass player." I felt something about the way he played bass was strange but didn't identify it right away. Eventually I realized, the guy's a left-handed bass player!

Drummer Jo (Jonathan) Jones was born in Chicago, Illinois on July 10, 1911. He was raised in Alabama, studied music for twelve years, and became proficient on piano, trumpet and the saxophones. When he left school he joined a carnival and toured the Chautauqua circuit working as a single and tap-dancer. In the late 20's he joined Walter Page's Blue Devils until he moved to Omaha, Nebraska where he played drums with Lloyd Hunter. In 1933 he moved to Kansas City and joined the Count Basie Orchestra, remaining until 1936. He then played with Walter Page in the Jeter–Pillars Orchestra in St. Louis. At the end of 1936 Page and Jones left to rejoin the Count Basie Orchestra. Jo Jones served in the US Army during WW II, 1944-'46, and then rejoined Basie until 1948 when he played with Jazz At The Philharmonic, with Illinois Jacquet and Lester Young prior to making the record with BILLY TAYLOR in 1951.

Toward the end of 1951 BILLY played piano and organ on an album featuring himself, Joe Holiday, tenor saxophone, Jordan Fordin, alto saxophone, Earl May, bass and Charlie Smith, congas in an album entitled Mambo Jazz which was released by Prestige Records. The tunes recorded were Besame Mucho, I Wouldn't Want To Walk Without You and Fiesta.

BILLY TAYLOR: The Street sort of folded gradually. The decline had begun around late 1946 and early 1947. Why? Well, with so large a number of hangers-on, those hangers-on were finding a lucrative market for all the vices – drugs, et cetera – and were preying on the school kids and others who came down. They didn't care too much about traffic from the musicians themselves. Then too, the Street was close enough to the East Side so that people from the East Side used to come down 'slumming,' and they were available too to those pushers and to the guys looking for a fast buck. And the club owners didn't help much either, because of their own greed and the fact that they didn't police their clubs better. By their greed, I mean the small tables and the big cover charges didn't build up good will. And the owners got into booking wars. If Dizzy was working at the Onyx, The Deuces would have Roy Eldridge and Charlie Shavers. Or if Bird was at one club, another club would get all the other alto men available – like Pete Brown and fifteen others. That sort of thing was wonderful for listeners, but it didn't help music, having that kind of battle of attractions. 13

BILLY eventually returned to 52d St., even though jazz had largely moved away by then, but it wasn't until Marian McPartland had given up her lease on Hickory House. Her tenure changed the famous jazz club from a Dixieland room to a showcase for piano trios. Even though BILLY worked there steadily for five years, he didn't break her record.

What made 52d St. was not just the number of music clubs, but the variety of the music you could hear and the interchange between musicians. Color was no hang up. When BILLY took a job, he was free to hire anybody he wanted. Drummer Shelly Manne used to sit in at various clubs wearing his Coast Guard uniform. The only thing people thought was that he was a good drummer. Race was not an issue. At Café Society downtown, owned by Barney Josephson, great care was taken to insure a good quality sound system, in-tune piano and good lighting. The shows were well-presented as compared with those in effect on 52d St. However, it was felt that the clubs on the Street were informal and intimate which allowed for great rapport between artist and audience. The Street changed the character of American jazz.

BILLY TAYLOR: It was exciting to be a part of that. That period was a time when I think the musicians who are now legendary, like Miles and Coltrane and

Charlie Parker and Dizzy Gillespie and many others, actually were shaping the language we use today. What they were doing was looking for the manner in which they were going to speak the language as individuals. They were standing on the shoulders of the Art Tatums, the Lester Youngs and the people who preceded us. These musicians came up with ideas that were not only very sound but were really the kinds of things that people have been building on ever since.

BILLY'S activities on "The Street" had brought him to The Deuces, The Downbeat, The Onyx, The Famous Door, Kelly's Stables, The Royal Roost and the Hickory House. He continued writing articles on jazz for Down Beat magazine, Saturday Review, Esquire and other journals. He enjoyed the joy, what was then common practice, of 'sitting in' with various groups and playing with great musicians like Sid Catlett, John Levy, Denzil Best and others. In addition to his trio playing he formed and recorded with his own quartet and quintet. He became the house pianist at Birdland and played with Charlie Parker, Dizzy Gillespie, Georgie Auld, Roy Eldridge, Slim Gaillard, Terry Gibbs, Gerry Mulligan, Howard McGhee, Lee Konitz, Oscar Pettiford, Kai Winding and others. He met and enjoyed playing with bassist Earl May who would work with BILLY for nearly a decade.

The best was yet to come as during the remainder of the 50's BILLY would form his own trio which set the pace for that instrumentation we have all come to love and admire over the past fifty and more years.

IV

THE BILLY TAYLOR TRIO

The most immediate reaction to cool concepts came from musicians who were from the bebop generation. – BILLY TAYLOR

MARY LOU WILLIAMS: In '52 I came back with a trio of my own to the Downbeat. The owner then was Morris Levy, the man who owned Birdland. He had a brother – the one who was killed at Birdland. Irving was my friend, and I was very fond of him. He was the manager of the Downbeat. I alternated with BILLY TAYLOR. After the Downbeat, I was sent to Europe (in 1952) on a goodwill tour. I was sent to England to break the ban that prevented American musicians from playing in England or English musicians from playing here. This had never happened in thirty years. I was supposed to stay there for nine days and I wound up in Europe for over two years: eleven months in England and then in Paris. The Europeans had the same attitude toward jazz as the people on 52nd St. They respected the artist and loved the music. When I came back to the United States in '54, the Street was gone. 1

ARNOLD SHAW: "By 1948 the Downbeat name was gone from the brownstone at 66 West, and in its place was the Carousel, a club that traded on skin, not music, and the unbuttoned humor of B.S. Pully. The name Downbeat appeared again, not on The Street but on West 54th, where in '52 someone established Le Downbeat (no less). Studious-looking pianist BILLY TAYLOR and mallet-murdering vibraharpist Terry Gibbs occupied the small bandstand during much of its two-year storefront existence." 2

On April 18, 1952 BILLY formed a band that recorded Alone, To Be Or Not To Bop, Lonesome And Blue and Paradise. The record was never released. The excellent personnel included Taft Jordan, trumpet, George Matthews, trombone, Doc Clifford and George James, alto saxophones, George Berg and Stan Getz, tenor saxophones, Bill Doggett, organ, Earl May, bass, Charlie Smith, drums and BILLY TAYLOR, piano.

Drummer Charlie (Charles) Smith was born in New York City April 15, 1927. He was raised in Long Island and played with various groups in and around New York City until he joined a trio (Hank Jones, piano and Ray Brown, bass) who were accompanying Ella Fitzgerald in 1948. Smith than played with Erroll Garner, George Shearing, Slam Stewart, Benny Goodman, Oscar Peterson, Artie Shaw and others prior to joining the BILLY TAYLOR TRIO in 1952.

RUDOLPH (RUDY) TAYLOR: The problem they had with Charlie Smith was every time they got ready to play the question was: "Where's Charlie?" Charlie was out chasing the girls. When they played in D.C. Charlie would be walking down the street around 2:00 in the morning with some young lady. He was a character.

HERB WONG: I knew about BILLY TAYLOR through his records first when he had this trio with Earl May, the bass player, and I were very impressed with him. That was in the 50's. I played those records a lot – they were pretty special. And there was a great photo of him wearing the glasses that he still wears, actually, not rimless. I remember the first time I saw the picture on the LP. I said: "Man, this cat looks like a scholar!" He looked really studious, young, and very interesting. So than I had a trip in the mid-50's that took me to New York. I was actually visiting eleven national parks; my other interest, you know (bird-watching). So when I got to New York I went to Birdland and he was playing. I thought: "Oh man, there's the guy!" I don't remember what it was but he seemed to be (I went there more than once) a utility pianist. It wasn't his trio. He was playing with a variety of different people – he was the house pianist. That's when I realized that he was extremely elastic and was able to adapt to a variety of styles – pretty amazing, almost like a chameleon – always with a certain amount of flair, too. His body language was also interesting to me. I met him casually at that time as a fan. He was very cordial as usual.

The BILLY TAYLOR SEXTET consisting of Chuck Wayne, guitar, Earl May, bass, Charlie Smith, drums; Frank Conlon and Manny Quando, bongos/conga; and BILLY TAYLOR, piano, recorded Cuban Nightingale, Tiboro, Makin' Whoopee and Moonlight Saving Time for ROOST RECORDS on May 2, 1952.

BILLY TAYLOR: Actually what had happened was that I had, prior to this, played with Machito. He had a big band and this was at a time – I got the gig when I was working with Walter "Foots" Thomas who had a studio together with Cozy Cole on 48th St. One of the gigs I played with this guy was at La Conga nightclub, down in Times Square. At La Conga they had a group of Cubans – we were the relief band. The union said they had to take one night off and bring in a relief group. The relief band had to be a Latin band. This was my first real, nightly, saturation with Afro-Cuban music and they were wailing. Anytime I wasn't playing I was sitting there listening and soaking it all up. So the piano player got drafted and the leader hired me. That's how I got into Latin music. That's where this record came from. I got to know those guys. When the Latin piano player came back I didn't have a gig so I would go down and listen to those guys.

A quartet was formed by BILLY TAYLOR to record for BRUNSWICK RECORDS on July 11, 1952 in New York City. The personnel was made up of Chuck Wayne, guitar, George Duvivier, bass, Sid Bulkin, drums and BILLY, piano. The quartet recorded Three Little Words and Oscar Rides Again. Oscar Pettiford played 'cello on the latter.

George B. Duvivier, bassist, was born in New York City on August 17, 1920. He studied violin at the Conservatory of Music and Art and was the assistant concertmaster of the Central Manhattan Symphony Orchestra when he was 16. While he attended New York University he studied bass and composing-arranging. During 1940-'41 he played with Coleman Hawkins and in the 1942-'43 years played with Eddie Barefield and Lucky Millinder. In 1943 during WWII he began serving in the U S Army. When he was released in 1945 he began writing for the Jimmie Lunceford Orchestra. In 1950 he toured Europe with Nellie Lutcher.

During the 50's BILLY recorded for various record labels including Riverside, Roost, Prestige, Impulse, ABC Paramount, Sesac, Capitol and Mercury. A number of well known performers were in the Capitol stable at that time including Nat King Cole, Peggy Lee, Frank Sinatra and George Shearing.

DAVE BRUBECK: One of the first New York jazz musicians that I got to know as a friend when I came from the West Coast to play at Birdland was BILLY TAYLOR. That was close to fifty years ago. We have remained friends ever since. I've always felt closeness to BILLY because we have parallel interests. We both love playing jazz and we are also interested in writing various forms of music such as a string quartet or pieces for orchestra and chorus.

In the autumn of 1952 the BILLY TAYLOR TRIO with bass man Charlie Mingus, drummer Marquis Foster and pianist BILLY TAYLOR played at STORYVILLE in BOSTON and recorded Ladybird, I'm Beginning To See The Light, All The Things You Are, Laura and What Is This Thing Called Love for ROOST RECORDS.

Charles Mingus, Jr. was born in Nogales, Arizona on April 22, 1922. His family moved to the Watts area in Los Angeles where Mingus grew up. He began studying trombone, then 'cello, switching to bass when he was 16. He studied bass with Red

Callender and Herman Rheinschagen, a former New York Philharmonic bassist. He also studied composition with Lloyd Reese. In the early 40's he played with Buddy Collette, Lee Young and Louis Armstrong. By the mid-40's he was playing with Kid Ory, Alvino Rey and Lionel Hampton. In the late 40's Mingus wrote compositions including "Mingus Fingers" and led various groups under the title Baron Mingus. In the early 50's he worked with Red Norvo prior to joining BILLY TAYLOR.

BRIAN PRIESTLEY: Mingus came with an enviable reputation as a bassist, and a less enviable one of being able to throw his weight around . . . Because Celia was already working as a secretary Mingus could weather the lack of income from playing, but he was offered some casual engagements and, after appearing at Birdland with Miles Davis and BILLY TAYLOR, he was free to travel to Boston for a fortnight with the BILLY TAYLOR TRIO. TAYLOR described the association as follows: "I was influenced by Ellington, and so was he. I knew many Tatum voicings, and so did he. We learned a lot from each other. I taught him what a montuna was, and he taught me not to make the drums and bass subservient to the piano in a trio". Although Lennie Tristano did exert a minor but undeniable influence on Mingus's thinking about group approaches to improvisation, it is perhaps not surprising that Mingus found more freedom as a bass player alongside the many other pianists he gigged with, including on several occasions in 1953 the bebop giant Bud Powell (for whom he created several introductory bass figures), and especially BILLY TAYLOR. 3

GEORGE WEIN: When I opened my club in Boston, Storyville, one of the first groups I brought in from NY was BILLY TAYLOR and his trio. BILLY'S trio at that time featured Charles Mingus on bass. It was a fascinating week. My feeling about BILLY personally is one of the true gentlemen in any field that I've ever had the privilege of meeting. Musically, he fits well into the panorama of great pianists that bloomed throughout the 50's and the 60's.

NAT HENTOFF: Back in the 50's I was on a radio station in Boston and, among other things, I had a jazz program and BILLY came in to George Wein's Storyville Club. Mingus (Charles) was a pretty powerful presence all by himself. BILLY was very impressive as well. Not only the technique but also he had presence and you could tell it was BILLY TAYLOR. In other words he had his own signature. We talked and then I got to know him in New York. I became the New York editor of Down Beat a couple of years later and ever since then we've talked and I've heard him on CBS Sunday Morning.

BILLY formed his own trio in earnest with bass player Earl May and drummer Charlie Smith in 1952. That trio remained intact for three years.

PHIL SCHAAP: Musically it's uncanny what he can do. He's able to play perfectly in a number of genres. BILLY is one of the people who helped codify the piano-led trio. In the 40's the trio, as we knew it, didn't really exist – the piano, bass and drum trio didn't exist. There was piano, guitar and bass; Tatum had it, Tristano used it, Nat "King" Cole had it, Clarence Profit started it. BILLY would be an impossible person to invent because you would say: "Too perfect!!"

The trio with Earl May, bass, Charlie Smith, drums and BILLY TAYLOR, piano, did a record date for PRESTIGE RECORDS on November 18, 1952 in New York City. The tunes were They Can't Take That Away From Me, All Too Soon, Accent On Youth, Give Me The Simple Life and Me.

On December 10, 1952 the trio, Earl May, bass; Charlie Smith, drums; and BILLY closed out the recording year by playing Little Girl Blue, The Man With A Horn, Let's Get Away From It All and Lover for Prestige Records.

EARL MAY: Somebody sent a copy of that record to me recently; that's got to be the fastest record. I thought that couldn't be me, but it was. Lover was so fast. I can't believe how fast we played – of course we were much younger then, really young.

In the December 31, 1952 issue of Down Beat Magazine BILLY TAYLOR'S recorded album of the autumn of 1952 was reviewed thusly. The tunes on the album were Laura, Ladybird, All The Things You Are, I'm Beginning to See The Light and What Is This Thing Called Love. The album received a four star rating (the top rating at that time). The reviewer said the album was recorded at George Wein's Boston Storyville Club, supervised and annotated by Nat Hentoff. "The typically fleet and fecund series of improvisations by BILLY with Charles Mingus and drummer Marquis Foster. It looks like a record month for the North Carolina piano flash who also steals top honors on Jazz Times USA." The record was recorded on Roost RLP406. In that same issue of Down Beat BILLY placed in the reader's piano poll after Oscar Peterson, George Powell, Bud Powell, Erroll Garner, Dave Brubeck and Lennie Tristano.

ALAN BERGMAN: I have some of those 10-inch Prestige L.P.'s from the mid-50's, the trios with Charlie Smith and Earl May. I first heard BILLY live at the Hickory House when I was studying for the bar examination. Maybe before then, I was in college, around '56 or '57 at The Composer and at the Embers. I don't recall if I ever heard him at Birdland – that was before my time.

BILLY began to spend more and more time serving as a spokesman for jazz. He gave workshops for teachers and lectures for the general public. He was extended an invitation by Yale University, which he accepted, to attend a conference to explore ways to improve the teaching of music in public schools. Only two jazz musicians attended the conference, BILLY TAYLOR and Mercer Ellington. The conference lasted for two weeks and resulted in a long list of recommendations that were forwarded to the Department of Health, Education and Welfare, the agency that funded the meetings. Although no formal action resulted from the conference, BILLY gradually got involved in radio and television.

In 1953 Down Beat Magazine presented BILLY TAYLOR with the New Star Award, the first International Critics Award for "Talent Deserving Wider Recognition".

BRUCE LUNDVALL: BILLY'S wonderful. I first saw him play at Birdland in 1953 with his trio and many times thereafter. I didn't know him then but he was one of the most articulate people as well as one of the best musicians. And he had some records – I remember buying "Too Blue" and some things like that, Afro jazz things that were really great little records. I think they were on Prestige or Roost, no Prestige I think. Anyway, I got to meet him much, much later and he's always been a real huge supporter of the music and just continues to play at the top of his game. He's one of the nicest, friendliest men and lives his life for this music and dedicates his life to it.

The first record date for BILLY in 1953 was finished on May 7 in NYC. BILLY added three bongo and conga players (Machito's rhythm section) to the trio, Jose Manguel, Ubal Nieto and Chico Guerro, while retaining Earl May on bass and Charlie Smith on drums for an album that was released under various titles, among them, MAMBO JAZZ, for PRESTIGE RECORDS and ORIGINAL JAZZ CLASSICS. The tunes recorded included I Love The Mambo, Candido, Early Morning Mambo and Mambo Azul.

JIMMY HEATH: I was working with the Symphony Sid All-Stars – Miles, J.J. Johnson, Milt Jackson, Kenny Clarke and Percy Heath – in 1953 at a place on 54th street, the Downbeat. BILLY'S trio was opposite the Symphony Sid All-Stars. BILLY had Earl May, bass and Charlie Smith, drums; a left-handed bass player and left-handed drummer. So it looked like we were looking in a mirror or something. It was the first time I heard BILLY play.

On November 2, 1953, in New York City, the BILLY TAYLOR TRIO with Earl May, bass, Charlie Smith, drums, and BILLY, piano recorded Cool And Caressing, Who Can I Turn To?, My One And Only Love, Tenderly, I've Got The Whole World, Bird Watcher, BT's DT's and Hey Look for PRESTIGE RECORDS.

The final record date for 1953 occurred on December 29 in New York City and featured BILLY, Earl May, bass and Charlie Smith, drums. The tunes recorded were That's All, The Little Things, Nice Work If You Can Get It and The Surrey With The Fringe On Top. The record was released by Prestige.

During 1953-54 ERNIE ROYAL and HIS PRINCES recorded an album for URANIA RECORDS. In addition to Ernie Royal, trumpet, the band included Sidney Gross and George Barnes, guitars, Oscar Pettiford, bass, Osie Johnson, drums, and BILLY TAYLOR, piano. They recorded Flowin', Fascinating Rhythm, Stompin' At The Savoy, Stardust, Taking A Chance On Love, Handful Of Stars, It's A Grand Night For Swinging and What Is There To Say.

On July 30, 1954 The BILLY TAYLOR TRIO with Earl May, bass, Charlie Smith, drums, and BILLY, piano, recorded an album entitled CROSS SECTION for PRESTIGE, later released by ORIGINAL JAZZ CLASSICS. The tunes included were Time For Tex, Moonlight In Vermont, I'll Be Around, Biddy's Beat, Eddie's Tune, Mood For Mendez, Goodbye and Lullaby Of Birdland.

The BILLY TAYLOR QUARTET with Earl May, bass, Charlie Smith, drums, Candido Camero, conga drums and BILLY, piano did an album on September 7, 1954 entitled THE BILLY TAYLOR TRIO WITH CANDIDO for PRESTIGE RECORDS, later re-released by ORIGINAL JAZZ CLASSICS. The tunes were Dectivity, A Live One, Mambo Inn, Bit Of Bedlam, Different Bells and Love For Sale.

> FRAN RICHARD: I've been familiar with BILLY and his music since I was a teenager. I used to hear him in various hotels and rooms in the city. One time I took two classical-type music lovers to hear BILLY. One of them said: "He's playing the music of Chopin or Mozart." I said: "No, he's playing SWEET GEORGIA BROWN!!" I'll never forget it. Nobody could believe what he or she was hearing there. I couldn't believe what he was doing there. Everything under the sun came in, you heard it, and then it got incorporated. That's the thing about hearing some really excellent jazz musicians. Any great improvisers; you can hear how their brain works. We don't get that so much on the concert side. It's all pretty much pre-studied and pre-learned.

On November 6, 1954 BILLY played piano with the COLEMAN HAWKINS BAND as they recorded Lullaby Of Birdland, Get Happy, Blue Lou, Stompin' At The Savoy and Just You Just Me for JAZZTONE RECORDS. The personnel were Hawkins, tenor saxophone, Emmett Berry, trumpet, Eddie Bert, trombone, Milt Hinton, bass, Jo Jones, drums, and BILLY TAYLOR, piano.

> EDDIE BERT: BILLY TAYLOR and I recorded with Coleman Hawkins in 1954. That was for JazzTone Records and Milton Hinton was on it, Jo Jones and Emmett Berry. Milt Hinton took pictures of that date and they're in his

book. That recording turned out great – all head arrangements, no music, and it won all kinds of awards. Coleman Hawkins had just come in from Europe on a plane and he was oiling his horn. Forty-five minutes into the date the producer said: "You don't have any music, you haven't played a note and the tenor player is oiling his horn!" In three hours we recorded all the tunes. It was more fun in those days – it's not like that now.

BILLY joined with Milt Hinton, bass, Jo Jones, drums, and Coleman Hawkins, tenor saxophone to record with COLEMAN HAWKINS QUARTET on November 6, 1954 in New York City. The group recorded If I Had You, Ain't Misbehavin', Cheek To Cheek, Undecided and Honeysuckle Rose for JAZZTONE RECORDS.

The BILLY TAYLOR TRIO with Earl May, bass, Percy Brice, drums, and BILLY TAYLOR, piano played at TOWN HALL in NEW YORK, on December 17, 1954.

The concert resulted in an album for PRESTIGE RECORDS entitled BILLY TAYLOR TRIO IN CONCERT AT TOWN HALL. They played A Foggy Day, I'll Remember April, Sweet Georgia Brown, Theodora and How High The Moon.

Drummer Percy Brice was born in New York City on March 25, 1923. His aunt was an actress and his mother played piano. During the WPA in the 30's Brice studied piano and violin. He was primarily a self-taught drummer. In 1944 he played with Luis Russell and during 1945-'46 with Benny Carter. In 1947 he played with Mercer Ellington and Eddie Vinson from 1948 to 1951. During the period 1951 until late 1954 Percy Brice worked with Tiny Grimes, Oscar Pettiford, Lucky Thompson and after hours at Minton's with Chocolate Williams. He joined BILLY TAYLOR in 1954.

EARL MAY: I remember my daughter being there in Town Hall. She was about two years old. She was up in the balcony, wiggling and keeping time with the music so that nobody could pay much attention to the music, they were so busy watching her. That was a good date. I wish I had the bass I was playing on that date. I bought it for $300; good fiddle. I was just so fussy and dissatisfied with what I was doing that I put it all on the bass but I remember that date.

BILLY, Johnny Windhurst, trumpet, Jimmy Shirley, guitar, Earl May, bass, and Percy Brice, drums on March 15, 1955 accompanied singer BARBARA LEA on some singles for RIVERSIDE RECORDS. The tunes recorded were Love Is Here To Stay, Love Me, As Long As I Live and Come Rain Or Come Shine.

EARL MAY: That was her first record date. She brags about that now.

In 1955 the TAYLOR'S welcomed their second child KIM into this world. TEDDI TAYLOR had previously given birth to son, Duane in 1951. Duane ultimately graduated from Grinnel College. KIM graduated from Yale University with a degree in law (Juris Doctor). She and her husband both teach law at New York University. She specializes in criminal law.

> KIM TAYLOR THOMPSON: We (my brother Duane and I) had wonderful childhoods. My father (BILLY) used to take us to see jazz events where we met big stars like Dizzy Gillespie and Sarah Vaughan. We didn't realize dad's standing in jazz at that time. We didn't even realize how famous the people we were hearing and meeting were. My brother, Duane, was extremely talented in many artistic areas. He moved to California and passed away in the 80's.

A TOUCH OF TAYLOR was the title of the album recorded by Billy's Trio, which included Earl May, bass and Percy Brice, drums, on April 10, 1955 in New York City. The album released by PRESTIGE RECORDS included Early Bird, Abientot, Memories Of Spring, Ever So Easy, Day Dreaming, Radio Activity, Purple Mood, Long Tom, A Grand Night For Swingin', Blue Clouds, Live It Up and Daddy-O. Each of the tunes recorded were written for a different disc jockey.

> EARL MAY: The tune "Daddy-O" was written for the disc jockey in Chicago named Daddy. He was trying to play theme songs of a lot of jazz disc jockeys so he could get his records played. Smart guy, very smart.

Around the middle of 1955 BILLY changed the name of his music publishing company to Duane Music, Inc. It was originally called Soundpost Music.

> JIM ANDERSON: My first remembrance of BILLY TAYLOR was when I was a child and he was doing the Captain Kangaroo Show. That was in the mid-50's. I was a kid in Butler, Pennsylvania. It was the children's show of the day and BILLY had a band on the show. He was doing those kinds of television shows regularly.

The BILLY TAYLOR TRIO with Earl May, bass, and Percy Brice, drums, made an album for PARAMOUNT RECORDS on January 1 and 2 of 1956. They recorded But Not For Me, All The Things You Are, Cheek To Cheek, Between The Devil And The Deep Blue Sea, I Only Have Eyes For You, It's Too Late Now, More Than You Know, Satin Doll, Then I'll Be Tired Of You and You Don't Know What Love Is.

PERCY BRICE: Playing with BILLY was very enjoyable –he was our favorite, you know. I did a lot of recording with BILLY during '54, '55 and '56. He used to write out our parts on whatever we played – occasionally he would ask us to write out what we were playing, not necessarily everything but a guide. Earl May was playing bass then; I think BILLY'S a big time player. BILLY'S a wonderful person. We never had any incidents, we were a very clean trio. It was wonderful playing with BILLY. It was my first trio experience. He treated everybody well – he's that kind of a guy.

On January 22, 1956 BILLY, Earl May, bass; and Percy Brice, drums, made an album, BILLY TAYLOR AT THE LONDON HOUSE. The tunes were Gone With The Wind, I Cover The Waterfront, It Might As Well Be Spring, Our Love Is Here To Stay, The London House, Midnight Piano and Stella By Starlight. The album was released by ABC Paramount.

EARL MAY: The LONDON HOUSE was a live record date.

In the December 3, 1955 issue of the Chicago Daily News an announcement indicated "THE BILLY TAYLOR TRIO OPENED AN ENGAGEMENT." The author, Sam Lesner wrote: " . . . Wednesday at the London House and the jazz music to be heard there during this engagement will have the ring of authenticity. TAYLOR, as a Washington, D.C. youth spent many days at the Library of Congress studying jazz recordings. TAYLOR is the author of eight pamphlets on the history of jazz styles. Like Don Shirley, a magnificent jazz artist who played a recent engagement at the London House, BILLY TAYLOR believes that original jazz did not have a musical form. It was an expression in the American musical idiom that should have developed it's own sound musical form but didn't and the noisemakers and exhibitionists took over. Both TAYLOR and Shirley treat the keyboard with affection and clear understanding of the same qualities of the piano; which is basically a percussion instrument. It's beautiful jazz that TAYLOR and his trio offer. TAYLOR won a large following of Chicago jazz enthusiasts in an engagement last year at another jazz haunt. London House however has turned out to be a sort of Carnegie Hall for jazz artists with dinner as part of the main attraction. The distinctive restaurant has become a jazz music mecca in the few months since it launched its after dinner music policy."

BILLY recorded Indiana with bass man George Duvivier and drummer Percy Brice in March 1956. The tune was included in the album EVERGREENS produced by ABC-PARAMOUNT RECORDS.

PHIL SCHAAP: I used to hear him when I was a little kid. I was born in 1951. My mother was a piano connoisseur. Percy Brice was playing with him when I first heard him. I was already a BILLY TAYLOR fan when he started doing jazz radio with LIB and NEW and the Basie guys were my friends, the older Basie alumni. BILLY did a show with them. I think it was 1961. I was either 10 or 11 and I got to meet him that day. The great Count Basie was there too; Dickie Wells, Earl Warren and Buddy Tate. I think the bass player was Gene Ramey. So I met him, probably as a three-year-old, got his autograph and things like that. When he played with the Basie guys I became a little more cognizant of him. I became very serious about jazz – initially I was a very inferior musician – but I started gaining more of a scholarly kind of approach and BILLY TAYLOR was like a magic thing because if I had invented someone like him people would say: "It doesn't exist."

The BILLY TAYLOR QUARTET featured the trumpet, alto and tenor saxophone wailing of Ira Sullivan in an album entitled BILLY TAYLOR PRESENTS IRA SULLIVAN recorded in November, 1956 in New York City. Joining BILLY and Ira were Earl May, bass and Ed Thigpen, drums. The album was produced by ABC-PARAMOUNT in New York City.

BILLY TAYLOR: I didn't even know Ira Sullivan was a trumpet player. He was funny. I was so enthused about his saxophone playing – I heard this guy go toe to toe with these guys in an after hours joint and thought WOW!!! He was just wiping these cats out. And I called Creed Taylor when I got back to New York and said, "We've got to record this guy," so the record that we did was to introduce Ira. The funny thing about it was that he didn't even play saxophone, didn't even come with a saxophone, and came with his trumpet. I had touted him as a saxophone player. I said, "Man, you got to play something." Zoot Sims showed up for the date and I said, "Hey man, let me borrow your saxophone."

Drummer Ed (Edmund Leonard) Thigpen was born in Chicago, Illinois on December 28, 1930. In 1951 he joined the Cootie Williams band at the Savoy Ballroom in New York. From 1952 to 1954 he was in the military service where he taught percussion at Fort Ord, California and then in Korea with the Eighth Army Band. When he was discharged he moved to New York where he worked with Lennie Tristano, Dinah Washington, Gil Melle, Jutta Hipp, Toshiko Akiyoshi, Johnny Hodges and Bud Powell before joining the BILLY TAYLOR TRIO in 1956.

ED THIGPEN: Oh, BILLY'S special. He's very special. I first met him in '56. And then I joined him in '57 or '58. My working with BILLY was what got me interested in getting more involved in jazz education because he was at the forefront in a lot of this stuff. Actually, the idea was started in Germany when we were doing free-bees all up and down the place for a long time wherever we would go and he was trying to promote jazz music. For me, BILLY'S consistency, his perseverance, leading when he wasn't even leading in a sense, is a good role model for me. A great role model in the sense of courage – carrying himself as a man, you know, and a gentle man; his ability to speak, his approach, a lot of things.

BILLY brought in Quincy Jones to conduct an album for ABC-PARAMOUNT, MY FAIR LADY LOVES JAZZ on January 8, 1957. The large orchestra included Ernie Royal, trumpet, Don Elliott, trumpet/mellophone/vibes/bongos, Jimmy Cleveland, trombone, Jimmy Buffington, French horn, Don Butterfield, tuba, Tony Ortega, tenor saxophone, Charlie Fowlkes, baritone saxophone, Al Casamenti, guitar, Earl May, bass, Ed Thigpen, drums, BILLY TAYLOR, piano, and Quincy Jones, arranger/conductor. The orchestra first recorded I've Grown Accustomed To Her Face. With Jay MacAllister replacing Don Butterfield on tuba, on January 22, the orchestra recorded With A Little Bit Of Luck, Wouldn't It Be Loverly? and On The Street Where You Live. On February 5 the orchestra returned to the studio and, with Gerry Mulligan replacing Charlie Fowlkes on baritone saxophone, recorded Show Me, The Rain In Spain, I Could Have Danced All Night and Get Me To The Church On Time.

On March 7 and April 10 BILLY joined Mundell Lowe, guitar, Gene Quill, alto saxophone, Les Grange, bass, and Ed Thigpen, drums to record It's A Grand Night For Swingin', Easy To Love, Crazy Rhythm, Blues Before Freud, Love Me Or Leave Me and You Turned The Tables On Me. Riverside, 238/ojc-1940 released the record.

In the March 7, 1956 issue of Down Beat magazine BILLY TAYLOR penned an article entitled "PROGRESSIVE JAZZ". The editor stated: 'Top Pianist BILLY TAYLOR Defines Jazz, Shows Its Role In Contemporary Music.' BILLY summed up his rather lengthy article by saying: ". . . Since one of the most distinguishing features of good jazz playing is that it is basically a form of creative expression against the limitation of a steady beat, no matter what techniques are used, progressive jazz must swing or it loses its validity as jazz . . . Progressive jazz is the latest development in jazz. It adds new techniques and devices to the mainstream of jazz, yet does not ignore the jazz tradition. And because it requires a greater skill and knowledge on the part of the musicians, it gives imaginative performers, and writers, new tools and materials with which they may create original music."

On October 25, 1957 in New York City the BILLY TAYLOR TRIO did a record date for ABC-PARAMOUNT. The trio, consisting of BILLY, Earl May, bass, and Ed Thigpen, drums, recorded Small Hotel, The More I See You, There Will Never Ever Be Another You, Sounds In The Night, Southside, Will You Still Be Mine, Round Midnight and I Never Get Enough Of You.

The BILLY TAYLOR TOUCH was the title of the tunes recorded for ATLANTIC RECORDS on October 28, 1957 by the BILLY TAYLOR TRIO in New York City. The bass player was Earl May and the drummer, Ed Thigpen. The tunes recorded were Can You Tell?, You Make Me Feel So Young, I Get A Kick Out Of You and Earl May.

WARREN CHIASSON: I had his albums in Nova Scotia before I came to the United States in the late fifties. During my first trip to Birdland he was playing in Birdland with his trio, about 1957 or '58, and prior to my coming to join George Shearing I used to go to New York and catch all the different jazz clubs. He was playing with his trio there and I just marveled; I remember the tune that he was playing, "Moonlight Saving Time", an old standard. I marveled at his technique. He covered the whole piano and that made a big impression on me. So I would say that I was well aware of BILLY TAYLOR'S mastery of the piano at that early stage. I do recall him really stretch out on "Moonlight Saving Time".

BILLY organized a nine-piece band to do an album for ARGO RECORDS on November 17, 1957 in Chicago, Illinois. The album was entitled BILLY TAYLOR AND HIS ORCHESTRA and included Willie Cook and Clark Terry, trumpets, Britt Woodman, tuba, Johnny Hodges, alto saxophone, Paul Gonsalves, tenor saxophone, Harry Carney, baritone saxophone, Earl May, bass, Ed Thigpen, drums, and BILLY TAYLOR, piano. They recorded Buddy's Best, Theodora, Mood For Mendez, Daddy-O, Cue-Blue, Day Dreaming, Can You Tell? and Time For Tex.

BILLY TAYLOR: Clark Terry was working with Duke Ellington in Chicago and I did an album in which I used a lot of guys from the Ellington Band. Johnny Hodges, Paul Gonsalves, people like that. They were all members of the band at that particular time and Clark had just gotten a flugelhorn and he took it out on the date. The guy he was staying with interrupted the date and said: "Hey, man, I got your horn, I got your horn!" Clark unwrapped it and played it. That was the first date he played it on – it just knocked me out!!

CLARK TERRY: You know I've been given credit for the resurrection of the flugelhorn. Not too far from Gary, Indiana is the home of the Selmer Instrument Company. I used to go there quite often with my Indiana buddy and go down and visit Keith Eckert, technical advisor to Selmer, and Keith, a real nice guy, used to feed his daddy home made wine in the basement where he had a workshop for experimental things. I always wanted to recapture that Jimmy Lunceford trumpet section sound – they all had flugelhorns. A few cats around, Emmett Berry had one, Shorty Rogers had one, and shortly after that Miles had one. Miles called his flugelhorn "fat girl". He'd say: "I have to take my fat girl home!" We'd try to put together a horn in Keith's basement and they'd send it to the main factory in Paris. Keith is the person whose name you see on a lot of trumpets called "K-Modified". So he'd send it back and they corrected it, all the technical aspects, the trigger, etc. and send it back to me at my friends house in Indiana. This happened to be the same day that BILLY TAYLOR was doing a date with the whole Ellington Band, except Ellington. The record was called "Taylor-Made Jazz" with BILLY on the plaid cover. The cover looked like a big slice of plaid cloth. This was November 1957. My buddy brought the flugelhorn to the record date. The first break we had I took it out and played it, real sparkling gold, and BILLY comes up and says: "Hey, you want to use that on the date?" and I said: "I intend to!!" The record date was on Ontario or Rush Street.

On December 16 and 17, 1957 the BILLY TAYLOR TRIO recorded an album for ABC-PARAMOUNT RECORDS. The trio consisted of Earl May, bass, Ed Thigpen, drums, and BILLY TAYLOR, piano. The tunes recorded were Round Midnight and I Never Get Enough Of You.

In 1958 BILLY began his disc jockey career on radio station WLIB in New York City. He also became the Music Director for the NBC TV Series "The Subject Is Jazz." That series was the first jazz series produced by the new National Educational Television and lasted thirteen weeks. The series featured BILLY leading a band that included Doc Severinson, Jimmy Cleveland, Tony Scott, Earl May, Eddie Safranski, Mundell Lowe, Ed Thigpen, Earl May and Osie Johnson. Some of the guest artists included Ben Webster, Willie "The Lion Smith, Jimmy Rushing, George Russell, Lee Konitz, Warne Marsh, Bill Evans, Duke Ellington, Cannonball, Langston Hughes, Nat Adderley, Toshiko Akiyoshi and Aaron Copland among others.

ED THIGPEN: That "The Subject Is Jazz" series was a very important series. When we did "The Subject Is Jazz" we went through everything from rhythm and blues to Ellington and Aaron Copland. I learned a great deal about a lot of things from BILLY. Those are important to me personally. Things like survival, ideas about perseverance, caring, making friends, having respect for the music in your class. He personifies all these wonderful attributes.

BILLY TAYLOR: We had some great guests on 'The Subject Is Jazz". We had Willie "The Lion" Smith doing ragtime. We had Ben Webster, Jimmy Rushing, Wilbur De Paris, Cannonball and Nat Adderley. We had Lee Konitz and Warne Marsh. On one program we had "The Influence of Jazz on Classical Music" with Aaron Copland. We discussed third stream. We talked about

"Jazz and Its Influence On Other Arts" and "The International Influence Of Jazz".

In June 1958 George Russell was the guest star on the NBC TV series "The Subject Is Jazz", introduced by Gilbert Seldes. The musical director for the series was the jazz pianist and scholar BILLY TAYLOR. BILLY had been so impressed with the Russell-Evans escapade on RCA's "Concerto for Billy the Kid" that he built the final installment of the program called 'The Future of Jazz,' around another performance of it.

HORACE SILVER: I first met BILLY in the late 50's. I've always admired his mastery of the instrument, and always liked his compositions. He's a fine pianist and also a fine composer. I played opposite him a couple of times at Birdland on different gigs. Sometimes I was a sideman with some band and sometimes he was a sideman with some band and I played there one time with his trio and my quintet. His drummer, Charlie Smith, and me used to hang out and we would go after the gig to the place around the corner from Birdland, The Ham and Eggery.

We would go in there after the gig at 4:00 in the morning, eat breakfast and talk music until the sun came up. I used to enjoy doing that. I was friendly with Earl May, BILLY'S bass player, too. I would marvel at his playing bass backwards, with the left hand or something.

Another great thing about BILLY is that he's been an ambassador for our music throughout the world for many years. I, for one, am grateful for what he's done to perpetuate the music. I always remember one thing he said to me that made me feel very good. I said to him "when I first started out, recording with Stan Getz and all that, that I sounded a lot like Bud Powell – I was trying to emulate Bud." BILLY said "I heard you when you first came to town and when you played with Stan Getz and it was evident that you dug Bud, but I always heard something of you in there," and that made me feel kind of good. When I made the records with Lou Donaldson I realized that Bud was in there but there was something of me in there and I tried to develop that. BILLY heard that right away.

MICHAEL ABENE: I was first aware of BILLY when I was a teenager, late 50's, early 60's. It's kind of interesting because I remember the fact that I can always tell his playing, the sound he gets out of the piano; it's a sound that I always knew was him. He would play like a fugue. He would get two lines together, kind of counterpoint lines. I probably heard him at Newport. I was there with the Newport Youth Band and it's possible that I first heard him then like 1958-'59. I was playing in the Newport Youth Band with Eddie

Gomez, Jimmy Owens, Eddie Daniels and others. When I was in the Newport Youth Band the instructors were Marshall Brown, John LaPorta and Lou Mucci. BILLY was one of the first guys I heard being so positive about the future of jazz education. At that time little was happening in jazz education when I was a kid. It was very far and few in between. New it's become like the norm.

ONE FOR FUN was the name of the album the BILLY TAYLOR TRIO recorded for ATLANTIC RECORDS on June 24, 1959. Earl May, bass and Kenny Dennis, drums were with BILLY on the album. The tunes recorded were Summertime, One For You, That's For Sure, A Little Southside Soul, Blue Moon, Poinciana, At Long Last Love and When Lights Are Low.

Drummer Kenny Dennis (Kenneth Carl Dennis) was born in Philadelphia, Pennsylvania on May 27, 1930. In the 50's he played with Jackie Davis, Earl Bostic, Erroll Garner and Sonny Stitt prior to joining BILLY TAYLOR.

ED THIGPEN: Without BILLY TAYLOR I wouldn't have been as prepared as I was to play in the Oscar Peterson Trio. BILLY taught me how to, he gave me a certain freedom that allowed me to develop at my own pace. The appreciation of all ballads, the exposure to the repertoire, the American song, we would experiment; I was able to exploit my hand drumming, things not to do, talk over the composition, the story you wanted to tell, etc. So I learned a great deal from him.

EARL MAY: BILLY was like a big brother to me. He really looked out for me. He was the one who put me on to Charles Mingus. I studied with Mingus and that really helped me a great deal. BILLY was really wonderful. It was always a pleasure to go to work. He was so great fun to be with all the time; never put you down. If you hit a bad note he was right there – he was trying to help you all the time. He was a friend – we were real close. I really felt like we were related, like a big brother; it was really wonderful. I still feel the same way. I've never met anybody in my life like BILLY. He has been a part or the head of more programs than you can shake a stick at.

After 1958 the great pianist, arranger/composer/conductor Lalo Schifrin came to the United States from his home in Argentina. He mentioned BILLY TAYLOR as a reason he had for coming to America:

LALO SCHIFRIN: DR. BILLY TAYLOR is a true master of this genre of music which: "it doesn't mean a thing if it doesn't swing." He was one of the reasons why I decided to embrace jazz with passion and conviction and he is one of the reasons why I came to this country. BILLY TAYLOR represents the essence of the whole history of jazz and I have no words to express my admiration and respect for his work as a performer and as an educator.

In New York City on July 20, 1959 an album entitled BILLY TAYLOR WITH FOUR FLUTES was recorded for RIVERSIDE RECORDS. The personnel were Phil Bodner, Herbie Mann, Frank Wess and Jerome Richardson, flutes, Tom Williams, bass, Dave Bailey, drums, Chino Pozo, conga, and BILLY TAYLOR, piano. They recorded The Song Is Ended, Back Home, One For the Woofer, Kool Bongos and Blues Shutters. Flutist Bill Slapin came in to replace Jerome Richardson on the tune Blues Shutters.

Dave Bailey (SAMUEL DAVID BAILEY) was born in Portsmouth, Virginia on February 21, 1926. Dave was raised in Philadelphia, Pennsylvania. During WW II, 1942-1946 he was an officer in the Army Air Force. In 1947 he moved to New York City and studied at the Music Center Conservatory on the GI bill. He was an early follower of Art Blakey and Max Roach. During 1951-'53 he played with Herbie Jones. Prior to joining BILLY TAYLOR he played with Johnny Hodges, Lou Donaldson, Al Sears, Charles Mingus, Curtis Fuller, Horace Silver, Ben Webster and Gerry Mulligan. Bailey became a professional musician in the late 40's. He played with BILLY at the Hickory House, and toured with him, in the early 60's. Ben Tucker was the bass player at that later time.

RAMSEY LEWIS: I met BILLY TAYLOR at the very first recording session I ever did. He came by to wish us well. I'd always admired him and he was one of the pianists whose records I bought early on. His technique, his sense of melodic lines and harmony, and his piano tone – he has one of those good piano tones. 4

BILLY'S final record date during the 50's was completed on July 24, 1959 in New York City. The album, a philosophical extension of the previous one, was entitled TAYLOR MADE FLUTE and was produced by RIVERSIDE RECORDS. The personnel included BILLY, piano, Tom Williams, bass, Al Heath, drums, Jerry Sanfino, Bill Slapin, Jerome Richardson and Herbie Mann, flutes. The seven-piece group recorded St. Thomas, Oh Lady Be Good, How About You? and No Parking. On the final tune Seldon Powell replaced Herbie Mann.

Drummer Al Heath (Albert "Tootie" Heath) was born in Philadelphia, Pennsylvania on May 31, 1935. His older brothers are Percy and Jimmy Heath. In 1958-'59 Al played with J.J. Johnson and with several trios including those led by Cedar Walton and Reggie Workman.

LONNIE LISTON SMITH: I was born and raised in Richmond, Virginia and while I was in high school, around 1959-1960, they always talked about

BILLY TAYLOR. As you know BILLY TAYLOR graduated from Virginia State University. Everybody was telling me that BILLY TAYLOR was giving a concert at Virginia State. Being still in high school I didn't drive, didn't know how to get there or anything, so I hitchhiked all the way down to Virginia State and I heard the concert. But, man he did something that set me back – he played "I'll Remember April" with just his left hand. That just threw me. I took it personally. I took stock of it and said "wow"!! I'm still working on my right hand and he's doing this with his left hand. It just threw me for a loop. I went out and bought all his records. I remember he was playing at the Hickory House and I bought this album with a picture of his trio standing outside the Hickory House. BILLY has this tweed coat on; I made my parents get me a tweed coat – the whole bit. He was a great influence on me when I was very young. Everybody talked about him. He was definitely one of the first! Out of all the jazz educators BILLY TAYLOR is the best because no one else has the background he has – experience all the way back to Art Tatum and anyone else you want to name. I really hope he sticks around a while because the younger kids really need to get the authentic theory of jazz from someone who has been there.

LARRY RIDLEY: I knew about BILLY TAYLOR in the late 50's and when I went to New York in 1959 I had his records and knew of him and the kind of work he was doing. At the time I knew of him working on, what we used to call, the East-side circuit with those particular rooms. I guess the Café Carlyle is one of the few remaining now in New York, with Bobby Short doing his thing, but we had the Hickory House and all those kinds of places. And I know BILLY used to work a lot of those places – the London House, etc. I don't recall the exact time I joined BILLY.

The 50's had been good for BILLY who was now enjoying his years as a 30 year old. He had alternated at the Downbeat Club with Mary Lou Williams, formed and led his own trio with Earl May on bass and drummer Charlie Smith. He had recorded with his own sextet, hired Charles Mingus to play with his trio for an appearance in Boston, placed in the Readers Poll of Down Best magazine among the top jazz pianists, won Down Beat's New Star award, was heard on more than three dozen recordings, began his jazz disc jockey career at WLIB in New York City and headed the NBC TV series "The Subject Is Jazz" and became a father to son, Duane and daughter Kim.

He looked forward to the sixties and to spending more time and energy in radio and television, recording and playing with his trio.

V

BROADCASTING – THE JAZZMOBILE –
THE DAVID FROST SHOW

Jazz has been ridiculed, distorted, fragmented, diluted, and deemed unworthy of serious study and performance by music educators, musicologists, historians and others who were not really qualified to evaluate the music. – BILLY TAYLOR

On February 4, 1960 the BILLY TAYLOR TRIO did an album for ORIGINAL JAZZ CLASSICS entitled UPTOWN RIVERSIDE. The bass player was Henry Grimes and the drummer Ray Mosca. The tunes recorded were Le Petite Mambo, Jordu, Just The Thought Of You, Soul Sister, Moanin', S'Wonderful, Warm Blue Stream, Biddy's Best and Cue-Blue.

Bass man Henry Grimes was born in Philadelphia, Pennsylvania on November 3, 1935. He studied violin in junior high school and played tuba at Mastbaum High School. In the early 50's he moved to New York City and studied at the Juilliard School of Music. During the 50's he played with Willis Jackson, Arnett Cobb, Lee Morgan, Bobby Timmons, Tootie Heath, Anita O'Day, Sonny Rollins, Gerry Mulligan, Benny Goodman, Lee Konitz, Sonny Rollins, Thelonious Monk and Lennie Tristano.

RAY MOSCA: The last time I saw Henry Grimes he was living in San Francisco around 1971 (I was with Oscar Peterson). Henry was a vagrant. He lost his bass, he lost everything – he had had a nervous breakdown. He had gone to Japan with Sonny Rollins and lost his bass, lost his "marbles". In San Francisco he was like a street bum. He had first come to New York with Gerry Mulligan from Philadelphia.

Ray Mosca (Raymond Mosca, Jr.) was born in New York City on July 26, 1932. He began playing drums with his uncles, who had played with Joe Venuti and Paul Whiteman, when he was 8 year old and at various parties in the Catskills when he was 14. At 16 he began to study with Jo Jones and at the Manhattan School of Music in New York City. During the 50's he played at the Desert Inn in Las Vegas and with Cy Coleman, Oscar Pettiford, Mary Lou Williams, Alex Kallao, Lennie

Tristano, Al Cohn, Zoot Sims, George Wallington, Hampton Hawes and George Shearing. In 1960 he joined the BILLY TAYLOR TRIO.

RAY MOSCA: I was with BILLY from the time I left George Shearing. I was with George from 1957 to 1960. I used to play opposite BILLY. I was with Mary Lou Williams before Shearing. I met BILLY in 1955. I played opposite him at the Embers in New York; I was with Cy Coleman. I went from Cy to Mary Lou Williams and then George Wallington, Hampton Hawes, etc. I joined BILLY with Earl Mays and played about six months with Earl. Doug Watkins came in and then Henry Grimes. We made a lot of records together. I used to know about BILLY when Charlie Smith was with him – I'm a New Yorker. When I was a kid I used to go to the Downbeat Club where they were working. I couldn't go in because I was about fourteen years old.

BILLY TAYLOR, with Henry Grimes, bass and Ray Mosca, drums, made another New York City recording on March 26, 1960. The album was entitled WARMING UP and was produced by RIVERSIDE RECORDS. The tunes were Warming Up, Easy Like, That's What It Is, Coffee Break, Native Dancer, Afterthoughts, Easy Walker, Lonesome Lover, Don't Bug Me, You Know What I Mean, Uncle Fuzzy and No Aftertaste.

NANCY WILSON: BILLY was a part of my musical life. When I first went to New York I met BILLY and his wife, Teddi, in the late 50's, early 60's. I had his records and knew who he was. He and Teddi were kind to me. They took me in, fed me, took me to their house. I knew their children. They were just so kind. I got to know what a genius he was later. It was he and his wife who were such a great family who nurtured and took me in and were kind to a young girl from Ohio. They were so nice to my husband and me.

The Christmas, 1960, Vol. 18, Nos. 10-12 release of the journal, SESAC MUSIC, featured an article by Jack Francis entitled " MEET THE DISC JOCKEY". The article featured BILLY TAYLOR, who was personified as one of the 'Prophets of Jazz'. The author claimed that BILLY "is making tremendous strides in his efforts to get the listening public and jazz musician on the same thinking plane. It's not that the 36-year-old pianist, composer, arranger, author and recording artist is making with a 'crusade,' but rather doing his bit to bring the audience close to jazz. This applies to his records, personal appearances and as host on The BILLY TAYLOR Jazz Show heard each Saturday from 4 p.m. to sign-off over New York's WLIB. BILLY'S excellent choice of jazz selections plus his intimate knowledge of the performers and their art, makes one of the most informative and listenable shows on the air today. WLIB is to commended for its good judgment in letting TAYLOR have complete control of his shows. The station's confidence and cooperation have paid off in one of the most tasteful programs in the metropolitan area . . . With more than 15 active years on the jazz scene, BILLY TAYLOR is certainly well suited to his role of 'Jazz Spokesman' for WLIB. At this writing, in addition to THE BILLY TAYLOR JAZZ SHOW and the Pepsi Jazz Corner, which is heard 3 times daily on WLIB, BILLY is enjoying one of his long engagements at the Prelude, one of New York's most famous jazz spots. Truly, BILLY TAYLOR and jazz swing well together."

KENNY WASHINGTON: BILLY'S the one that inspired me to become a disc jockey. When I was in junior high, back in the 60's I used to come home at 4 o'clock in the afternoon and turn on WLIB. He was so hip on the radio, not one of those slick talkers but you could tell he definitely knew about the music so he was able to educate listeners. He had a very friendly type voice and later on, as I got to know him, I realized that his voice is actually like he really is, a very together person. He would explain what was happening on the records, and also the thing that knocked me out, he wasn't longwinded. He'd say what he had to say about the music and he was concise. BILLY made anybody who was listening understand what was happening. Of course at that point, he had 20 plus years of experience in terms of playing with all these different people. He played with everybody from Hot Lips Page on, Stuff Smith, all of them, Charlie Parker, Dizzy, and you knew this man knew what he was talking about. And consequently he played the best music on radio. So when I come on the radio today, I try to play the highest quality music possible. 1

In 1961 BILLY began a long tenure as pianist at the HICKORY HOUSE in NEW YORK CITY. That year the trio won the "Trio of the Year" from Jet Magazine.

ARNOLD SHAW: The house pianist after Marian McPartland was BILLY TAYLOR of Greenville, North Carolina, who must have been a Cheshire cat in an earlier existence. Although BILLY made his 52 St. debut at the Three Deuces, he is remembered for his pianistics at Popkin's place. Willis Conover of The Voice of America thinks back to the many hours when he sat listening to BILLY. In his memory, they were not entirely pleasant hours because "waiters, management and even the audience seemed rather insensitive – talking, shouting and generally paying not attention to Billy's superlative playing." Conover adds: "How he managed to remain so cool was a mystery to me. But he did have an extremely well balanced orientation toward the condition under which the Negro lives and works in our society. I put it to him once. And do you know what he replied? 'My father was a minister, and he persuaded me that if I kept my own inner strength, nothing would bother me. And nothing has!"

Hickory House outlived the bop era – BILLY played modified bop – as it had the swing era. John Popkin watched all the great music clubs disappear after they hopped from location to location on The Street. He watched the invasion of the strippers during the war and the gradual deterioration in the fifties. For a time, he remained the western outpost of a block that was known as Chow Mein Lane, it housed so many Chinese restaurants. Eventually, as the towers of huge office buildings shadowed The Street, he and Jimmy Ryan's, east of Sixth Avenue, remained the sole vestiges of a golden era of jazz, exuberant entertainment and gentle togetherness. 2

MARIAN MCPARTLAND: I have very happy memories of the Hickory House and of John Popkin. Most of the time he'd sit behind our table in his own particular spot with his back to the room, studying the racing form. I realize that underneath all the brusque remarks, he had quite a feeling of affection for me and I certainly did for him too. I was in the club on the last night before the place was sold and torn down. BILLY TAYLOR was on the bandstand, and he invited me to sit in; but I felt so sad that I just couldn't play. I knew that with this room went almost forty years of jazz history. I never went back, and I've never been in the new place. I don't think I could stand it. And now, Mr. Popkin is gone, too, and with him some wonderful memories and wonderful music. It's hardly surprising that the Hickory House was like home to him. At times it was like a home for me, too. I'll always think of it with great nostalgia. That has never been another place like it. And there never will be. 3

RAY MOSCA: We used to work six nights a week, six hours a night, from 9:00 to 3:00 at the Hickory House. We worked there 35 weeks a year for about three years. We used to split it with Marian McPartland. She would do 35 and we would do 35. They had a solo piano player opposite us. In those days it was Bernie Nero (now known as Peter Nero). We traveled also. We played the London House in Chicago, in Detroit, Cleveland, Toronto, etc. We used to travel about eight or ten weeks a year. That's why I joined BILLY because we stayed in town mostly. When I was with George (Shearing) we did one-nighters every night – for fifty weeks a year!

ARNOLD SHAW: Hickory House was not a haven for bop, big bands or hot drummers so much as outstanding keyboard artists. Joey Bushkin, who worked with Marsala's Chicagoans in '37, was the first of a group that included Billy Kyle in '39, Jess Stacy in '40, and Mel Powell in '41. There were also Hazel Scott, Marian McPartland, Martial Solal, BILLY TAYLOR and others.
4

BILLY played with several different bass players and drummers during his long tenure at the Hickory House. During this period bass player Ben Tucker and drummer David Bailey worked with him for about a year.

DAVID BAILEY: As a musician BILLY is impeccable. As a person he is one of the most decent human beings I've ever known in my life. We had a ball, Ben Tucker and me; we used to have good times. When I was with BILLY everything was taken care of; everything was in order. We never had any problems, anything like that, inasmuch as we worked mostly at the Hickory House and that was a pretty steady gig. Everybody used to come to hear us. There were several things that we enjoyed the most. We used to play places like Augustana College out in Cedar Rapids, Iowa, which is one of America's most conservative schools. The people that we played for use to give receptions after the concerts and a bunch of them would grab BILLY and a bunch of them would grab me and Ben Tucker and we were all very articulate and that shocked them. They thought that all we could do was play but they found out that we had things to say and that we had theories and philosophical approaches to life and other things and that we were really well rounded human beings aside from being fine jazz musicians.

JIMMY OWENS: What Dizzy Gillespie did for the big bands in the operation of Afro-Latin music BILLY TAYLOR was doing that for the small groups, at the same time. His group in 1948, after Chano Pozo died, had Candido (Candido Camero De Guerra). They were doing that kind of stuff and BILLY was writing that type of music. At that time Charlie Smith played drums, they used to work at the Hickory House; they worked at the Hickory House for many, many years. That was his place.

PHOEBE JACOBS: I frequented the Hickory House when I used to do freelance work with Duke Ellington. Twice a year he worked at Ralph Watkins Basin Street on the west side and then they moved over to the east side. It was a perennial that Duke Ellington came in twice a year with the band and his favorite place in New York was the Hickory House. Not only was he an admirer and fan of BILLYS, but also he loved the calf liver. Mr. John Popkin was the proprietor and naturally was very cordial and attentive to Duke. In fact he even permitted Duke to come in with his little dog Davy – a French poodle that Joe Glaser gave him. Davy would sit under the table absolutely quiet; he had beautiful manners. BILLY was the pianist there and was one of the first people to bring jazz an image of dignity and professionalism and a lot of style, a lot of style and he was very popular.

KETER BETTS: I didn't meet BILLY until he was at the Hickory House in the early 60's. I was with Dinah Washington and Ed Thigpen left us and went with BILLY. When I went with Dinah we used to work Birdland about two or three times a year (they always had three acts) and BILLY was on with his trio, Ed Thigpen, drums and bassist Earl May. I know the first night we opened with them I kept thinking: "Something's wrong with that bass player." The second night all of a sudden it dawned on me; it wasn't that he was playing from the left hand side; his bass was strung up right-handed.

In New York City on January 3, 1961 the BILLY TAYLOR TRIO with BILLY, piano, Doug Watkins, bass, and Ray Mosca, drums recorded You Tempt Me, Did You Dream Too? You're All That Matters, Interlude, You're Mine You, My Heart Sings, I Sigh, Here Today And Gone Tomorrow and All Alone for MOODSVILLE RECORDS and released under the title INTERLUDE.

Doug Watkins (Douglas Watkins) was born in Detroit, Michigan on March 3, 1924. He attended Cass Tech High School where his schoolmates were Donald Byrd and Paul Chambers. In 1953 he joined James Moody and played in the Detroit area with the Barry Harris trio backing visitors Charlie Parker, Coleman Hawkins, Stan Getz, etc. Moving to New York in 1954 he played at Minton's and with Hank Mobley and Kenny Dorham before joining Art Blakey's Jazz Messengers. In the late 50's Watkins worked with Horace Silver and Charles Mingus. Watkins was ultimately killed in Arizona when his car struck a slow-moving tractor.

CLEM DEROSA: I first heard about BILLY TAYLOR when he was playing at the Hickory House. Marian had been there and I had never really heard his name although I knew he had done some playing with Charlie Parker and Dizzy, and I went down to hear his trio. I can't remember the bass player but I remember that Grady Tate was the drummer. It was just really a creative group. The thing I liked about it was that he played tunes, and developed jazz from the tunes, but they were very tasty arrangements all the time. Grady was doing some singing also and then finally ended up doing some solo albums as a vocalist. The Hickory House was one of the last ones to close. From that point on whenever I was in the city and had a chance (they were in there six nights a week) I would go by. They had a bar and the band was inside the bar so there was a good opportunity to see the band up close by sitting at the bar.

RAY MOSCA: We played a lot of concerts also with our trio. Then BILLY broke the trio up and became a disc jockey, WLIB, I think up in Harlem. We stopped working in clubs for a while. We made a lot of records with that trio. We had a lot of laughs. When I left BILLY I went with Dorothy Donegan and stayed with her for twenty years. I used to go down to Washington, D.C. and play with BILLY in the Women in Jazz Series.

WAYNE ANDRE: I first heard THE BILLY TAYLOR TRIO at the Hickory House on West 52 Street in Manhattan in the early 60's. I enjoyed the trio and was especially impressed with his great technique that, along with creativity, he maintained throughout his very fruitful life.

CLARK TERRY: I met BILLY shortly after I joined the Navy in 1942 and got to know him well when he was at the Hickory House. When I first heard him I realized right away he was awesome. From that point on I realized he could sit down there and scare a lot of people to death.

The JIMMY JONES ORCHESTRA with BILLY TAYLOR completed an album for MERCURY RECORDS in 1961 in New York City. The orchestra included Clark Terry, flugelhorn, Jimmy Cleveland, trombone, Julius Watkins, French horn, Jay McAllister, tuba, Phil Woods, alto saxophone, Frank Wess, tenor saxophone, Jerome Richardson, baritone saxophone, Les Spann, guitar, George Duvivier, bass, Dale Johnson, drums, BILLY TAYLOR, piano, and Jimmie Jones, arranger/conductor. The orchestra recorded Something Big, I'm Seeing Rainbows, Ordinary People, The Cocoa Bean Song, What's Wrong With Me?, Nothing More To Look Forward To, Another Time, Another Place, Happy Is The Cricket and The Sun Is Beginning To Crow.

BILLY TAYLOR: I started Clark Terry in the teaching thing. He was working at NBC in New York and I used to use him any time he was available because he was one of my first call musicians – anytime I had a big band or anything like that; he, Frank Wess, Phil Woods, and a few other guys. I would call them and then set the date. Clark would add so much to the trumpet solos, the trumpet section in those days. When Clark was on the staff we did a TV Show together and I said: "Hey, you're going to have to talk because we're going to be talking about jazz and everything and you're going to say something." He said: "Yeah man, I'll just play." I said: "No, no man, as articulate as you are you can talk. I'll ask you some questions and it'll be cool." He got on there and he has never stopped doing it. He realized how easy it was for him at that time, but before he had been, like all of us, in places where people ask all the wrong questions.

CLARK TERRY: BILLY was responsible for my getting involved in jazz education. He was doing a clinic in Cleveland, Ohio back in the 60's when I first went to work for NBC. He wanted to go visit a school so we went and I've been involved since then. He started it all! He started all this jazz.

Guitarist Jim Hall joined the BILLY TAYLOR TRIO resulting in the BILLY TAYLOR QUARTET recording Don't Go South, Empty Ballroom, Impromptu, Muffle

Cuffle, Paraphrase, At The Carrousel, Capricious and Free and Easy for MERCURY RECORDS in 1962. The album included Bob Cranshaw, bass, Walter Perkins, drums, and BILLY on piano.

> WALTER PERKINS: It was very enjoyable working with BILLY. We did an album called IMPROMPTU. Everything was beautiful. I really enjoyed playing with him. BILLY is a beautiful pianist and a very nice person to work with.

Bassist Bob Cranshaw (Melbourne Robert Cranshaw) was born in Evanston, Illinois on December 10, 1932. He took piano lessons beginning at age five, drums from age nine and played bass in high school and college. He attended Northwestern University, Roosevelt University and Bradley University and majored in music therapy. During the Korean War he served in the US Army where he played tuba. In 1950 he was a founding member of Walter Perkins' MJT + 3. During the 50's he played with Eddie Harris, Carmen McRae, Joe Williams and Junior Mance prior to recording with the BILLY TAYLOR TRIO.

Walter Perkins, drummer, was born in Chicago, Illinois on February 10, 1932. He attended DuSable High School and Wilson Community College on a basketball scholarship prior to serving in the military in the early 50's. When he was released from the service he studied at the Cosmopolitan School of Music in Chicago. During the mid and late 50's he played with Coleman Hawkins and Ahmad Jamal prior to forming MJT + 3 with Bob Cranshaw, Willie Thomas, Frank Strozier and Harold Mabern. He moved to New York City in 1960 and worked with Carmen McRae and Sonny Rollins before playing with the BILLY TAYLOR TRIO.

In 1962 the BILLY TAYLOR QUARTET with guitarist Jim hall made an album for Mercury Records in New York. Joining BILLY and Jim were bassist Bob Cranshaw and drummer Walter Perkins. They recorded Don't Go South, Empty Ballroom, Impromptu, Muffle Cuffle, Paraphrase, At The Carrousel, Capricious and Free and Easy.

In his role as "disc jockey" BILLY was hired by radio station WLIB to do a daily jazz program. The show met with great success and led to an offer from New York's top independent, middle-of-the-road, station WNEW that gave him a much larger audience to share his expertise in jazz. BILLY remained at WNEW for two years before returning to WLIB. He also began doing concerts in schools where he reached pre-teen youngsters as well as high school students. Also in the early 60's, BILLY served as music director for a pilot television comedy show headed by David Frost, THAT WAS THE WEEK THAT WAS. The show was an American version of a show previously aired in England with the same title.

HERB WONG: BILLY was on radio and I was on radio (in the 60's) so we had some kindred interests. That started our friendship. We crossed paths in so many different ways. One particular incident was with the late Bill Barron (Kenny's older brother). Billy used to come to the NAJE* conventions every year, one of the few Afro-Americans, as a matter of fact, but he was consistent. He was at Wesleyan College up there in Connecticut, head of the Afro-American studies music program, so he said to me a couple of times: "You know, I want to do something special on campus. I've been coming to these NAJE conventions and I'm really motivated to do something. So, can I call you sometime and just chat about it?" I said: "Sure", and I suggested something dealing with creativity and the widening world of music. So he festered with that, he liked that, and so he sent a proposal to me and I said great. So I said: "Now, you've got to get BILLY TAYLOR." So we got BILLY TAYLOR, Max Roach and others that had other cultural performers, Gamelan, Asian, etc. So that lasted about four or five days. It was very exciting to note the different kinds of expressions but Billy was the person that stitched these things together. He would be able to segue these things so everybody could view that as a global situation and that mixture of all these different streams from different cultures was all part of our music.

BILLY joined with the OLIVER NELSON ORCHESTRA to do an album for CAPITOL RECORDS, Right Here, Right Now, during 1962-'63. The large orchestra included John Bello, Snooky Young, Joe Newman, Thad Jones, Ernie Royal, Doc Severinsen and Clark Terry, trumpets; Wayne Andre, Britt Woodman, Quentin Jackson, Tony Studd and Urbie Green, trombones; Phil Woods, Jerome Richardson, Romeo Penque, Stan Webb and Danny Bank, saxophones; Ben Tucker, bass, Grady Tate, drums, BILLY TAYLOR, piano, and Oliver Nelson, arranger/conductor. They recorded That's Where It Is, Lot Of Livin' To Do, Right Here, Right Now, I Believe In You, Easy Walker, Afterthoughts, Stolen Moments, Give Me The Simple Life, Something Always Happens, Soul Sister, Freedom and I Wish I Knew.

Bass player Ben Tucker (Benjamin Mayer Tucker) was born in Nashville, Tennessee on December 13, 1930. During high school days he studied tuba prior to majoring in music at Tennessee State University where he began playing acoustic bass. Prior to serving in the military, he played in various clubs in Nashville for two years. In the mid-50's, when he was released from military service he joined Warne Marsh in Los Angeles where he also played with Art Pepper and Carl Perkins. He

---

*NAJE – National Association of Jazz Educators was founded in 1968. In 1989 the name was changed to IAJE – International Association of Jazz Educators. In 2001 the acronym remained the same, IAJE, but stood for International Association for Jazz Education.

moved to New York City in 1959 and played with Chris Connor, Herbie Mann, and Roland Hanna prior to joining BILLY.

Drummer/singer Grady Tate was born in Durham, North Carolina on January 14, 1932. He studied percussion while serving in the US Air Force from 1951 until 1955. When he received his discharge he attended North Carolina College prior to moving to Washington, D.C. where he played with Wild Bill Davis in the late 50's, early 60's. He then moved to New York City and worked with Jerome Richardson, Quincy Jones, Cy Coleman, and Les Crane before joining BILLY TAYLOR.

> GRADY TATE: I met BILLY at a time when I was new in town and relatively new to the recording industry. We'd worked in different recording scenes together, doing jingles or a record date and enjoying the way one another played. BILLY reformed his trio and used Ben Tucker and me. We worked the Hickory House for six or seven years, six nights a week, and of course, concerts. That was during one of my busiest periods, when there was a very active studio scene in New York and I'd do three record dates a day and then go right to work at night with BILLY. 5

BILLY left station WNEW in New York City and returned to WLIB where he had begun his career as "disc jockey."

> HERB WONG: We had very lengthy conversations. I hitched a ride to New York with him because I knew he was close by and he had no problems with that. He thought it would be a nice opportunity for us to actually sit down, and while he was driving, to talk about a whole bunch of stuff. So I found him to be such a consistently affable person that I said to him: "Your personality has a semaphore. I think it has a really tight connection to the expression that you have in your music." He said: "Well, I've thought about that and maybe it does because it's a reflection of my feelings and my life and if that's the kind of person you think I am maybe you're right about that." So that was one of the things that I know came out – I was curious about. I actually went back to talking about his early work and how he was motivated to excel and to improve and to always try to do something fresh. So, all those strengths we know about that today – they have been lifelong streaks. So he was very kind and brought me back to the city before he went back to his home residence.

In New York City in 1964 BILLY TAYLOR recorded MIDNIGHT PIANO for Capitol Records. The orchestra members included Joe Newman, Barry Galbraith, Tony Studd, Phil Woods, Urbie Green, Snooky Young and Clark Terry. Oliver

Nelson did the arrangement which included From The Heart, It's A Grand Night For Swinging and You Tempt Me.

JIMMY OWENS: My first encounter with BILLY was in 1964. I was working with Charles Mingus. I first had the record he did with Ira Sullivan that came out in the late 50's and there was a record BILLY did that I had, with Duke Ellington musicians. Clark Terry was on it, and Clark had told me a story, in 1961-'62 that that was the first time he had played the flugelhorn, on that recording session with BILLY TAYLOR. I knew of BILLY at that time. In 1964 I was working at Birdland with Charles Mingus. We worked at Birdland two weeks, one week beside John Coltrane's great quartet and one week beside the BILLY TAYLOR TRIO, that was Earl May and Grady Tate. It was from that time that I got to respect him, not only as a musician but also as a very warm person. I was 21 years old and he gave me warm feelings right off as somebody who really cared for younger musicians. I was always an inquisitive musician when I was fourteen or fifteen years old and it extended right into my professional career.

I was born and raised in New York City, in the Bronx. It's really different growing up in New York and being part of the learning jazz situation because I was at all the clubs, even when I couldn't get in and in Birdland it was possible for me to get in – the original Birdland, 52nd St. and Broadway. They had a place for teenagers. You could go in and you came down the stairs, made a right turn and another right turn and there were some tables right up there and that's where they served you soft drinks and everything. The peanut gallery was over by the bar. So that particular time being around BILLY TAYLOR for a week was very interesting, and that was the first time I heard Grady Tate sing. All of a sudden I hear this voice singing "Body and Soul" and I'm looking up on the stage and I don't see anybody standing up in front of a microphone singing; and it's Grady Tate with a microphone, and he's playing the drums, and he's singing "Body and Soul". So, from there, I got friendly with BILLY. I was constantly on the road and in 1966 I gave up the road, stayed in New York, and people like Clark Terry and Jimmy Nottingham and other trumpet players helped me. That allowed me to get friendlier with BILLY.

BILLY initiated a workshop series for jazz promoter George Wein at the Newport Jazz Festival and Hunter College; was appointed to the advisory board on jazz at Lincoln Center in New York City, and accepted an officer's position with NARAS (the National Academy of Recording Arts and Sciences).

GRADY TATE: Out of necessity, BILLY taught me how to play very quietly with intensity because in his playing, he would be from the very light to something more bombastic. But it wasn't the kind of bombastic playing you'd do with a big band so I had to cut the volume in half at all times, yet the intensity had to remain there. I leaned how to do that playing with BILLY. He didn't turn around and demand it of me, it's just that when you're a drummer, you have to be quick enough to decide to play softer or louder, more fills or less fills. BILLY taught me a hell of a lot about dynamics. He also taught me about programming. He knows how to program a set with changing of keys and different tempos and styles. 6

BILLY'S 1964 tune, I WISH I KNEW HOW IT WOULD FEEL TO BE FREE, was selected by THE NEW YORK TIMES as 'one of the great songs of the sixties' and became the theme song for the movie 'Ghosts of Mississippi'. Although the tune from the title of the album was written in 1954 it was not popularized until the civil rights movement of the 60's. Many of the country's top recording stars contributed more than 30 different recordings of "I Wish I Knew How It Would Feel To Be Free" including Lena Horne, Harry Belafonte and Nina Simone, Leontyne Price, John Denver and the jazz-rock band Cold Blood.

REVEREND DALE LIND: In the fall of 1962 I was in college in New York in my intern year and met BILLY at the Hickory House. My predecessor, Reverend John Gensel, who started the jazz ministry, took me to the club – that was one of our stops - and I went back on my own to see him quite a few times. He was playing with Grady Tate and Ben Tucker. The first recording I heard of him was "I Wish I Knew How It Would Feel To Be Free". It was a '45s release with "Sonny" on the other side.

In the Thursday, July 14, 1964 issue of the Christian Science Monitor columnist Amy Lee wrote a column called "TELLING TONES" featuring BILLY TAYLOR. She said: "Pianist BILLY TAYLOR is seldom at a lost for words or notes. One of the few occasions he had real difficulty talking was when he played the part of Jelly Roll Morton on a television show. In a recent interview, he said: 'I had a problem playing in Morton's style and talking at the same time. I even find it hard to talk to my own playing.' The articulate pianist, composer, arranger, lecturer does not find it hard to talk about his playing or that of others or for that matter almost any topic from Scott Joplin and ragtime to Stockhausen and electronic music, from civil rights to his son's chemistry experiments. 'I wanted to go into radio because I thought it was one way I could make a contribution to greater understanding' he said. 'Many musicians find it hard to communicate in words. I felt I had some talent for it and should use it.' He first put this talent to work in 1959 with a jazz show on Harlem's WLIB. In

September 1962 he moved downtown to WNEW where he conducts a nightly jazz program in prime evening time. Now he just plays records and talks. 'Back in college I was on radio too, just playing, not talking.' His concern with education motivates everything he does and says. This is not surprising. By his senior year in college he was making quite a bit of money with his dance band. In fact, so much more than a salary attached to a teaching job offered him. 'I just laughed.' Mr. TAYLOR readily acknowledges his debt to those who have helped him to shape his career and ideals. 'Many wonderful musicians looked after me and advised me when I first came to New York. Jo Jones, Basie's great drummer was one, Art Tatum was like an older brother. Lots of younger musicians had help from the older ones and it's the same today. It's just that you never hear about it; the same as you seldom hear about peaceful integration or the good side of Harlem.' Two teachers greatly influenced BILLY TAYLOR also. One was a woman, professor of music at Virginia State. 'She helped me to see I should be spending more time in music.' Another was a supervisor of bands at three Negro high schools in Washington, D.C. He accepted BILLY as a piano pupil when the boy's early musical influences compounded of his 'proverbial musical' families, Bach, Scarlatti, etc. Baptist church choir music and an uncle's jazz piano playing made him uncertain of his musical whereabouts. 'He taught me the same principles apply in all music. He would relate a ninth chord as Debussy used it, for instance, to the way Gershwin used it. I don't agree with those who try to make music complicated. They used to say bop was complicated. It never seemed so to me, in fact the first instruction book I wrote was on bop.' Another in his eleven book instruction series he plans to redo is the one on ragtime. 'Ragtime is really very difficult to play. It was as much of a protest to its day as our music is today. I don't like to hear musicians say: "electronic music, I don't understand it!" and dismiss it. Of course they understand it. They know music and they know what's going on. What they mean is, they don't like it and they don't want to listen to it. It's all right if they want to reject it but only if they first listen to it. As musicians we have to reevaluate our whole approach. This is the day of electronic music. Every musician should ask himself: 'Who am I? What am I trying to say?' He must think in this way because before going he on stage must think how he can truly communicate with his audience. If he doesn't succeed he cannot excuse his failure by saying, The audience doesn't know anything about jazz. He needs to look into his own performance.'"

LLOYD PINCHBACK: I had heard BILLY'S tune, "I Wish I Knew How It Would Feel To Be Free"; I didn't know he had written that tune for many years. I had heard Nina Simone and several others doing it, but I didn't realize BILLY had written it.

In the 60's BILLY TAYLOR took the blindfold test for Down Beat Magazine. The record to be adjudicated was the Bill Evans Trio playing the Sonny Rollins classic "Oleo". BILLY was always quick to compliment other pianists. As stated in Peter Pettinger's book, BILL EVANS: HOW MY HEART SINGS: "The pianist BILLY TAYLOR reacted enthusiastically to this track in his Down Beat Blindfold test: 'Sounds very much like Bill Evans – very adventurous. I like his playing. He's one of the few guys around now- even though he plays quite a lot in hornlike lines when he's playing, with drive like this – who has two very good hands . . . Actually, he has two styles of the moment – a ballad style and an up-tempo style. His work is very personal. Five stars for this." 7

GRADY TATE: Aside from being such an incredible musician, he's also an incredible human being and I think that was the greatest lesson he taught me, the respect for a decent human being. He's a very nice man. I've yet to see BILLY lose his cool. He can be perturbed, as everyone can, but he has himself under control and that too was another lesson. He's a great person to grow up under, it's an accumulative effect that BILLY has on you. If you're around him often enough as I was and that just begins to rub off on you, the niceness and gentility. It's just something you have to see. I can't describe it, adequately. 8

In the mid-60's BILLY was appointed to the Harlem Cultural Council where council member Daphne Arnstein proposed a project which would take music to the people of New York; BILLY insisted that the music be jazz. A float was borrowed from the Budweiser Co, which also gave a grant of $10,000 and converted it to a bandstand on wheels. The Jazzmobile delivered jazz to the people who were unable to afford admission to routine jazz concerts. Some of the original artists who performed were Cannonball Adderly, Carmen McRae, Dizzy Gillespie and Duke Ellington. The concept rapidly developed adding lecture-demonstration programs in the public schools, free outdoor summer concerts, and Saturday workshops.

JIMMY HEATH: I heard BILLY around but our paths were not crossing all the time. I was doing other things and he was busy with his music until we ended up hooking up at the time that Daphne Arnstein and BILLY hooked up with the idea of Jazzmobile in the 60's. At the first press conference at a bank on 125th St. a meeting was held with all the people who were interested in the Jazzmobile program. BILLY was picked as the Executive Director of Jazzmobile and I taught at the Jazzmobile under BILLY and then Paul West who ran the program for awhile before he went to Henry Street to run that program and than David Bailey.

KETER BETTS: I played with BILLY at the Caverns in D.C. for about a week with Lou Rawls in the mid-60's. We had a ball! I still do a lot of school things – I'm still at Wolf Trap with Head Start – this will be my 23rd year. It's introducing young people and people from all walks of life to jazz and making them more knowledgeable about jazz.

During the 60's BILLY lectured at Yale and at MENC (the Music Educators National Conference). He wrote original compositions for PBS productions of The Electric Company and Sesame Street; served as music director for Tony Brown's Journal and lectured and demonstrated on the CBS Captain Kangaroo Show, Rainbow Sundae, Exploring and Dial 'M' For Music. He also served as the spokesperson for several companies including L'Oreal Hair Products, Canada Dry, Campbell Soup and Coca-Cola. To make certain that all of his business bases were covered he established BILLY TAYLOR PRODUCTIONS.

WAYNE ANDRE: I got to know BILLY, the man and the musician, when I, a trombonist, was a member of the big band on the weekly PBS (Channel 13 in New York City) show called Black Journal hosted by Tony Brown. We performed instrumental features and accompanied singers. What I remember most, aside from the great musician he was, is his judging (acceptance of, if you will) musicians based on their ability. I only knew BILLY as one musician to another and I had the highest respect for him.

LARRY RIDLEY: We did a lot of things with Jazzmobile That whole thing that BILLY did in establishing Jazzmobile was really very, very important because it brought the music to the community. The whole idea started out basically sort of like a second line concept, the New Orleans funeral marching kind of thing. We had this float that would go through various parts of the street with a final destination where we'd end up playing a regular concert. The kids would be running after the float – it was really nice. They stopped doing that a few years back and now the program is stationary, with different block associations and things like that. So it's great because he had the foresight to see the idea of getting the community involved and that part has been beautiful. The only down side is the thing that I see a lot of these guys who for years would come to the Jazzmobile concerts because they (the concerts) were free and I would tell them: "Hey, I've got a concert coming up and why don't you guys come by?" They'd start hemming and hawing. I'd say: "Well, you guys" - you know they'd come with their coolers, beer and everything else, their lawn chairs, and they'd sit up and check out the music. I'd say: "Well, you know, we've got to pay the rent too!"

BILLY TAYLOR: The Jazzmobile float was redecorated with a New Orleans-type motif and fitted with a Wurlitzer electric piano and a sound system that would amplify the music as the float moved through the streets. With the enthusiastic cooperation and support of the New York City police, the sanitation department, the mayor's office, community organizations, and the Musicians Union, the New Orleans tradition of tailgate jazz was updated with a six-piece bebop band. They led hundreds of curious jazz fans of all ages and ethnic groups to the site of Jazzmobile's first free street-concert. 9

The Jazzmobile concept received wholesale interest by musicians and educators through the world and was enthusiastically emulated. The concept lasted through the 20th century and into the 21st.

BILLY TAYLOR: Using pragmatic approaches to its basic programs, Jazzmobile became the prototype of the New York City summer street programs and the model for many subsequent lecture-demonstrations and workshop-clinic programs presented by other jazz organizations all over the country. 10

The only jazz organization designated as a major cultural institution by the New York State Council on the Arts, Jazzmobile utilized its considerable jazz experience and resources in the field of education. During the 1976-77 fiscal year, Jazzmobile received a grant from the Department of Health, Education, and Welfare and the U.S. Department of Education to plan and execute an arts program which was designed 'to reduce the adverse effects of minority group isolation.' In this Emergency School Aid Act (ESAA) program, Jazzmobile applied the principles of jazz improvisation and the talents of professional artists in music, dance, visual arts, poetry, and the theater to the problems of a target group of a thousand youngsters who were up to three years behind their peers in reading skills. The idea was to give the students a better sense of their importance as individuals by having them actively express themselves through the arts. LeRoi Jones's Black Arts group presented the new music in the streets of Harlem in 1963-65, attracting an audience of people who left their houses out of curiosity at first and stayed out of interest, but one of the first positive attempts to take jazz back into the black community originally had less to do with collectivism and education than with advertising. The Harlem Commmunity Council instigated the Jazzmobile, which started operations in 1964, and was the first of many mobile theatre projects. It is just what its name implies – a bandstand set up on the back of a truck. It was originally sponsored by Coca Cola and Ballantine beer and, for a nominal fee; musicians took their music each summer into Harlem, the Bronx, Brooklyn and other culturally deprived areas where many of the younger blacks had never heard jazz before. Every Saturday, a staff of experienced musicians . . . conduct a series of sessions at the Jazzmobile Workshop for students whose ages range from fifteen to fifty with a syllabus that includes everything from instrumental basics to big band orchestrations. The students, surrounded by the mandatory posters, proclaiming the evils of narcotics, are impressively serious about their music. 11

JIMMY HEATH: I did a lot of workshops with BILLY during the Jazzmobile period. We would do these jazz-lecture concerts in the schools here in New York. There was a program that presented these jazz-lecture concerts and we would do an evolutionary kind of concert where BILLY would play ragtime, boogie-woogie stuff and we'd come all the way up to whatever was happening and that was a great experience. Also we did street concerts and went upstate and did some things in Albany and Schenectady and places like that with Jazzmobile.

DAVE BRUBECK: BILLY'S efforts to educate young people and his Jazzmobile program has been enormously important in promoting jazz in New York City and elsewhere.

CLEM DEROSA: There was a jazz organization that was developed in New York City called Jazz Interactions, I think was the name of it, and I was part of that and BILLY was part of it. Reverend Gensel and Alan Pepper, who owned the Bottom Line, was also part of that organization. BILLY was deeply involved with that, very influential. Dave Bailey was there. Then there was a spin-off of that; BILLY was involved with Dave Bailey and Paul West, bass player, and they really developed a very successful Jazzmobile program. BILLY was involved with that for a long time, and, of course, I see him often at conventions. He spent a lot of time working in education. He was one of the few that saw the opportunities for young people in education.

In BILLY'S interview with Dick Miller, August 27, 1989 (The Dick Miller Show, WMUB, Miami University of Ohio), Miller pressed BILLY for information regarding the project:

DICK MILLER: I know that there is something that is very near and dear to your heart and has been for over twenty-five years, that's the Jazzmobile. Why don't you tell out listeners something about the Jazzmobile.
BILLY TAYLOR: Well the Jazzmobile started about twenty-five years ago and our thought was to really get the music out to people, to bring the music right to their doorstep, to bring it in to the schools and community centers, and so forth. I realized from my own career that a lot of people who I related to, who related to me, simply couldn't afford to come to the festivals, or come to the many concert halls and places where I was playing. I wanted

to work out some way that they could hear the music also and Jazzmobile seemed to be an excellent vehicle in more ways than one.

DICK MILLER: And you got a new album out.

BILLY TAYLOR: Yeah, it's interesting. The album is interesting to me because the material itself came from a residency that we performed up in New Hampshire and Jazzmobile takes the improvisatory aspects of jazz and applies them to education in many ways. So we go off and we give lecture-concerts, lecture-demonstrations, master classes, workshops, and so forth in, all the way from grade school through university. This was at a university where we were working with a tremendous choreographer. Most of the pieces on the recording were things that were designed to be danced by the people in her dance corp. We taught the music to some of the students; she taught the dance to some of the student dancers and they performed the work for us after we performed it for them. So it was a very exciting project and this was several years ago; this was the first chance we had to record the material that we've been playing for a while. The guys who recorded it are pretty much on the staff. As a matter of fact, Jimmy Owens, trumpet player, runs the Jazzmobile workshop. He's the guy who designs the classes, oversees the whole project.

In 1965 the BILLY TAYLOR TRIO played a concert in TOWN HALL in New York City. The program resulted in an album entitled BILLY TAYLOR TRIO AT TOWN HALL. The tunes recorded were Sweet Georgia Brown, Theodora, Foggy Day, How High The Moon and I'll Remember April.

JIMMY OWENS: I started to do workshops with the Jazzmobile because BILLY had started Jazzmobile in the 60's. During '69, '70, '71 and '72 we had a Saturday workshop. We would see somewhere between three and four hundred people from age 12-13 up to 60 and 70 years of age. Any players, they would come. At first it was free, then an initiation fee was put in place, something like $20 to register. That would run for like twenty weeks, twenty-five weeks of a year, teaching, every Saturday. BILLY had Chris White, bass player with Dizzy Gillespie, as the director of the workshop and later Paul West became the director of the workshop. After that, Dave Bailey became the director of the workshop. I was teaching in the trumpet workshop. The trumpet teachers at that time were Lee Morgan, Kenny Durham and myself. Lee Morgan would go away and he would send in somebody or we would get somebody to replace him. It was a fantastic experience for the students. It was all from BILLY'S mind that this is what should happen – just like Jazzmobile; the actual mobile was from his mind. That's why he is such a great leader when it comes to education.

In 1966 BILLY hosted a jazz TV show on channel 47 in Newark, New Jersey.

JIMMY OWENS: In going to performances of Jazzmobile BILLY started to use me on some of the Jazzmobile groups that he put together, big band. His quintet, he was using Joe Newman, and then he replaced Joe Newman with me. We recorded an album called THE JAZZMOBILE ALL-STARS. So BILLY, at that point, hired me; was constantly calling me for Jazzmobile and other things; now we're talking 1966-'67-'68, in that period. So I was doing things with him off and on, as well as lots of other stuff, and I got to really appreciate him more when he and I would get together and talk because I saw how alike I was to him, without knowing his life. One of the things he really felt was important was to educate musicians who are interested in learning about things like business, and they didn't know very much about business, many of them. When BILLY found out and I found out about that with BILLY we were both amazed at that was what this young guy was doing and I was amazed at what BILLY TAYLOR had been doing. It was a lot different than Dizzy Gillespie or Slide Hampton, other people that I was friendly with and had come up with. Donald Byrd was like that. Donald Byrd was one of my teachers when I was fourteen year old in high school.

Jazzmobile eventually became a major producer of concerts and special music events including the anniversary concerts of Sarah Vaughan and Milt Jackson, "Jazz in July" at the University of Massachusetts, and toured its groups as part of various international jazz events in France, Holland, Belgium, Canada, Japan and England.

DAVID BAKER: I knew about BILLY during my college years. I knew about Jazzmobile. I'm not sure about the exact year of its formation. By the time I came back to teach, a gap of about seven or eight years, I knew through that and about the time I was a little further along, very active and he was one of the first blacks to have a studio orchestra (in the 60's). In the 50's there was so little activity. I knew about recordings by BILLY. Also, I'd heard about him from another mutual friend, Joe Kennedy. And the next thing I knew BILLY had that piano show and he started to really blossom into one of the premier educators.

BILLY joined GERRY MULLIGAN to do a tune from Newport, Rhode Island for NIPPON COLUMBIA COMPACT DISC entitled GERRY MULLIGAN on July 1, 1966. Players in the MULLIGAN BAND included Rudy Braff, trumpet, Bud Freeman, tenor saxophone, Gerry Mulligan, baritone saxophone, Benny Moton, bass, Osie Johnson, drums, and BILLY TAYLOR, piano. The tune recorded was Rose Room.

DAVE BRUBECK: One experience I had with BILLY stands out in my memory, probably because I was so nervous about playing solo piano for the first time in public. Somewhere in the early sixties George Wein decided to have a piano workshop one of the afternoons of the Newport Jazz Festival. To everyone's amazement it drew about 2000 people. BILLY TAYLOR was the moderator. And what amazed me about BILLY was his ability to not only explain to the audience the different styles of piano as exemplified by the performers that afternoon – Willie "The Lion" Smith, Thelonious Monk, Toshiko, George Wein, Joe Sullivan and myself – but also to play examples of the different approaches, so that the audience was well prepared to understand each artist as he or she took the bandstand. I recall that John S. Wilson in the New York Times called the afternoon "the highpoint of the festival", and it was due in great part to BILLY'S eloquence with both the spoken word and at the piano keyboard.

In 1967 the BILLY TAYLOR TRIO recorded the album I WISH I KNEW HOW IT WOULD FEEL TO BE FREE in New York City. TOWER RECORDS was the producer. The personnel with BILLY were Ben Tucker, bass and Grady Tate, drums. The seven tunes comprising the album were I Wish I Knew How It Would Feel To Be Free, Pensativa, Morning, TNT, Hard To Find, Lonesome Lover and CAG.

FRAN RICHARD: So it seems like BILLY was always there – the Jazzmobile, etc., he was always playing. He was on the Board of ASCAP before my time at ASCAP. I wish I had been here when he was on the Board – it would have been wonderful. BILLY impresses everyone. When you grow up in this city (New York) he was always a presence in the music life. I can't remember – my father took me a few times (I can't remember the place) to a different club. BILLY has touched many people. If only tangentially, they know him. They recognize his voice and they recognize his face and because of all the ways he participates in the cultural life.

On April 23, 1967 John Coltrane appeared at a benefit concert for and at the new Olatunji African Culture on East 125th Street in New York City. BILLY was the M.C. and recalled the two sets on that Sunday: "John called me and asked me to do that. Olatunji was right around the corner from the radio station, WLIB. I knew Olatunji's work and on the station we played him a lot. He was really trying to do something to awaken the community to his view of the African heritage, which was a lot deeper than many people had delved into it prior to him."

The question posed to the people was about Coltrane's music and sound. "There was such a crowd that after he played they had to empty the room and bring in the next group, so if there were questions it was after the second set. His music was always so passionate at that period that I had to digest it. There was just so much going on. The volume in the room was much higher than I was accustomed to, but I enjoyed it. The difference between John Coltrane screaming and doing some of the kinds of things he was doing in that period – it took me years to realize that he had learned how to do that in rhythm-and-blues bands, and he was using that kind of a cry, that kind of utterance on the saxophone, in a totally different way, than many guys who came along after and said, 'Oh, physically he'd doing this to make that sound.'" Coltrane wasn't doing it for effect. It represented his entire history. 12

PHIL SCHAAP: In the early years I would be perhaps a more cognizant fan but he was this magical jazz person. He started Jazzmobile and I was so young I was going to those things on my bicycle and he was on the air. And I use to rely on him for a great deal of good judgment on the hard bop records. Records were spinning out of Blue Note like they were issuing ten LP's a week and I was buying one a month – one out of forty albums to pick from. I followed his guidance, good judgment on Horace Silver records.

On May 31, 1967, at composer/arranger Billy Strayhorn's funeral, Father Norman J. O'Connor, a Catholic priest active in the jazz world, said a prayer, and the service ended with BILLY TAYLOR and Ray Nance, on piano and violin, performing TAKE THE 'A' TRAIN as a dirge. 13

LARRY RIDLEY: I don't recall the exact time I joined BILLY; it just seemed like all of a sudden we were working together. But I remember BILLY on so many different fronts because BILLY was always active in so many different areas rather than just being a regular jazz musician. He was very much involved in being on various panels, like the National Endowment for the Arts; he was a disc jockey at a radio station. He just was a gentleman who was involved in so many different ways, all of them being very positive. And he's always been that kind of a person, always giving, and BILLY was a mentor to me, in many respects because through him and David Baker (I came up around David when I was much younger in Indianapolis) where we all grew up (Freddy Hubbard, Slide Hampton, etc.). I was always impressed with BILLY and how he was always very well spoken, very articulate and always a champion for the music, and I don't think BILLY gets the credit that he really justly deserves for all the things that he's done for the music.

BILL MCFARLIN: BILLY'S relationship with and support of IAJE (International Association for Jazz Education) began in the early days of our founding as the National Association of Jazz Education in 1968. He was an outspoken participant in the MENC (Music Educators National Conference), Tanglewood Symposium, also held in 1968, which addressed integrating jazz with music education on a more formal basis, and has volunteered thousands of hours to our work. Many people talk a good game, but BILLY is always the first in line when it is time to get things done. I have asked BILLY to do many things through the past twenty years, and he has never said no!

DAVID BAKER: I met BILLY about the time of the first TANGLEWOOD and then I got to know BILLY, the educator – his piano book and then through David Bailey we formed the NATIONAL JAZZ SERVICE organization; BILLY was on the board of directors of almost everybody by that time; anything to do with culture, I got to know him in that capacity. And then when he started to do the stuff on Sunday morning. Those things were probably an oasis in a really dead land on Sundays. And I can remember being astounded at how many people BILLY could come up with who were really not well-known at the time, because of BILLY they became well-known. Through the years we became really good friends.

In 1969 BILLY TAYLOR began a three-year tenure as Music Director for the David Frost Television Show. Several prominent personalities raved about the BILLY TAYLOR ORCHESTRA on the show: SAMMY DAVIS, JR: "Man, that has to be just one of the greatest bands I've ever heard. They're really cooking." LOUIS ARMSTRONG: "Pops, now you're really swinging along back there." PEGGY LEE: "Now that's really a great, great band." MEL TORME: "Wow . . . the sound he gets from that group is just wild."

BILLY TAYLOR: When I worked on the David Frost Show for three years I had the opportunity to develop a jazz sound, we used a lot of head arrangements. Johnny Carisi wrote the basic book, although a lot of other writers including Harold Wheeler, added arrangements as well. I wrote some of the music myself. The basic concept was the same kind of thing Basie had (when he had his smaller band). The guys in the band came up with some great things. We had the best of both worlds.

LLOYD PINCHBACK: My first awareness of BILLY TAYLOR was his work on the David Frost Show. Seeing the black musical conductor of a nationally distributed TV broadcast was somewhat striking because he was the first to my knowledge. This was also at the end of the Civil Rights movement of the 60's. David Frost and BILLY TAYLOR seemed so well matched; both seemed to be genuinely nice people. The mutual respect these two have for each other was visibly evident.

CLEM DEROSA: I think the David Frost Television Show that he did was very influential and that ran for a long time. I was always impressed with the way it was done and I think that's one thing about BILLY that I always remember; there's a dignity about what he does, he brings that to everything he does including his playing, his speaking, and he put a lot of time into jazz education, starting with the Jazzmobile. I think that's part of his legacy.

JIMMY OWENS: In 1969 BILLY called me to be a part of the David Frost band. That band was a very unique band from the standpoint of the bands that were on television. The Dick Cavet Show Band and the Johnny Carson Show Band were all big bands, four trumpets, four trombones, and five saxophones. BILLY put together this band of two trumpets, one trombone, and three saxophones, alto, tenor, and baritone, all doubling. Frank Wess, Hubert Laws, and George Berg saxophones, Morty Bullman, trombone, Dick Hurwitz and myself, trumpets. The rhythm section was BILLY'S rhythm section that was, at that time, Bobby Thomas and Bob Cranshaw. Cranshaw stayed there for about three or four months and then he left the show. The show ran for three years, 1969 to 1972. It was a very interesting situation, business-wise, because the way that the contract was negotiated – we were not on staff, the band was not on staff. The musicians on the Cavet Show and Johnny Carson were on staff and their base pay was about $280 a week. We (the Frost Band) were not on staff - they could fire us and say: "Don't come back tomorrow!" Whereas with the other shows they would have to give them a ten-week notice, we made $580 a week, a big, big difference. So Hubert Laws then left and he was replaced by a saxophonist by the name of Al Gibbons. BILLY had asked me: "Who can I get who plays tenor, flute, and clarinet?" and I said: "Al Gibbons is real good." Well, he knew Al Gibbons from Al being in some of the bands in New York and what not, big bands. So he took my suggestion and called Al. Al came and played with the band. Al must of stayed about a year and a half and then he started having some mental problems, paranoia, and he wound up leaving the band and was replaced by Shelton Powell. So at that point we had another great saxophone section of Frank Wess, Shelton Powell and George Berg – every double you can imagine. We played every kind of music. Because the members of the band were so musically versed, we could play anything. Whether it was Bette Midler, who came on and had no music, first time on television, or it was an opera singer who came on and had a piano part. The other pianist besides BILLY was Johnny Lesco and would make an arrangement right then and there for people to play. Johnny Lesco is still around New York; he does a lot of Broadway conducting, writing, etc. The contractor of the show was Marty Grupp; his father was a great trumpet teacher. Marty took BILLY'S suggestions. The band was a 12-piece band, with six white musicians and six black musicians, which was unlike any band on television. All of the bands had one or two black musicians and they had many more musicians.

BILLY really started to get into learning how to conduct; that was his major problem when we first started the show, he was not a conductor of the musicians. He started to learn how to conduct, getting himself together enough to really do the band. We would warm up the audience – had to be to work at 5:15, and we would rehearse from 5:15 to 6:30; then we were off from 6:30 to 8:00. Eight was the show's downbeat. When we were putting the music together, Manny Album wrote some of the arrangements; he did the first arrangements for the band of some of BILLY'S compositions. The theme, which was called OK BILLY, was written by somebody in England, somebody who David Frost knew, was arranged by Manny Album. Manny did a number of arrangements for the band during the whole life of the show. Other writers included Jimmy Heath, Frank Wess. I wrote a number of things; and we used to warm up the audience fifteen-minutes or so before the show started. The audience was always gassed because when they heard us play they were amazed because they didn't think they were coming to a concert; they thought they were just coming to a TV show.

So that show lasted for three years. Sometimes we worked five days a week, five shows, or we would do six shows, two on Wednesday. For about a year we worked three days a week. The show was at a theater on 44th Street, called the Little Theater. I later did some research and found out historical facts about the Little Theater. Bessie Smith used to sing in that theater and Coleman Hawkins was accompanying her and Louis Armstrong was accompanying her in this theater. We had everybody on the show – more jazz artists than Cabot, Mike Douglas or Johnnie Carson ever had. Because BILLY, being in the know, and because David Frost and the whole business structure respected BILLY, when BILLY said: "We should have so and so on the Show," they arranged to get that person on the show. Like a show with Duke Ellington, Willie "The Lion" Smith and BILLY TAYLOR, playing on two pianos – Willie "The Lion" Smith played one piano and Duke and BILLY shared. Louis Armstrong was on all the time. BILLY didn't have to push that. People like Eddie Harris, etc. So it was a very, very wonderful experience. We were on screen quite often; at least twice a week we were on screen. They would move the band to such a way where the TV audience could see us during the show. So I got to be much friendlier with BILLY during those years.

DAVID FROST: Every guest I had on the show raved about BILLY TAYLOR and his orchestra, not just the people who really knew their music, who really knew their bands, but people like me who may not know that much about music but who certainly knew what they liked.

NNENNA FREELON: I was first aware of BILLY when I was a little girl; he was on TV! My mother was a culture woman – she's the kind of woman who pointed out anyone who was African-American who was doing something. It was in the late 60's (the David Frost Show) and they gave him a little feature every time. I don't think she was pointing him out to me be because of his musicianship as much as because he was in the spotlight, doing the right thing, that kind of thing. It impressed me that he was treated with such respect. He was an articulate person. You didn't see that many black persons on TV at that time. So I first heard him play on television. I don't believe we had any of his recordings.

BOBBY THOMAS: I played drums in BILLY'S trio and in the band on the David Frost TV show and the thing about his piano playing is that his musicality is always first class. When we played ballads, the voicings he would use, especially with strings behind him, would just be superb. He has that way with chords. And when it came to the up-tempo things, he would razzle dazzle you so it was always enjoyable playing with him. The band on the TV show was not quite a big band, we had ten pieces including Frank Wess on woodwinds, Hubert Laws on flute, Jimmy Owens on trumpet, Barry Galbraith on guitar, Bob Cranshaw on bass, a few others and we had wonderful charts by a lot of the really great arrangers and composers in the city. We got to play some great music and back up everybody who came on the show. It was fun and a challenge to be able to play different music every day. You just went through it once and then you shot it, that was it! But the caliber of musician that we had in that band could pull it off, there's no doubt about that. I've always appreciated BILLY'S very intense love for teaching and the way he's constantly promoting jazz as America's classical music, which is one of his favorite sayings. A lot of our appearances would turn into question and answer type concerts. There was always a lot of information he would give out and pass on to the audience, especially to the young people, because we did a lot of college gigs and each college gig was always a workshop. Then we would listen to their bands and combos and critique them so they could walk away with something. 14

Bobby (Robert Charles) Thomas was born in Newark, New Jersey on November 14, 1932. He played in various army bands before studying at Juilliard.

After playing briefly in Newark he worked with Nat Phipps in the early 50's and Sir Roland Hanna and Illinois Jacquet in the late 50's. During the 60's and 70's he played with Gigi Gryce, Ray Charles, Quincy Jones, Herbie Mann, Cy Coleman, Gerry Mulligan, Hubert Laws, Junior Mance and BILLY TAYLOR.

DAVID BAKER: I was familiar with people on the David Frost Show – that show was a major breakthrough. Every civil rights organization of any kind was quick to tout that as a major breakthrough. People like Joe Wilder, Clark (Terry), and all the guys would ultimately be ensconced in the real world.

JIM ANDERSON: As an adolescent growing up I was very aware of BILLY on the David Frost Show. David would say: "Hit it BILLY!" This was while I was a student in high school in the 60's. I also remember BILLY doing commercials for Cold Power – he wrote the music and would also say: "Hi, BILLY TAYLOR for Cold Power Detergent!" I was 16 or 17 years old and would drive around Pennsylvania hearing BILLY on the radio selling detergent. I was very aware of who BILLY was.

LOREN SCHOENBERG: When I was first aware of BILLY TAYLOR I was a young person growing up a Metropolitan area in the 60's. I used to watch the David Frost Show. BILLY had that great band. I didn't know anything. And as I became a professional jazz musician and hanging around New York City in the early 1970's it became clear that this man that I first saw on television – how many African-American Bandleaders on major talk shows were there? – and having a band I began to discover that the musicians in that band (the BILLY TAYLOR band on the David Frost Show) were the really greatest players and I was just really knocked out that there was already this intersection between commercial music and these great jazz artists' ability to deal as the house band for a TV talk show. And also the fact that on occasion they would get to play. I do remember, as a kid, seeing Duke Ellington on that show and BILLY playing with him. That's probably the first time that I really saw him play the piano because most of the time he was leading the band on that show.

When the David Frost show went off the air BILLY returned to radio WLIB as station program manager and disk jockey hosting two jazz programs.

BILLY TAYLOR: With the help of Del Shield and Ed Williams we built the biggest jazz audience in New York. Radio and jazz go together in a special way and we exploited that fact to the fullest.

The BILLY TAYLOR TRIO with Ben Tucker, bass, Grady Tate, drums, and BILLY, piano recorded an album, TODAY, for Prestige Records (later released by Pausa Records, Sleepin Bee) in 1969. The tunes recorded were La Petite Mambo, Theodora, Paraphrase, Don't Go Down South, Brother and Where Are You.

BRUCE LUNDVALL: I've worked with BILLY on projects such as years ago, when I was with Columbia Records, we did a 52nd St. project. He was part of that. The idea was to commemorate 52nd St. in terms of the clubs that were lining the Street up and down. So we had, at the time, the cultural envoy to the major, and we had a committee with Dizzy Gillespie. BILLY TAYLOR was part of it, a number of us at Columbia Records, and we finally got the mayor and his counsel to agree that we could tear up the sidewalk and put these plaques in and we had a big celebration when we unveiled the plaques. Every year there were supposed to be another six. It lasted for two years and then it disappeared but that's something that needs to be done again. Now the plaques are scuffed so badly, you can't even see them in the summer. They need to be replaced probably with some solid brass ones. Anyway, we'll get BILLY involved with that and I'm sure it will be done.

JIMMY OWENS: In 1969 when I started to do some workshops through this organization that we started, called the Collective Black Artists of New York, BILLY was there to aid in any kind of workshop that I needed him. When I said: "I want to talk about copyright; I want to talk about publishing; I want to talk about owning your own publishing company, will you address panel sessions?" Stuff like that.

On the 23rd of October 1969 the Petersburg Alumni Chapter of Kappa Alpha Phi presented a certificate to BILLY "in recognition of academic excellence and achievement."

DAN MORGANSTERN: I remember doing at least one feature piece on BILLY when I was with Downbeat and interviewed him when he was musical director for the David Frost Show. I remember Louis Armstrong and Bing Crosby were guests on the show.

BILLY began to expand his educational interests, became an adjunct professor at C.W. Post College in New York and visiting professor at Howard University. He received his first honorary doctor's degree; this year from Fairfield University. By 2003 he received twenty honorary doctorates from many of the nation's most prestigious universities. He finished a long tenure as pianist at the Hickory House in New York City, left WLIB to serve as a disc jockey at station WNEW where he reached a much larger audience, wrote compositions for PBS productions of The Electric Company and Sesame Street, served as Music Director for Tony Brown's Journal and lectured and demonstrated on The CBS Captain Kangaroo Show, Rainbow Sundae, Exploring and Dial "M" for Music. After a while he returned to WLIB, began doing school concerts, initiated a series of workshops for George Wein at Hunter College and the Newport Jazz Festival, was appointed to the advisory board on jazz for the Lincoln Center in New York City, and became an officer with NARAS (National Academy of Arts and Sciences). He established Jazzmobile and was appointed to the Harlem Culture Council, served as pianist-conductor for the David Frost Television Show, lectured at MENC (Music Educators National Conference), and hosted a jazz TV show on channel 47 in New York.

LOREN SCHOENBERG: As I moved to New York it became more apparent to me – the more deep I got into jazz music, reading about it, studying the piano myself – although I'm a saxophone player – that eventually this was someone who was much more than just a bandleader on a famous television show or that he was much more than just the leader of a trio. I began to hear all about Jazzmobile. And slowly, as I got more and more into the jazz world, I began to realize that there was hardly any corner of the jazz world in which BILLY TAYLOR wasn't a part.

At the end of the 60's decade BILLY began a three-year tenure as Music Director for the David Frost TV show. During the 60's BILLY wrote his most performed tune, "I Wish I Knew How It Would Feel To Be Free" that went on to be the featured music in a successful movie production.

BILLY was on a roll. His creativity was blossoming through his piano playing, his writing, his teaching, and the huge audience he was building for jazz through radio and television. He had amassed a large following of devotees and friends. He felt that a closer contact with students would be even more rewarding. He was going to begin to reap that reward during the seventies.

VI

DR. TAYLOR! – NATIONAL PUBLIC RADIO – MEDIA RECOGNITION, AWARDS

Jazz, a unique American phenomenon, is America's classical music. – BILLY TAYLOR

In 1970 BILLY TAYLOR was appointed to the National Council for the Arts by President Richard Nixon and worked with Maurice Abravenel, Eudora Welty, Beverly Sills and Nancy Hanks. Virginia State University honored BILLY with an honorary doctorate.

MARQUITA POOL ECKERT: I was first aware of BILLY TAYLOR when I came to New York around 1970. I knew of him because of the Jackie Robinson Foundation, the David Frost Show and Jazzmobile. I heard him play in person at a Jackie Robinson Foundation event. I sort of grew up listening to jazz. I got married in 1975. My husband and my father were both into jazz. The first jazz records I recall hearing were Django Reinhart, the Modern Jazz Quartet and Erroll Garner, "Concert By The Sea" or something like that. I used to wear them out. At one time my father had an interest in a jazz club in Chicago called Birdland. It lasted about two years, I think. They had a problem getting a liquor license and ultimately it was closed because of that. Around that time I went to work at a show called "Like It Is" on WBAC-TV, a black public affairs show. I used to book the talent sometimes. I had an ear in that camp always. So somewhere around that time with the Jackie Robinson Foundation, the David Frost Show and Jazzmobile was when I became familiar with BILLY.

One very practical education aid, the Jazzmobile (a vehicle equipped to present jazz concerts in the open air) gained popularity in the 1970's. Pianist BILLY TAYLOR and drummer Dave Bailey, and others had organized the traveling unit in the 60's that toured New York City.

COBI NARITA: I first came to New York in 1970. I met BILLY and he was so kind and I started an organization of my own (Universal Jazz Coalition). He was always so helpful. He's just a big, big man in his heart and in his soul.

I heard him play right away – that's how I met him. Every time he played I went to hear him play. He always had a couple of young people in his group and whenever he had a young person, boy did that young person grow! He always had established musicians with him also. I love him. He's always been very, very sweet and very, very kind to me. I was a brand new person starting a brand new organization. He would answer questions. He would involve me in the things he was doing.

In New York City in 1970 the BILLY TAYLOR TRIO recorded the album OK BILLY! for BELL RECORDS. The orchestra was comprised of the personnel from the David Frost Show: Dick Hurwitz and Jimmy Owens, trumpets, Morty Bullman, trombone, George Berg, Frank Wess and Al Gibbons, saxophones-clarinets, Barry Galbraith, guitar, Bob Cranshaw, bass, Bobby Thomas, drums, Marty Grupp, percussion, BILLY TAYLOR, piano-leader. Tunes recorded included By George (the David Frost Theme), O.K. Billy, Somewhere Soon, Tell Me Why, Dirty Ole Man, If You Really Are Concerned Then Show It, Break-A-Way and After Love, Emptiness.

DEREK GORDON: I first heard BILLY play on television on the David Frost Show and others and I was familiar with the album "My Fair Lady Loves Jazz". I grew up with the Platters, Josephine Baker, that sort of thing, Dinah Washington, etc. That was the music from my parents' era and so I sort of grew up with that music; then eventually got into Motown and all of that stuff but I always had a great appreciation for great ballads, whether they were instrumental or vocal. BILLY has such a lyric quality when he plays a ballad – it's just beautiful. I'm a singer but not a singer when BILLY plays.

The March 4, 1971 release of Down Beat contained an article, "TAYLOR-MADE FROSTINGS", written by Dan Morganstern who touted the David Frost TV Show: "When it comes to bands (an important ingredient in all talk shows), Frost's show certainly is in a class by itself. While the big three boast large, smooth, well-oiled orchestras mainly made up of studio veterans, the Frost band is smaller (11 pieces), younger, hipper, and admirably well balanced, musically and racially." He went on to cite BILLY'S involvement in radio when he said: "He also misses one area of activity that took up much of his time before he joined the Frost show. 'The one thing I really miss is being on the radio. It took me time to realize that. There were things I was able to do in the community (TAYLOR was program director of Harlem-based station WLIB and conducted his own jazz show) – I hope to be able to get back into radio when possible,' he says. While he was at WLIB, TAYLOR, at his own expense, conducted a series of seminars for jazz musicians dealing mainly with economics and business problems, and it made him happy that some participants, at least, 'got information that put some money in their pockets.' In general he feels that young musicians today are 'much better trained and prepared and are looking into business aspects of jazz. They're joining AGAC, ASCAP and BMI and learning to protect their music. It's a far cry from the days when I used to sell songs for $25-30 outright.' But then, BILLY TAYLOR today is a far cry from the gifted young pianist struggling to be recognized. 'It took me years to live down my reputation as a good accompanist.' He recalls. 'On 52nd Street, on the Birdland scene, almost every job I was offered was tied to a singer. I even had a row with George Wein at Newport one year about that. I really like to play for singers, but that wasn't all I wanted to do. That was one reason I never made a big effort to get into the studio thing.' If he's in it today, and in a big way, it's because his reputation has grown to the point where the Frost people called him – not he them. Success has not spoiled BILLY TAYLOR."

In the early 70's jazz concert promoter George Wein began to explore additional venues for which to present his festivals. Having been successful at Newport and in Boston for several years he called Phoebe Jacobs.

PHOEBE JACOBS: George Wein called from Boston in the early 70's, around 1971 and I spoke to him and Charlie Bourgouiso and they said they were contemplating doing the jazz festival in New York City. What did I think? At that time I was the manager of Special Events for Rockefeller Center. I would take care of the lighting of the Christmas tree, entertainers like choral groups, musicians; I would do things in the Rainbow Room and the Rainbow Grill and the skating rink and there were little restaurants there where they would have special parties where they needed music of VIP's to be entertained like dignitaries that came to America or to New York and the Rainbow Room was naturally a showcase for scenery and view and opulence and elegance. So I was always involved. Like when Duke Ellington was going to Russia we entertained the United Nations and when there was a president in town we would do a special luncheon at the Rockefeller Center Luncheon Club. So I was involved there and when they called me I said: "I think it would be sensational to come to New York", and I called BILLY TAYLOR. I said: "BILLY, what do you think?" And he said: "Oh, that would be fabulous!" So when I spoke to Charlie Bourgouiso again, who still works for George Wein, I told him I spoke to BILLY TAYLOR and I spoke to Milt Hinton and a couple other musicians, and they all thought it was sensational. And when I spoke to the people at Rockefeller Center, Mr. Jerry Brodie who was then our managing director said: "By all means. Let's not only suggest they come; let's give them a press conference." So when we prepared the press conference, again with BILLY TAYLOR'S help, because he was then head of Jazzmobile, he agreed and we extended the invitation.

NNENNA FREELON: I remember I was in Boston in Cambridge in the 70's and he came through, probably when I was in high school. I remember that there was a concert involved and I remember his name.

On April 26, 1971 an interesting article appeared in Newsweek magazine. The author, unidentified, wrote about the studio bands used by Johnny Carson, Dick Cavett, Merv Griffin and David Frost. As he wrote about the latter show he said: "To jazz buffs, the handpicked personnel of the TAYLOR group is a pantheon of high-powered virtuosity.

'Their jazz background gives the guys the ability to have a complete conception of something very quickly. You don't have to spell it out and that's what TV is all about,' says TAYLOR. 'I can say, 'Give me an ending in B-flat,' and it comes out sounding like an arrangement. The things we're able to do come from playing together.' With 32 records to his credit ('They're the best-kept secret in the music business/) TAYLOR has some reveling insights into jazz music. 'When jazz sells, it's called pop,' he laments. Brubeck's 'Take Five' was a jazz tune that was sold as pop. Bossa nova was a form of West Coast jazz the Brazilians picked up.' He points out that his band's strict musicianship should be comment enough on the notion that jazz is untrammeled freedom and reliance on pure feeling. 'It's not just winging it,' he says, 'it's a lot of hard work.' And he feels that if record companies promoted jazz as they do rock, jazz would be as popular among youth as rock. 'Whenever they run into trouble,' he says of the record industry, 'they drag out the old jazz standbys. They know they can sell jazz.' As a musician with some of the most impressive credentials around, TAYLOR'S comments cannot be taken as mere sour grapes."

COBI NARITA: When I first read up on him they were comparing him to all the great pianists and I just feel that he's always played the way he wants to play and the way he wants to sound and he's not trying to sound like anybody else or be like anybody else or beat anybody else. He loves playing – look at his face when he's playing! I love to go hear him play simply because he enjoys himself so much. But everyone else tells me, but I'm not a musician, that he's a fine, fine piano player.

By 1971, the Jazzmobile was receiving grants from the New York State Council on the Arts and other bodies, and in ten years it had progressed from a summer session of ten free concerts to a year-round program which also presented public school lecture/concerts conducted by pianist BILLY TAYLOR as well as a weekly workshop clinic for aspiring young musicians held at IS 201, a Harlem school. 1

On August 20, 1971 BILLY became a member of the Century Club of the Virginia State College Alumni Association, Petersburg, Virginia.

DAN MORGENSTERN: I got to see BILLY in a number of different situations. He was very much in evidence on the jazz scene and I got to see him on television. We got to know each other well over the years and worked together on many different occasions in many different situations. He was a member of the National Council of the Arts and I was on the Jazz Panel at the National Endowment for the Arts so we had a professional connection there.

"HOW MR. TAYLOR BROKE THE ICE WITH MR. FROST" was the title of a lengthy article about BILLY in the September 1971, Vol. 5 #2, edition of ASCAP Today. This article was copyrighted in 1971 by THE NEW YORK TIMES CO. and reprinted by permission. The article written by Barbara Campbell opened with: "The waiters all know him at Sardi's now, and when he left the restaurant after a drink and a light supper the other night the autograph hunters hanging around the outside, scanning faces of diners for the famous, forced pieces of paper into his hands. 'Hey, BILLY, c'mon, sign right here,' they said. The tall, scholarly looking black man wearing horn-rimmed glasses and a quiet gray business suit took each piece of paper patiently and signed his name, BILLY TAYLOR. Five nights a week, as music director of the David Frost Show on nationwide television, TAYLOR is saluted by Frost with the now famous phrase, 'Okay, BILLY!' It's his signal to sit down at the piano and, along with his 12-piece band, swing into the theme of the show. 'By George, it's the David Frost Show.' The music comes curling from under his light touch in the same manner in which he has played jazz in clubs across the country for 25 years . . . During the winter TAYLOR and six members of the band, along with a guest artist, tour the city's schools. He also runs a jazz workshop every Saturday for 110 blacks at I.S 201 in Harlem, where he has persuaded jazzmen to act as consultants. He persuaded Coca-Cola, the State Council on the Arts and Chemical Bank to fund the program at I.S 201. 'We give the students individual attention. If the kid is a pianist, we sit right down at the piano with him and show him just what he is doing wrong,' said TAYLOR. 'There is so much work to do with young people. They feel that nobody is listening to them. I try to show them how not to waste their time and talent and how to make the establishment work for them. The question they ask and I try to answer is, can you do it with music?'"

HILTON RUIZ: I had BILLY'S records before I met him and was one of his fans. He was playing all over the place. He's had a great impact on my playing. He's kept his playing up to date. He can play almost any style that there is. He's one of the originals.

On February 22, 1972 Black Variety, the Jazz at Home Club of America, in an article written by M. Montgomery entitled "JUST JAZZ" explored the use of the term jazz, quoting Ahmad Jamal and BILLY TAYLOR who said: "Much to the chagrin of people I've worked with, I've insisted in all the things that I've done on labeling what I do as jazz. When I used to work at the London House in Chicago, the Marienthals, who owned it, would insist on never mentioning the fact that all the pianists who worked there played jazz. It was a real jazz piano room but they never mentioned the word jazz in their releases or in their treatment of the artists. It used to drive them up the wall when I was going on a radio show, promoting my appearance there, and the disc jockey would say, 'Well, Mr. TAYLOR, how do you classify your music? What do you think it is?' and I would say, I play jazz! 'Really' the disc jockey would say, startled because he'd been playing my records on WCFL or one of the other stations out there that didn't think jazz worthy of programming and I guess in some cases they felt they'd been suckered into it because somebody had told them, 'Oh, BILLY TAYLOR is a fine pianist – plays like Eddy Duchin only a little more rhythmic.' 'It just annoyed me,' BILLY said, 'that people would carve out special categories and proceed to discriminate because they made arbitrary distentions between that and something else.'

In 1972 BILLY was a co-founder and officer of the Black Communications Corporation. This corporation purchased radio station WGOK in Savannah, Georgia. BILLY also continued his work in broadcasting, as Music Director for Tony Brown's BLACK JOURNAL TONIGHT (PBS).

JIMMY OWENS: I was always an activist and BILLY TAYLOR helped form me in the kind of direction that was going to be important for jazz. Just being around him, I learned. The two most important mentors I've had, from the standpoint of an overall outlook, were Donald Byrd and BILLY TAYLOR. BILLY TAYLOR was instrumental in getting me involved with the National Endowment for the Arts. The person in charge of the National Endowment Music Program, Walter Anderson, had a good relationship with BILLY because BILLY was on the National Council, appointed by President Nixon. BILLY was always talking for jazz and, what was called at that time, the Jazz-Folk-Ethnic section. By the time I got there in 1972 we had $50,000 for jazz for the whole United States. When I left in 1976 we had put together lots of stuff and we had $850,000! Some of the activists on the panel made it grow that fast; David Baker, Larry Ridley, John Lewis, George Russell, Milt Hinton were some of the people there at the time. I served for four years and then they rotated me to serve on the classical music panel, so I looked at opera, symphony orchestras, etc., and BILLY TAYLOR was partially responsible for getting me in there by talking my name up to Walter Anderson saying: "You should have Jimmy Owens involved with this. He's a good activist."

In 1972 BILLY was appointed by then New York Governor, Nelson Rockefeller, to the New York State Commission on Cultural Research and by New York Mayor John Lindsay to the New York Cultural Council. The National Council on the Arts was responsible for advising the National Endowment for the Arts on the distribution of millions of dollars of government funds to encourage and support cultural endeavors in the United States.

DAVID BAILEY: BILLY was the one who got me to leave flying a Lear Jet for F. Lee Bailey to cover Jazzmobile. I flew a Lear Jet into La Guardia (airfield) one night and found out he was playing at Basin St. West, or some place like that, and went to see him; this was in 1973. He asked me if I would consider leaving that job and coming to take over Jazzmobile. I told him no. I had worked for Gerry Mulligan and had gone flying the Lear Jet for F. Lee Bailey and managing F. Lee Bailey's airport up in Marshall, Massachusetts. BILLY always respected me. I would take care of business; no nonsense and that kind of thing. After due consideration one night about 41,000 feet above Chicago I thought about it; music was so important to me, more important than that which I was doing. I finally gave in and left the cushy job, flying a 3-million dollar Lear Jet, and took a pay-cut that I won't even mention for the love of the music. I accepted the job in a one-room office on 125th St. in the YWCA. We are now (2002) in a building on West 127th St., which is worth about 2 ½ million dollars, heavy into Arts and Education and those kinds of things. It's a tribute to the vision of people like BILLY, Daphne Arnstein, Evelyn Cunningham, and the early fathers of this organization; people at the Harlem Cultural Council because at one time Jazzmobile did not have it's 501-c3 and it was the recipient as the conduit of the first grant that Jazzmobile got; $10,000 from Ballentine Beer to do ten concerts in Harlem. BILLY had gone up to Boston with James Brown to help quell the riots in Boston. Dr. Kenneth Clarke had predicted that there would be a riot in Harlem and Jazzmobile was supposed to be the balm that calmed the people in Harlem. I guess it worked, because there wasn't a riot.

A booklet entitled "Billie Holiday Remembered" was published in 1973 as a collection of memoirs about Billie Holiday. BILLY TAYLOR'S commentary was the most memorable. He stated: "Billie Holiday was a unique artist even though her roots were firmly planted in the traditional jazz she grew up with. She was an innovator of the finest order. Her sound was very personal and her conception of how to sing a song was more of a jazz conception than almost any other singer's of her period. Her charisma as a performer was unequaled. She was an extremely beautiful woman; the force of her personality and the depth of her talent enabled her to reach audiences on a level that transcended music. Though her personal life was tragic, her performances, both on record and in person, changed the direction of jazz singing. She was a superbly creative woman." 2

LARRY RIDLEY: We were playing on one of those jazz cruises, on the Rotterdam, in the 70's and, I'll never forget, we were in the middle of the ocean and a storm came up. The ship started to sway; we were playing, and sliding back and forth across the stage. I had to catch myself, hugging the bass and wondering when the piano was going to slide across the stage. That was a panic.

In the August 6, 1972 issue of Time Magazine David Gahr penned an article on BILLY TAYLOR entitled "O.K., BILLY!" Mr. Gahr said, among other things: ". . . Every summer since 1965, when he helped found it, TAYLOR has made sure that the truck-borne bandstands of Jazzmobile have brought performers like Duke Ellington, Carmen McRae, Dizzy Gillespie and TAYLOR himself to the ghettos of New York and fifteen other U.S. cities. As Jazzmobile's fundraising, talent-coordinating president, TAYLOR also gives two lecture-concerts a week in New York City's public schools and conducts a piano class in a workshop program at Harlem's Intermediate School 201 on Saturday. He is a get-it-done member of a dizzying array of cultural boards and commissions from the Harlem Cultural Council to the National Council on the Arts, which elected him to a six-year membership last summer. He has taught the history of jazz at the Manhattan School of Music, and is working toward a Ph.D. in musicology at the University of Massachusetts. He has made more than 30 recordings (some of which, he concedes, 'are among the best-kept secrets in jazz'), written a dozen books on jazz piano playing and composed 300 songs."

DEREK GORDON: I don't think you grow up African-American in this country and not be aware of BILLY TAYLOR, a musical icon. I am old enough to be BILLY'S son. I've always known who he was. A song that I first heard performed by Glen Yarborough, of all people, "I Wish I Knew How It Would Feel To Be Free", also particularly strikes me. That's who I first heard perform the song. I first heard the song when I was in college in Baton Rouge, Louisiana (LSU) and for many years adored the song but for many years did not know that BILLY had written the song. Then to eventually not only find out that it was his but to have the opportunity to work with him has been one of the greatest experiences of my life. I was in college around 1972-'73.

Pittsburgh's COMLETE ENTERTAINMENT GUIDE of August 19, 1972 announced the coming of pianist BILLY TAYLOR with the title "COOKIN' IN THE ATTIC". It went on to say: "Considered one of the great jazz pianists of our day,

BILLY TAYLOR has been acclaimed both here and abroad. (Winner of Down Beat magazine's award for best pianist in their first annual critics' poll) TAYLOR is best known for the superb job that he recently did as musical director of the David Frost Show where he was seen by millions every day. That show sent the stock of BILLY TAYLOR up one hundred per cent . . . Noted for his versatility, BILLY'S artistic style has simplicity untrained ears can enjoy. Besides being heard in this country, TAYLOR is a great favorite in Denmark, Sweden, Norway, Holland, Belgium, Switzerland, France and Germany."

The New York weekly publication TWILIGHT featured a picture of BILLY TAYLOR with an article entitled "JAZZ IS ALIVE AND WELL IN NEW YORK" in the April 21, 1973 issue. The author, not identified, went on to say: "There are over 70 jazz night clubs in and around the City and great jazz artists are performing in an ever widening variety of situations. Some are teaching in public schools holding workshop clinics in community centers, and some are even serving as artists in residence in prep schools and colleges. WRVR, New York's major all jazz station features a wide variety of jazz styles ranging from early jazz styles to the most avante garde. Other radio stations such as WLIF-AM and WBLS-FM, feature a wide variety of jazz artists mixed with rhythm and blues, Latin and gospel artists . . . New York City has an unparalleled position as the foremost center of jazz activity. It has long been the focal point of this most American of arts and is giving inspiration and joy to the delighted music lovers who are fortunate enough to live, work in, or visit its environs."

On May 7, 1973 BILLY TAYLOR AND HIS ORCHESTRA appeared at the Lincoln Square Neighborhood Center, Philharmonic Hall, in New York with Jerry Stiller and Anne Meara, Melba Moore, Ben Vereen and others. The program described BILLY as "a pianist, composer, arranger, actor, author, lecturer and radio and TV personality . . . Winner of Downbeat Magazine's Award for Best Pianist, honored by Fairfield University with a Doctorate in Humanities, elected a Yale Fellow and recently appointed to the National Council on the Arts. BILLY has been acclaimed and appreciated wherever music is heard. In spite of an almost impossible schedule, BILLY TAYLOR has maintained his first role as a jazz artist and performer."

In the August, 1973 magazine Encore, Candace Womble wrote an article about BILLY entitled, "MULTI-TALENTED BILLY TAYLOR." Among other things, BILLY said: "It's important that black writers write about our musical tradition. Unfortunately, not enough is being written about black music by black writers. For instance, when I want students to go to the library to do research on the history of black music, there are few books I can honestly recommend. The research undertaken by these youngsters proves that the books written by Gilbert Chase and many others are inaccurate; they do not reflect what black music is all about. Therefore, it is necessary that black writers document how they feel about black music and artists like John Coltrane and Fats Waller. My writing is being neglected because I play much more now. Since I've been working on my doctoral thesis, 'The History of Jazz Piano', at the University of Massachusetts, I've become interested in and fascinated by the compositions of older pianists like Scott Joplin and James P. Johnson. Many of their devices are cropping up in my own work. I haven't included their compositions in my performances yet, but I'm sure that much of Fats Waller's influence is evident. Not many black students are interested in playing with classical orchestras, but they realize that the world of music is vast and that they should learn as much as possible about all kinds of music. Most of them want to express some aspect of their own music. They rebel against the New York Philharmonic and most major symphony orchestras because great black composers are not programmed along with the great white composers. For example, although black composer Ulysses Kay is tremendously respected in other parts of the world, his compositions are not played in this country along with those of Copland and Gershwin, white 'American-style' composers. Most colleges, however, are aware of black composers, and piano works of black people are included in piano study courses. Nevertheless, it's difficult to get hold of these works because they're not published as extensively as they should be. Most black music teachers who are aware of these problems try to surmount them, and their students are more aware of black composers than whites are. This is unfortunate because I don't want my music played by only black people; it's music and should be played by any capable person."

ROBIN BELL STEVENS: BILLY was one of the lucky ones who was so committed to the music that he was willing to make any sacrifices he had to make to be able to do that – to make his music to support his family and to be able to play the music, be loyal to the music. And to spread the music as far and wide as he could just to kept the importance of the music alive.

The September, 1973 release of Black Stars magazine featured an article by Peter Bailey entitled, "BILLY TAYLOR KEEPS JAZZ JUMPING". Among other things, Bailey said: "To the distress of many devotees of black music, one important segment of that music has had a difficult time penetrating a large part of the black community. For too many folks, that music, jazz, conjures up images of dark, smoky, dope-infested night clubs, while for others it has become a kind of intellectual exercise that pseudo-experts, many of them white, write doctoral theses about. For years, jazz musicians have waged a battle against these negative images and one of the most active, determined and persistent fighters has been 52-year-old jazz pianist-composer WILLIAM E. 'BILLY' TAYLOR. The youthful looking, North Carolina born-Washington, D.C. raised jazzman, who has been a professional musician for over 30 years, has devoted much of that time, not only playing jazz which he calls 'America's classical music', but also promoting it. A list of his organizational affiliations and other activities offer a good example of what he has been doing to promote his favorite music. Probably his pet project is the Jazzmobile, a showcase setup that brings programs of jazz music to residential areas . . . With all this lecturing, advising, teaching and managing, does the brother have any time left to play jazz? 'I sure do,' insists TAYLOR with a smile, as he proceeded to show a schedule that lists appearances in night clubs around the country, at concerts and jazz festivals and even a stint as guest soloist in four performances with the New Jersey Symphony Orchestra. 'I'm first of all a performer,' he continues, 'and like to play. My writing (his most famous composition being the song, I Wish I Knew How It Feels To Be Free) is only an outgrowth of my playing. I involve myself in all those activities because I believe in the growth and evolution of jazz. I have been able to earn a comfortable living playing nothing but jazz which says to me that there's an audience out there if its intelligently dealt with.' He sternly rejects what he considers the prevailing myth that jazz musicians are supposed to be poor. 'It's much easier to create on a full stomach,' TAYLOR asserts."

In 1974 BILLY led the band for the New York Repertory Company. He also played at the White House State Dinner at the request of President Richard Nixon.

> JOHN DUFFY: When I founded MEET THE COMPOSER on July 1st, 1974, with the help of the State Arts Council and the American Music Center and people like Cecil Taylor, Steve Reich, and other good people, our board of directors was comprised of BILLY, Aaron Copland, Leonard Bernstein, Richard Rogers and Virgil Thompson – they made up the composer wing of the board; then Steve Reich, Fran Richard and others. BILLY was an important voice. We had a special jazz program for commissions and we had a proposal in to A. T. and T. The trustees of A. T. and T. said they felt that jazz was a popular music and that jazz musicians made a lot of money so they were going to turn us down. Then I asked Leonard Bernstein to write a note to me that I could submit to them (I knew they would listen to someone of his reputation) and he wrote a glowing letter about the significance of jazz that we submitted. A. T. and T. turned around and they funded us.

An undated award was presented to DR. BILLY TAYLOR by the governor of North Carolina and the chairman of North Carolina Awards Committee that read: "Achievement is man's mark of greatness. A North Carolina award in the Fine Arts is presented to DR. BILLY TAYLOR."

In January, 1974 an article appeared in Parent Magazine entitled "HOW BILLY TAYLOR HELPS TEENAGERS BEAT THE BLUES: A Visit With An Extraordinary Jazz Musician Whose School Concerts And Seminars Are Capturing The Interest And Refining The Talents Of Music Loving Young People." The article went on to say: "BILLY TAYLOR 'speaks' music. And though the eloquent language –

principally expressed in jazz piano – of this extraordinarily gifted and accomplished musician is steeped in the blues and born out of the rich laments of black spirituals and work songs, BILLY'S musical voice is not blue at all, but joyous. Joyous for his hearers as well as himself and surely for the many kids with whom he works, helping them to express themselves through the universal language, music, and thereby to establish meaningful communication – and community – with others. BILLY'S elegant, sophisticated compositions and his flawless piano technique (the kind that makes it all seem effortless, and easy) reflect, of course, a lifetime of work and study. In spite of his ever-crowded schedule (a full program of live performances, musical director of the David Frost show during its long TV run, other TV and radio work, membership on federal, state, and city councils, to mention only a few of his many activities) BILLY finds the time to work extensively with young people in their neighborhoods. . . BILLY'S enthusiasm for his school workshops stems from the kids' own enthusiastic response. 'The boys and girls in that class have been so turned on by the potential of really being able to express themselves musically that we see a new door opening for them. You want to help speed that process if you can.'"

The April, 1974 edition of the magazine PISCES featured an article entitled "JAZZMAN – BILLY TAYLOR: PIANIST AUTHOR, TEACHER" . . . The author said: . . . "He told me how lucky he was to have married her (Teddi) 26 years ago; gave her credit for raising their children; praised her as the first person he always turned to for an honest opinion; and cited her support during the most hectic periods in his career. By the time his tribute ended, I had decided I was talking with a very nice guy – a man of constant activity who remains deeply in touch with the basic human values of life. . . 'What I'm going to do tonight,' he says – referring to an upcoming concert at Boston's National Center for Afro-American Artists – 'is play from about 10 'til about 4 or 5 in the morning. I'll go back to the hotel and maybe lay my head down for a minute or so, catch a plane out of here at 8 or 9 and from 11:30 until 4 tomorrow I'll by teaching in New York. And the reason I do this is because the kids that are involved are so turned on by the potential of being able to express themselves . . . and you see a whole door opening for somebody.'"

In the September 23-29 printing of Cue Magazine the author, under the heading, "INTO THE OLD BASKET", talked about BILLY and the Jazzmobile: "BILLY TAYLOR was busy as usual. The jazz pianist with the dazzling smile and even brighter improvisations had about 15 minutes, he said, before he rushed from his office to Lincoln Center and Jazzmobile's last concert of the summer season. It was Jazzmobile and its pressing problem that were foremost on his mind. The Jazzmobile is homeless. It isn't a question of just finding a parking space for a big truck, either. 'Most people think that we're just a summertime program, because that's the time when we have the big names and get the publicity. But we're a year-round program with our Jazzmobile school concerts and the student workshops.' For the past five years, the Jazzmobile, of which BILLY TAYLOR is president, has had a couple of rooms in a Harlem YMCA on West 125th Street. One serves as an office for the executive director, David Bailey. The other houses a library of scores and records. The library is especially important in the workshop program. But the Y decided to close. 'We were trying to get together enough money to buy the building,' Mr. TAYLOR explained. 'But we couldn't raise it. We're supposed to be out of there right now, but we haven't anyplace to go.' In discussing the two-part program that lays just ahead, Mr. TAYLOR said: 'We play concerts at two or three schools each week and visit about 120 different schools every year. The second part of a workshop program, where guys such as Jimmy Heath and Jimmy Owens teach young people to play. This year we're off to a really good start because we have about 600 applicants. Some will turn out to be beginners. This doesn't mean they can't play, just that they aren't ready for our workshop.'"

ALAN BERGMAN: BILLY always kids me about being a player (drummer). I actually never played with him but we used to play at the same place. Bill and George Simon used to have a band that played a cocktail hour at a place called Eddie Condon's on 54th Street. I was at ABC then, so this was in the mid-70's, and when George couldn't make the gig, I was the drummer who filled in. They hired a professional piano player, sometimes John Bunch, sometimes Ram Ramirez (composer of "Lover Man"), and a professional bass player. BILLY also played occasionally as a guest pianist, he still does that for some reason. The nights that I was there were not the nights that BILLY was there. Now I play more classical music – I play with orchestras around town.

On April 25, 1975 Clark College issued the following: Citation to WILLIAM EDWARD TAYLOR. BILLY TAYLOR, you have accomplished within a few years what for many would have required a lifetime. You have been extremely productive in your work and your contributions to the arts and to the humanities. Your creative talents have manifested themselves in many ways, as a concert pianist, arranger, author, actor and lecturer. You have been unselfish in your devotion to cultural and artistic endeavors. You have done more than your share in generating conditions and environments to further music and jazz as avenues of expression and understanding and to promote better racial relationships. Your presence here at Clark College these last few days is further manifestation of your willingness to share your talents and your experience and genius as a musical scholar. Your versatility is matched by your human touch and that touch is firmly entrenched in your compositions, "I Wish I Knew How It Would Feel To Be Free", "Theodora," "We Need Peace and We Need Love." You stand tall among the music greats and as a creative spokesman for America's most indigenous music – jazz. You honor Clark College by allowing us to honor you. (signed) Vivian W. Henderson, President.

ALAN BERGMAN: BILLY'S tune, "I Wish I Knew How It Would Feel To Be Free", is a very successful tune and we've had some great things happen in music publishing with that tune including a motion picture called THE GHOSTS OF MISSISSIPPI. BILLY'S tune is used not once, but twice – in the main credit and the end credit. I was very pleased to place that tune in that movie. I also set up international publishing for BILLY.

August 1975 marked a milestone in the career of BILLY TAYLOR. He received the DME (Doctor of Music Education) from the University of Massachusetts. His doctoral dissertation, which would become a published book later, was entitled THE HISTORY AND DEVELOPMENT OF JAZZ PIANO: A NEW PERSPECTIVE FOR EDUCATORS. This text, which would later become available to the public through publication by Wm C. Brown Co., was entitled JAZZ PIANO.

JIMMY OWENS: A friend of mine who was teaching at the University of Massachusetts, Dr. Roland Wiggins, had been approaching me about going back to school and getting an advanced degree and we finally set up some meetings and I said: "This is something a number of people should be involved in" and I named Chris White, the great bass player with Dizzy Gillespie, Bill Barron (Kenny's older brother), BILLY TAYLOR, and myself; people who could be a resource to starting a program like this. Roland took it to the Dean, and whatnot, and they started one of the first, if not the first, but one of the first universities without walls; a situation where we had managed to get credit for our past experiences. I had not been to college. By 1971, when we started this program, I had played with everybody, as well as being a bandleader. I worked with Duke Ellington, Count Basie; I was in the original Thad Jones-Mel Lewis Band, with Art Blakey, Max Roach, Lionel Hampton, Slide Hampton, and you know by '71 I'd had about sixty or seventy records that I was on, with people like James Moody, Erie Klaus, Herbie Mann, and numerous other people. So that particular program got BILLY TAYLOR his Ph.D. degree and the same with Bill Barron because they both had credits in the Master's degree program. We got a Master's degree for Chris White and for myself in Education. We were up on the campus an average of twice a month, or for a weekend, sometimes, where we gave workshops, not together, but individually. Sometimes we put ourselves together. BILLY created his working relationship with the University of Massachusetts. At that point another school, the School of Media, took our idea and managed to get Bill Cosby in the program and that's how he got his Ph.D. in the study in that program. Yusef Lateef finally came in the School of Education and we brought in a couple of other people. This is very important – again, this is BILLY TAYLOR giving back to his community.

JIM ANDERSON: The first time I met BILLY I was doing a recording with the Detroit Symphony Orchestra. About 1977 there was a performance of BILLY and his trio with the Detroit Symphony. I think Dorati was conducting; it was a David Baker piece that had been written for BILLY'S trio and the orchestra. I think it was Black History Month – a concert at the Edsel Hall in Detroit. It was unbelievable!

In the October, 1975 release of Radio Free Jazz, Christian Renninger wrote an article headed; 'DR. BILLY TAYLOR, 'FEDERAL FUNDING (FOR JAZZ) HAS BEEN GOOD, BUT I THINK IT CAN GET BETTER!' Renninger goes on to say: "In this statement lies the drive, the desire, the interest, the spirit and the excitement of this incredible man who, at this stage of a remarkable career, just may be the greatest friend jazz has." Renninger quotes BILLY: 'Now is the time when everyone interested in jazz as American music should be striving to get it into focus, look at it not as the kind of thing you or I like, but rather say, hey, it's a big thing that includes a lot of styles, a lot of different contexts, but it's all one thing. It's still under the umbrella of jazz. I have a lot of trouble with the fact that as an artist becomes more popular he's generally read out of the jazz fraternity. Therefore people can say: 'Jazz doesn't sell,' or Jazz is elitist – when it does sell it crosses over into popular.' MALARKY!!! 'To me, a guy who plays jazz is a jazz player. Errol didn't change when he became popular. Ella Fitzgerald didn't stop singing jazz. Louis all his life sang jazz – he did a lot of other things too – but all his life he was a jazz musician. I want all these things to be recognized for what they are.' Closing the article, BILLY had this to say about his teaching: 'It's not for me to forward any conception, but I like to help them discover for themselves, and they can come up with things so meaningful – the same kids who were only listening to rhythm and blues are now relating to things that are highly instrumental, highly abstract, a different point of view in terms of electronic instruments – the response to something highly artistic is just tremendous. Like: 'HEY, JAZZ IS GOOD!!'"

DR. FRED TILLIS: I really got to know BILLY on a closer basis because he picked up his doctorate and I was on his committee. In a way I supervised his dissertation because, there was another guy involved, Roland Wiggins, who was on the faculty of the School of Education, and I wasn't. I was in the music department (University of Massachusetts); the usual mess, all of this compartmentalization, but I was the musician associated with the department and also on that committee because that's one of the things I was doing here.

A lengthy article by Len Lyons was published in the March 10, 1977 issue of Down Beat magazine. He interviewed Bill Evans, Ramsey Lewis, Patrice Rushen, Paul Bley, McCoy Tyner, Josef Zawinul, Chick Corea, Herbie Hancock, George Shearing and BILLY TAYLOR. The article was termed, "PIANO PANORAMA: INSIGHTS INTO THE IVORIES." BILLY TAYLOR had this to say: 'There have been some definite advances recently in the exploration of the acoustic piano, usually by means of devices used in other areas. For example, Chick Corea recently did some serious exploration of his Hispanic background (My Spanish Heart) using different styles of music. Keith Jarrett has been looking into textures more usually associated with impressionistic concert music. His touch reflects that kind of interest. The late Erroll Garner left a legacy of things that are currently being explored by pianists who found his rhythmic technique applicable to contemporary playing. I think we'll see more of this because after the death of a famous jazz artist, and a great one, his records are played more often and people see again the elements that made him important. In my own work on the acoustic piano – especially solos – I'm doing some things that I don't hear anyone else doing. And in the trio, I've actually gone back to some things I did when I was working with Mingus; using a wider range of technical things in the left hand without getting in the bass player's way. I see a tremendous interest growing in the tonal possibilities of the acoustic piano, too, mostly because of the new systems of full keyboard amplification.'

DAVID BAKER: BILLY is one of the giants. He is so unselfish in sharing all the things that he does. He's amazing. For BILLY to have reached his age and still be as active and full of energy; still playing; he's been through a bunch of stages when he was known primarily as an educator, a player, as a person who had served on the National Endowment For the Arts, as a council member (I had known him in that capacity, too). The fact that BILLY is so articulate and I thought, "This is really great!" at the time when he went back and got his doctorate. I thought: "Boy, this is the kind of role model jazz musicians could emulate." He's kept his hands in everything.

In 1977 BILLY began directing the JAZZ ALIVE program for NATIONAL PUBLIC RADIO, a position he held through 1982.

TIM OWENS: I was first aware of BILLY TAYLOR in 1977 when we made a pilot; we did five pilots for the JAZZ ALIVE series and he was one of them. I had actually heard of him before that. I'm just not exactly sure when. I had heard, since I was into jazz, the name. I just couldn't put it in focus. As soon as we started working on JAZZ ALIVE together; at our first meeting there was nice camaraderie, a nice working relationship. He's warm, he's charming, he's hopeful. He doesn't let his ego get in the way; very unusual. BILLY realized that I (I was 28 at the time) didn't have quite the history, quite the knowledge. So he was really instrumental and probably the most instrumental person in giving me a jazz education from an appreciation point of view, especially. I don't play myself. From an historical point of view, he really opened my ears and opened my head up to the history 'cause, what better teacher? Here's a guy who was on 52nd St., played with everyone. And so when we wrote our JAZZ ALIVE scripts, he knew virtually all of the people. So he was able to bring his own experience into JAZZ ALIVE. So that's one of the elements I think that made him a great host, a great radio host. He also had had broadcast experience on WLIB in New York City. So he already knew how to communicate with an audience.

BILLY understands that the radio audience is only one person, in the sense that when you're communicating through a microphone to a listener, you're communicating only to one listener, because there is only one listener who's going to hear you and even though there may be a number of them, you have to talk to that single person. And he understands that concept. Then, combined with that, he's warm, he's friendly, he's knowledgeable, he sounds authoritative, he's engaging, he's enthused, and you put together all those ingredients and that really makes him absolutely special as a broadcaster. We used to say that anything we would do with BILLY was golden. And so much of that is just the sound of his voice. It's not even so much as what he says often. When I hear often is: "Oh, he sounds so nice." "He sounds like somebody who would be a nice friend." "I want to be with him." "I want to listen to him." So anyway we worked on JAZZ ALIVE together for five years.

JIM ANDERSON: I was the original technical director of JAZZ ALIVE so we did about six or eight pilots with different people. I remember Paul Anthony did one, BILLY did one, there were a couple of other people, maybe Tony Brown may have done one; then we sent them out to stations to give them a different sense of what they would sound like. But BILLY has the presence and the personality that could come across on the microphone. At that time he had not done broadcasting for maybe a few years, was more concentrating on his playing. So in the fall of 1977 Tim Owens, BILLY and myself were the main team of the original JAZZ ALIVE show. So I had done the original recording with Ella Fitzgerald, the premier show that they ran; Ella Fitzgerald, Stevie Wonder, etc. BILLY, at that time, was an elder statesman. After we had done the recordings we would go off and have dinner and, being with BILLY, you would just get a history of music, a very personal history of what he had done and all the people that he got to know.

JAZZ ALIVE was the title of an album the BILLY TAYLOR TRIO cut for MONMOUTH-EVERGREEN RECORDS in 1977. The tunes were Suite For Jazz Piano and Orchestra, Ivoire and Echoes of Ellington.

TIM OWENS: When we did radio JAZZ ALIVE, BILLY was available to us not only as a host but as a musician, so that we were able to augment some of the groups that we recorded with BILLY. What better situation to have a host who is a great broadcaster, a great communicator, a great educator, and he can also perform, and work with other musicians and other egos out there? - people who respect him, who will do as he asks. They do leave their egos at the door when he's around.

The office of the Mayor of Galveston, Texas issued a proclamation which read: "By the authority vested in me, by the City of Galveston, Texas, I do hereby proclaim October 18, 1977 as BILLY TAYLOR DAY and the city of Galveston urges each and every citizen to honor this great jazz musician and educator, a member of the National Council for the Arts, who will be in residency here, October 16-18. In testimony whereof, witness my hand and seal of the City of Galveston this the 13th day of October, AD 1977.

JOHNNY GARRY: I came to Jazzmobile in 1977 and BILLY would take me on the road with him when he had special things he was doing. I went out on the road with him a lot. He goes to colleges. That's where we should be doing that now. The guys should be going into schools to tell the students early what jazz is. A lot of people don't know what jazz is – what it means. It's an expression of what you feel. I do mine on the stage because a stage is like a beautiful lady. I like to dress it up, make the musicians happy with the sound.

On December 1, 1977 Arnold Jay Smith penned a lengthy article for Down Beat Magazine entitled "BILLY TAYLOR and DAVE BAILEY: MAGNETIZING THE ARTS." Smith opened his writing by stating: "Living and working in a city like New York is unique since the Apple has more of everything than any other place in the world. With more of everything comes more of the detrimental-to-life factors like crime, poor housing, bad air and angry folks. But every sickness has its medicine. And often the bitter pill can taste sweet. Jazzmobile, a non-profit result of HARYOUACT (Harlem Youth in Action), is a trailer, a wagon, or a float, as Jazzmobile president BILLY TAYLOR calls it. Aboard this four–wheeler have sat the most praised musicians in the world. . . Actually, Jazzmobile was formed when TAYLOR, wanting to bring some culture to Harlem youth after it was cut out of the original HARYOUACT, pressed his big band (he had just recorded with Oliver Nelson at that time) to play in the street. 'It was to be a one-time only performance, but you know what happens when we get a bug in our heads.' TAYLOR said. What happened was that the artists who had been consulted regarding the value of the arts for HARYOUACT, and then totally disregarded out-of-hand, became incensed and formed the Harlem Cultural Council. 'The Council was looking for visibility, and the float seemed to be just the thing,' TAYLOR went on. 'The float was not the idea of the principals of Jazzmobile, but of the World's Fair, N.Y. 1964-65 Corporation, who had Greyhound design one for the Dept. of Sanitation Band under Paul Lavalle, which toured the Flushing Meadow Fairgrounds for two years. Some of our original board members saw that that float was so vastly popular at the Fair that they quickly pressed for one for us. Greyhound was not willing to lend us theirs, but Ballantine Beer got us one.'"

ARNOLD SMITH: When did Jazzmobile begin branching out to other forms of music? Was it accidental? BILLY TAYLOR: 'No. It was intentional because our concept of what jazz is may be a bit more universal than many people's. Dave and I have many differences as to what constitutes specific areas of jazz. But, again, we respond to the neighborhood itself. One neighborhood may ask for Sun Ra, as one did. Another group may ask for Tito Puente, as another did. If we can't get one, then we suggest another in that style. We try to match the music with the neighborhood. We combine our thoughts about the neighborhood with their requests.' Dave Bailey: 'I think that's a salient point. Sometimes we are criticized for having a myopic view of what jazz is about. It is never Jazzmobile imposing its will, but a response to what the music is. We had had Norman Connors as well as Sun Ra, and a lot of mainstream.'" 3

With Victor Gaskin, bass, Curtis Boyd, drums, and BILLY, piano, the BILLY TAYLOR TRIO did an album, LIVE AT STORYVILLE for WEST RECORDS on December 2nd and 3rd, 1977. The tunes they recorded were Misty, Night In Tunisia, My Heart Sings, Naima, Birdwatcher, Lush Life and I Wish I Knew How It Would Feel To Be Free.

Bass player Victor (Roderick) Gaskin was born in the Bronx, New York on November 23, 1934. His father played calypso flute and was born in the Virgin Islands. Victor studied guitar with his father and uncles and with Charlie Richards beginning in 1944. During 1952-1954 he began playing tuba while serving in the US Marine Corps. On his release he began to study double bass, working with teacher Al McKibbon from 1960 to 1962. In the later 60's he studied with Stuart Sankey, Al Brehm and Ralph Pena. He played with Eli Fountaine II, Kin Bradfrord-Betty Roche, Mike Wofford, Paul Horn, Harold Land, Cutis Amy, Roy Ayers Oscar Brown, Les

McCann, Thad Jones-Mel Lewis, Duke Ellington and many others. Prior to joining BILLY TAYLOR he worked with Richard Davis in the 70's.

Curtis Boyd was born in Brooklyn, New York on June 9. 1940. His father was a singer and piano player. Boyd studied at the Brooklyn Academy of Music and the Chicago Conservatory of Music. He took arranging lessons from Adolph Sandole. In the 50's and 60's he played with Cedar Walton, Julian Priester, Wymon Kelly, Frank Strozier, Kenny Durham, and Joe Williams. During the 70's and prior to joining BILLY TAYLOR he worked with Chris Woods, Al Cohn, Helen Merrill, Chick Corea and others.

TIM OWENS: We had a public radio conference in 1978 and I was asked to put on a jazz program in San Francisco at the GREAT AMERICAN MUSIC HALL. I asked BILLY to perform there, to play solo, and he brought the house down and he hadn't performed solo in a long time. So it was great for him to play alone. His left hand is as strong as his right hand; it's nice to be able to work with somebody who has all those attributes.

In December, 1977 Sepia Magazine featured an article on BILLY entitled "BILLY TAYLOR – THE FORCE WHO KEEPS JAZZ ALIVE". During the interview Mark Ribowsky wrote: "Through the years TAYLOR played with them all. He was with Dizzy Gillespie's first band at the Onyx Club. He took Errol Garner's spot with the Slam Stewart trio (and lost it when he and Theodora got married in '46, went on a honeymoon, and found another guy playing his piano when they got back – ('Slam's wedding present, he grins'). He toured Europe with Don Redman; then joined Artie Shaw, Billie Daniels, Charlie Parker, Art Blakey, Terry Gibbs and a score of others who played Birdland. 'I think I set the house record for the longest continued run there,' TAYLOR says. 'I was soloist, a leader of trios, quartets, quintets, sextets, everything. It was like a picnic every night.' Later there was the David Frost Show on television – 'No idea how I got that job, but a lot of people have taken credit and I've thanked everyone of them. To be the first black conductor on national TV and present jazz coast-to-coast was a dream come true. We had some fabulous musicians – Jimmy Owens, Dick Hurwitz, Morty Bullman, Frank Wess, Sheldon Powell, Bob Cranshaw, Bobby Thomas. We even had Hubert Laws on reeds for a while until he went on to bigger and better things'. Later, TAYLOR repeated that role as a big band leader of the PBS series, Black Journal. 'Sometimes the times weren't too good,' said Says BILLY TAYLOR, looking back over his brilliant career. 'Sometimes we didn't have much to eat, didn't live in the best of surroundings. That's the sacrifice any musician has to make for a while. But at least I was playing my jazz. Somehow, the world didn't seem too bad if I could be doing that.'"

An album entitled BILLY TAYOR TRIO IN LIVE PERFORMANCE was completed in 1978. The great bandleader Stan Kenton died in August, 1979. Shortly before he passed away he remarked: "BILLY TAYLOR was the most important figure in jazz."

DICK HYMAN: Although that period has long passed, I remember subbing for BILLY once with the Indianapolis Symphony in 1979 when he became ill. Our careers have been parallel in a number of ways – from clubs to television, concert halls and production.

As the 70's began to wane, BILLY continued to tour with his trio, doing appearances at a record number, but began to play fewer crowded jazz clubs in favor of concerts at larger venues, including performing arts centers and concert halls. BILLY'S trio welcomed this change and began to reach many larger audiences.

During the 70's BILLY received his second honorary doctor's degree. This year his alma mater, Virginia State University honored TAYLOR. He co-founded and became an officer of the Black Communications Corporation that purchased radio station WGOK in Savannah, Georgia and was appointed to a six-year term to the National Council On The Arts by President Richard Nixon. He formed a new trio with Larry Ridley, bass and Bobby Thomas, drums, founded BILLY TAYLOR Productions and was Music Director for Tony Brown's "Black Journal Tonight" on PBS. BILLY led the band for the New York Repertory Company and played at the White House for President Nixon at a State Dinner. In 1975 he received an earned doctorate (DME) from the University of Massachusetts. His dissertation, "The History and Development of Jazz Piano: A New Perspective For Educators", would become the definitive book on the subject, published by Wm D. Brown Co. and entitled "Jazz Piano". He also began directing the Jazz Alive program for National Public Radio, began a lecture series at Howard University and played at the White House State Dinner for President Gerald Ford.

VII

CBS SUNDAY MORNING – AUTHOR – MORE MEDIA RECOGNITION, AWARDS

The music will continue to evolve as national music, but its international effect will become even more clearly defined as jazz musicians from other countries become more involved in expressing themselves through this art form. – BILLY TAYLOR

TIM OWENS: We often did live broadcasts. Once we were at the Chicago Jazz Festival, the second night of the Festival, and we were broadcasting live. This would have been 1980, I think. BILLY opened the show from the stage and I was out in front of the stage, in front of the audience, there to cue him when the broadcast would start. So I'm holding my hand and I wave and he waves back. I'm saying: "No BILLY!" I'm throwing him the cue to start the show and he's smiling and waving back. I finally had to have somebody run up to the stage to say: "Oh, we're on the air." Then BILLY, in his inimitable way just recovered beautifully. When he gets into these awkward situations he's always great at recovering and that's kind of neat to see. He's great in that environment.

DR. FRED TILLIS: For more than twenty years BILLY has been associated with our Jazz In July program. It was born out of something I said to BILLY: "You know BILLY, we have Tanglewood that's running all the time, it's famous, money and all that stuff; we don't have a program and that's what we would like to do here." We were on the same page, emphasizing improvisation for youngsters. That was the idea then. In the late fifties Tanglewood had a symposia but they kicked that out. They stopped it. 'They only did it for a year or two. So I said: "Hey, this is a nitch for us!" That's how it came about. BILLY had been doing Jazzmobile and I kept up with him when he was in New York doing that. So, I told him about wanting to do this and he really didn't want to get involved in big bands, which was fine. There were a lot of good big bands, but getting at the heart and soul of the music through improvisation really excited him, so that's why we called it the Jazz In July workshop in Improvisation. So we've been partners in that and became closer and closer as friends, plus then I got involved with his doctoral committee. Somebody threw him a curve ball in the School of Education and that's when I was able to exercise, because I had been there longer, as long as any, and I played the leadership role.

The editors of Down Beat Magazine supported Stan Kenton's statement about BILLY by awarding BILLY with the Lifetime Achievement Award in 1984.

JIMMY OWENS: We played the Olympics in 1980 in Lake Placid. BILLY organized a big band, a masterful band. It had great musicians of all ages, and Frank Foster was commissioned to compose a piece for the 1980 Winter Olympics, which he did. We performed the piece seven or eight times in the period that we were up there – we stayed a number of days.

JIMMY HEATH: During the Winter Olympics in up-state New York at Lake Placid, we stayed up there for a week or more. It was a great experience and it was under the Jazzmobile banner. BILLY stepped off the stage backwards and we thought he was going to kill himself. He was backing up and BOOM! It was indoors in a concert hall and I don't think he hurt himself. It was just funny to see a guy with so much poise. (He won't think it's funny but he remembers it, I'm sure.)

In December 1980 in New York City the BILLY TAYLOR QUARTET recorded the album WHERE'VE YOU BEEN? for CONCORD JAZZ RECORDS. The trio with violinist Joe Kennedy recorded Where've You Been? Night Coming, Tenderly, Ray's Tune, Antoinette, I'm In Love With You, All Alone, I Think Of You and Capricious.

JIM ANDERSON: I remember when we started doing JAZZ ALIVE, every once in a while he would perform on the show and once on New Years Eve, 1980 we were at Blues Alley and BILLY came and knocked on the door to my truck and said: "Hey! Come out here and listen!" Blues Alley used to have a speaker out the alley – and Billy said: "Check this out!" There was a guy who had wandered into the alley with a harmonica and was jamming with the sounds and I looked at BILLY and said: "I think you're getting better." He looked at me and said: "Well thank you!"

On May 16, 1981 Berklee College of Music presented the following to BILLY: "Upon recommendation of the President, Dean and Faculty, the Board of Trustees have conferred the honorary degree of Doctor of Music upon WILLIAM E. (BILLY)

TAYLOR with all the honorary privileges and responsibilities pertaining thereto. Given at Boston, Massachusetts and signed by Richard Bobbitt, Dean and Lee Eliot Berk, President.

TIM OWENS: We put on a concert in Los Angeles in 1981, a concert in tribute to jazz in Los Angeles. BILLY had spent some time in Los Angeles, and he did so often times with a bass-less group so there was a duo with himself and a drummer. Sometimes he would perform in that context. So we put him on in that context. I also put him on leading an all-star group with Marshall Royal, Red Callender, Lawrence Marable, Barney Kessel, some really fine, fine players, and BILLY knows how to be a musical director; his years with David Frost. So you can count on him to bring together the forces in the way that he does that makes for great programming. So we were able to do that on several occasions, for him to be an MC and a performer. We had a concert in Disney World and I presented him between the Ramsey Lewis Trio and Nancy Wilson. I was always enamored with his solo playing. Although he didn't appear very often as a solo pianist, I was always struck by his solo playing.

In October, 1981 Keyboard Magazine published an article by BILLY TAYLOR entitled "AN ART TATUM RECOLLECTION AND ANALYST." As a former student and colleague, BILLY adored and highly respected Art Tatum. He opened his article by stating: "Although jazz piano playing has gone through some dramatic changes in recent decades, I think it's still true that any jazz pianist today, who does not study Art Tatum's innovations is limiting himself or herself as an artist. You might not necessarily want to emulate his style, but if you look at the ideas in his music, even during his last years when he was very ill, you will learn something about the potential in jazz piano that still has yet to be realized, with all due respect to the people who are playing today. The heights to which Tatum carried solo jazz piano playing have yet to be matched." In closing BILLY said: " But despite his obvious stylistic preferences, I still think there's no question that Art summed up all of the music that went before him, while very effectively pointing the way to the many musical innovations of the future. Of course there were other pianists with similar vision, some of them not as well known today as they should be, like Clarence Profit, who was harmonically comparable to Tatum and who had a big influence on his inner voicings, and Marlowe Morris, who was as close to Tatum stylistically as anybody back in the 40's. Still, no matter who you name in the annals of great pianists, known and unknown, the fact remains that Art Tatum was the greatest jazz soloist ever to raise the piano stool."

RAMSEY LEWIS: I'm always looking for things to do that I haven't done, or a different way to do something I have done. So I'm talking to CBS and they say, 'What about two pianos?' I said, Now that's an idea. So I called BILLY TAYLOR and he says, 'Hey, how you been doing? I want you to be on my show.' I said, 'Great!' I came to New York and we were supposed to do enough for an hour or more. I mean, we just got on so beautifully that, in fact, during the interview on the show we both said maybe we should do an album – sort of jokingly, but honestly. And afterward, we talked about it and we figured that at some point in the future we would do that. But our schedules and what have you just didn't work out. Meanwhile, I signed with CBS Masterworks and I did another album with James Mack with the London Philharmonic called CLASSIC ENCOUNTER. I could say that album – no work of art is perfect, to the artist – is one of the several of the sixty-odd albums I've done that came close to what I really wanted to say. 1

In the November 22, 1981 issue of the San Diego Union, Art Section, an article appeared by Robert P. Lawrence. The headline stated: "LA WAS ALWAYS KEY TO JAZZ" He said: "When jazz folks get together and talk about the great music towns of America the discussion usually begins with New York and wanders over the map from there. New Orleans figures prominently in the conversation for historic reasons and so will Kansas City and Chicago. Few fans will bring up the name of Los Angeles over motion picture soundtracks, singing commercials and rock and roll records. Except as a good place for musicians to make money, Los Angeles is not normally regarded as one of the important centers for jazz in the world. But pianist and scholar BILLY TAYLOR will be out to change that notion this Thursday, Thanksgiving Day. For nine hours, from eighth a.m. to five p.m. TAYLOR will chart the history of Los Angeles jazz from 1920 to the present, from Jelly Roll Morton and Kid Ory to Al Jarreau and the Crusaders. TAYLOR will undertake that sizeable task as master of ceremonies of 'Central Avenue Breakdown,' the conference of jazz history survey broadcast by national public radio and carried locally by KPBS-FM. TAYLOR, who for the past four years has been the genial host of NPR'S weekly 'Jazz Alive' Concert Series, called Central Avenue 'absolutely crucial to the development of jazz on the West Coast. 'That's where LA jazz had its happening', he said in an interview from New York, 'the heart of the jazz effort was on Central Avenue.' It is often believed that the importance of regional movements has been overstated. TAYLOR emphasized the role of LA, as an incubator, for it was the place where Jelly Roll Morton began to get his act together in the early 1920's. Now obviously the stuff was created in New Orleans, but he lived in Los Angeles for four or five years and it was during that period, just before he went to Indiana to make his first piano records that he actually got all his stuff focused and got ready to do his thing. During the 1940's TAYLOR believes LA was, if anything, behind New

York in terms of musical development. 'I had come to LA from New York, he remembered, where everybody was getting into bebop. Everybody in the East had heard Dizzy Gillespie and Charlie Parker and knew something was afoot. On the West Coast they were aware of it but didn't have a handle on it because none of the guys who played it had been out there for any length of time. Miles Davis had come out West, J.J. Johnson had come out, Max Roach had come out, but it really hadn't been a part of what guys were familiar with. They hadn't heard enough of the records; they weren't generally available . . . When you had the swing broadcasts from all the ballrooms it wasn't happening at the moment. That has always been used as an example of what people talked about as West Coast Jazz and East Coast Jazz. It was a lot of malarkey. The West Coast Jazz in those days was the Modern Jazz Quartet that was an East Coast group. One of the swingingest piano players who played in the funky East Coast style was Hampton Hawes who lived on the West Coast.'"

JOHNNY GARRY: I was with BILLY when he would go to colleges. I went to Eugene, Oregon with him, way out there. I had never heard of Eugene, Oregon and I'm 78. He was saying: "That's where people train for the Olympics," and I was saying to myself: "Who the hell's going to know what he's taking about in Eugene, Oregon?" But he played with the symphony. Everybody knows him.

In 1982 The Wm C. Brown Co published BILLY'S book, JAZZ PIANO. It had been originally written in 1975 as the dissertation for BILLY'S doctoral degree under the title THE HISTORY AND DEVELOPMENT OF JAZZ PIANO: A NEW PERSPECTIVE FOR EDUCATORS.

WARREN CHIASSON: The JAZZ PIANO book that BILLY wrote is very, very specific and very nicely organized. His tutorials are fabulous. That's really a wonderful book.

DAVE BRUBECK: BILLY TAYLOR has reached many thousands with his appearances on the CBS Sunday Morning show, bringing a variety of jazz artists to the attention of the general public. Entertaining, performing, and educating . . . that seems to be BILLY'S theme. I have great respect for him as a scholar, as he is one of the few jazz musicians who has really earned his doctorate degree rather than given an honorary one.

JIMMY OWENS: I'm very happy to have been around him for all of these years because I've learned about how to really give back. BILLY'S book! Just the way it's laid out; more history books should be laid out that way no matter what instrument they're talking about. Because he could talk about it from a first hand basis, that's what made it great! That's one of the things that make BILLY TAYLOR a great educator. Not only does he have the history but he knows how to put that history into context to teach whoever; this young person, and much older, elderly person. And that's what, in my opinion a great educator is. Unfortunately we don't always have that in jazz education. We have people who have gone through school to school to school and come out and become a director of a jazz program and have no real history and even for some of the musicians who come out and play in a professional situation; they may have played in Woody Herman's Band or Maynard Ferguson's Band or one of the big bands and whatnot, but there is a world of difference in what BILLY TAYLOR has set as the standard, from the standpoint of musicians who have interacted with and some of the other people that we can look at out here (attending the 29th conference of IAJE in Long Beach, CA, Jan., 2002).

The violinist, JOE KENNEDY, joined with the BILLY TAYLOR TRIO, Billy, piano, Victor Gaskin, bass, Curtis Boyd, drums, to record Take The A Train and Let Us Make A Joyful Noise for the album YOU TEMPT ME for TAYLOR-MADE RECORDS on June 24, 1981 in New York City.

HERB WONG: When I was president of NAJE ('82-'84) BILLY came to the conferences – he was always around. He was omnipotent, was everywhere, and he would come and play. He was playing for our organization for a long time. Then, of course, he became more of a spokesperson and would host things. But he was always available to lend a hand or give you an idea or tell you about somebody else, never forcing anything; just a beautiful way of sharing. That's the kind of remembering I have of BILLY forever. It was also around that period ('83) that Jazz Times magazine, which was originally called Ira Sabin's Free Jazz USA – that's the original name – when BILLY was around doing things for the magazine's first conventions. So he was already into that area before it became more feverish. That's when I started to notice how he was expanding his work and image to whatever was happening.

During this period BILLY formed his own record company. TAYLOR MADE, but after producing five albums he decided that he wanted to be more involved in the music rather than the business. He also continued to work as a performer on radio and television as well as in live performances and record dates. He hosted his own show for BRAVO, "JAZZ COUNTERPOINT", featured such artists as Marian McPartland, Ramsey Lewis, George Shearing and others and two radio shows, TAYLOR MADE PIANO (based on BILLY'S book, JAZZ PIANO) AND

DIZZY'S DIAMOND. The TAYLOR MADE PIANO show generated more requests for tapes than any previous NPR program.

JIM ANDERSON: We did a series called "Taylor Made Piano" in 1981-'82 and we worked on it for quite a few months. BILLY got a Peabody Award for that show. BILLY wrote a book based on the radio show Taylor-Made, Jazz Piano, his doctoral thesis. We did essentially the history of jazz piano according to BILLY. When I listen to players today there is so much of BILLY in so many players. They don't realize how influential he was – just as they don't realize how influential Nat "King" Cole was. BILLY is fun – I don't want to say BILLY is un-fun; BILLY has been very influential. I don't think people realize how much he has contributed to the style of piano playing. You hear it all the time. When I hear it I know it's BILLY right there. It crosses generations – certainly in the James Williams generation – people in their 50's. I even hear it in people like Kevin Hayes, people in their 30's. He's so modest about these things. I don't think he would ever say: "That's my influence right there." But sometimes he's not appreciated for that. In 1982 BILLY became art correspondent on the TV program "CBS Sunday Morning". He termed the program "the best show on television. This is the most effective presentation that I have been able to make on television about people that I think are important in jazz. I'm really proud of it." To date BILLY has presented more than 250 artists in profile including Quincy Jones (which earned BILLY an Emmy in 1983), Ella Fitzgerald, Dave Brubeck and many, many others including Festival Productions president George Wein, talent-discoverer John Hammond and the Village Vanguard founder Max Gordon. BILLY'S sixth anniversary with "Sunday Morning" was celebrated with performances by BILLY'S trio and a live segment from Moscow featuring Charles Kuralt and BILLY in a discussion of Russian and American jazz.

CHARLES OSGOOD: I was assigned to do a piece about BILLY TAYLOR for Sunday Morning about twenty years ago (1982) so I did the piece – BILLY was performing at a club in New York, so I went down there and interviewed him at the place. I same back and everybody loved the piece so much, they loved the music, the way he talked about it so much that he became a regular on the show. I had heard him as a listener, but I had not met him personally and had no professional connection with him until then. I was always told that my biggest coup for Sunday Morning was bringing BILLY TAYLOR in. Charles Kuralt was anchoring the show at the time and thought: "We've got to get this guy!" He was so articulate and came across with that great voice. He knew everybody in jazz. There could have been nobody better to be a regular jazz contributor than BILLY.

MARQUITA POOL ECKERT: I think he is a real treasure just by virtue of the musical life that he has led. He is a living example. He is a treasure and he doesn't mind spreading the goodies around. I think we're all the better for that! The fact that he shares what he knows with the rest of us. It's been an exciting experience working for him. One of the things about the job that I do (Producer, CBS Sunday Morning) is that I learn things and working with BILLY is just one of the greatest rewards in that regard because it's something I'm interested in and he brings so much to it and I don't really think I could have the depth of the experience I have had working with him if I worked with someone who didn't know as much. He knows everything from the very beginning.

On Saturday March 1982, Mannie Faria in the News-Times penned a review of a performance by the BILLY TAYLOR TRIO. The headline screamed 'TAYLOR TRIO DAZZLES JAZZ LOVERS." The author went on to say: "It is a given that jazz is truly an American form of musical expression. What is not always so obvious is its connection with music of other cultures. While anyone will readily agree that jazz has its roots in Black America and as a result can be traced to African rhythms, it might have a hard time connecting it with the music of the Middle East, India or Southeast Asia. But BILLY TAYLOR can make the connection. His trio has just completed a six-week, seven-nation tour and the music he encountered has already become part and parcel of the jazz he plays. The BILLY TAYLOR TRIO gave amble evidence of this in its concert at Western Connecticut State College last night. Throughout the pieces were the rhythms of the Arab and Indo-Pakistani and African. The surprising thing was how well it all worked within the framework of jazz. And maybe the truly American art form expression is ready to go international. He was very much the teacher last night giving his audience a trip through straight improvisation, rearrangement, experimental material, a taste of foreign rhythms and finally his 'Suite for Jazz Piano and Orchestra' done only with his trio in a way to make you feel he left out nothing. He chatted with the crowd between selections and at the start of 'Suite for Jazz Piano' stressed the improvisatory nature, not only of jazz, but of classical. He pointed to the cadenza improvisations done by Bach and Mozart before they ultimately wrote passages for others to play and then he proceeded to improvise. TAYLOR'S reworking of Richard Rogers' 'My Romance' was a pleasure to hear. His laid-back, easy piano style reminded me of the late Vince Giraldi.

JIMMY HEATH: When BILLY got on television, CBS Sunday Morning, he did a program on me and interviewed me that I really appreciated him doing because a lot of us get left out. He's always very conscious of who's around who didn't have the opportunity that others have. He's always been a person to acknowledge other people.

In July 1982 the Ovation Magazine turned over its Viewpoint column to BILLY TAYLOR who headed his statement with: "IS JAZZ AMERICA'S CLASSICAL MUSIC?" This was a theme that BILLY had championed for many years. He concluded his column with: "Jazz is an important cultural contribution. It speaks most eloquently of the American concept of individual freedom within a planned structure. It can speak to or for anyone. Since it originated as an American cultural expression, Americans have a responsibility to document and record its evolution and development. We should report and applaud the achievements of the creative musicians who write and play jazz. In addition, we should know what there is to know about the music and its creators and support it in every way possible. We do this for European classical music in order to give present and future generations a clearer, more accurate conception of its cultural importance, and we should do no less for jazz, America's classical music."

ALAN BERGMAN: I didn't meet BILLY until the Jazz Times Convention in New York at the Roosevelt Hotel in the mid-80's. He was around and he was a player. BILLY was one of the very few clients that I actually pursued. I went up to him and introduced myself. I said to him: "I'm a lawyer. I represent a lot of jazz people and I've been a fan of yours and an admirer for a long time and I think that I can really help you." I invited him to lunch at the Princeton Club and than we started working together. BILLY was very involved in those early days of Jazz Times and Ira Sabin and we used to meet up in my office at 40th and Madison. I was a partner of a law firm in the late 70's , early 80's, and we had a big conference room and Ira used to come up with pastrami sandwiches. BILLY was there, Ira was there and I was there, and a few other people.

The Jazz Times release of April 1983 featured an article by Joe Blum. Blum said: "Jazz didn't exist when I was a music major in the 1960's, at least as far as academia was concerned. To graduate you had to memorize eighty pieces of standard classical repertoire (at Brooklyn College), and if your composing was even remotely 'jazzy' in tone, you were most likely reprimanded by your instructor. Ten years later I taught at Brooklyn College, by which time they had a full-fledged Jazz Studies Department, headed by Chuck Israels, and offered (bless my soul) a degree with a concentration in jazz. Now I'm not going to say that BILLY TAYLOR is solely responsible for the vast changes that have occurred in academia over the past two decades, but he certainly has had an awful lot to do with them . . . Consider the variety of experiences – BILLY TAYLOR has done enough to keep any interviewer busy for days and I've hardly begun to cover it all! For example, besides working in the usual jazz venues, TAYLOR also makes about twenty guest appearances each year with symphony orchestras playing his own compositions (such as 'Suite for Jazz Orchestra and Piano'). His most recent orchestral work is 'Peaceful Warrior', written for the Atlanta Symphony in February 1983. He has also gone on tour for the State Department."

ROBIN BELL STEVENS: Rachael Robinson (widow of Jackie Robinson) and I went to hear BILLY play in the old jazz club called Fat Tuesdays. This was in the early 80's. He was there with his trio. He did a couple of solos and we were there just listening to the music and we just looked at each other and I said to Rachel: "That's what I call music!" And she smiled at me and said: "Yeah!" That's what I think about his music. He can take a song and make it his own. His style has his signature. He can play a ballad and make you forget where you are – he can just carry you away with the music. He's a great pianist.

On March 26, 1983 the University of Central Florida issued the following: University award presented to DR. BILLY TAYLOR for his outstanding artistry and contributions to music; KALEDISCOPE I.

NNENNA FREELON: I first met him personally in 1983. He came to North Carolina Central University in Durham, N.C. in 1983 to adjudicate some jazz ensembles. I was just starting on my journey as a professional singer and he was gracious enough, although I was not a student at North Carolina Central I was invited to participate. He listened to a local pianist and myself do three tunes. He wrote beautiful notes that were so useful to me. He didn't say: "You are fabulous," or "Wonderful!" He gave me some constructive criticism, some things to work on, some recordings to listen to, he suggested a few, and after he had gone through all these big bands, he made all his comments to me; he wrote them down on a piece of paper. Afterwards, I was so shy but I invited him to my house. At this time my husband and I were in a very small house, we had three children; my youngest child was about one. As soon as I asked him I started to take it back because he was such a great man I thought: "No way" and he said: "Yes!" I said I'll cook; I'll make some greens. I couldn't believe he said yes. So he came to my house. I cooked a big dinner; some of the local musicians came over. He's so warm and so wonderful and so supportive. I'll bet I didn't know fifteen songs at that time. I was just starting out.

On July 6, 1983 The Campus Connection publication of the University of Massachusettspublished an interview with BILLY TAYLOR by Stanley Winter. The title of the article was "BILLY TAYLOR TALKS JAZZ". BILLY is quoted as saying: "I've been trying to have people understand that hey, this music is not only great to listen to, but it's something I should know more about." The author of the article went on to say: "Classical, swing, modern, fusion, Latin . . . all variations on the same theme . . . jazz spoken here. The popularity of jazz seems to be on the increase, on college campuses and throughout the country. And one man who has been spreading the language of jazz is pianist, composer-arranger BILLY TAYLOR. TAYLOR is one of the many internationally known faculty members of the 6th annual Jazz in July workshops, which start next Monday at UMass. BILLY TAYLOR is a major figure on the jazz scene, known for his work both as an educator and musician. He's the author of over 300 songs and a dozen books on jazz piano. One of the prime movers in National Public Radio's 'Jazz Alive' series and the music editor of 'Sunday Morning With Charles Kuralt,' TAYLOR has introduced and defined the jazz idiom to audiences across the country. In closing, the author asked TAYLOR the following: "There are many different forms of jazz. Are the workshops specialized in any particular area?" BILLY replied: 'The principles are the same. You can learn about jazz by applying the same sort of principles to electronic instruments, or other kinds of instruments. The people attending these workshops want to learn more about the particular instrument they should play, what style I should be interested in playing, the components of a jazz style, developing an exciting improvisation. The basics.'"

HILTON RUIZ: Around 1982-84 there was series in New York City at the Village Gate called "SALZA MEETS JAZZ". One night I had my band there and BILLY was the jazz soloist. He came in and played a few numbers with the band. There were two pianos on the bandstand and we got off on some Latin mambo and he came in there and played it like – man, he just played all over it. He was right in the idiom and we had a ball. It was wonderful because he was able to fit right in. He came in and played with two hands and all these chops together. He was wailing! That was the first time we played together and after that I continued to see him at concerts and other places.

On July 9, 1983 an invitation was sent by Anne Dhu McLucas which read: "We cordially invite you to a reception in honor of Oregon Festival – guest artists: BILLY TAYLOR TRIO and the Turtle Island String Quartet. Eugene, Oregon.

DAN MORGENSTERN: Where he gets the energy from I don't know. He's active on so many fronts and he has always been somebody who has known how to put the music in its best perspective. When he was on the radio he was a wonderful disc jockey (now they are called 'on the air hosts!') He's a wonderful presenter, a great MC. He's a great interviewer. He's a great writer, His book, Piano Jazz, is a wonderful book. Some people get their doctorates in an 'honorary way' but he earned his.

The August 8-19 1984 issue of Harlem Week featured an article written by BILLY TAYLOR entitled "JAZZMOBILE: TWENTY YEARS OF PROGRESS." BILLY traced the 20-year history of Jazzmobile describing the start-up years, the development of various programs, the struggle for funding, and the attempt to set up not-for-profit record and music publishing companies. He summed up the 20-years by saying: "For twenty years Jazzmobile has been a cultural catalyst, serving as a vanguard institution which provides leadership, creative programs and a role model for other outreach organizations. We have come a long way and are proud of our achievements and appreciative of the support we have received from great jazz artists, our sponsors, public and private, and the communities we serve. We hope to expand our programs and services by providing more innovative programming to our clientele and by building on the jazz traditions we have helped to establish. It's a matter of pride for us to be based in Harlem, the best known black community in the world, because we believe the positive changes which are taking place in that community are reflected in the upward mobility of Jazzmobile.

"FOR THE LOVE OF JAZZ" was the headline of a Ted Dyer article published in Personality Magazine in January 1985. Mr. Dyer began: "There is little in the unassuming manner of DR. BILLY TAYLOR to suggest that he is the premier spokesman for jazz today. A dapper dresser who favors conservative hews of blue and gray. Horn rimmed glasses, and a modest Afro, the 6-foot-1 TAYLOR looks much younger than his 63 years. Whereas the stereotypical jazz musician is a leather-faced black man with a whiskey-baritone voice, TAYLOR'S demeanor is downright professional. His lectures on jazz, punctuated by frequent trips to the piano, are models of clarity." Following the long, in-depth, interview, Mr. Dyer closed with: "Perhaps the most amazing thing about TAYLOR, when the full scope of his activities is finally grasped is that he always finds the time and energy to play jazz – a full-time task for the average mortal – despite a schedule of non-performing and performing commitments substantial enough to anchor a battleship at sea. How does he do it? TAYLOR gives much of the credit to his wife, Teddi, whom he married in 1946, and who shouldered the lion's share of responsibility in raising their two children. 'She's a remarkable woman,' says TAYLOR. 'She's very sensitive and understanding. In the fifties, I was practicing eight to ten hours a day, and working at night, and she said, "Go for it." 'Because of her natural sensitivity to the arts, she has been one of the biggest support factors in my life. I'm very lucky. She does more than her part.' BILLY TAYLOR puts fun into listening and the almost full house proved it, demanding two encores and a standing ovation. Next year's show will have a tough act to follow."

HILDE LIMONDJIAN: I remember listening to BILLY TAYLOR on WLIB in the early eighties; I worked late. One night, listening and working, it occurred to me that BILLY TAYLOR would be a wonderful addition to the Concerts and Lectures series (The Metropolitan Museum of Art). I called WLIB while BILLY was playing a record, spoke with him, and found him very receptive to the idea.

In the May 18, 1985 edition of Billboard it was noted that the Nestle Corporation that did concert promotions with Concord jazz artists, Dave Brubeck, Marion McPartland and BILLY TAYLOR was pushing a new Maragor Bowl – Bowl Instant Coffee.

The March 1985 edition of Down Beat magazine contained an article written by Jim Roberts. Under a formal picture of BILLY were the headlines: "BILLY TAYLOR: PRIMARILY PIANO." Mr. Roberts begins his article with: "BILLY TAYLOR is a great jazz musician. That might seem obvious, but it sometimes gets overlooked in the midst of his many achievements. It would be hard to name a single person who has done more recently to further the cause of jazz than TAYLOR. As an educator, writer, and radio and television personality, he has spread the world to millions of people all over the world. He holds a doctorate in education and has taught improvisation in countless master classes and, recently, on video tape as well. He founded the Jazzmobile in 1964 and continues as the organization's president. He wrote JAZZ PIANO (William C. Brown Co., 1982), the definitive book on the subject. TAYLOR is perhaps best known for his role as host of the JAZZ ALIVE! series, a much-lamented victim of short-sighted budget cuts by National Public Radio. He was also the music director of David Frost's 60's television show, and these days he can often be seen on the CBS news program, SUNDAY MORNING. But BILLY can play, too. He considers himself a piano player, first and foremost. Although his life's work has been acknowledged with numerous awards – including a Peabody, an Emmy, and the DOWN BEAT Lifetime Achievement Award – there has been little recognition lately for his skill at the keyboard." At the conclusion of the article Mr. Roberts posed the following question to BILLY: "In all your playing and your educational work, what would you say is the most important message that you're trying to get across to young musicians?" BILLY: 'The most important message, I think, is that those of us who are fortunate enough to be born in America are blessed with a country and a living situation that allows us tremendous personal freedom. And that personal freedom is certainly expressed in the most succinct way in jazz. And so what I try to tell everybody that I come in contact with is that this is a very precious thing. We're in danger of losing it because we have thrown it away by ignoring it. We are in danger of having it redefined because Europeans and other people recognize the value of it, and they're defining jazz on their own terms. But the thing that I'm most anxious to get across, from a personal point of view, is that I really want people to hear me play. I would like people to be familiar with what I do. Many people only know me from my records of the '50s, so they don't know what I've been doing for the last 20 or 30 years. Now, I think, not only as a human being, and I hope I'm expressing that better as a musician.'"

MARQUITA POOL ECKERT: If you have a story (CBS), he's got the back-story to that story. He's like a walking encyclopedia. He is actually sometimes better than the music encyclopedias.

On June 30, 1985 BILLY wrote an article about Art Tatum entitled "A TRIBUTE TO ART TATUM" that was published in the Toledo Magazine (Ohio). He opened by saying: "Art Tatum was probably the most lasting influence on my development as a jazz pianist. When I was first interested in jazz piano, I was interested in Fats Waller, who was an influence on Tatum. I didn't know that at the time. But Art would always say, 'Fats Waller. That's where I come from.' He really loved Fats Waller, and really, in his own mind, he became a kind of super Fats Waller. He did what Fats did, twice as fast and with much more technical facility. Waller himself had a beautiful touch, and I'm sure that had an influence on Art's ideas about pedaling and the things that made his piano sound so unique. Art used his foot almost as another hand. He did things, which, in his time, had not generally been done by a solo jazz pianist. But he did it for color and to use the instrument to its fullest potential . . . He listened to classical music. I'd pick him up at his hotel sometimes, and he'd have the radio on, listening to classical music. He liked Chopin, Liszt, Tchaikovsky – the really showpiece piano things. He loved Chopin. Chopin is so pianistic, and I can hear little things of Chopin in his improvisations. Some of the things that he liked just became a part of his language . . .

Art Tatum, to me, was the epitome of great jazz artistry, not only because of his technical facility, which is so obvious, but also because of his harmonic sense, for the time (he was playing) – the adventurous harmonies he was using, the way he reharmonized music. When you realize the liberties he took with rhythm, in terms of his solo work, he made a remarkable giant step. He pointed the way to what many of us are doing now."

ROBIN BELL STEVENS: One of the more interesting things we (BILLY and I) did together was when we went to Dakar Senegal, in West Africa. They took a group of people over there for a concert that we called "An Afternoon Of Jazz" – Jazz '85 in Dakar. Rachel Robinson (widow of Jackie Robinson) had sold her house so in 1985 we didn't have a place to do the concert for the

Jackie Robinson Foundation, so the idea came up to go to West Africa and everyone loved the idea and I think they said: "We'll go raise some money", so we could go, and I did, and so I got BILLY TAYLOR and Aaron Bell to be the co-music directors for it. It was an interesting experience because one of the things that we got to do on the trip, other than the concert that was phenomenal, was the ability for a number of people to go who were on their first trip to Africa. BILLY brought his wife, Teddi, along and she was just absolutely taken by all the things that there were to do. We went on tours, half-day city tours, and I would have to say probably seeing BILLY TAYLOR'S face when we went to Goree Island. Goree Island was the last stop off point for the Africans that were stolen from their villages and then sold into slavery. We were all taken into this room that was maybe twelve feet by ten feet, if that big, and told that there could be as many as fifty people squeezed in there at a time and to see everyone's face, to see BILLY'S face as the tour guide, historian actually, was telling us the story and then showing us the one window at the back. BILLY said: "What's that? At least they had some air". The tour guide said: "Actually, that's called the door of no return." And we all looked sort of puzzled and he said: "Many of the people that were captured took that route – jumped through that window to try to swim back as opposed to being sold into slavery and the reason it as called the door of no return is because most of them didn't make it." Just to see BILLY'S face when that story was told. He was no longer the great jazz musician, he was just another descendent from Africa.

The July 24, 1985 edition of the Valley Advocate published an article by Jim Roberts entitled "DR. BILLY TAYLOR'S ART OF JAZZ." He starts out by saying: "For aspiring jazz musicians in New England, there is no opportunity to learn that is more important than the annual Jazz in July program at the University of Massachusetts in Amherst. At the workshops and master classes held on the UMass campus, young musicians have the chance to learn from some of the acknowledged giants of jazz, and they can hear many of these virtuosos play during the Bright Moments Concert Series that is held in conjunction with the program. Now in its fourth year, Jazz in July traces its roots to the Leonard Bernstein Festival held at UMass in the summer of 1978. Later known as the American Music Workshop in Jazz, the program has grown in scope each year. Although the success of Jazz in July is the result of a collective effort, no one has made a contribution more significant than DR. BILLY TAYLOR. TAYLOR'S summer visit to Amherst always includes a concert, but the bulk of his time is spent teaching. His knowledge of jazz, and especially of the history of jazz piano, is encyclopedic, and his patience, good-humored approach is applied evenly to students of all abilities. Not surprisingly, pianists come from his classes with a better technique and a deepened appreciation for the music itself. 'As I travel around, I'm always coming across people who have taken part in the program..' says TAYLOR, 'and I get feedback as how effective it is. That's why I keep coming back. – it works. I feel that I have the ear of the people whose consciousness needs to be raised, in terms of the support that jazz should get, whether we're talking about the National Endowment for the Arts or funding organizations or UMass or other schools. I do what I can in that context. In many cases, because I don't have a vested interest – I'm not on the faculty, I'm not connected with the institution - what I say is taken in the spirit in which I give it,' says TAYLOR. 'I'm really delighted about that. It's worked!'"

NNENNA FREELON: I kept in contact with him and wrote him frequently and he encouraged me to apply to the program that he has at UMass, "Jazz In July". I attended two years in a row. I got a scholarship the first year; I think I got a scholarship both years. It was the mid-80's. I got a chance to work with BILLY more intensely as well as with Yusef Lateef, Dr. Tillis and others. Our friendship; I know him more as a mentor than a friend. His musicianship you just can't question. I believe who you are is what you play. DR. TAYLOR'S humanness comes through in his playing. That's what I relate to. I love him.

On August 10, 1985 Billboard Magazine announced: "The University of Michigan is holding a symposium on Black Music, August 9-15. More than 250 composers, performers and historians have registered. The emphasis will be on more classically influenced composers such as William Grant Still, although BILLY TAYLOR is lecturing on the topic of 'JAZZ, AMERICA'S CLASSICAL MUSIC.'"

In September 26, 1985 Billboard Magazine columnist Peter Keepnews talked about BILLY in his column "Jazz Blue Notes" when he said, referring to the Jazz Times gathering: "BILLY TAYLOR, pianist, composer, commentator, educator, activist, who as the convention's keynote speaker and guest of honor, was seemingly ubiquitous at the Roosevelt and never less than articulate, charming and optimistic."

The following appeared in the Daily News of the Hungarian News Agency, MTI Budapest, Thursday October 30, 1985. A picture of BILLY was featured with the caption, "JAZZ MAN AS FORUM DELEGATE." "The TV gala at the Budapest Op on Monday night, when the Budapest cultural forum went public for once, is still a talking point, with various comments on the quality and originality of the performers. But there is little doubt that among the show steakers was the BILLY TAYLOR JAZZ TRIO. It must have been the first time the Budapest Opera House resounded to jazz, and it was not a bad debut for the idiom at all. Always smiling and kind to friends and enthusiasts of jazz, BILLY has now exchanged the opera stage for the halls of the Budapest Convention Centre. He is a member of the US Forum delegation and serving on one of the SWB's this week. It's his second visit to Hungary. The first was during an American astronautical exhibition, a couple of years ago, and BILLY said he was very willing to accept an invitation to represent his country here." 'I have very strong feelings about cooperation between nations when it comes to sharing the culture that is unique to each nation, and hope that I can be of some service to my government and to the governments of other countries, so that we can understand one another better.' "Inevitably, the conversation turned several times to the BILLY TAYOR jazz trio's gig at the Opera." 'I was thrilled because the diversity of the presentations was very exciting, to hear young people singing and playing and to watch them dance. One does not see so large and diverse a group ever, and I was very proud to hear them. As regards ourselves, we played an original composition, 'Walking In The Light', a six-movement jazz suite inspired by the Bible. The rapport with the audience was very exciting. I was delighted that they liked my playing. In this context, and the context of the forum here, it is important to stress that jazz is international and now all over the world. In any country you will find a unique means of self-expression. I experienced the same thing during my earlier visit here in Hungary when I heard some very fine Hungarian musicians at the Miskole Jazz Festival. At the forum', BILLY says, 'the atmosphere seems to be quite friendly, and I hope we can get down to more specifics. I like to discuss very much, with the members of the other delegations, a way in which we can be more cooperative and share our cultural riches. I mean here the specific ways in which we can share television programs, any of the suggestions that seem to work for all concerned. The Hungarian Jazz Society has invited us to meet with them on Thursday; which will probably end up in a real jam session and on Friday we have been asked to give yet another concert here at the Forum for the delegates after all the weeks' sessions are over.'"

> MARQUITA POOL ECKERT: BILLY is extremely conscientious about what he perceives to be the facts, from his point of view. In other words he won't just say something because it sounds good. I write sometimes for him but I never write anything that I think he won't say or anything that he won't agree with. A – he won't say it or B – I'll write a script and we'll sit down and go over it line by line.
>
> You know: "What do you think? Is this accurate?' for accuracy. He always has a certain perspective regarding accuracy – there is a certain perspective that he has by virtue of having been there. Whereas somebody like myself, I don't have it because I wasn't there. So it's almost like a column when he does this (CBS Sunday Morning) – much more personal.

In the October 26 issue of Billboard in 1985, columnists Sam Sutherland and Peter Keepnews penned an article in their column, "Jazz Blue Notes". They said: "Headquarters and offices are in place for the recently formed National Academy of Jazz, along with the governors, on the six-month old organization's regular and honorary boards and the NAJE's agenda makes it clear that the fledging group is looking beyond Southern California in terms of its presence. Steve Allen who has been appointed to the Honorary Board of Governors has donated office space for the non-profit organization in Van Nuys. Other members of that group include Louis Bellson, Ray Brown, Benny Carter, Chick Corea, Gary Giddings, Gerry Mulligan, Oscar Peterson, Buddy Rich, Artie Shaw, George Shearing, BILLY TAYLOR, Mel Torme, Sarah Vaughan, Joe Williams and Phil Woods, among others.

On October 29, 1985, Lifestyles magazine, had an article featuring BILLY TAYLOR and Ramsey Lewis entitled "JAMMING IN RYE" subtitled "Jazz Greats Join Forces For TV Taping". The article, which was written by Harcourt Tynes opened: "Last Tuesday musical sparks lit up Wainwright House, the picturesque mansion in Rye that overlooks Long Island Sound. As the musicians played their Steinways, clusters of spectators tapped their feet and bobbed their heads. The atmosphere was definitely Greenwich Village jazz club. The musical duo, BILLY TAYLOR, the elder statesman of New York jazz pianists, and Ramsey Lewis, the jazz playing sensation from Chicago provided the feverish action. Many Westchester residents were on hand to witness the event, however, Wainwright House is too small for staging public shows. While a busy TV crew taped the show called 'Jazz Counterpoint' which will be shown on cable television in February, the show with TAYLOR acting as host and Lewis making a guest appearance will be aired on UA-Columbia cablevision of Westchester. Two other Westchester cable companies, American Cable Systems and Adams Russell also will carry it. The pair played one fast-paced duet after another for an hour and a half in a fashion few other musicians can duplicate. These are performers who achieve all sorts of musical miracles the moment they touch a keyboard. Good jazz musicians, most of whom are instinctive improvisationists, frequently team up with each other for very workable, unrehearsed, jam sessions. But very few of them succeed as well as TAYLOR and Lewis did. Even the two musicians were excited about it. 'It was simply excelerating,' said Lewis who was a Chicago school boy working part time at a neighborhood record shop and an avid BILLY TAYLOR fan during the early 1950's when he first heard about TAYLOR."

The Wednesday, November 6, 1985 issue of Variety indicated that "You Made Me Love You", a tribute to Harry James will air December 1 on PBS. The special, produced by Nebraska ETB network of cultural affairs unit, was taped on location at L. Mars Peony Park with Joe Graves leading the Harry James Orchestra, Helen Forrest as guest and BILLY TAYLOR as host.

In Jazz Times Magazine of November 1985 the following was printed: "The choice of BILLY TAYLOR as the keynote speaker and unofficial host of the convention (Jazz Times Convention) was a master stroke. BILLY TAYLOR is a jazz renaissance man in every sense of the word. Besides being a master performer his advocacy of the jazz art form has crossed over into the educational support system world as well. As leader of his own trio, director of Jazzmobile, television show host, educator and former member of the National Council on the Arts (a presidential appointment) BILLY'S personal jazz world touched nearly everyone of the many bases covered at the convention, from performance to media to support. For people beyond those which I moderated, there are only a few I can offer commentary on having been working on my own sessions during the conference."

The Billboard Magazine of November 9, 1985 featured a column by Sam Sutherland and Peter Keepnews entitled "Jazz Blue Notes". It was announced that: "The first steps have been taken toward setting up an ambitious fund raising organization that will enable jazz musicians to do their part, on a grand scale, in the ongoing battle against hunger. The Jazz For Life project, the brainchild of a group of University of Michigan law students has held a number of meetings to discuss organizing a three-day jazz festival, at as of yet an unspecified future date, that would involve participation in both the local and national level and, the organization promised hopefully, hopefully to feature 'the most prominent artists in the jazz world.' Proceeds will be earmarked for long-range developmental projects in hunger-these programs in both Africa and the US. A formal steering committee met in New York on September 14 with such familiar names as BILLY TAYLOR, David Baker, and Herb Wong participating.

In the December 1985 edition of Jazz Times, it was announced "Teddy Wilson will be the guest on BILLY TAYLOR'S show, 'Jazz Counterpoint', to be seen this month on the Bravo pay cable TV channel. In January BILLY'S guest will be Tommy Flanagan."

In 1986 Betco Records released a cassette entitled LET US MAKE A JOYFUL NOISE featuring the BILLY TAYLOR TRIO with Victor Gaskin, bass and Curtis Boyd, drums. The tunes included Take The A Train, Tom, Vaguely, You Tempt Me, Let Us Make A Joyful Noise/Spiritual, Rejoice, Prayer, Celebrate and Walking In The Light.

In Down Beat magazine, January 1986, Art Lange reviewed his visit to the Fourth Annual Jazz Times Convention in New York City and said: "Dr. BILLY TAYLOR set an upbeat but cautious tone in his address warning against complacency and he went on to accept a limited public awareness of jazz, he suggested that everyone involved in the making and marketing of jazz question first their own motives and goals, and then work to expand the music's visibility and effectiveness citing such slow to change concerns as radio and T.V. exposure, conditions and fees for working musicians, education and . . . activity as areas for improvement."

Billboard Magazine's February 1, 1986, Volume 98, Number 5, printed a commentary by BILLY TAYLOR entitled "JAZZ AMERICA'S MUSIC: WE'RE WASTING A NATIONAL RESOURCE". In the article BILLY pointed out that the music business had been "callous, negligent, thoughtless, incredibly stupid and unbusinesslike" in the treatment of jazz. He felt that there was no excuse for the lack of industry support for jazz. He closed his statement by saying: "Millions of people in Eastern Europe watched and listened to the music of Bach, Handel, Debussy, Kodaly, folk, opera, the music of the Renaissance – and contemporary jazz. The reaction to jazz was an excellent indication of the appeal that jazz has for audiences attuned to the nuances of European classical music, as well as its own indigenous music. I agree wholeheartedly with the member of the Polish delegation who stated: 'I hope we will not build new borders when technology has given us the means and the opportunity to cross old ones.' Hopefully, greed, shortsightedness and inertia will not prevent the music business from developing a more effective approach to the business aspects of jazz. We are wasting a very valuable national resource."

HILDE LIMONDJIAN: When he came to our stage (The Metropolitan Museum of Art), he had an almost immediate rapport with our audience. Since his first year on our series in 1986, his audience has steadily grown as he has reappeared on our stage every year since. BILLY'S concert days are special here at the Museum, and we never cease to appreciate his appearances here with the trio.

In San Antonio, Texas, the major newspaper, The San Antonio Light mentioned BILLY in its midweek calendar of Wednesday, February 19, 1986. Headed by "TAYLOR JAZZES THINGS UP" the article went on to mention "Trinity Music Fest Features A Master Musician." The article further stated: "TAYLOR calls jazz, 'America's Classical Music." The reason, he says, is not only because jazz is a musical melting pot, but also because it champions the individual player. 'It takes all the aspects of our culture and puts it in a context that is unique to the United States. As I travel the world, I see that this is the music that captures the essence of who we are and what we're about. In a jazz performance, the highest priority is placed on individuality. A musician is allowed to do his own thing – no other music does that to that great an extent. Typically, there is a five piece group, and you set the key and tempo. But once you start, each musician has the obligation to do something of his own to make the effect special.' TAYLOR agrees that the barriers between 'black' and 'white' musical forms are being broken down. But there's still a ways to go. The Atlanta Symphony, 'one of the most conservative elements in the community', commissioned his piece entitled 'Peaceful Warrior' which is on Friday's concert program. It premiered two years ago. 'And I dare say two years ago I wouldn't have been invited to Trinity, but here I am. And it's going to be a terrific program.'"

Two days later, Trinity University's own newspaper, THE TRINITORIAN announced the concert, "BILLY TAYLOR, TRINITY MUSICIANS JAZZ UP MUSICFEST VI TONIGHT." BILLY said: 'I was the first to make the statement that jazz is classical music. I don't consider it black classical music, but American classical music. Black music has contributed much more to the culture of this country than many of us realize. All the popular music had its origins in the same kind of musical experience that gave us the spirituals, the blues, and, of course, jazz.' . . . "Joining TAYLOR are drummer Keith Copeland and bassist Victor Gaskin. The Stieren Arts Enrichment Fund sponsors MusicFest VI, coordinated this year by Greg Fried. All events are free and open to the public."

In the March 9, 1986 issue of the New York Times it was announced that "BILLY TAYLOR, jazz composer, pianist, conductor, professor and lecturer, will perform with his trio on Saturday at 8:00 P.M. in the Rocklin Center for The Arts in West Nyack, New York. He will also tell about a recent world tour. In Shanghai the auditorium where he was to play it was so cold that his wife asked the interpreter when the heat would be turned on? 'When the people arrive' was the answer. Meaning that only the audience would warm the place. So Dr. TAYLOR kept his overcoat on at the keyboard."

On April 2, 1986 the Board of Trustees of the University of Massachusetts issued a proclamation: "To all whom these presents shall come, greeting: Be it known that we hereby confer on WILLIAM EDWARD TAYLOR, in recognition of distinguished attainments, the honorary degree of Doctor of Fine Arts, with all the rights, privileges, and dignities appertaining to that degree. As given at Amherst on April 2, 1986 and signed by David C. Knapp, President of the University.

A group called Project Return gave BILLY an award on January 19, 1987. The award read: "For your dedication to the ideals of Martin Luther King and your stance against drug abuse."

On the 26 of January, 1987 the President of St. John's University of the state of New York conferred upon BILLY the degree of Doctor of Music, honorary. "Upon the recommendation of the faculty of the College of Liberal Arts and Sciences . . .

On March 9, 1988 BILLY received a letter from James H. Harding, Jr. who was a special advisor to the mayor of the City of New York which stated: "Dear BILLY: I am delighted that you were able to be a part of the February 2nd opening of 'Black Visions '88: Lady Legions In Jazz." I hope you enjoyed yourself as much as we enjoyed having you here. "Lady Legions In Jazz" is not only a Black History month; it is also a great way to pay our overdue tribute to some very special women. Best Wishes and Warmest Regards." (signed) Jim.

Victor Gaskin, bass, Bobby Thomas, drums, and BILLY TAYLOR, piano made up the BILLY TAYOR TRIO that recorded WHITE NIGHTS and JAZZ IN LENNIGRAD for TAYLOR-MADE records in LENINGRAD, SOVIET UNION on June 13 and 14, 1988. The trio recorded Pensativa, Morning, Secret Love and My Romance.

Drummer Bobby Thomas (Robert Charles Thomas) was born in Newark, New Jersey on November 14, 1932. He attended the Juilliard School of Music in New York City and played in Army bands during the late 40's and early 50's. On his release he played in Newark with Nat Phipps and in the late 50's with Sir Roland

Hanna and Illinois Jacquet. During the 60's and 70's he played with various groups including Wes Montgomery, Gigi Gryce, Cy Coleman, Junior Mance, Hubert Laws, Don Ellis, Herbie Mann, Gerry Mulligan, Quincy Jones, Ray Charles and others.

JIM ANDERSON: We were doing a trio recording in Minnesota on the Taylor-Made label, BILLY and I. We were going through takes and I said: "I think take two is better for Victor and Bobby." BILLY answered: "When it's their record we get take two!!"

The NATIONAL ENDOWMENT FOR THE ARTS at the annual meeting of the International Association for Jazz Education named BILLY an ARTS AMERICAN JAZZ MASTER at the annual meeting held in Detroit, Michigan in 1988. Carlton College conferred upon BILLY an honorary doctor's degree.

NANCY WILSON: He's one of the greatest teachers. He's a great speaker aside from being a brilliant musician, that's a given . . . we all know BILLY TAYLOR can play the piano, but his knowledge is what has been so valuable. He's so giving of it. He knows so much and he's witnessed so much and he's willing to share it. BILLY has history – there is so much there. I got more from this man, because I've never considered myself a jazz singer. I'm a song stylist – I sing songs.

On August 1st and 2nd, 1988 BILLY made a solo album in New York City entitled SOLO for TAYLOR MADE-RECORDS. He recorded All The Things You Are, Bit Of Bedlam, Old Folks, More Than You Know and Gone With The Wind.

The January 1989 issue of Essence Magazine, Volume 19, Number 9 Scott Gutterman featured a picture of BILLY with this statement: "For more than 40 years jazz has been BILLY TAYLOR'S life. In addition to his status as a gifted pianist and composer, TAYLOR, 68, is America's unofficial 'Ambassador of Jazz,' playing and speaking on behalf of the music in schools and concert halls from the Soviet Union to South America. He also boasts an extensive radio and television career, as well as a doctorate in Black History and Music from the University of Massachusetts at Amherst. As president and founder of Jazzmobile, a traveling concert hall featuring musical greats such as Dizzy Gillespie, TAYLOR helps bring jazz back to black communities in New York State free of charge all summer long. Of the music he loves, TAYLOR says: 'Jazz takes all the elements in our culture and puts them into perspective. It celebrates the individual freedom that we prize so dearly in our society.' Despite his feeling that record companies have neglected this 'great American art form,' the good doctor still finds reasons to be hopeful about the future of jazz. 'You've got a whole contingent of young people coming along who are extending the tradition and who deserve attention. And people out there are responding and asking to hear this music that belongs to them.'"

In May 1989 BILLY received his sixth honorary doctorate from Clark College.

Radio show host Dick Miller interviewed BILLY on the Dick Miller Show on August 27, 1989 and alluded to the CBS Sunday Morning Show:

DICK MILLER: You know I've always been a big fan of the Sunday Morning Show that you appear on with Charles Kuralt* on CBS and I think our people would like to hear you have any comments on that show because it is a wonderful show and especially I always enjoy your segments on it.

BILLY TAYLOR: Thank you. I appreciate that. I am delighted to be on the show; I've been on the show about eight years now. It started when they did a profile on me. They liked it and they asked me if I was interested in doing that same kind of thing on other people, and I was, so I've been doing it every since. What they base the show on is Kuralt's strength. He's a very eclectic man and he listens to all kinds of things. He's very interested, not just in people, but in the environment, a wide range of interests, which are reflected by the magazine format of the show. So we sort of play to his strength. The thing I love about it when I go on with him to introduce one of the artists that I'm talking about; he always asks the questions that the guy sitting out there on Sunday morning having coffee would ask, and he sets it up in a way that makes the story much more understandable.

DICK MILLER: Well, it's very homey.

BILLY TAYLOR: Absolutely.

DICK MILLER: Yes. It's great. I missed you last Sunday.

BILLY TAYLOR: Well, you know, every now and then folks have to go to church and do other things on Sunday.

DICK MILLER: I think the last one was about two weeks ago. You had Max Roach on.

BILLY TAYLOR: Yeah, Max Roach.

DICK MILLER Was that a tape segment?

BILLY TAYLOR: Well, that part of it, the part where I'm actually dealing with the artist is taped because what we do is over whatever the period of time is, we will go and try to get sort of information from the artist and about the artist, and usually I interview the artist and a lot of what we present comes from that interview. The guy will say: "Oh, I like to do this" so we'll get, like Charlie Byrd said: "I like to go sailing" so we got a picture of him sailing. And other things; Peggy Lee was very proud of these really champion roses that she grows, big as cabbages, really gorgeous, so we showed her in her garden.

---

*Charles Kuralt eventually left the Sunday Morning Show and was replaced by Charles Osgood.

And this is a world-class singer that knows people know has great aesthetic opinions and taste. That just gives us another side of it, hopefully.

BRUCE LUNDVALL: The CBS Sunday Morning Show with BILLY has just been terrific. Every time an artist appears on that show of course we see the records sales increase. He's extraordinary. He's just one of those guys we're all fortunate to have among us as a musician and as a spokesman for the music.

SHELLY BERG: My dad had an extensive record collection and BILLY TAYLOR was one of the people he pointed me to because of BILLY'S apprenticeship with Art Tatum and his kind of progression to the history of jazz piano. I always think of BILLY TAYLOR as a way of listening to the whole history of the piano. You are listening to a two-handed piano player who understands what's going on now but has lineage all the way back to Tatum. So my dad had me listening to BILLY TAYLOR a lot. I met him in 1986. I was a finalist in the Great American Jazz Piano Competition and BILLY was the head of the judging panel. That competition is always held in Jacksonville, Florida and the winner plays on a large festival they have there. So that was when I met BILLY when he was judging there. I was not the winner of that competition but BILLY was very encouraging to me at that time. Every since then he almost took me under his wing; he's always been there for me for advice and encouragement. Years later he said: "Those other judges just didn't like any piano players that swung!" So he's been great to me ever since.

On June 11, 1988 Carleton College, through President Lewis, presented BILLY with the honorary Doctor of Humane Letters, honaris causa. "Given by the authority vested in me by the State of Minnesota and the Board of Trustees of Carleton College."

Marian McPartland did a lot to further the jazz piano tradition through channels other than performing live or on records. For years she taught jazz to schoolchildren at various clinics and workshops around the country. Since 1979 she has hosted MARIAN MCPARTLAND'S PIANO JAZZ SHOW, a thirteen-part series broadcast annually on National Public Radio. These shows include her elucidating commentary on music and conversations and spontaneous duets with such guests as Oscar Peterson, George Shearing, BILLY TAYLOR and several other pianists.

In January 1989 BILLY concluded a series focusing on his own work at the Metropolitan Museum of Art in "Self-Portrait". The January 4-10 issue of Variety Magazine indicated that BILLY had returned from a vacation in Barbados in time for a December 29, 1988 "Piano Spectacular" gig in Sarasota, Florida. Another event in January, the Florida National Jazz Festival, featured a broad spectrum of performers at Jacksonville, Florida. BILLY served as one of the judges along with Bob James, Amy Duncan and Jazz Times owner Ira Gitler.

The January 1989 edition of Jazz Times indicated that the BILLY TAYLOR TRIO had played at the Jazz Ministry at St. Peter's Church where Lionel Hampton was saluted with the first Duke Ellington/Shepard of the Night Flock award. With BILLY were bassist Victor Gaskin and drummer Bobby Thomas.

In September 1989 BILLY was invited to Juilliard to be part of a one-day symposium entitled: "The Color Of the Performing Arts." The school invited Arthur Mitchell, director of the Dance Theater of Harlem, BILLY TAYLOR and actor Raul Julia to speak at the symposium.

> LARRY RIDLEY: We had lot of nice things happen when I was playing with BILLY. We played at the White House for President Gerald Ford, the state house dinner for the Premier of Pakistan, a special thing for him. We had a nice time doing that. We played something kind of East Indian in flavor and I played a bowed solo. After we finished President Ford jumped up on the stage and congratulated me saying:" That was just marvelous". We did a lot of great things – we toured a lot and Freddie Waits was the drummer with us at one point. Bobby Thomas was the drummer most of the time early on and then Freddie Waits came on. We did a lot of great things. We went somewhere in Missouri – Joplin or some city like that, and we played a concert at a school. To get there we flew in a very small plane. And there we were, the three of us with the bass, drums, and with BILLY sitting up in the front with the pilot and a tom-tom sitting on his lap.

The March 18, 1989 printing of the Indianapolis Star featured a reprint of an article previously written by Leonard Feather and published in the Los Angeles Times. The article entitled "TAYLOR TAKES JAZZ CONCERT ON ROAD TOUR TO SPREAD WORD" began: "It is doubtful that any individual now active has had a greater impact on the appreciation of jazz than the genial, protean pianist and educator BILLY TAYLOR. Once a month on average, during Charles Kuralt's Sunday Morning show, he is seen on CBS-TV interviewing a jazz personality, reviewing and analyzing the artist's work, and generally spreading the word for this music in a style that is accessible to the millions who tune him in regularly . . . Of all his good works the one dearest to TAYLOR'S heart has been Jazzmobile, beginning in 1965 as a project to bring live music to the streets of Harlem. It has expanded into a series of workshops and seminars. 'We now have our own building. We're trying to fashion it into a small recording studio combined with a rehearsal hall, so that young musicians who cannot afford to go downtown will have a place to try out their ideas. Jimmy Owens, who was a trumpeter in my David Frost Show band, is supervising this logical extension of our workshops. What I like about it is that people come from all over Harlem every Saturday to 127th Street and Madison Avenue, and despite all the bad-mouthing you hear about how dangerous Harlem is, we have about 65 percent female students; we also have a large percentage of Asians. The age range is from 11 to 67.'"

>   CHIP JACKSON: I first met BILLY around 1988. His drummer, Bobby Thomas, who was with him for a long time, got a gig at TAVERN ON THE GREEN. He hired Frank Wess and BILLY and me. That was the first time I met BILLY and played with him and we had a ball, we just had a great time. So about five years later when BILLY was going to make a change Michael Abene recommended me, and BILLY said, "I remember Chip from about five years ago. We had a ball on the gig."

BILLY TAYLOR and THE JAZZMOBILE ALL-STARS recorded nine BILLY TAYLOR tunes and Ceora for TAYLOR-MADE RECORDS on April 5th and 6th, 1989 in New York City. The personnel included Ted Dunbar, guitar; Frank Wess, soprano and tenor saxophones, Jimmy Owens, trumpet, Victor Gaskin, bass, Bobby Thomas, drums, and BILLY TAYLOR, piano. The released album was entitled THE JAZZMOBILE ALL-STARS.

>   SHELLY BERG: BILLY'S just about the most wonderful person that you can ever meet. Even when he meets you for the first time you get the sense that he really cares that he's meeting another human being. So I think that he's a wonderful person. I think that arguably there isn't anybody who has been more important to jazz education than BILLY TAYLOR. He's made it a life's work and continues to make it a life's work in a variety of ways. He's amazing too because he has such energy and vitality and he's unchanged in all the years that I've known him. I only hope that the same things will happen for me.

BILLY TAYLOR has a great deal of love and respect for his peers. In Gene Lee's book "Oscar Peterson: The Will To Swing" BILLY had this to say about Oscar: "He is not only a virtuoso pianist, he's a remarkable musician. The thing I admire about him is that he is always growing. His phenomenal facility sometimes gets in the way of people's listening, but he has a big heart and he plays beautiful things."2

In the April, 1989 edition of the Richmond News Leader BILLY had this to say in commenting on the music played at the Apollo Theater: "The repertory is no more trying than any European repertory – it took a lifetime to create. You have to take what's meaningful to you. There are certain things in Monk, in Ellington, Don Redman, Eubie Blake, Art Tatum. Jazz basically is a personal expression. That's why there's so much of it. Jazz is improvised in that it is spontaneous composition anytime you play. It's the structure that one learns from an Ellington, a Monk, or a Coltrane."

In June 1989 the BILLY TAYLOR TRIO, with Victor Gaskin on bass and Bobby Thomas on drums, appeared with the Richie Beirach Trio at Indigo Blues. The Jazz In July workshop was held on the campus of the University of Massachusetts in Amherst and featured BILLY TAYLOR, Max Roach, Victor Gaskin and Yusef Lateef.

On Sunday, July 16, 1989 an article in the New York Times entitled, "DOES THE JAZZ OF THE PAST HAVE A FUTURE?" written by Richard M. Sudhalter, stated "BILLY TAYLOR, one of the most eloquent and widely quoted spokesman for the black jazz tradition has gone on record as saying he sees the absence of black players in traditional jazz as part of a larger breakdown as jazz, in general no longer plays a central role in black culture. 'Until the 60's,' he said, 'jazz seemed to be part of the general fabric of black expression. It was played at social gatherings; it was functional. I remember seeing kids doing the Madison and other dances popular then to Miles Davis. The revulsion of the old Uncle Tom images and postures, coupled with an emerging militancy in black awareness drove entire generations away from the jazz past.'"

On July 8, 1989 BILLY presented a Creative Award to Lionel Hampton during the 25th anniversary bash of the music and performing arts unit of B'Nai B'rith. In August the BILLY TAYLOR TRIO played at the Lincoln Center Out-of-Doors North Plaza of Lincoln Center in New York City. In August there was a Jazzmobile concert at Grant's Tomb, 122nd St. and Riverside Drive in New York City.

JON FADDIS: It's always wonderful to work with BILLY because he's a fantastic musician and he really knows the history of the music, which is something I really respect. He likes to have fun when you play, and I like that too. As an educator, I take a lot of things that BILLY has already done and developed and try to use them when I got to work with kids as well. For example, his book "Jazz Piano". I try to apply those same principles with trumpet players; Players; listening to those who come before you and going through the different styles. He's very knowledgeable about what pianist did this with his left hand and this with his right hand and how they did this, things like that. I remember BILLY talking about meeting Jelly Roll Morton and going to hear him for the first time and Jelly Roll was older at that time and said, here kid, check this out and threw something at BILLY. Jelly Roll was doing all this great stuff in the key of D flat, which is a difficult key, BILLY was sitting there wide eyed and in awe, so having had those experiences, I think that's something else that he brings to his music and to the audiences that he performs for. And of course BILLY'S very, very knowledgeable and intelligent when it comes to like jazz and politics and education because he's been doing that for years, the ramifications of budget cuts and things like that, and I don't know of a better spokesperson for jazz at this point, as far as all of those things go, he's right in there and knows what he's talking about. 3

In September 1989 there was a "Back To The Rose Garden" fund raising bash in Washington, D.C. that was formed to reaffirm the commitment made by President Johnson in 1965 when he pledged the creation of the American Film Institute. Those who took part in that event included Alan Arkin, Phil Donahue, Douglas Fairbanks, Jr., Goldie Hawn, Norman Lear, Steve Martin, Brooke Shields, Sissy Spacek, Marlo Thomas, Cicely Tyson and BILLY TAYLOR among others. That same month, September, the BILLY TAYLOR TRIO played with the Bridge Festival Orchestra. Jeff Levenson, who reported in Billboard Magazine stated: "In jazz where improvisation is all, styles of playing can be as different as personalities that fashion them. Recent columns focusing on pianists Bud Powell, BILLY TAYLOR and Harry Connick, Jr. inspire just a start: demeanors that are intrinsically introspective, scholarly or brash may very well translate into corresponding musical attitudes as demonstrated by myriad jazz persons who boost the talent (and courage) to be themselves, diversity and talent is it's own reward."

The Preview Section of the Greeley Tribune on September 21, 1989 contained a headline, "JAZZ PIANIST BILLY TAYLOR STILL LEARNING". The article written by Tribune staff writer Lisa Greim said: "After 40 years in the business, jazz pianist BILLY TAYLOR hasn't stopped learning – and doesn't plan to. He's a teacher, composer, arranger, conductor, author and activist on behalf of jazz. 'I learn as much as I try to share,' he says. TAYLOR, who will perform Friday evening in Greeley, has just started his own record label, put out his first-ever solo album and teamed up with Ramsey Lewis on another recording. Honored by a raft of organizations from the White House to the Union of Composers of the Soviet Union, TAYLOR has dedicated himself to promoting jazz as "American classical music." . . . He's hoping that the new series of recordings will let people know that there's an active, growing musician behind the years of stumping to raise interest in – and money for – jazz performance and education. 'Most people are much more aware of me from my other activities.' TAYLOR said. 'One of the reasons I'm focusing on recording is so people will have that aspect of what I do available. Many people that I work with find their point of reference to me, musically, is 30 years old.'"

On Sunday night in October 1989, the finale was held in honor of Duke Ellington's 90th birthday year presented by the Schomburg Institute for Research in Black Culture. It started in the New York Public Libraries Ester Hall on 5th avenue with Brooke Astor, Mercer Ellington, Charles Rangel, Sherry Bronfman and Liz Rohatyn. They segued over to the Shubert Theater where another star cast of characters took to the stage including Ed Bradley, Honi Coles, Dick Gregory and BILLY TAYLOR. Also in October the Melotones Compact Big Band, under the direction of Gordon Grinnell, played a free concert of Duke Ellington music at Horton Plaza Sports Deck. The program included some of the great masterpieces of the band built into its library at the encouragement of arts historians and critics, e.g., DR, BILLY TAYLOR, Leonard Feather and Whitney Balliett.

Also in October the National Jazz Service Organization (NJSO) was organized to nurture the growth and enhancement of jazz music as an American art form. It was a not-for-profit benefit corporation organized under the laws of the District of Columbia and its Director was Willard Jenkins. David Baker was the President of the Board of Directors and some of the people on the board included Muhal Richard Abrams, Fred Brown, Nancy Clarke, Ritchie Cole, Peter Duchin, Congressman John Conyers, Larry Ridley, and BILLY TAYLOR. The same year Congressman John Conyers, Jr. authored and worked nationally for the successful passing of House and Senate Resolution 57 that declared: "Jazz was an American National Treasure." In November BILLY TAYLOR was featured at Jazz At Noon that was held at the Savoy Grill on East 54th street. On Friday, November 10 1989, BILLY TAYLOR was the guest pianist with Bill and George Simon's swing band at the Red Blazer Two on Wes 46th St. in New York City.

> JOHN DUFFY: The National Jazz Service Organization: David Baker was the President, BILLY was on the board, David Bailey, James Jordan of the New York State Council For The Arts; and I kept fighting for that organization but they didn't make it. They just petered out. The problem with jazz has been that it's not organized like symphony orchestras in terms of boards and service organizations, people with money to support the organization of it. In jazz, people are more independent, not part of a larger group. They do gigs, traveling, struggling in terms of supporting a family, etc.

In the November 1989 issue of Variety Magazine it was stated: "The jazz ministry at St. Peter's Church will honor jazz impresario George Wein November 16 with the presentation of it's Duke Ellington 'Shepard of the Night Flock' award. The prize is named for Duke Ellington and pastor John Garcia Gensel, for whom Ellington composed a tone poem, 'The Shepard Who Watches Over the Night Flock'. Concert participates will include Lionel Hampton, Howard Alden, Ruby Braff, Doc Cheatham, Dizzy Gillespie, George Shearing and BILLY TAYLOR."

In November 1989 The Jazz Link (Vol. 11, Issue 18) featured an article written by Alex Henderson carrying the title "DR. BILLY TAYLOR: A TAYLOR MADE JAZZMOBILE INNOVATOR". As part of the title, the following statement by DR. TAYLOR stated: "Many musicians have found it easier to earn a living outside the United States but the United States is bum-rapped. People don't realize how much support is really here." Of interest were the following questions and responses:

Henderson: "Do you often find that young listeners start off enjoying Pat Metheny or Grover Washington, Jr. and end up enjoying Charlie Parker or John Coltrane as well?" TAYLOR: 'To me, your entry point isn't as important as where you ultimately take it. Pat Metheny is a very fine musician. He does some very worthwhile and interesting things, and I'd like the students to listen to him or any other musician of that caliber and ask themselves, 'What makes him special? Why is Pat Metheny reaching so many people?' He's not reaching them because he's playing three chords.' Henderson: " How does the level of support in Japan and Western Europe compare to the United States?" TAYLOR: 'I know of five cities that had city-sponsored jazz festivals around Labor Day weekend last year; Detroit, Chicago, Atlanta, Milwaukee and Washington, D.C. I told one of my researchers to find out how many people went to the festivals. She came back with a figure of five million, based on police estimates. That's a lot of folks over one weekend, and that's only five cities we were looking at. I was very pleased. I had no idea the numbers were like that.'"

ALAN BERGMAN: I think BILLY is very, very musical – I think he's a two-handed piano player. He's very lyrical and he has a distinctive style. You can especially tell BILLY TAYLOR from the way he plays ballads. BILLY is an historian, a teacher, and it comes out in his playing. He has definite views about drummers. He has great technique.

The Jazz Times magazine of December 1989 stated: "DR. BILLY TAYLOR was host for a five part series during American Music Week in early November. He covered the field from Louis Lonnie Chatmon all the way to John Blake via George Venuti, Stuff Smith, Eddy South and the Mississippi Sheiks as well as Claude Williams, 'cellist David Darling and even L. Shank Shankar.

BILLY'S travels took him to Miami University in Ohio, radio station WMUB, where Dick Miller interviewed him, on the Dick Miller Show, on August 27, 1989. The topics that follow were not included previously:

DICK MILLER: You, BILLY, more than any other jazz artist can be credited with bringing jazz to the forums of national radio and television, and that's the truth.

BT: Well, I've been working hard at it and I really appreciate people like you and others who are just helping get the music out to people. You know, it really bothers me that National Public Radio is the only game in town, for the most part, when it comes to putting jazz and other kinds of music, other than what's on the charts, out there for the public. When you look at radio stations around the world that are owned and operated by the country that they're in and realize that they have one outlet; China has one outlet for all of those people; Russia has one outlet. Here we have hundreds all over and we don't really use them to the extent we should, as a free country. DM: That's very true what you say about Public Radio being, probably ninety-nine percent, Pubic Radio being the ones that are running jazz, and stuff from the big band era. BT: And giving information. Considering the fact that our information is not censored, we still only get such a small amount of it fed to us in sound bites. When you listen to the news on NPR and you listen to the information given about what's going on, it's very refreshing.

DM: Yes. You know you're talking about in China, only have one medium, I guess that's true in Russia too, isn't it? BT: Yes. There are a lot of places. Many places, one doesn't think about normally, in Holland; in Germany they have one state owned and operated station. DM: I guess it's the same in England with the BBC and in Sweden with Radio Stockholm. BT: It has advantages in that they present state orchestras that play all kinds of music, much more world music than we seem to, except on NPR. When I travel around a lot I really am chaffing at the bit that we don't do a little more because it's our choice.DM: I know you travel an awful lot and I tell you what; you wear an awful lot of hats! You're a pianist, you're a composer, a recording artist, an arranger and conductor, an actor, an author, a teacher, a lecturer, radio and television personality; boy, that's a lot of hats! BT: (laugh) It sure is. DM: I love that comment you made when you said: "Everything I do stems from the fact that I'm a pianist-composer." BT: That's true. That's where it all starts for me and all of the other things that I do come from the fact that I like to express myself. All of the other things I do come from the fact that I like to express myself in musical terms and I like to share my experiences with as many people as possible. DM: I see. You also have your own recording label now. BT: Yes. I'm kind of pleased that the Arabesque people, the people who own Arabesque, decided that they wanted to tip a toe into the water of jazz so they asked me to do some recording for them and bring some of my friends along so that's what I'm in the process of doing. DM: And that's how Taylor-Made records came about. BT: Absolutely. DM: Well, that's great. It really is. Carol Conover, from your agency who very kindly set this whole thing up, is really a doll, I'll tell you. BT: Oh, yeah. She's a wonderful lady and really does a tremendous job. Well, first of all she understands music; she understands the nuances what one goes through to perform, especially in the jazz arena. People like that are hard to come by. DM: Yes. She's on top of things, she really is. She makes sure you're where you're supposed to be at the time you're supposed to be. BT: This is correct. DM: You are the recipient of two Peabodys and an Emmy Award. Can you tell us a little bit about those?

BT: Well, the Peabody that I'm proudest of came about from, what I think, is the best radio series I've every done, in my entire career. It traced the history of jazz using the piano to tell the story and I played a lot of recordings and played a lot of things on the piano and it was the 13-week series. It's based on a book that I wrote called JAZZ PIANO, in which I literally traced the styles of the music. I have a lot of problems with the "Great Man" theory of the arts, whether it's classical music, folk music, or jazz, whatever. It's every easy to say: "This great artist took the music from one place to another." Well, in my opinion what usually happens is a great artist epitomizes what's going on in his or her period and this is not to demean the talent of the artists. But in jazz, especially, if you say Louis Armstrong did everything, you could make a point by quoting the tremendous volume of, the tremendous part of the vocabulary that he personally put into use, by virtue of his recordings; but that would leave out, if you say he did it all, that would leave our Red Allen, Cootie Williams, that would leave out Bix Beiderbeck and people who did other things that were very important to the jazz vocabulary. Now, one could argue that what he did was more important than anyone else, but there are so many other things that I see, as a pianist, when I look at, for instance, two musicians who co-existed, Fats Waller and Earl Hines. Both were kind of coming into focus at the same time, equally influential on other pianists, yet totally different. If you say Fats Waller did it all, you ignore the tremendous things that Hines did, and I don't think you can do that.

DM: Yes, that's very true. You've also appeared at the White House on three different occasions.

BT: Yes, actually about five. We've been invited to perform there and I was really quite excited. As a matter of fact last night in listening to the Army Chorus at the dinner I attended, it reminded me of the time I performed with the Chorus. I performed something at the White House at a Christmas program. I wrote a piece called "Stable Down The Road" and they did it and it was just phenomenal, for me, to hear a vocal group of that quality do music that I had written; it was just terrific. So, playing at the White House is kind of like a command performance, it's a lot of fun.*

DM: Yes, and you've also been on three State Department tours.

BT: Yes, and that has caused me to hold some of the opinions that I hold because in traveling; for instance, we went on a State Department tour to about seven countries in the mid-East. We got to India, Pakistan, Egypt and a lot of other places and it was an eye-opener for me to see how American music, jazz in particular, was accepted; how knowledgeable many of the people were, and yet how much I could learn from them in terms of their music and their aesthetic approaches. There's so much that we could exchange if we in America were more diligent about sending our best artists over to various places to as many places who their best artists here, the Chinese, the Indians, the people from South America, the Soviets; they really send their best dancers, best singers, best actors, a lot of folks. If the states send them, and I think they ought to do that, because it makes a big point to a lot of folks

---

*Around that same period BILLY TAYLOR was also commissioned to write a dance suite, eventually entitled "For Rachel" at the University of New Hampshire and a piece entitled "Impromptu" for the Kentucky Symphony. He also composed the score and lyrics for an off-Broadway production of Wole Soyinka's "The Lion and The Jewel" and some dance music for the original production of "Your Arms Are Too Short to Box With God". To date he has written more than 350 songs that include "I Wish I knew How It Would Feel To Be Free" and "Urban Griot."

as to who we are and what we're about and I think they would understand us a lot better.

DM: I read another article. You received an award at Carnegie Hall and it had something to do with the Jazzmobile. BT: Oh in June, yes. It was a very nice gesture on the part of George Wein who decided that he would dedicate the Jackson concert to me and use the money to assist Jazzmobile in an attempt to bring music to more people around the city of New York and the State of New York. DM: Well I noticed in that article something that I never knew. It said: "Among those attending the concert and dinner last night at Carnegie Hall was actor and jazz pianist Clint Eastwood." I never knew Clint was a jazz pianist. BT: Well, as a point of fact, he wasn't there but he, at one point, when his acting wasn't quite as well accepted as it later became, he was a professional pianist, played cocktail lounges, played light jazz like Erroll Garner. The picture that he produced, "Play Misty For Me" was no accident; he really knew the work of Erroll Garner. DM: Well maybe that's why he directed and produced "The Bird" I guess. BT: Yeah. DM: I never realized that he was a jazz musician. Interesting. Maybe there are a lot of hidden jazz musicians out there. BT: There are. DM: And I'm sure there are a lot of them who couldn't make it and they are doing other things. BT: Well, you know a lot of guys have an interest in the music and do other things. Dudley Moore really can play the instrument. He does other things. DM: He's quite a composer too.

BT: Yes he is. I just received a CD the other day from Andre Previn who decided that he's been away from jazz long enough and wants to dip his feet back in the water, so he got together with Joe Pass and Ray Brown and put out a trio record. The music is reaching out for a lot of folks. Reclaiming a few folks.

DM: Reclaiming is about right. Well BILLY, I know that you've got a busy schedule. I can't thank you enough for spending a few minutes with us today.

BT: Well, it's a pleasure to talk to you and I'm delighted that you are keeping the flame burning in your neck of the woods.

DM: Well we are – we're trying.

At the end of the 80's BILLY signed a recording contract with GRP/Impulse records. And would record some of his greatest records including "It's A Matter Of Pride, Dr. T, which featured Gerry Mulligan, a re-release of the previously recorded "My Fair Lady" and "Homage" that would feature the Turtle Island String Quartet; and which received a Grammy nomination in 1996. He had received five more honorary doctoral degrees from the Berklee College of Music, the University of Massachusetts at Amherst, St. John's University, Carlton College and Clark College. His book, "Jazz Piano", was published by Wm C. Brown Co. and he was named art correspondent for the television program "CBS Sunday Morning". He was named an Arts American Jazz Master by the National Endowment For The Arts and formed his own record company, "Taylor Made".

BILLY was nearing his seventieth birthday. He had appeared in many states and in many countries. His live performances and radio and television exposures had made him a known music and visual personality. Dozens and dozens of journal and newspaper articles had been published. The nation's capitol would soon issue a beck and call and he would become intimately associated with an international jazz association as he continued to record and appear with his trio throughout the world.

**ALL PHOTOGRAPHS COURTESY
OF THE LIBRARY OF CONGRESS
AND
DR. BILLY TAYLOR**

Billy & Teddi celebrating

Billy & Teddi greet the New Year!!

Billy & Teddi with Grand-daughter, Ayo

Working at WLIB radio station as a 'Disk Jockey'(DJ)

Radio station interview

Perusing through records

Billy on the piano

Billy Taylor

Billy Taylor

Billy Taylor

Ramsey Lewis & Billy Taylor

Billy Taylor on The David Frost Show

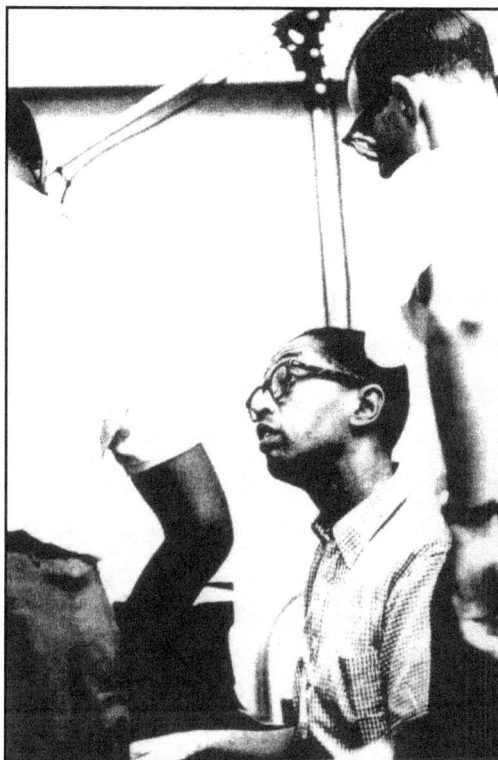

Arranging compositions

Jazz Mobile

Stuart Pope, Gerald Marks (ASCAP Board Members)

The womenfolk

VIII

EDUCATION – THE KENNEDY CENTER INTERNATIONAL ASSOCIATION FOR JAZZ EDUCATION

Through teaching and serving as artist-in-residence, I have learned much from many students who were inquisitive, perceptive, sensitive and extremely talented. – BILLY TAYLOR

DAVE BRUBECK: I am personally grateful that BILLY has been so kind to my son, Darius, giving him advice and counsel, and whether BILLY realizes it or not, really helping him make some vital career decisions. I am sure there are many younger musicians who have also been influenced by BILLY'S guidance.

In 1990 BILLY teamed up with Ramsey Lewis to do a two-piano album "We Meet Again" for CBS Masterworks, Ramsey's record company at the time. Critic Ron Wynn said: "BILLY TAYLOR takes the date, but Lewis shows chops he seldom taps these days."

RAMSEY LEWIS: CBS Masterworks called me and said, 'What do you want to do for your next album?' Well, by now BILLY TAYLOR and I have gotten with each other and we'd started playing some concerts. That was going so well I said to CBS Masterworks, 'I want to do a two-piano album.' 'You do?' I said, 'Yeah.' They said, 'Who with?' I said, BILLY TAYLOR.' 'Great! But we have to have a concept. What's the concept?' I called BILLY. He says, 'Well, we sort of already have a concept.' I said, "What?' He said, 'On our tour now we were playing great compositions written by great pianists who also happened to be great composers.' I said, 'You're right! There's the concept!' I called CBS back. I said, 'Here's the concept.' They say, 'I love it!' I called Chick Corea and he says, 'I'll write something for you!' It's called 'We

Meet Again.' That's the name of the album. So we ended up doing pieces by Duke Ellington, Bill Evans, Denny Zeitlin, Oscar Peterson, and Chick. 1

In February and March, 1990 the Festival In The Sun that was touted as the "American Southwest International Celebration of the Human Spirit" took place at the University of Arizona in Tucson. The featured artists at that conclave were violinist Isaac Stern and 1jazz pianist-composer BILLY TAYLOR among others. In the February 1990 issue of Jazz Times it was announced that the 1989 Samuel Sacks award for distinguished and dedicated service to the musical community went to DR. BILLY TAYLOR. "The honor is bestowed by the ASCAP Foundation in behalf of the New York Community Trust."

MARQUITA POOL ECKERT: I think he has done an enormous amount for American music because for one thing he studied it so not only does he have a natural talent but he's also studied it. He is a great example – I mean a GREAT example for other musicians. He sort of draws people into the musical tent and the music is more than just hearing notes, it sort of speaks to the whole social context. Obviously straight ahead jazz is the thing that he likes to do and yet the way he plays it's not just a narrow definition of it. There's more to it than that. I've never experienced his playing with anyone who didn't come away amazed.

On March 12, the Juilliard Quartet and the BILLY TAYLOR TRIO played a concert at Orchestra Hall. "The famed Juilliard Quartet has been a strong advocate of music by American composers. This concert features the Quartet with pianist BILLY TAYLOR, a jazz veteran who had played with Charlie Parker . . . TAYLOR impressed the audience by playing 'The Man I Love' with only his left hand hitting all the bass notes and the melody. It wasn't until Hilton and Rosengarden joined in at the last of the tune that both of TAYLOR'S hands touched the keyboard." In the March 18, edition of the Daily News, Pablo Guzman indicated that during the tenth anniversary of the Tito Puente Scholarship Fund designating deserving talent to the Juilliard School of Music a dinner dance was held. In addition, Tito Puente and BILLY TAYLOR performed.

DAVID BAKER: I think BILLY is one of the great piano players. He certainly fits the legacy of Tatum. BILLY was a part of all the music of the 40's. I admire him very much because he's been so unselfish in giving back to the field –all the wisdom and ideas gained through some really hard years. He's been so active in every aspect of jazz education. He and Marion McPartland have done as much as anybody.

In the Chicago Tribune of March 11, 1990 BILLY talked about string players and their role in jazz. "He said: 'When most people think about the best jazz players they don't think about string players so this was a chance to get the record straight. When you listen to 'Homage' you'll hear a pseudo gypsy melody and that's a reference to Eddie South who was a great jazz artist but also used to play some terrific gypsy music. He studied in Budapest and really knew the style. There's also a 'cello melody that recalls Oscar Pettiford who played both 'cello and bass. There's a viola solo, which is based on the kind of thing that Stuff Smith used to do down in the lower register of the violin and there are some 'cello passages along the lines of what Slam Stewart used to do when I worked with him.' It almost goes without saying that TAYLOR has constructed the piece to allow for vast improvatory solos and even the notes he put on the paper to be reshaped by the players if they are so inclined. Yet nothing strikes more terror in the heart of a classically trained musician than the prospect of having to play something that's not on the page. 'Yes, we've all been asked to embroider what BILLY has written and that's what we're trying to do' said Mann.' Truthfully the only authentic jazz player among us is Joel (Joel Sminoff), Juilliard Quartet's second violinist. He has some really long and wonderful licks in this piece. As for the rest of us squares, we're trying to do the best we can.' BILLY went on to say: 'One of the great misconceptions people have about improvisation is that it has to be absolutely spontaneous composition. But if you consider Louis Armstrong's performances over the years it is obvious that he worked out some of his improvisations too. You'll hear essentially the same solos from Louis on the same piece over and over again. It's true that if you're a jazz player who improvises every night of your life you become very good at it, so that you don't have to figure it out way ahead. It's like having a conversation with someone – the words just tumble out. The same thing happens in jazz. But that just isn't quite possible for this venture.' TAYLOR is the first to acknowledge that his experiment is not unique. Musical chemists of every kind have been attempting to mix jazz with the classics since 1920, occasionally turning up real gold. Darius Milhaud's Le Creation de Monde, 1923; George Gershwin's Rhapsody In Blue, 1924, and Leonard Bernstein's Age of Anxiety, 1949, stand among the best. And though the critical jury hasn't yet waved in on TAYLOR'S effort there seems to be little doubt the musical public adores such cultural ventures. BILLY TAYLOR said: 'I was just looking for something that would be fun to play, tough to play, and fun to listen to. I'm not trying to come up with some kind of twelve-tone piece, something that was completely inaccessible – that's not the way I play or the way I write. But if we can make a few sparks fly by putting my trio and the Juilliard Quartet together I'll be happy.'"

IRA SABIN: BILLY was really my inspiration for the Jazz Times Conventions. Ever since the first one, back in 1979 when we were still Radio

Free Jazz, BILLY'S been involved. He's been my advisor, always coming up with great ideas. I just took his ideas and ran with them. BILLY'S been responsible for a lot of the formats, topics of discussions and the selection of the early guests of honor. He has always helped. Any time I was really in a bind, I'd call BILLY and he'd come up with the answers. Over the years he's been the guest of honor, the keynote speaker, he's delivered the welcoming address several times and has been the moderator of numerous panels and he's even been a panelist as well! I've known BILLY for quite a number of years and I've always been amazed at the fact that he can do so many things at one time and still do them all well. One time I asked him how he did it and he said, "Well, you do something, you give it all you've got, then you finish it and go on to the next thing!" It was a tremendous piece of advice, but sometimes very hard to follow. 2

The Thursday, April 26, 1990 edition of THE HONOLULU ADVERTISER ran an extended article on BILLY TAYLOR: "For more than thirty years BILLY TAYLOR has spread the musical message as the ambassador of jazz. 'I've been working in the non-profit area since the late 50's for thirty ideas. We have to have more exposure, more attention; we have to get to know the music, know its history. Only then will we know its full potential. Jazz is quite popular in Europe and Asia,' says Taylor. 'It's big in the Soviet Union and in South America but in this country many people seem to loose sight of its importance; in the sense it's unappreciated here by the very people who promote, program and present the music. Yet the fans of the music, and there are legends, buy CD's, listen to the music, support jazz. The numbers are quite large but the problem for jazz is perpetuated by the myth that it's not enjoying the popularity it should. Sometimes I wish there were several of me to do all that I want to do. My preference is playing piano and writing music. I was convinced many years ago, and based on my own experience, that there are many ways to learn other than in the classroom. I find that many of the lasting lessons, the most effective teaching is often from the bandstand.'"

LOREN SCHOENBERG: And then there is his piano playing, which is a whole other thing. The fact that you go back to his early years; his apprenticeship with Art Tatum, and all those things. We did a concert once with David Baker and BILLY at the Kennedy Center and BILLY was great. So we did this gig and BILLY sat at the piano and had this marvelous arrangement of "Take The A-Train." BILLY has this thing in the left hand where he does "Take The A-Train" with four note chords. More than a 10th between the pinky and the left thumb, and it's not just straight parallel harmony in the key of "C", like most people must go up and throw in an F# if they have to – but he really finesses the piece.

On June 1, 1990 the President and Trustees of Long Island University conferred upon BILLY the degree Doctor of Arts. The citation read: "Jazz great, you have played with the best and won raves for your artistry. Your songs are part of this nation's musical gift to the world. The thing that we most applaud is when you share your talents by teaching arts to others." Signed by the President and the Board of Trustees.

MARQUITA POOL ECKERT: I like him very much. One of the things I like a lot about BILLY is that he is such a gentleman. I put a lot of stock in that. He is a real gentleman. He's firm, he knows what he wants; he's focused; he's directed; but he does everything in such a way that you feel guided or steered not pushed. By virtue of the fact that everyone likes him so much, he gets probably most of what he wants just because he's such a nice guy.

In October 1990, in the Weekender magazine of the Century, Daily Times, there appeared an article entitled "THE CHEMISTRY WORKS – RAMSEY LEWIS AND BILLY TAYLOR TOGETHER." The cover story, written by Pat Banks Mitchel who said: "It's not always easy to get old friends together. Everyone is so busy with a schedule of things to do, but when it works its sheer chemistry, that's the teamwork of Ramsey Lewis and BILLY TAYLOR. They will meet at Penn State in Eisenhower Auditorium Saturday at 8:00 P.M. 'It's just the two of us and it swings!' Talking from his home in New York, TAYLOR recalls how Ramsey just called him up and asked casually if he had ever thought about doing something with two pianos. In 1986 these two fast-tempo jazz pianists decided to make time and play a few gigs. Their first appearance together happened in Kansas City, an outdoor music festival in front of 50,000 people. 'That was the most exciting road test!' TAYLOR said, 'the response was immediate.' Next came an album called "But We Meet Again". To date TAYLOR and Lewis still have their own trios and separate musical careers but whenever possible they get together. TAYLOR said, 'It's the first time in months we've played together. Eighty percent is improvised.' He emphasized that while the actual notes may be improvised the structure isn't. They leave room to stretch and have a good time, the chemistry works. They don't even have to look at each other. It's what TAYLOR calls 'spontaneous action.' 'I take a melody, then Ramsey takes a melody.' They listen and pick up clues from the other; still it's a challenge. 'When two piano players try to play together, the problems are multiple, especially for two who lead their own groups,' TAYLOR explained. As part of the new School of Music Lecture Series, 'Music Today', DR. BILLY TAYLOR will hold a discussion at 2:30 P.M. today in the recital hall of the music building on the Penn State campus.

JOHN DUFFY: In 1991 the Sierra Club commissioned me to write music to draw attention to Southeast Utah. CBS Sunday Morning wanted to do a special and they sent BILLY out. He flew out to Salt Lake City, then in a small plane to Southeast Utah. We were out in the wilderness somewhere in these canyons and he's talking to me with the CBS recording engineers and photographers there, and every now and then the tourists would come by, two or three people, and each one of them said: "Hey, BILLY TAYLOR!" way out in the wilderness of Utah. "We see you – we heard your program – we love your program – we see you on CBS Sunday Morning or we saw you on David Frost!" and it was wonderful. He's just a sterling person and a mentor, educator, and a guy who cares deeply and is a great spokesperson for the arts, for music, and of course for jazz.

The BILLY TAYLOR QUARTET consisting of Fred Tillis, soprano and tenor saxophones; Victor Gaskin, bass; Bobby Thomas, drums; and BILLY TAYLOR, piano recorded a CD for DIGITAL PRODUCTIONS entitled AMONG FRIENDS in February of 1991 in New York City. The QUARTET played The Holidays, Confirmation, When Lights Are Low, It Don't Mean A Thing and Harlem Blues.

DR FRED TILLIS: When Victor Gaskin and Bobby Thomas were with BILLY we made a CD. By his being here at the University of Massachusetts at the Jazz In July Workshops what happened is that, by that time I must have been the Director of the Fine Arts Center, or whatever I was doing in administration and he would hear me blow a little bit. He said: "You know Fred, people know you did administration but they don't know that you can play your instrument." He really poured me out of the closet. When I first met him in 1970 the University of Massachusetts had no jazz at all. My composition teacher said: "Fred, I need to find somebody to give some courses in jazz." All he knew was that I was a composer in the Western European tradition. So I set up the first courses in jazz. He wanted a faculty advisor but he had enough respect for me to go along with the program; so that's how we started. It took nine years to get the major through the faculty. I started the big band because that was one way to get people who wanted to play and added a Jazz History and Afro-American music course. I had one ally – a music librarian who played clarinet. Anyway, it was in this context that I said: "I want to do a summer program." BILLY was very interested in doing it and we started a Jazz In July Workshop in Improvisation. That's a very long title but at least it's a title in which only Jazz In July sticks now. I think it started in 1979.

CLEM DEROSA: I would put BILLY in the category of being a jazz ambassador among Louis Armstrong, Clark Terry, etc. I think that's the title, in my mind, I would give him. I remember when he was serving on the committee for the National Endowment for the Arts and, it wasn't that I was in touch with BILLY that frequently, but I would always hear after that he had done good things to help education, to help jazz. I don't remember him teaching in an institution, that kind of a structure. He has that kind of playing facility that from playing back in the 30's you had to use both hands.

In the February 1991 release of Down Beat, John McDonough wrote a piece entitled "BILLY TAYLOR: THE PLAYER'S ADVOCATE". He begin the column with: "Recently BILLY TAYLOR – pianist, educator, composer, and probably the most articulate performer/spokesperson jazz has ever had - was on CBS TV's SUNDAY MORNING. In addition to the usual chat with host Charles Kuralt, he also played with his trio. A few days later, TAYLOR was back at the West Side Broadcast Center, where CBS News New York operations are headquartered.

> 'I saw your piece last Sunday.' A colleague said. 'Good.'
> 'Thanks,' replied TAYLOR. 'Glad you liked it.'
> 'By the way,' the man added, 'you play very well for a news correspondent.'

TAYLOR smiled to himself and walked on. But that's what happens when you lead a double professional identity. You're a kind of one-eyed Jack. Half the world never sees the other side of your face. Most readers of DOWN BEAT know TAYLOR to be a very good news correspondent for a pianist. But the fact is that most of the world probably thinks of him as an erudite, young music critic who has lucidly discussed jazz on TV since 1981. They are, of course, wrong on all counts. AT 69, TAYLOR is not especially young, despite his Dick Clark veneer. Second, he rarely criticizes. And although his erudition has carried both himself and the cause of jazz education a far way, he is fundamentally a fundamentalist bebop piano player . . . Today TAYLOR observes the overwhelming influence of Wynton Marsalis on many young players with pleasure. Does the next decade hold a long line of Marsalis clones, as the '30s produced a string of little Armstrongs? Perhaps, he says, but that's not all bad. 'Wynton offers the young black player a great deal more to use than, say, Miles, who is too much of a self-created individualist to be a real role model. Wynton, on the other hand, has that sense of professionalism, department and control. It is a different, more purposeful kind of coolness. It says achievement is cool and this is music to be taken seriously. He's a renaissance man, and that's what's needed now.' And, of course, it takes a renaissance man to know one."

BILL MCFARLIN: When organizing a tribute for BILLY'S 70th birthday at the 1991 IAJE conference in Washington, D.C., I had the opportunity first-hand to see how may lives BILLY had touched. How many careers he has nurtured and inspired. And how many cultural organizations he has encouraged and supported. Everyone lined up for BILLY'S parade and our toughest job was deciding who could have podium time. The late Charles Kuralt, host of CBS Sunday Morning, prepared a heartfelt tribute and BILLY'S longtime friend and musical partner, Ramsey Lewis, served as host.

On the 19th day of March, 1991, the mayor of the city of Houston, Texas, Catherine Whitmore, issued a proclamation announcing BILLY TAYLOR Day . . . Whereas, the city of Houston commends Young Audiences for bringing DR. TAYLOR to Houston, and extend to him a warm and exuberant welcome, we proclaim March 19, 1991 as BILLY TAYLOR DAY!!

NAT HENTOFF: Musically, that story tells itself. You're always interested in what BILLY'S doing musically. It's like his personality; the way he thinks is the way he talks and the way he is, is the way he plays and it's lucid, clear, full of emotion but very controlled, but not to the point where it's robotic. He has immediacy in his playing.

In the April, 1991 issue of New Times, it was stated that: "BILLY TAYLOR is a dazzling jazz pianist who is one of the worlds best, and he will perform for you in another concert brought to you as part of Cuesta Colleges Jazz Week. TAYLOR had won various awards including an Emmy, two Peabodys and a National Association of Jazz Educators "Man of the Year" designation. He'll tickle the ivories in his own unique and professional style on the concert on Thursday, April 25 in the Cuesta auditorium. He'll play with bassist Victor Gaskin and drummer Bobby Thomas." Also in April BILLY appeared with the Manny Albam All-Star Band in Peekskill, NY at a Saturday, 8:00 P.M. concert at the Paramount Center. On May 20, 1991 BILLY addressed the graduating seniors in Steele Hall at Fredonia State University College.

JANE IRA BLOOM: BILLY'S a really special guy. We've been friends ever since he did a feature on me for CBS Sunday Morning back in the 80's. He means what he says and he's an extremely sincere individual. I think people sense that no matter what he does, whether he's communicating with other musicians or with audiences who are learning about music, it's his complete sincerity and it's a very rare and wonderful thing in the jazz world. I've played a few concerts with BILLY, one time at the Kennedy Center and one time at the Metropolitan Museum of Art in New York, and he's just a completely open and embracing musician. He embraces the contemporary aspects of my music, he's fascinated with all the electronics in the things that I do, which is very different from the musician world that he works in, but he finds musical interests in all kinds of interesting places; it's an open mind. It's a treat to play with him too. I don't even think about age with BILLY, he's young in mind and heart, that's how I look at him. I always go to these events where he's paying tribute to someone, giving out awards and they say, DR. BILLY TAYLOR will now present an award. It's great to finally pay tribute to him!! 3

An honorary Doctor of Music degree was given to BILLY by The State University College at Fredonia, May 18, 1991. The degree was headed State University of New York, and went on to declare: BILLY TAYLOR, you have brought a more profound understanding and appreciation of jazz to literally tens of thousands of Americans through your teaching and broadcasting; at the same time you have contributed significantly to the art of jazz as both performer and composer. Through countless workshops and clinics with young musicians in colleges across the country you have helped a new generation of artists to emerge, and you have worked to bring to these musicians a new audience by taking jazz to the great public through your CBS Sunday Morning Show. The archives of this program are the history of jazz recorded in light and, most appropriately, in sound. They store the scores of interviews you have conducted with jazz artists; with their help you have opened the subtleties and nuances of the music to us all. As a pianist, you have performed with Art Tatum, Dizzy Gillespie, Cozy Cole, Charlie Parker, Miles Davis, Stan Getz and Art Blakey, as well as in solo performances and with symphony orchestras. Your playing won for you the first International Critics Award for best pianist in Down Beat Magazine's annual poll. As a composer, you have written some three hundred songs, among them the renowned, "I Wish I Knew How It Would Feel To Be Free" recorded more than thirty times by artists as diverse as Leontyne Price and Nina Simone, we will hear it today in a new arrangement by faculty of our own School of Music performed by the Symphonic Winds and College Choir. Your work has been honored at the highest levels. You have served at the pleasure of the President of the United States and the National Council on the Arts, you have performed at the White House for visiting heads of State, and Howard University has established the BILLY TAYLOR collection in its Center for Ethnic Music. The State University of New York is proud to join such distinguished company, presenting you with the degree of Doctor of Music. DR. BILLY TAYLOR, you have helped us all to understand a little better how good it can, "Feel To Be Free."

JOHN DUFFY: When BILLY was 70 there was a big celebration, I believe it was at the Kennedy Center, with people honoring him there. Scott Simon was one of the speakers – I think Dave Bailey and David Baker were too – and BILLY was commissioned, through Meet The Composer, to write a work for his trio and the Juilliard String Quartet. He worked with them on improvisation.

In January 1992 BILLY began serving as MASTER OF CEREMONIES for the JAZZ MASTERS awards presented annually by the NATIONAL ENDOWMENT FOR THE ARTS at the annual meeting of the INTERNATIONAL ASSOCIATION FOR JAZZ EDUCATION. He continues to present these awards. On May 1, 1992, calling BILLY TAYLOR the "quintessential eminent scholar" in the field of jazz, the President of the University of North Florida at Jacksonville, Florida, Adam W. Herbert, presented BILLY with the honorary degree, Doctor of Humane Letters.

REVEREND DALE LIND: BILLY has been very helpful to St. Peter's Church. He is on our advisory board. We have a full time jazz ministry at St. Peter's, the only one in the country. He's active in so many things. Every year at the International Association for Jazz Education he has a booth for himself, and one for Sunday Morning and St. Peter's Church as well.

On July 22, 1992 the President of the United States of America, George Bush, awarded the National Medal of Arts to BILLY TAYLOR. The document read: "For his world class jazz artistry, which so many have experienced both live and through radio and television; his frequent service as an ambassador for American Arts abroad; and his staunch advocacy for richer cultural opportunities for every American."

NNENNA FREELON: He recommended me for the Eubie Blake Award after Columbia Records signed me in the 90's. He has sat on panels where I've received grants. He's been in the background supporting me, not just with opening doors but also with some real constructive criticisms, as far as repertoire goes; as far as your listening goes; as far as editing what you do. When you first start out you want to sing everything thats available. He acts with gentleness – not in a way that would so deflate you that you feel like you just want to give it up. He's always encouraging. BILLY'S contribution to American music is unparalleled because of the human being that he is. He could have kept his gifts to himself or made them such that they reflected back on his own genius. Because he has spread it around, he has been so giving and so open with both his knowledge and his talent, he's just made a huge impact. If you look in terms of his musicianship you see excellence; if you look at his role as an educator you see excellence. He has the ability to make it plain and just demystify this music that some would have us believe is so esoteric and hard to understand. I've watched him work with eighth graders and just make it so plain that you would almost have to be blind not to be able to see it. That's a real gift!!

In the Variety Magazine of October 1, 1992 writer Jim Butler talked about Ramsey Lewis and BILLY TAYLOR combining forces to perform jazz classics. He had this to say: "The only thing limited in the expression of a great pianist is in only having two hands and 88 keys. That obstacle is effectively surmounted when Ramsey Lewis and BILLY TAYLOR join forces. BILLY TAYLOR was quoted as saying: 'When the university invited us to perform, Ann Black (OPAS, executive director) asked if we could do something special for the occasion. I welcomed this as an opportunity to play homage to my mentor, Art Tatum. When I first heard him I thought he was using two pianos so I wrote a two-movement suite. Tatum liked to play out of tempo but with a lot of harmony and the first movement reflects that. The second movement is a melody in octaves, a tricky little thing he liked to do. It was interesting for me to try to do something different with his style because he often did it with mine. Turnabout is fair play.'"

TIM OWENS: I put a concert on at the Joseph Papp Public Theater in New York City. It was to be a concert around BILLY, a tribute to BILLY. We called it BILLY TAYLOR and FRIENDS. We constructed a big band, had Frank Wess, BILLY'S longtime friend book these all-star musicians and I also augmented it. I said: "BILLY, we want to have special guests. Who do you want to have?" and he said: "I want Johnny Hartman, Milt Jackson, etc, etc." and of course everybody agreed to do it. "I want Dexter, etc, etc." Anyway, Dexter and Frank did a jam together. They did a tenor battle on "It's A Grand Night For Swinging" and one of the things I remember was just Frank blowing Dexter all up and down the stage . . . winning that battle. Jimmy Owens was in the band, Jimmy Heath was in the band; quite a long list of notable names.

In 1992 Gerry Mulligan joined the trio on baritone saxophone to record an album entitled DR. T for GRP RECORDS. The trio consisted of BILLY, piano, Victor Gaskin, bass, and Bobby Thomas, drums. The quartet recorded I'll Remember April, 'Round Midnight, Line For Lyons, Cubano Chant, Lush Life, Who Can I Turn To? Laurentide Waltz, You're Mine, Just The Thought Of You and Rico Apollo.

The March 1993 issue of Down Beat Magazine featured a review of that album, DR. T, written by Owen Cordle. Mr. Cordle gave the album three and one-half stars (four being the highest rating) and said: "It transpires that the good doctor does his neatly swinging trio thing exactly as usual here. The trim, tastefully decorated lines, the smooth reharmonizations, and the ability to swing with a sense of decorum are part of it. So, too, is his polished tone, expertly reproduced by the TAYLOR, Grusin, and Rosen crew. Mulligan adds luster to the date with warm readings and improvisations on three tracks. On his 'Line For Lyons,' we have not only his bouncy lines but also TAYLOR'S e.s.p. like accompaniment. On Monk's venerable 'Round Midnight' and TAYLOR'S 'Just The Thought Of You", Bari and piano are a congenial match of romantic melodists. The trio tracks range from a meditative 'Lush Life' (with a fine arco opening by Gaskin) to a pair of festive Latin numbers: Ray Bryant's 'Cubano Chant' and Mulligan's 'Rico Apollo.' TAYLOR'S impressionistic beginning to 'I'll Remember April' beautifully sets up the group's dapper signature sound. For those seeking eloquence and comfort in the jazz mainstream, this album is it."

ED THIGPEN: BILLY is very linear. He has wonderful comping skills. I have some records at home of BILLY playing with Coleman Hawkins and different people and he comps his head off. And the solo things! He also dared to just be himself. So his contributions to this music, and this continues today, are endless. He's a gentle warrior, I call it. He's got his stuff together. BILLY is always open to new things. Another thing that's great about BILLY – there's NO scandal with him, no booze, no drugs. I never heard him curse; it wasn't part of his vocabulary. It was how he was brought up. He was brought up in a time when virtue was a plus.

BILLY contributed some historical information for a column written by Sonia Alleyne in Black Elegance of June-July, 1992. The article dealt with Black Women in Jazz and was entitled "IMPROVS ON A FEMININE SCALE." While the emphasis was primarily on women of more contemporary vintage, BILLY had this to say: 'I did a history of jazz for an educational audiovisual and while we were going through some assorted photos, I found pictures of women playing the saxophone and other instruments. This was back in the early 1900's, in the ragtime days.'

HERB WONG: BILLY came to San Francisco to the Herbst Theater in the 90's. I wrote a very extensive set of program notes about him. So he came after a concert that was held there by Max Roach and his string quartet. Well he had his double quartet there, and BILLY was the next major jazz artist, so I was asked to do that. I'd done it for Max and so I did it for BILLY. BILLY liked to come to the Bay area because his daughter lived in Palo Alto. A couple of years ago there was a special event dealing with some achievement, something special about his daughter that he came to Palo Alto. Once in a while we see him coming to Stanford or he goes to the city (San Francisco); he has not played in clubs. He usually plays in big venues (in the Bay area). BILLY is very generous as a player – ego less - in the sense of his playing. He's very generous in sharing space and time for improvised solos – very deep humanism in him. He has this philosophy, I think, that more warmth and communion results from greater sharing rather than the other and that leadership can be quiescent, can be subtle. Back in San Francisco's Herbst Theater, a major venue but not one that has huge, huge capacity, more medium capacity, allowing for more attention, and usually there is a series of performances, usually one with a major jazz artist, the category that BILLY fitted in to in the series. After his engagement there, I remember going back stage with my wife Marilyn to talk to him and he had a lot of family members there and I had not met them before and that's when he introduced me to various members of this family and I said: "Oh, where did they come from?" and he said: "Right down the peninsula where you live, in Palo Alto by Stanford," and I said: "I'll be darned!" and he said: "That's why I always enjoy getting the opportunity to come to this area."

According to the New York Press, in 1992, the BILLY TAYLOR TRIO played at South Street Seaport's Summer Pier on Front Street in New York.

The March 1993, Vol. 23 #2 edition of Jazz Times printed a feature by Ken Franckling entitled, "BILLY TAYLOR'S 50 YEARS IN JAZZ." Mr. Franckling opened by stating: "Time flies when you're having fun. How else to explain the nifty calendar trick that shows it was 50 years ago this summer that BILLY TAYLOR, fresh from Virginia State College, arrived on the New York jazz scene – when Swing Street was in its heyday. When you consider his resume and his itinerary, it is also clear that the youthful TAYLOR, in spite of his 72 years, has not slowed down in his multi-pronged role as a jazz ambassador – through playing, writing, teaching and broadcasting. 'One of the exciting things for me is that I've lived through and participated in a lot of the history. It not only was a privilege, but it has reshaped my life,' TAYLOR says. 'When I first came to New York, my first job was working with Ben Webster in one of those legendary 52nd Street quartets with Sid Catlett on drums and Charlie Drayton on bass. This is stuff I had dreamed about. It just was a wonderful time to come to New York and to be accepted.'

An album, IT'S A MATTER OF PRIDE was recorded for GRP RECORDS in 1993 in New York City by BILLY TAYLOR TRIO with FRIENDS. Joining BILLY, Christian McBride, bass, and Marvin "Smitty" Smith, drums, were Stanley Turrentine, tenor saxophone; Grady Tate, vocals; and Ray Mantilla, conga drums. The group played ten compositions by BILLY TAYLOR.

Bassist Christian Lee McBride was born in Philadelphia, Pennsylvania on May 21, 1972. His father, Lee Smith, is an electric bassist and his great uncle, Howard Cooper, is a professional bass player. Christian played his first job with Lovett Hines when he was 13. He studied at the High School for Performing Arts in Philadelphia from 1985 to 1989 and took private lessons from Neil Courtney of the

Philadelphia Orchestra. He attended the Juilliard School of Music in New York City during 1989-'90. Prior to doing the 1993 record date with BILLY TAYLOR, McBride played with Bobby Watson, Roy Hargrove, Freddy Hubbard, Benny Green and Benny Golson. He was also a member of the group Superbass with Ray Brown, John Clayton, etc.

Marvin O. "Smitty" Smith II was born in Waukegan, Illinois on June 24, 1961. His father is also a drummer and was Smitty's teacher for 2 years. After attending the Berklee College of Music, Smith played with Jon Hendricks, Frank Foster-Frank Wess, Hamiet Bluiett, Kevin Eubanks, David Murray, John Hicks, Bobby Watson, Slide Hampton, Ray Brown, Ron Carter, Dave Holland, Hank Jones, Art Farmer, Benny Golson and others. In the early 90's he recorded with Sonny Rollins, Donald Byrd and toured with the group Sting.

MICHAEL ABENE: I produced two records of BILLY for GRP Records. I got to know him really well through those records. The first record we did was the first time he played with a new rhythm section; his regular guys had been with him for years. He had Christian McBride (bass) and Smitty Smith (drums). The first rehearsal he had he sounded like a twenty-year-old playing with these guys. In fact Grady Tate was singing on a couple of tunes. Grady came in on the rehearsal and couldn't believe it. Grady said: "Yeah!!" He couldn't believe it and BILLY sounded like he was rejuvenated. There was nothing wrong with the other guys. You can play with guys for so long and you kind of fall in with certain things. Stanley Turrentine was on some of the tracks and Grady. Smitty went out to the west coast to do the Tonight Show right after that and Chris was so busy doing his own things. That's when I recommended Chip Jackson. The other drummer at the time was Steve Johns.

In 1993 the Denver Post featured a column by Critic-At-Large Jeff Bradley. Mr. Bradley boldly announced, "BILLY TAYLOR PLAYS JAZZ PIANO BETTER THAN EVER AT POPS CONCERT." He then went on say: "BILLY TAYLOR is best known these days as a presenter on Charles Kuralt's 'Sunday Morning' program. But at the age of 72, the jazz pianist is playing better than ever, as he showed last night in a Colorado Symphony pops concert at Boettcher Hall. The best moments came when TAYLOR joined with bassist Chip Jackson and drummer Carl Allen for some trio jazz, including a rollicking gospel encore that earned them a standing ovation. Earlier, they played a 20-mintues set of three tunes, opening with TAYLOR'S richly chorded intro to 'I'll Remember April' and including a gorgeously voiced treatment of Billy Strayhorn's 'Lush Life' and an up-tempo blues featuring exciting strummed chords by bassist Jackson. TAYLOR is also a composer, and the main work in the two-hour show was his 'Suite For Jazz Piano and Orchestra' dating from 1975. Based on a lovely theme developed in the first movement, the writing for warm strings, rich woodwinds and jazzy brass reminded me of Michel Legrand. The second movement, 'Well It's Been So Long,' gave the trio a chance to wail."

On May 3, 1994 BILLY appeared before the US HOUSE APPROPRIATIONS SUBCOMMITTEE in Washington, D.C. to make a case for funding for the National Endowment for the Arts. This partial report was printed in the bulletin of the American Council For The Arts under the title UPDATE: "Good morning Mr. Chairman and members of the subcommittee. Thank you for the opportunity to testify on behalf of the American Council for the Arts regarding 1995 appropriations for the National Endowment for the Arts. I would also like to thank you for the chance to discuss an issue I feel quite strongly about – the arts as a catalyst to transform the lives of our young people. The arts have the capability to transform a potentially destitute young mind just as they have the capability to transform our socially destitute nation. I have seen this transformation occur, one child at a time. My life as a jazz performer, music educator and teacher has witnessed how an instrument, a paintbrush, or a dance class can positively affect the life of another young person."

"This leads me to what I would like to focus on today: the case for arts in education. During the past few years, critical links have been found between solid arts programs and quality education. For instance, in 1990, the Florida Department of Education found a direct correlation between an active fine and performing arts program, a lower dropout rate and increased student motivation. In Pittsburgh, the Manchester Craftsmen's Guild apprentices young at-risk, inner-city students in the arts, while also teaching them other subjects like math and English. Seventy-five to 80 percent of those students graduate to a higher education in all fields, not just in the arts. And right here in Washington, D.C., at the Duke Ellington School for the Performing Arts, students graduate at an unbelievable 99 percent rate while 90 percent go on to higher education. These studies demonstrate how the arts engage young minds to perform well and stay in school".

"How does this happen? Why is there such a powerful discrepancy between those who study art and those who do not? R. Craig Sautter, professor at the School for New Learning at DePaul University in Chicago, concluded that students who took more than four years of music and arts scored an average of 34 points higher on the verbal section of the SAT and 18 points higher on the math section than the students who took these subjects for less than one year. Jerrold Ross, director of the five-year-old National Arts in Education Research Center at New York University, said: 'There is a naturalness of the arts to childhood. The symbol of the arts in sound and sight are things that children deal with and respond to automatically, unlike the symbols of reading, for example. Students have a natural and immediate link to the things that arts are made of.' In other words, an education in the arts maintains higher levels of interest because it speaks directly to the student. It builds community within school walls, encourages the much-needed respect of teachers, and most importantly, keeps interested students in school."

"Mr. Chairman, on a broader scale, when we examine the United States and its effectiveness to compete globally, we find that our chief competitors, Japan and Germany, devote extensive time to the integration of arts in education. In secondary schools, Japan requires 5 credit hours of arts education while Germany requires 7-9 hours. Meanwhile, the United States only requires 0-2 hours. Simultaneously, Corporate America has sounded the alarm to educate a creative workforce, one that can adapt quickly to a changing marketplace. A recent Labor Department report declared that arts education provides for the core competencies our future workforce needs to succeed: creativity, cooperation, self-esteem, and problem-solving. Employers are becoming more interested in workers who have had some experience in the arts. Finally, the movement towards arts in education appears to be the will of the people. In 1992, an ACA-sponsored Harris poll determined that 90 percent of Americans felt that the arts are an important part of education, while almost 60 percent felt it should be required for graduation".

After providing additional rationale BILLY summed up by stating: "If we agree that NEA (the National Endowment for the Arts) is a strong candidate to promote these changes, then this Congress cannot continue the current process of stagnant funding. We need to choose to invest in the successes described here today and place the NEA in the forefront of this initiative. The NEA has already been cat - $4.23 million – since the President's proposed budget from last year. This cut translated into the elimination of two NEA programs, bringing the total to sixteen programs eliminated since the 1990 fiscal year. The arts-in-education program was forced to be trimmed by over half a million dollars. Along with the cuts and level funding over the last decade, the NEA's purchasing power has decreased 46 percent since 1979. Chairman Alexander has said that the NEA has spawned hundreds of arts organizations since its inception and would need a budget triple its current size in order to serve them all. This occurs at a time when private industry in America is tightening its belt and finding fewer dollars to donate for the arts. Corporate giving has decreased 18 percent since 1985."

"Mr. Chairman, with these sources of funding drying up, the arts community and educational institutions need to look to Congress not only for a funding increase, but to send a message to the states and Corporate America that funding for the arts is a positive solution to many of today's problems. Therefore, on behalf of the American Council for the Arts, I would like to recommend a funding level of $200 million for the National Endowment for the Arts for Fiscal Year 1995. With this modest increase in funding, the National Endowment for the Arts can lead the national agenda for reform in education, crime prevention and the improvement of local economies. And most importantly, it can transform the lives of our future American leaders, one child at a time."

Katherine A. Martin, Dean of the College of Fine and Applied Arts, University of Illinois at Urbana-Champaigne, Illinois stated: "I recommended BILLY TAYLOR for the honorary degree of Doctor of Musical Arts." This was presented to BILLY by the president and chancellor of the University, and chairman of the Board of Trustees. "By the authority of the Board of Trustees of the University of Illinois and upon the recommendation of the Senate at the University at Urbana-Champaigne, BILLY TAYLOR has been admitted to the degree of Doctor of Musical Arts and is entitled to all rights thereto appertaining. Signed by all appropriate officers on May 15, 1994."

DAN MORGENSTERN: BILLY is somebody who has made such an enormous contribution over the years. He's still vital, still a presence on the scene. He was one of the first jazz musicians to really involve himself in making the music more noticed by writing about it, by being what he is always referred to, as being one of the most articulate spokesmen for the music, and has used his considerable influence over the years. At the same time he has managed to have a great career as a player. It's just amazing at how much he has managed to do.

In May 1994 the Gallery of Sound Gazette featured a column by Joe Middleton that opened with the headline: "JAZZ LEGEND MAKES LOCAL APPEARANCE." Joe Middleton opened by saying: "GRP recording artist DR. BILLY TAYLOR recently appeared in Scranton under the sponsorship of the local African American Arts Alliance headed by Dr. Ada Harrington Belton from Keystone Junior College in La Plume. This afternoon gig allowed us to recall an earlier meeting with the famed jazz personality about 15 years ago at the Deer Head Inn in Delaware Water Gap. TAYLOR was doing a piece on Johnny Coates, Jr. for his then National Public Radio series, 'Jazz Alive.' . . . In the April issue of the Gallery of Sound Gazette, we reviewed DR. TAYLOR'S latest album for GRP, 'It's A Matter Of Pride.' Coming soon is the re-issue of a legendary jazz interpretation of Broadway's 'My Fair Lady', called 'My Fair Lady Loves Jazz.' The collection features the 1956 BILLY TAYLOR TRIO and an all-star band arranged by Quincy Jones. In closing our conversation, DR. TAYLOR told us, 'I've really looked at the field. There are a lot of things I've been able to do. But there's a lot more things I want to do.' That's certainly something to look forward to from this 72-year-old master of the art form."

DAVID BAKER: BILLY is such a voracious reader – one of those people in search of all the information and knowledge you can acquire. He's the one for me, in a lot of ways, who had connected the dots. A lot of people have written about these things from an historical standpoint but have not been players. Players are so many times, incapable of articulating but BILLY has put both left brain and right brain together.

On March 18, 1994 American Weekly featured a picture on the front page and announced: "JAZZ GREAT BILLY TAYLOR NAMED ADVISOR TO KENNEDY CENTER." Kennedy Center President Lawrence J. Wilburn said: "Taylor's first endeavor at the Kennedy Center will be a joint project with National Public Radio (NPR), a series of 26 jazz programs with conversation and commentary to be taped at the Kennedy Center and aired on NPR member stations beginning in the fall of 1995. TAYLOR, who is celebrating his 50th year in jazz will serve as artistic director and host for the series which is tentatively titled 'BILLY TAYLOR'S Jazz at the Kennedy Center.' TAYLOR will develop a series of regional and national jazz programs and educational initiatives for the Center." TAYLOR'S renown as a jazz artist is the result of his talent; his fame as a jazz educator has grown out of his prodigious knowledge."

DAVE BRUBECK: BILLY'S involvement at the Kennedy Center in Washington, D.C. continues his good work of promoting jazz and bringing to the art form the prestige of the Kennedy Center. I respect his insistence that jazz be elevated to be recognized as America's truest art form.

BILLY continued to hold his position at the Kennedy Center and established a number of performance programs and education outreach activities at the center. The Millennium Stage at the center is one example of the successful projects he had established to bring jazz to the people. The first year BILLY did jazz programming for the Kennedy Center fifteen concerts were presented – in 1991 twenty-nine programs were given. The years presentations included a solo piano series, a collection of vocalists, an annual women in jazz festival and the BILLY TAYLOR Monday night sessions. The concerts have changed considerably beginning with well-known names, e.g., Lionel Hampton, Dorothy Donegan, Nancy Wilson, Woody Herman to groups headed by Cyrus Chestnut, James Carter, the Charlie Mingus Big Band, and tributes to musicians of the past, e. g., Thelonious Monk. He also developed a number of concert series including The Art Tatum Pianorama, the Louis Armstrong Legacy Series, the annual Mary Lou Williams Women In Jazz Festival, Beyond Category, Betty Carter's Jazz Ahead, and the Jazz Ambassadors Program. The president of the Kennedy Center, Lawrence Wilburn said: "BILLY'S been able, in his own non-preachy way, to develop and teach an audience. In his years here, we've taken the jazz program for zero to sixty. We've really brought the audience along."

DEREK GORDON: I actually met BILLY in 1993 or '94; that's when I began conversations with Mr. Horowitz who ran NRP about doing a radio project. Actually at the time they were looking for individual venues around the country who would be willing to do a show because eventually they wanted people to pay for doing the show; they could come and record the show and they would do maybe twenty different shows in twenty different venues or however many it took to make a season. And coming from the Kennedy Center's perspective my sense was that being one of twenty or twenty-six programs wouldn't really do a lot for the Kennedy Center, really didn't say a lot for the Kennedy Center and it wasn't an opportunity to build anything. What I proposed to Murray Horowitz was we could be interested in doing all of them or none of them. It would certainly be better for them if they knew one venue was going to do all of the shows and it had a hall and they weren't going to have to find twenty different people to agree to do it; and then it could be BILLY TAYLOR'S "Jazz At The Kennedy Center". My interest institutionally was to position the Kennedy Center in terms of jazz because I thought it was something that needed to happen. It had not happened in a significant way, although there had been occasional programs and occasional wonderful programs but there was no on-going consistent jazz presence at the Kennedy Center. So we brokered that deal and that show was the show with BILLY and that's how I got to meet BILLY and began to work with him. Shortly after that time, I approached our then president, Larry Wilburn, about the idea of really using this as a foundation upon which to build a real jazz program for this institution because it's the national center for the performing arts. It seemed a very obvious omission that we did not have a significant jazz program. To Larry's credit, he agreed and after a few minor starts ands stops I got the permission I needed to invite BILLY to be our jazz advisor and then to basically to coordinate all of the jazz programs here at the Kennedy Center and so in that capacity BILLY and I have been able to work together to build various series that we present; the Women's Jazz Festival as well as the radio show that we were doing at the time. And it's been such a tremendous education for me because BILLY knows everyone and everyone respects him.

Rutgers University, of the State of New Jersey, presented BILLY with the honorary degree Doctor of Fine Arts on May 20, 1994. Francis L. Lawrence, President, presented the degree to him.

DEREK GORDON: When we do a "BILLY TAYLOR and Friends" program (Kennedy Center) he is as comfortable with artists of his own generation as he is with the new kids who are just coming down the pike. He had an album out called "Music Keeps You Young" and I think that music has really kept BILLY young because his trio mates are all significantly younger than he is and every once in a while they change – not very often – but they challenge him, they keep him fresh. He always rises to the occasion. Even doing the radio show, he was basically working with a different guest every week and that meant every week he was adjusting to a new individual, maybe learning new music, maybe improvising and trying to feel the rhythms of another person and creating really what was a window on the creative process in the role of being an artist for all of the country to hear on the radio, or in the case of here in Washington, to see in the theater.

On May 23, 1994 The University of Illinois issued BILLY TAYLOR a plaque, which read: Be It Known That BILLY TAYLOR is enrolled as a life member of the University of Illinois Alumni Association and is entitled to all the rights and privileges thereof. Signed by William L. Blake, President.

CHRIS ANDERSON: Having gone to college in a recording program working alongside music students, and jazz being a music form that students study in college, we would hear BILLY'S name pitched around and having my uncle (Jim Anderson) working for him, I certainly heard his name in the early 90's. I began working for him in 1994 as a sound reinforcement man. That's when I first heard him play.

On May 24, 1994 Temple University conferred upon BILLY the honorary degree of Doctor of Music and was signed by the chairman of the Board of Trustees and the president of Temple University in Philadelphia. The citation read: "To WILLIAM EDWARD (BILLY) TAYLOR for an extraordinary lifetime of enriching our lives through music, the common language of humankind, and especially jazz, by the authority vested in Temple University by the Commonwealth of Pennsylvania, and with the consent of the University Board of Trustees, I confer upon you, BILLY TAYLOR, the degree of Doctor of Music, honoris causa, with all the rights, privileges, responsibilities and duties pertaining there unto." Signed by Peter J. Liacouras, President, Temple University.

JIMMY HEATH: My longest duration experience with BILLY was during the Jazzmobile because after that he went down to the Kennedy Center where I played with him and I played with BILLY at something at his alma mater, Virginia State University, with a big band for homecoming and they honored BILLY.

May 26, 1994 The John Hopkins University presented the George Peabody Medal for Outstanding contributions to music in America to BILLY TAYLOR accompanied by a citation.

LLOYD PINCHBACK: I'm really impressed with his music. He has a style of playing like counterpoint. He has one hand doing one thing and the other hand doing a completely different rhythm. Complete independence. I haven't heard any players do it in the same way that he does. BILLY is an educator. He spreads the word of jazz all over the world. He's taken American music overseas; since the early 50's he's been doing this; and just basically been spreading the word of jazz as an ambassador.

The May 28, 1994 edition of Billboard Magazine's Artist & Music Section' Jazz Blue Notes, a column by Jeff Levenson mentioned: "DR. BILLY TAYLOR has added three more honorary degrees to his collection (that makes an even dozen, plus one – an earned doctorate). They come from the University of Illinois, Rutgers University, and Temple University. The pianist also received a Peabody Medal for Johns Hopkins University, making him (I assume) the most-honored jazzman in academic history or the most academic in jazz history.

DICK HYMAN: We've shared the stage quite a few times for George Wein, the San Francisco Jazz Festival, Sarasota Jazz Society, and various places where we've played my arrangements for four pianos. He's had me on his television show at Kennedy Center and CBS Sunday Morning. Although we've developed different specialties, we come from the same Art Tatum-to-bebop background, and I think I can always identify his playing. And through all this time we've shared occasional social events with our wives – we are both long married. I very much admire BILLY for his playing, his career as a performer and educator, and because he stands for what he believes.

On Saturday, July 2, 1994 Stephen Holden reviewed a jazz festival at Carnegie Hall in New York and wrote an article for the New York Times entitled "HONORING BILLY TAYLOR'S LIFE IN MUSIC: Fifty Years As Pianist And Composer, Teacher, and Historian." Mr. Holden opined: "Midway in a concert at Carnegie Hall on Thursday celebrating BILLY TAYLOR'S 50 years in jazz, the pianist, composer and bandleader was presented with a plaque by his record company, GRP, praising his work as a musician, historian and educator. It was a fitting accolade for the man who founded the influential jazz education organization Jazzmobile 30 years ago. And during the show, which was part of the JVC Jazz Festival, Mr. Taylor played all three roles with an engaging ease and bonhomie. Where the majority of jazz musicians onstage simply perform their music without bothering to place it in a historical or stylistic context, Mr. TAYLOR provided annotation that was useful without being labored. The composer dedicated the evening's longest and most ambitious piece, 'Homage,' in which his trio was joined by the Turtle Island String Quartet, to the influential jazz violinists Eddie South and Stuff Smith . . . In all the instrumental combinations, Mr. TAYLOR'S musical personality shone through. A musical extrovert who is naturally and fluently melodic, he writes music that is bright, blunt and friendly and that rarely pauses to reflect. Both his trio and band arrangements favor instrumental textures that are full, yet clear and ringing. And on Thursday Mr. TAYLOR displayed a vivacious stage personality that matched his music. It was hard to believe that he will be 73 on July 24."

HILDE LIMONDJIAN: From his young days at the Blue Note to his active participation in projects that have kept jazz alive, such as Jazzmobile, to the way he has made jazz real and palpable to a wide audience through his work on CBS Sunday Morning where he brought us new, emerging talent as well as insight into great names in music (Duke, Ella, Aretha), BILLY TAYLOR has been a great champion of music.

The Vail Trail's Daily Options of July 22, 1994 highlighted an article by Jonathan Leseer. Mr. Leseer's piece was headed: "THE DOCTOR IS IN; JAZZ LEGEND BILLY TAYLOR COMES TO VAIL CELEBRATING 50 YEARS IN MUSIC." Leseeer opened with: "Does BILLY TAYLOR look more like a professor, an actor or a jazz cat? DR. T is all that and more, and at 72, he's just reaching the peak of his careers. On July 25, the eve of his 73rd birthday, TAYLOR will be tickling the ivories as well as the hearts and souls of Vail's music-loving population at Ford Park Amphitheater. The show, part of the Bravo! Colorado Music Festival, shouldn't be missed . . . Things have been going real well lately for The Doctor. He's got a new record label (GRP), and, after playing with the same trio for 20 years, TAYLOR is now playing with two new musicians: Chip Jackson on bass, and Steve Johns on drums. 'It makes us sound different,' he says. 'I wanted to go in new directions; not better, just different.' TAYLOR and his wife of 48 years, Theodora, also have a newlywed daughter, Kim, currently teaching law `at Stanford University. 'It's very nice right now,' he says, 'because when you get to be my age, people say, 'He's been around long enough to learn something – let's check him out.'"

NANCY WILSON: To hear him, as a teacher, and to get inside his head and know the things he knows and the things he's aware of . . . I had my more nurturing and most wonderful conversations with BILLY TAYLOR in a car driving from one place to another, especially since we were at NPR together during the 90's. Just to hear him talk about the early Washington (D.C.) days,

Ellington, and to drive through Washington, D.C. with him in a car and have him tell about back in those days – nothing can replace that.

The TURTLE ISLAND STRING QUARTET joined the BILLY TAYLOR TRIO to do an album for GRP RECORDS entitled HOMAGE on October 10 and 11, 1994. BILLY'S trio included Chip Jackson, bass, and Steve Johns, drums. The group recorded the ten-section composition Step Into My Dream.

Charles Melvin Jackson (Chip Jackson) was born in Rockville Center, New York on May 15, 1950. He studied at the Berklee College of Music in the early 70's and played with John LaPorta and Herb Pomeroy. During 1972-73 he worked with Gary Burton and played on the Woody Herman Band in 1973-74. During the latter part of the 70's he played with Chuck Mangione, Horace Silver, Betty Carter, Thad Jones-Mel Lewis and Hubert Laws. In the 80's Chip Jackson played bass with Stan Getz, Gary Burton, Elvin Jones, Al Di Meola and Elvin Jones. He played with Roy Haynes before joining the BILLY TAYLOR TRIO.

Drummer Steve Johns (Stephen Samuel Johns) was born in Boston, Massachusetts on November 25, 1960. Johns studied with Alan Dawson, attended the New England Conservatory of Music and played with Vic Firth, Fred Budda, Jim Pepper, Gary Bartz, the Count Basie Orchestra, Jimmy Owens, Nat Adderly and Thomas Chapin. Prior to joining the BILLY TAYLOR TRIO he worked with the Living Time Orchestra, Stanley Turrentine, Larry Coryell, Diana Schuur and the Mingus Epitaph Orchestra.

MICHAEL ABENE: The second record I produced for GRP Records was with BILLY'S Trio and the Turtle Island String Quartet. It was dedicated to players like Stuff Smith. I got be to pretty confident about certain things. We talked music and he was amazing because his hands, I've never seen anything with such a long reach. He's got an amazingly long reach and really pretty sense of playing ballads and everything, really pretty sense of music. I've seen him do like a 12th with his left hand; play three or four note chords with his left hand, rolling right along. 10ths are nothing for him from what I've seen! He's got a really nice touch and he is ageless. This, the second record we did was with Chip (Jackson) bass, and Steve Johns, drums, and the string quartet. This was kind of an interesting record. I didn't feel it was promoted really well but it was a great idea with the string quartet and BILLY'S trio. BILLY did all of the writing. My wife (Gretchen) contracted the date and we did everything through GRP. It was fun working with the Turtle Island group and BILLY did all the orchestrating. They tried to get a whole tour going, but it (the record) just wasn't promoted well enough. BILLY was really open-minded about things and I felt he was real easy, obviously a very bright guy. He had certain ways he wanted to do things that made sense and it was just a pleasure to work with him. When Larry Rosen asked me to do these records I said: "Yeah, I'd love to work with the guy," Just to talk to him and get in his head because knowing him as a teenager I respect his musicianship a whole lot.

In November 1994, BILLY'S record company, GRP RECORDS, INC., released a statement BILLY made in explanation of HOMAGE. BILLY stated: "In my formative years I was privileged to work with and be taught by many of the greatest musicians jazz has produced. This album pays homage to some of them. The title composition HOMAGE is my tribute to violinists Eddie South and Stuff Smith, bassist Slam Stewart, 'cellist and bassist Oscar Pettiford, percussionists Sid Catlett and Jo Jones and the pianist whose influence is omnipresent in all my work, Art Tatum. For me, no string players every played with more lyricism than Eddie South and Slam Stewart and no players ever swung with more conviction and power than Stuff Smith and Oscar Pettiford. No percussionists played more melodically or swung more elegantly than Jo Jones and Sid Catlett and it was Art Tatum's innovative harmonic devices that inspired me to explore the piano voicings such as those found in the second movement of HOMAGE. Each of these jazz masters liked to organize his music in ways that used improvisation as a compositional tool, so I constructed HOMAGE that way."

"In 1990, at the suggestion of the Juilliard String Quartet, I was commissioned by the Civic Center of Madison, Wisconsin to compose a piece for string quartet and jazz ensemble. It was an exciting opportunity to climax the 10th anniversary of the Madison Civic Center by premiering a jazz composition written for and performed with one of the world's greatest quartets. I am greatly indebted to Robert Mann, Joel Smirnoff, Samuel Rhodes, Joel Krosnick, Victor Gaskin, and Bobby Thomas for their contribution to the creation of this work; and to Tracy Silverman, Darol Anger, Danny Seidenberg and Mark Summer of the Turtle Island String Quartet, together with Steve Johns and Chip Jackson, for infusing their individual and collective spirits into the current version of HOMAGE."

"The second composition, STEP INTO MY DREAM, has a life of its own, but for me it is incomplete without the dancers who supply elements basic to its completion. When we perform together there is an interaction which gives the work an energy, a feeling of spontaneity and immediacy that changes with each performance. The dancers behave in many respects like jazz musicians, adding their creativity to ours and using their vocabulary to help us create a composition that is as much theirs as it is ours. Though David Parsons and I conceived and structured the work, we are indebted to Gail Gilbert, Jaime Martinez, Elizabeth Koeppen, Patricia Kenny, Christopher Kirby, Mathew Rodarte, Amy Marshal, Mia

McSwain, Robert Battle, Steve Johns and Charles "Chip" Jackson. STEP INTO MY DREAM had its world premiere at the Krannert Center for the Performing Arts/ University of Illinois at Urbana-Champaign on March 25, 1994 in honor of its 25th anniversary."

LOREN SCHOENBERG: I think he is one, as everybody knows, one of the great national treasures. Of course, CBS Sunday Morning with Charles Kuralt and Charles Osgood, all those years, all those profiles, all those magical things he's done, his radio show on WLIB that people still talk about. At that point it was like a shining light for intelligence and musical tastes, especially in the 1960's. I'm not even sure how many people have spoken or thought about his very important influence as a figure during those particular times. I was gratified when that album came out recently of Coltrane's last performance, in which BILLY was the M.C. BILLY was there because Coltrane wanted him there, and those marvelous TV shows BILLY did in the 50's, "The Subject Is Jazz." I don't understand why those things don't come out in a marvelously produced VCR; those things with Ben Webster, Tony Scott, Lee Konitz and Warne Marsh, all these things. BILLY did so many unique things. He is a unique figure; no one does all these things. And I can tell you from a personal level. When I was his guest at his lecture series at the Metropolitan Museum of Art, how incredible his skills were at putting people at ease and getting the best out of them and making audiences understand. That's why he's such a great teacher because he teaches without people even realizing that he is teaching.

The University of Pittsburgh presented an undated certificate to BILLY TAYLOR that read: "In recognition of your contributions to the growth and development of jazz." The document was signed by a number of university officials.

CHIP JACKSON: We went through some of BILLY'S music – kind of an audition, but not really. Really just to see what it felt like and BILLY loved it. We brought something fresh to what he was doing. We ultimately made several records. The first one was with a string quartet. It was called HOMAGE. Then we did one called MUSIC KEEPS US YOUNG for ARKADIA RECORDS and then the new one, URBAN GRIO. BILLY is really a pianist – he has total command of the instrument. I feel sometime when I'm playing with him its almost like playing with an organ player – there is so much going on there. He has such command of the piano.

A plaque inscribed as follows was presented to BILLY: "This official IAJE Award is presented to BILLY TAYLOR for outstanding service to jazz education at the 22nd International Conference, Anaheim, California, January 12-15, 1995, International Association of Jazz Educators.

JIM ANDERSON: At one point in the mid-90's BILLY and his trio and I were flying out to Sacramento to do a concert and BILLY sat and talked to me about Martin Luther King; about how it was like in the mid-60's in the middle of Alabama. I always liked those trips we would take because he would talk about those days and what it was like. He was with King and was reporting back to the radio station he was working with so he was almost acting as a reporter. He was a witness to so much.

In September 1995 BILLY spoke at the convocation of Appalachian State University in Boone, North Carolina. The title of his speech was "Jazz; A Metaphor for American Culture". He spoke about the positive influence teachers have had on his life. For him, he said: "Teachers have been an important part of my life. One of the things they do is to teach you how to think." His address focused on how people around the world have analyzed American culture through jazz. He used the example that jazz is democratic as each member of a jazz band is just as important as the other. He concluded his address by urging students to begin their search for the answers to the problems that plague modern society. "You personally can make a difference."

LARRY RIDLEY: Sometimes people who have been as diversified as BILLY has been, in wearing so many different hats and wearing them well – I think sometimes his musical attributes become overshadowed by his involvement in some of these other areas. But, without as doubt, you know like I've played with so many great piano players through the years, and been blessed with that in my experience, and BILLY'S right up there with the greatest of them and his music never suffers. I think that's always been the bottom line with BILLY. The playing. And that's like now, even with him doing what he does, like the occasional thing on CBS and being at the Kennedy Center and all those kinds of things, he still is very much BILLY TAYLOR, the piano player. He's playing better than ever! I was with him and his wife Teddi just a few months ago (we were at a function together) and he played something and I said to Teddi: "What are you feeding this guy?" 'Cause it seems like he's gotten stronger and he's playing better than ever. He's got a nice group – the trio that he has now (2002). Chip's a beautiful bass player.

TIM OWENS: We spent a lot of time on the road together; we took the show on the road a lot. BILLY'S always a joy to travel with, over dinners, etc. He's very much a conversationalist about a lot of different things aside about jazz. He's a very knowledgeable man. He's got a good opinion and he's always eager to meet people, make them feel comfortable, make them feel special. Whenever we did shows on the road, we almost invariably had receptions at each one. BILLY would be dead tired but would go into a reception, talk to people, wait until it was nearly over. He's always a very personal, very open, a very accessible person. That was the nice thing about working with him because we really needed that. He understood the value of promotion. I also used BILLY when I was working at WETA in Washington (D.C.). I created birthday tributes to jazz musicians and had BILLY TAYLOR narrate them for me. These were tributes to Duke Ellington, Kenny Clarke, Miles, etc; we did fifty-five of them all together. They were of very short duration but again BILLY would take the scripts, personalize them, and they were great!

The Kennedy Center commissioned BILLY to compose a work for jazz trio and symphony orchestra in 1995. The work "Theme and Variation for Jazz Trio and Symphony Orchestra" was premiered at the Kennedy Center on April 23, 1995 and featured the BILLY TAYLOR Trio and the National Symphony Orchestra conducted by Leonard Slatkin.

MICHAEL ABENE: From BILLY'S views on education and political views I think he probably hasn't gotten the recognition, as great a pianist as he is, because when you talk to pianists, most pianists talk about people like Herbie Hancock, Chick Corea, Bill Evans, and they seem to bypass BILLY'S contribution but if you talk to Herbie Hancock and you talk to Chick Corea they would say BILLY TAYLOR. He's always been in the forefront but for some reason most piano players say he has influenced them. He's made a fabulous contribution to jazz education and making jazz a "legitimate" music. He's always been outspoken about that. When he was a disc jockey he always had these positive views about the music and the thing I really like about him too, besides his musical demeanor, is his personnel demeanor – the way he carries himself. He always makes a terrific impression, he's very bright, and it's not like what you think of as a typical jazz musician from years ago.

On November 10, 1995 in the weekend edition of the Phoenix Gazette the headline stated: "TAYLOR-MADE, A CHAMPION OF JAZZ." The article by Salvatore Caputo declared: "DR. BILLY TAYLOR may be America's foremost jazz educator. He's not afraid to create forums for jazz to be heard and taught. But being an educator is not his primary role. 'While that's an important part of what I do; but basically I'm a pianist-composer.' TAYLOR says from his New York office. 'Every thing I do starts from there.' Everything included concerts by his trio today and

Saturday. His latest broadcasting project is BILLY TAYLOR'S JAZZ AT THE KENNEDY CENTER, 'Most of jazz audience doesn't get backstage at a festival or at a concert', he explains, 'They want to know basic things; 'How do you guys know when to start and stop? What comes first – do you learn the melody or the rhythm or the harmony?' TAYLOR doesn't think teaching the music in school will cut it off from its popular roots. 'I can say unequivocally, many of the kids that have gone through various kinds of schooling are better musicians than people who do not.' However, he doesn't discount such self-taught whizzes as Erroll Garner and Wes Montgomery. 'There were a lot of musicians who fell under that category who were wonderful musicians. School is not the only place you learn.' That's why jazz works to get jazz into the national media. BILLY is critical of TV's avoiding jazz saying: 'Only Bravo and Black Entertainment Television, two cable television networks, regularly present the music. Why is there so little jazz on the air? Greed is a one-word answer. They, the broadcasters, don't care about programming.

They just say, 'Hey, is this working? Fine, lets do a whole lot of that and make all that money.' So, either the successful is repeated. The worst part of what we get on radio and television is that it makes young people – who don't know any other point of reference – unaware of the fact that there is more to choose from. TAYLOR argues that kids do the best they can with what they're given and sometimes invent forms - such as rap - because they don't like anything they hear. Then they say: 'Hey, why are they doing that?' Because they haven't given them anything better.'"

COBI NARITA: For women, the main thing BILLY did was that he got the Kennedy Center to start a Mary Lou Williams Jazz Festival in, I think, 1995. But before that, he's always been supportive of women musicians, always. If he was booking anything he would book a woman's group in it. So you just can't say a bad thing about him; there's nothing bad to say about him.

NAT HENTOFF: I can't think of anything even remotely negative to say about him. He goes out of his way to help. He's been one of the few male jazz musicians who, for years, has been pointing out and trying to do something about the fact that female jazz musicians don't get their due regard. Like, for example, the Lincoln Center Jazz Orchestra. Wynton has not had one full time woman jazz musician. He (BILLY) helps younger players. He's just perfectly straight forward, lucid, he's almost unbelievably a good guy.

By the early years of the 21st century BILLY had established a number of programs at the Kenney Center including: Distance Learning By Satellite, What To Listen For In Jazz, Betty Carter's Jazz Ahead Program, Mary Lou Williams' Women in Jazz Festival, and the Jazz Ambassadors Program.

TIM OWENS: As to the genesis of BILLY TAYLOR'S "Jazz At the Kennedy Center", BILLY had been doing this thing at the Metropolitan Museum of Art in New York City, four or five times a year, where he would have a special guest in and they would play some and talk about the music. When we were creating jazz programming again on National Public Radio in 1994-95 I said: "Why don't we do something with BILLY?" So I went to BILLY and I said: "What do you want to do?" and he said: "Well I'd kind of like to do this thing I do at the Metropolitan Museum of Art, only I'd like to make it into a radio show." So that's how that sort of idea came about. We did a pilot in Pittsburgh at the Manchester Craftsmen's Guild and (Gerry) Mulligan was the special guest. They performed great together and it kind of gave us an opportunity to work the bugs out and then we partnered with the Kennedy Center. We were very, very interested in the educational component of this and we launched it and started recording in 1995 with Frank Wess as the first guest. We staged it as a radio show and it's been on since then. So that's how BILLY TAYLOR'S "Jazz AT the Kennedy Center" came about. I think he saw it as a forum, not only for himself and his trio to perform with all these different folks, but as a way of exposing people to names that are quite well known in the field but, more importantly, names that are not so known in the field. I think of various performers whose careers grew due the exposure received, people calling them for lessons, gigs, etc. That's the true educator. The extent to which you can take, create a show, and also add the national broadcast aspect to it, it's interesting. BILLY'S got an eye for talent or an ear for talent, and he is able to find these up and comers. It's an entertaining and fun show; it's a joyful show. Interestingly the audience for public radio is getting bigger but the number of stations carrying the programming is getter smaller.

The album MUSIC KEEPS US YOUNG, released by ARKADIA RECORDS, was completed on August 6 and 8, 1996 by the BILLY TAYLOR TRIO. Chip Jackson, bass, Steve Johns, drums, and Billy Taylor, piano played I Wish I Knew How It Would Feel To Be Free, Wouldn't It Be Loverly, Caravan and Body and Soul.

ALAN BERGMAN: BILLY is a jewel. He's made a great contribution to music in terms of having stayed with the trio format – he's discovered so many great players. He's a great composer; he's also made a contribution to race relations in America. He has in his mild, but firm way, always advocated a position for black musicians; he has given tremendous amounts of time and money to black colleges. He goes there, he plays, he conducts master classes, he takes young artists under his wings, he writes, he is totally devoted to that cause as he is totally devoted to the cause of jazz being America's Classical

Music, America's Treasure; he was involved with getting that congressional decree, and he still has this very idealistic view that jazz can become a popular art form. He has contributed so much to the music, the history, the education of young people, very much to race relations in a positive way; he has the ear of politicians, of educators, of writers, of media people; he has real roots in North Carolina, Washington, D.C., New York, and BILLY is one of the few, if not the only, jazz musician who makes a real good living just in the United States. He can command major fees in important venues like the Kennedy Center, the Metropolitan Museum of Art; he appeals across the board to a jazz and a classical audience. I think he's a very influential jazz artist.

In 1996 Lionel Hampton was saluted at the Apollo Theater for his long tenure in music. The New York Post talked about it in its Thursday, March 21 issue saying: "The amiable and informative BILLY TAYLOR was not only an ideal M.C, his piano playing was unusually commanding."

PHIL SCHAAP: He is so beautiful. The one thing that people don't realize about him – because he's got such friendliness – he has an unusual capacity for energy. It's subtle because of the smile. There was nothing subtle about Lionel Hampton's energy level but there's something subtle about BILLY'S. He's got a lot of energy. He's irrepressible.

KETER BETTS: In most fields people strive to learn more and run into a blank wall. They try to go over the wall but can't. They try to go higher and higher and try to got around it and its gets taller and wider and finally they are left with two alternatives. Either to go through it or stand there and be blocked for the rest of their lives. The ones that go through it come back periodically and reach through that wall and pull somebody else through. So BILLY'S main contribution has been as an educator; he takes his knowledge and his expertise and keeps coming back to that wall and pulling people through.

In the Aug.-Sept., 1996, Vol. 3, No. 5, edition of JAZZ PLAYER Bob Bernotas wrote an eight-page article on BILLY in which he asked: "What encourages you about the jazz scene today?" BILLY replied: 'The fact that we have so many young people who are so serious about it, who have done in their own way things which have broadened the audience to their generation and beyond. And I'm glad to see this magazine. Just to look at it, it would seem to be something that my students at the University of Massachusetts should be aware of, and I'm certainly going to make them aware of it. And this August-September 1995 issue, "Jazz 'Rhythmic Phrasing and Shaping," is very important. "A private lesson with Horace Silver," hey, I'll take that. "Hybrid Voicings and Constant Structures in Arranging," that's wonderful. These are things that I, as a teacher can hand to a student and say.

'Look, I want you to check out so-and-so-and-so. I've been talking to you about voicings, how I want you to voice. I want you to look at this 'Hybrid Voicings' article and show me what you learned from that. How is that different from what you do?' These kinds of things are invaluable. I'm so glad to see magazines like this coming out.'"

DAVE BRUBECK: BILLY is, above all, one of the greatest jazz pianists who has ever performed, and he continues to play in top form today.

ROBIN BELL STEVENS: BILLY'S contribution to American Music is on many levels. As an educator, and what he has done in creating – he created the jazz program at the Kennedy Center – by being the music director at the Jackie Robinson Jazz Festival, by his performances, by the lecture-demonstrations he has done, by the music and jazz programs he created at UMass in Amherst. I think that he has been able to be a part of a movement, that I believe is growing, of bringing jazz to the level where number one, it is respected as the art form that it truly is and, also as importantly, although BILLY has never verbalized it this way, I believe he is part of that mission as is Jazzmobile, where I now work. When I was growing up and I dare say a lot of people, if music was taught in your school, when you went to have your 'music appreciation' course it was a given that it was European Symphonic music. Jazz should be an important part of that curriculum.

Also during August 6 and 8, 1996 in New York City, BILLY did a solo album entitled TEN FINGERS – ONE VOICE for ARKADIA RECORDS. He recorded a number of tunes including Wrap Your Troubles In Dreams, Joy Spring and Tea For Two.

NAT HENTOFF: He did a solo album for Arkadia Records. I think it was his first and only solo album and I did the notes and it was a revelation because until then, although he had been extremely proficient and a wonderful accompanist, it was like he was young again. First of all, it's hard, unless you're an extraordinary musician, to hold attention as a soloist for an entire album. More than that; the ideas kept coming, the emotion was there, it was as if, I thought, as though as if he were liberating himself.

SHELLY BERG: I have some intense memories of BILLY. We went on some TV shows together when I was President of IAJE (1996-'98) and some of which he performed live on. He's such an amazingly polished player. My most intense memory of him was when his trio performed at an IAJE Conference and, I didn't realize it but, I guess he played at Billy Strayhorn's funeral and he played "Take The A-Train", as a ballad, at the funeral. Well, he played that at the IAJE Convention and, when an artist of the capability of BILLY, immediately transporting themselves back to a time and place . . . it felt like we were all at Billy Strayhorn's funeral again. It was so emotion-filled, so poignant. The nearly 3,000 people in the room were totally captivated and awed by the performance. Now he continues to educate the mass population through the CBS Sunday Morning and the Kennedy Center. So it's never ending for him. He's the perfect person to do it. Having gone on television shows with him and watched him extemporaneously speak or get up to MC a concert – there are very few individuals who are so brilliantly extemporaneous as BILLY is, and it makes him a fabulous ambassador for jazz music.

CHIP JACKSON: In the late 90's we played in Cuba and had a great time there at the HAVANA FESTIVAL. Chucho Valdez came up and played two tunes with BILLY – two pianos. The people just loved it. The two of them went at it, trading back and forth. With BILLY'S historical background, you know he played with MACHITO and is really into the AFRO-CUBAN thing. That was really fun! Of all the bandleaders I've ever played for BILLY TAYLOR is by far the finest human being.

The JazzTimes, October, 1996 release highlighted an article by Pret Primack headlined "DR. T AT 75: A TAYLOR-MADE TRIBUTE". Primack opened his writing: "BILLY TAYLOR has touched the lives of many during his half century plus in jazz as pianist, composer, author, activist, teacher, lecturer and actor, as well as radio and television personality. Although he turned 75 this July 24th (an event celebrated with a weeklong special guest extravaganza at the Blue Note in New York), he shows no signs of slowing down. In fact, he's as busy as he's ever been. Check out his current agenda: Three weeks a month, he performs as a solo artist or with his trio (featuring Chip Jackson on bass and Steve Johns on drums). He's also on the faculty at the University of Massachusetts where he received his doctorate in education (he has 15 other honorary doctorates at last count). And when the playing venue is collegiate, he manages to do an interview with the campus station and a workshop as well. BILLY has been on Public Radio for almost 20 years, hosting Jazz Alive, Taylor Made Jazz, Dizzy's Diamonds, Jazz Legacy and his current adventure, BILLY TAYLOR'S JAZZ AT THE KENNEDY CENTER. On television, BILLY continues to provide features on jazz musicians for SUNDAY MORNING, the acclaimed CBS program where he's enjoying a 15-year run. BILLY is also the jazz artistic advisor for the Kennedy Center, where in the past year, he's presented an Art Tatum Piano Panorama and a Mary Lou Williams Women's Jazz Festival. And let's not forget the appearances he makes with symphony orchestras and his compositions, which he writes on computer. The question is: when does this man sleep?"

WARREN CHIASSON: I've been on concerts where BILLY has played. Mark Morgan, who is a jazz promoter, gave a benefit for David Amram in Westchester in January 1998 or '99. David's house had burned down and there was a big benefit for him. Chuck Mangione, BILLY TAYLOR, and I, as well as others, played for him. I played with an all-star group. I've been meeting BILLY on the street and playing for him from time to time so I am very well aware of his mastery of the piano.

In 1997 Florida Memorial College in Miami, Florida conferred the honorary doctorate on BILLY.

CHRIS ANDERSON: What stuck me was his generosity as an employer. When I first started working for him out of college, the rate he paid me per day was significant, certainly relative to anybody else, and that was on an introductory basis. After I did a few shows for him he almost doubled the rate. I took a brief timeout working for him and had a friend of mine do his sound while I was off on another project. When I came back and started working for him again in 1997 he almost doubled my pay again – about $700 a day doing sound reinforcement. I was always impressed when he first hired me he said: "You're not the sound man as far as your treatment is concerned. You're the fourth member of the trio. If we get invited to dinner you're invited to dinner. The hotels that I'm put in you're put in. He was always very generous that way. He's also a walking jazz encyclopedia.

In the February 1997 issue of The Instrumentalist, Catherine Sell Lenzini conducted an interview with BILLY that resulted in an article entitled "SWING, BEBOP, and JAZZ AS PART OF THE CURRICULUM". Lenzini asked: "How do you defend jazz as an essential component of music education?" BILLY responded: 'Many jazz pieces are more difficult to play than most classical repertoire, and that's why jazz is generally not played well. People think jazz is easy because it's just eighth notes in some cases, but without an understanding of how those eighth notes should be played, the music sounds like a child practicing. When jazz is played well, it moves to a different level. I wrote HOMAGE for the Juilliard String Quartet, and the members approached this jazz piece in the same way that they approach the music of Bartok, Mozart or Beethoven. Their efforts took this piece to another level. There's no excuse anymore for omitting jazz from a music education program. Numerous books have been written about jazz on every level, and anyone who has had a reasonable music education can learn to teach jazz. There are how-to books and play-along records all over the place. David Baker of Indiana University has written extensively on how to play bebop, with in-depth books about the harmonic, rhythmic, and melodic structures that make up bebop phrases and bebop playing. Jamey Aebersold has a series of books and play-along recordings, so a music teacher doesn't even have to be able to play jazz to teach it. Any music educators who are not teaching the music that is certainly America's classical music are not doing their jobs . . .' Lenzini: "What aspect of jazz is the most important to include in music education?" BILLY: 'One thing we should learn from jazz is that it is inclusive rather than exclusive. Some jazz sounds like classical music, while other forms sound like country and western music. In India a few years ago I heard a type of Indo-jazz. I would like to see music educators become familiar with jazz as an artistic treasure of our society and teach it with ingenuity. We should take more advantage of our background and history because it offers so much to learn from and be proud of. People forget that jazz was the popular music of the 1920s and 1930s and we intertwined with Gershwin's music and many of the great Broadway and movie tunes. Jazz is the most influential music of this century.'"

CHRIS ANDERSON: It's unfortunate that I've only known him in the later part of his life – during his 70's and into his 80's. I have the same reaction that everyone else does when they hear him play – we can't believe what a master of music and of the piano that he is. It's additionally amazing whenever somebody recollects exactly how old he is. BILLY'S been on a jazz crusade. Despite what anyone else would do, he has kind of shouldered the responsibility of carrying jazz and exposing it to everyone and everybody and every possible audience he can. That seems to be a mission for him. He'll play all kinds of shows and he'll play the biggest and smallest show because his mission is to expose the art form to as many people as possible.

JIMMY HEATH: I was connected with Jazzmobile for many years and ended up a couple of years ago writing a piece called "Sweet Jazzmobile" that was performed at Avery Fisher Hall in New York City, but BILLY was the one who hooked me up with Jazzmobile and I was one of the instructors there.

In 1998 The University of Florida and The University of Delaware each honored BILLY was an honorary doctors degree. In 2000 Bard College and Pennsylvania State University became the seventeenth and eighteenth institutions to award BILLY honorary doctorates.

LLOYD PINCHBACK: I met DR. TAYLOR for the first time in the spring of 1999 at the Kennedy Center through his publicist, Lynda Bramble. We met to discuss the possibility of him donating his archives to the Library of Congress Music Division. I must admit that I was a bit nervous this being my first one-on-one with a celebrity, and then I was there to begin the process of "begging" for his collection. Nonetheless, it was a successful meeting owing largely to his congeniality. That was my first impression of BILLY TAYLOR and of course that impression remains. He's just a real nice guy, unspoiled by his success; unpretentious, a concerned humanitarian.

HILTON RUIZ: Around 1999 there was a concert of a piano choir under the direction of Stanley Cowell. There were nine grand pianos – BILLY TAYLOR was one of the pianists. I also played as did Stanley Cowell, Joanne Brackeen, Mulgrew Miller, Geoff Keezer, Nat Jones; a bunch of great piano players. This was held at a concert in Maryland at a college. We rehearsed in New York but the concert was held in Maryland. BILLY played great!! I respect BILLY. I think he's one of the greatest piano players I've ever heard. He can adjust to any situation. He's got all the tools.

In New York City during 2001 the BILLY TAYLOR trio with Chip Jackson, bass and Winard Harper, drums recorded the album URBAN GRIOT for Soundpost Records. Pieces included Local Color/Can You Dig It? Reclamation, Gracias Chucko, Etude, Conversion, Spoken, In Loving Memory, Like A Heartbeat, Invention/Looking For Another Theme, Transformation and A Duke-ish Blues.

Drummer Hiram Winard Harper was born in Baltimore, Maryland on June 4, 1962. He began playing drums when he was five and played with his brother's rock band when he was eight. He worked with Dexter Gordon, Johnny Griffin, Betty Carter, Stan Getz, Ray Bryant, Houston Person and the Tommy Flanagan Trio before joining BILLY TAYLOR.

WINARD HARPER: BILLY is a walking history of jazz - he's very important in that way, to the music and to all of us. He's been around and played with a lot of cats; he passes that history on. That's what the music is. We travel a whole lot; we do those things at the Kennedy Center, in schools, etc.

BILLY TAYLOR: When I was commissioned to write a piece for students, the Wharton Center at the University of Michigan suggested I combine some of the things I do while touring. They wanted to set it up at their school and at five other schools in the state. They suggested that they would premiere the work and then we could perform it at the other schools. So I wrote something that could be expanded to be used with students at workshops and master classes emphasizing the use of the fourth interval, in the melody or harmony, or both. As I began to put the music together I thought: 'It's kind of like a griot (the griots in Africa were the storytellers, the educators, the historians, the musicians). All this grew out of rhythms the kids dance to and a piece we play for kids called; 'Can You Dig It?'

During 2001 the University of North Carolina awarded BILLY'S nineteenth honorary doctor's degree to him.

JOHN DUFFY: In 2001 in Rockport, Maine the Bay Chamber Concert (I'm on the board of that) and Tom Wolfe (who runs that) wanted to have BILLY up here. I called BILLY and we commissioned him to write a work for the first desk wind players of the orchestras across the country. So BILLY played one of the most fabulous sold-out concerts, people standing, etc. It was artistry on the highest level. He and I had a chance to drive around, have lunch, and it was nice to talk together.

FRAN RICHARD: BILLY called me to do a panel at the Kennedy Center (it was either on the 4th of July or Memorial Day) on the weekend. I didn't want to go but I went. It was about how people can survive in spite of the fact that they have record companies, and they don't get any money from them (the same old story as always); but BILLY is such a marvelous catalyst also, ambassador, able to bring all the different forces together in a way that is beautiful. It's always beautiful to deal with him.

CLARK TERRY: I did an album with fourteen piano players. I had everybody, BILLY, Tommy Flanagan, Junior Mance, Barry Harris, Monty Alexander, everybody you can think of. BILLY was outstanding!

MICHEAL ABENE: BILLY has a terrifically open mind about music and I think he's the kind of a guy that when he was 80 years old he was talking about: "Well, yeah, in four years I'm going to do this, and five years this," and I'm thinking: "Now, wait a minute, 80 years old; that's a terrific attitude, just a really positive attitude. He's done some wonderful things for jazz.

In the Volume 3, Number 4 issue of JAZZ IMPROV magazine publisher Eric Nemeyer spoke to BILLY about the Urban Griot release. When asked about the premise for the album BILLY responded: "Well I was commissioned to write something which would be used for students. So, the Wharton Center, in Michigan, said it would be a good idea, they thought, to combine the many things I do when I was touring – they wanted to set up something at their school, and then at five other schools in Michigan. So they said, you know, you like to work with students, so whey don't you write something, and we'll premiere the work at our hall, and then we'll take it around . . . and you can work with the various students that are connected with the other places, that are similar to ours, in terms of presenting organizations. Because all these presenting organizations have ties with local schools, and they have outreach to the local schools, so this would be helpful to them."

CHIP JACKSON: BILLY is always considerate about sharing solos and the spotlight. When I played with S.G. he would always stand by me and talk to me when I played a solo – taking the attention away from me and centering it upon himself. BILLY never hogs the attention. He is wonderful to work for!

BILL MCFARLIN: I'm very proud that BILLY chose the recording of his performance at the January 2001 IAJE Conference in New York for his newest CD. He had a number of options, including his trio's performance at the Village Vanguard, but he chose to release a "Live From IAJE" recording because it would bring more attention to the importance of jazz education. This is just like BILLY! Always bringing a broader vision to every project with which he is associated.

On February 25, 2001, an article appeared in the St. Petersburg Times by Philip Booth that discussed a forthcoming concert featuring BILLY and his colleague for many years, fellow-pianist Ramsey Lewis. BILLY, in his typical fashion, praised Lewis: "Because he's so popular and has had hit records, people don't realize what a fine pianist he is. Not only is he classically trained, but also a lot of things he did that made his music popular came from the fact that he's a solid musician. When we play together, we switch roles. He tends to get more classical and I tend to get funkier."

JIMMY COBB: We're from the same place – Washington, D.C. that's where I grew up. I'm 73, BILLY'S 80. I knew about him; he was already gone by the time I started to play, he was already in New York playing. We never worked together – he called me a couple of times but I never made it. BILLY is a very brilliant man, he's good for music and he's done a whole lot for music. He's made a very large contribution. He's explained the music to a lot of people. We never got that close except for being from D.C. and all that. BILLY is a very pleasant guy. I did an interview for BILLY at the CBS studio on 57th Street this year with a lady that had a show – maybe a half-hour interview.

DEREK GORDON: It's truly been a blessing for me to work with BILLY (at the Kennedy Center) and through BILLY to meet Betty Carter, Cleo Laine, Alan and Marilyn Bergman, and any number of legends in the music industry that we work with as well as people like Regina Carter, Stephan Harris or Russell Malone. We just started our new jazz club here at the Kennedy Center, our newest venture, and in a club setting; the community has responded tremendously to the concept. We have been able to introduce some new artists to the Washington, D.C. audience who might not have been able to be presented on other venues. BILLY was here for the opening weekend and is so supportive.

BILLY does the distance-learning program a couple of times a year with us, a satellite based program where he brings guests to perform with him and to make the art of making music transparent to young audiences. It's beamed into schools all across the country. He's not afraid of new things.

In mid-year, 2001 Playback Magazine announced that IAJE and ASCAP commissions honored BILLY TAYLOR by celebrating his 80th birthday (July 24, 2001) and commissioning two works to be premiered at the annual IAJE conference in January, 2002 in Long Beach, California. "An established jazz composer will be awarded $7,500 and an emerging jazz composer who has not reached their 35th birthday by June 1st, 2001 will be awarded $3,000." Past recipients of the ASCAP-IAJE commissions were ineligible. A tribute was given to BILLY TAYLOR at the Schomburg Center in New York

MARQUITA POOL ECKERT: I learn when I listen to him. Hearing him play, it educates your ear. I do mostly jazz (CBS) – we do other people as well – we do pop, we do classical, so when I do a story with him it forces me to listen more carefully to what's going on, and even though I'm not a student of music whenever i do a story with him I learn something more about music, not just about the person we're doing but about music. He gave some of his papers to the Schomburg collection. It was on a Sunday afternoon and he played with his trio. Yikes!!! He just took off. First of all there was not a seat in the auditorium vacant and it was not like it had been heavily advertised or anything. He just took off and he plays with such technique. I don't know how anybody can think that fast. There is a certain lyrical quality about what he does. He makes these connections; things that you wouldn't even think: "How did he do that?" So I'm always amazed at this facility.

We did a story in 2001 about Miles Davis. We went to St. Louis (CBS) and walked through the exhibit, it was wonderful. It's really great!! We went to the exhibit with the curator – we were shooting, kind of a walk and talk. You know, you walk in front of a photograph, the guy explains what it is, the next thing I know the tables were turned and BILLY was taking the curator through the exhibit, telling him the background of all the bands, the people that Miles Davis had worked with. And this guy was just completely turned around – he didn't mind it either; he was a young guy who had done a great amount of research and he did a terrific job, the exhibit was really, really good. It's just that BILLY knew much more, all the background and everything, so he would stop and explain about Billy Ecktine's band, 52nd St., Bill Evans; it was an amazing thing.

LLOYD PINCHBACK: Other than his recordings, my first time hearing BILLY TAYLOR was in concert at a celebration held in his behalf at the Library of Congress in October 2001. By then, however, I had already been impressed with his ability. I heard him in practice at our first meeting at the

Kennedy Center in April 1999, and again while he was inspecting an instrument before his performance at the Library of Congress concert. During his inspection, he played a very interesting version of Duke's "Take The A Train." There was the familiar melody superimposed on a rhythmic counterpoint. The piece was not immediately recognizable to me, but then . . . a beautiful interpretation of a well-known classic. TAYLOR is unquestionably a consummate musician and brilliant lecturer and educator, dedicated to the craft of making music and sharing it with the masses. An ambassador of jazz.

Bebop continued to thrive despite the deaths of some of its outstanding contributors, J.J. Johnson (deceased 2000), Milt Jackson (deceased 2001) and Ray Brown (deceased 2002). Fortunately, we still have founders like Hank Jones, Max Roach and BILLY TAYLOR still with us and functioning. Many children of those who have passed have flourishing careers in music. Many of their musical grandchildren have established their careers as well; others are busy building local reputations and soon will be heard from on recordings issued by major companies.

JIMMY OWENS: BILLY is like a second father to me. I did a concert in New York with my quartet (June 8, 2001) at the Ethical Cultural Society and I dedicated the concert to the people that have affected me in my musical life; I'm 58 years old now. The people that I honored at this concert were Hank Crawford, BILLY TAYLOR, Donald Byrd, and Miles Davis; four people that have had a marked effect on the musical and business life of Jimmy Owens. All kinds of things I've been involved with with BILLY have been wonderful, wonderful experiences. When we started to do school concerts, sometimes we would do four or five concerts in a week, two on three days or something like that in a week. The group was his trio, which at that time was Victor Gaskin and Bobby Thomas, me and Frank Wess, me and Frank Foster, me and Jimmy Heath, according to who or who could not make it. Frank Wess would play alto or tenor; the others would always play tenor. My experience with BILLY TAYLOR has been thoroughly rewarding. He taught me about education – I've learned so much about performing – and we've played at someone memorial service and a few times I'd say: "Hey, BILLY, let's play a duo." We like to do that. We've done that a number of times. I hold BILLY very, very high, with high regards, as being a very, very caring person, very gentle and I love the way he is so spry at eighty years old. Last year (2001) my other half, Stephanie, said to me: "I love how BILLY is just so spry," as he walked up on the stage to introduce John Lewis, the three Jazz Masters in New York (2001 at IAJE). Just as he got to the top step he tripped, he didn't fall, he caught himself and she just said: "He's so spry, look at the way he walks."

CHARLES OSGOOD: I think he certainly has been the most, maybe along with Wynton Marsalis, the most visible spokesman for jazz. I don't know what is more important. I think to him the music has always been the most important thing. He's gotten great joy out of it and given great joy to a lot of people. He has been doing what he's been doing for such a long time and he seems still so youthful. His face is almost unlined; his smile is as bright and pleasing as ever, everything about him. He's just been doing this for such a long time. When you read about how long he's been doing it it's sort of stunning considering that he's been doing it lately and so well. Because of his outgoing and friendly nature, and because people respected him as a musician, he really did get close to everybody. Sometimes he would do a piece about Ella Fitzgerald or something like that and . . . . . he'd just be sitting in the background playing.

BILLY missed the 29th annual meeting of the International Association for Jazz Education held in Long Beach, California in January 2002. It was rumored that he had had a mild stroke that partially paralyzed his right side (temporarily) but did no damage to his brain cells or speaking ability. That meeting was held on January 9-12.

Fran Richard, Vice President of ASCAP (American Society of Composers, Authors and Publishers) flew out to Long Beach to introduce BILLY at the IAJE January meeting. Just prior to the evenings festivities she was told BILLY could not appear.

FRAN RICHARD: During the conference (IAJE) when they told me he doesn't want anybody to be alarmed, and he doesn't want any rumors and he just couldn't make it and I'm thinking: "He's always here! I mean what's happened? What's wrong?" So I got up and said: "He regrets very much he couldn't be with us and he's honored." Then I got home and they told me that he had had a stroke.

BILLY TAYLOR: All of the doctors and professional people I talked to don't give any credence to what I'm saying but I had some work done on a tooth, over the Christmas holidays. It had broken off. I felt fine. I went in and they did some work on my tooth and the next day I couldn't get a feeling. I felt something's wrong, something's wrong with my hand. So I went to the doctor, my personal doctor. So he said: "Go to this laboratory and do some tests, etc." I felt O.K. So I got up after I had the tests and started to walk away. My wife, who was with me, said: "Wait a minute, sit back down. Get up. Sit back down again." She could tell, whatever it was, that there was something wrong. The doctor put me in the hospital. I lost the mobility in my right side. I couldn't feel one of my right hand fingers.

The Sunday following the IAJE Conference, January 20, BILLY was honored at the Kennedy Center, in honor of his 80th birthday, (which, of course had already occurred in July, 2001). The event was a sold-out affair and was highly successful.

DEREK GORDON: Having spent all this time working with BILLY it was a tremendous joy for me to have the opportunity to put together his 80th birthday celebration. I invited all of the artists and they agreed to come. After the stroke, we didn't know what was going to happen. Certainly we knew he was not going to be able to be here and initially we weren't getting all the information so we were really unclear as to what was happening and we began to get some of the information and finally I was able to talk to the family. The most immediate concern was that BILLY was going to be OK. But then to deal with all of these wonderful performers and the excitement and the spirit of celebration that was going on and knowing that he couldn't be there. We were able to get NPR to arrange a live feed into his hospital room so that he could actually hear it as it was going on. It was a terrific show.

JOHNNY GARRY: I was fortunate enough to attend the show they did for him in Washington, D.C. That was lovely, it was sold out. They had Cleo Lane, Nancy Wilson, Dee Dee Bridgewater, Cyrus Chestnut, Charles Osgood, Arturo Sandoval, Kevin Mahogany, Regina Carter and others. It was great!!

CHARLES OSGOOD: I emceed his tribute at the Kennedy Center last spring, the birthday party. They piped it in so he could hear it. Everybody in the world was at that thing. It was sad that he couldn't be there but I'm glad that he's able to do pieces for us again and I know he's looking forward to being able to play the way he used to.

During 2002 honors for BILLY TAYLOR continued to pour in. On February 2 the University of Massachusetts held the 13th Annual Gala and Auction at the Hotel Northampton. The honoree was DR. BILLY TAYLOR, America's Ambassador of Jazz. In the place of BILLY, the special guest was BILLY'S longtime friend and retired head of the UMass Fine Arts Center, Dr. Frederick Tillis.

CLEM DEROSA: From the age of 60 on BILLY has always looked young. He's always had a young attitude. He has a wonderful image for us. My association with BILLY now is essentially through IAJE. I'm not in the loop of the Kennedy Center and other activities that BILLY is involved with so I only see him once a year at wherever the conference (IAJE) is. I've always admired him and I've always been glad that he's in our corner.

MICHAEL ABENE: I love the way he carries himself; he's a pleasure to listen to, he keeps on going. He's so positive. I love it! I was so sorry to hear about BILLY'S stroke. Here's a guy who is so vital and looks terrific. He writes some very pretty melodies too. My youngest son has done some music copying for some of his books and I perused them thinking: "These melodies are really pretty, real sing-able kinds of tunes."

By March 2002 BILLY was on the mend, having therapy every other day, practicing, and preparing to teach his summer classes, Jazz In July, at the University of Massachusetts. His spirits were high and he looked forward to getting back into the groove of playing and teaching.

RAY MOSCA: I'm so surprised that BILLY had a stroke. He never did anything wrong, never smoked, drank, etc. – a very clean-living guy, nice family, lovely wife and kids. I guess it was stress.

In the May/June, 2002 issue of the Jazz Education Journal, and in an attempt to keep his fans abreast of his recovery, BILLY released the following statement:

A MESSAGE FROM DR. BILLY TAYLOR

"Three months ago while I was preparing to travel to Long Beach to be with you all, I experienced symptoms which have since been diagnosed as those of a mild stroke. Thankfully, I was home in New York when they occurred, and I was able to get to a doctor quickly. This meant that the after affects of the stroke were kept to a minimum, and for that I am most grateful. During the past few months I have been hard at work getting my hands together, but the hardest part has been to be away from you folks and of course, from the music. As many of you know, I am used to keeping a rather busy traveling and performance schedule. So, to say that I am anxious to get back to work is a bit of an understatement. I anticipate that this will be happening in the very near future. In the meantime, my sincere thanks to all of you for your many thoughtful cards, gifts and letters. It means a great deal to know that I have been in your thoughts. Until then, straight ahead! BILLY TAYLOR"

EARL MAY: A couple of Sundays ago (May 2002) BILLY was up at that church in Mt. Vernon and he played. They were celebrating Frank Wess' birthday (which was in January). That was the first time he played so he's really doing well. Then he drove down to Philadelphia. They were honoring him down there; he drove himself. During the nine years I played with BILLY we used to play at the Tijuana Club in Baltimore.

BILL MCFARLIN: During my tenure as Executive Director of the International Association for Jazz Education I have had the honor of working closely with BILLY on the annual National Endowment for the Arts American

Jazz Masters Awards, which he hosts at our annual conference, and have also worked with him on other N.P.R., IAJE, Kennedy Center, Disney, and CBS Sunday Morning projects. He never ceases to amaze me with his energy, professionalism, and commitment to education.

By July, 2002, BILLY felt that he had not totally regained his health and made the decision not to teach the Jazz In July session at UMass. He employed a new therapist and was optimistic about regaining full control of his right hand that was operating at about 95%. His left hand remained strong and, according to BILLY, was 100% healthy.

EDDIE BERT: He got a lifetime achievement award from WLIU in Long Island and I did too. We got it together in July (2002). He seemed to be doing all right. He played the piano at an affair about two months ago. They had a thing for Frank Wess in Mt. Vernon and BILLY played "All The Things You Are". So he is still playing.

JOHNNY GARRY: In August (2002) at the Old Mt. Morris Park (because of the stroke he hadn't been around) I had the pleasure of introducing him and when he came to lecture, all the people (it had rained that day) stood up. I called him later and said: "Out of all the things you've done, it was so great to see people stand up for you." He's something else. He's a hell of a nice guy. I've never heard him swear; I've never seen him mad. He's always looked out for me.

By the middle of August BILLY began to be optimistic about his full recovery.

BILLY: My right hand is improving – I just got back from therapy this morning and I'm wood shedding. I have to go back and play those scales and arpeggios. When I worked on touch with Richard McClanahan (Teddy Wilson's former teacher) in the 40's, and he had me doing some things on touch that I was really very proud of, I could feel the difference, and somewhere along the line I became such a pawn of what I do that it's hard for me to go back and redo that because I had been playing (in '44 or '45) and had all that stuff under my fingers. So this has required me to retrain myself to do with touch. So when I started to play again I couldn't do it. I said: "Wait a minute; what is that?" Because I knew I had it but it wasn't as firm as I hoped it would be. But now it's coming. It's all in my head. I just have to reroute those nerves or whatever.

At the end of the summer BILLY'S old friend Lionel Hampton passed away.

MARQUITA POOL ECKERT: We (CBS) were doing an obituary on Lionel Hampton so I talked to BILLY on the phone in the morning – it was Saturday (we do the show in a day) – and I said to BILLY: "What do you think? Can we do something? And so he said yes. So I started asking some questions about Lionel Hampton and he told me a lot in less than five minutes, including years, dates, etc. I then go on my way into Barnes and Noble figuring I'll stop and I'll get various books. I'm looking up Lionel Hampton and don't you know that everything that BILLY told me including the exact year is there. So my experience with him is that he knows everyone and he knows the history of everyone.

CHARLES OSGOOD: He's done so many pieces that are moving (CBS). He did one just recently after Lionel Hampton's death. We've missed him!

On September 24, 2002 BILLY'S publicist Lynda Bramble, Creative Music Artist Management and Publicity, released BILLY'S new CD, "Live at IAJE". The release began by stating: " BILLY TAYLOR is nothing if not resilient. The multi-talented octogenarian who suffered a mild stroke in January of this year, has bounced back better than ever with the release of 'BILLY TAYLOR TRIO LIVE AT IAJE', (SoundPost Records) which was recorded live in New York City during the 28th annual conference of the International Association for Jazz Education. Longtime member and staunch supporter of IAJE, TAYLOR along with Chip Jackson (bass) and Winard Harper (drums) pulled out all the stops that evening, presenting a vibrant, dazzling set of TAYLOR originals as well as a beautifully executed version of the popular standard, 'Body & Soul', featuring an exquisite and flawless left-handed solo by TAYLOR.

BILLY commented on the music involved on the CD: "IMPROMTU is a piece I wrote many years ago. It starts with an up tempo Latin theme followed by a second theme which is actually a walking tempo variation on the first theme. The second section features a driving Chip Jackson solo followed by Winard Harper's solo, which goes through various tempi eventually leading back to the original theme and tempo for a piano ride out. BODY AND SOUL is favorite standard I originally learned from a Coleman Hawkins record. I like to play it modulating through different keys. I used to play it in all twelve keys. This version settles for two, starting it out in Bb with a piano chorus using only the left hand and then modulating to Db for Chip's solo with a final piano chorus. CONVERSION is a new piece written for Chip. About a year ago I heard him fooling around with the changes to 'Out Of Nowhere' and I suggested I write a feature for him. Chip plays the melody and a swinging solo. I follow with a piano solo before Chip restates the melody and adds an exciting cadenza to close. TITORO was originally Tiroro, named after a famous Haitian drummer we played with on a trip there in the late 40's. It became a favorite of Latin musicians and Tito Puente recorded it with a big band and called it TITORO. It is now one of our signature tunes and a feature for every drummer I have had in the trio from Charlie Smith to Winard Harper. Each has incorporated some form of hand drumming into his solo. Here Winard brings it up to date with his version. The last tune is the Third Movement from SUITE FOR JAZZ PIANO AND ORCHESTRA. It is something I do often as a piano feature. The introductory trio portion is actually the string part in the orchestra version. In the extended piano improvisation I try to make two hands sound like one, one hand sound like two and two hands sound like four.

By the end of September BILLY continued to attend the therapy sessions and to gradually appear at various fund raising events, primarily as a speaker.

BILLY TAYLOR: I'm not going to do any playing until the first of the year. I'm going to do a New Year's Eve program, "Billy Taylor and Friends" at the Kennedy Center. I'm kind of shooting for that. I keep putting it off, and putting it off, and so it's settled into that instead of something else because once I start I'm going to be playing. So I want to make sure that I'm ready to get my feet wet.

PHOEBE JACOBS: I saw BILLY last night (Sept. 26). He attended THE NIGHT IN HARLEM. He was honored; they named an award for him, the BILLY TAYLOR HUMANITARIAN AWARD. He looked stunning and was functioning beautifully. He walked to the stage beautifully. He was just doing fantastic and he got an ovation that was unbelievable. Everybody was standing in the theater when they announced his name.

MICHAEL ABENE: I was talking to the bass player (Chip Jackson) and he said BILLY'S going to play for the first time on Saturday (Oct. 17, 2002). It's kind of a special thing; a fundraiser for some cause. He just was going to play two or three tunes. I was surprised when Chip told me that.

The University of Michigan at Flint informed BILLY that they would award him an honorary doctorate on May 4, 2003. He also received an honorary doctorate from George Washington University.

CHARLES OSGOOD: Twenty honorary doctorates may be a world's record!! So he's doctor, doctor, doctor, doctor, etc. Because he has been a regular on CBS Sunday Morning and because he's been here for such a long time I'm sure he has fans everywhere he has worked but I can tell you everybody here is a big BILLY TAYLOR fan.

JIM ANDERSON: I think he could have been a much larger success, but in terms of his family, that was a lot more important to him. Most of his formative years were spent in New York at various clubs and on radio and he was not out there peddling himself. He was more of a family man than most jazz musicians would be and he yearned for a far more stable life. I think ultimately it was better for him. I was so happy to get out and spend a couple of afternoons with BILLY recently (July, 2002) to edit the taped performance of the IAJE concert for a special edition to be played on radio.

DEREK GORDON: I think the biggest dilemma is to categorize him. Everybody knows him as an educator. Part of that also reflects on his career as a broadcaster. He has such a great ease in speaking about the music and speaking with people about music – it carries through both in television and on the air so he's certainly a consummate jazz educator. But in preparation for the 80th birthday celebration to find the wealth of music that BILLY has composed – it's a tremendous body of work. To talk about BILLY I have to use Duke Ellington's expression, "beyond category". He really is a triple threat, and on top of that he's probably the nicest guy I know.

JIMMY HEATH: I think he has contributed to the repertoire as well as being a spokesman for the music. He's so articulate and a presenter of what this music really means from the beginnings. He is an historian and a great representative of the music (even before Wynton Marsalis!). BILLY was THERE!! He was there around Art Tatum, the ragtime guys, Willie the Lion, and all that; and the kids, they only listen to the records and read about that era. BILLY has that as part of his life!

COBI NARITA: He is absolutely one of the forerunners in American music. Remember, the National Endowment recognized him and the Kennedy Center recognized him and every time he had a chance to do anything he would put jazz music, this music called jazz, into whatever was going on. So he actually had more music played and performed at places than would have been if he had never been around. He has made a great contribution to the performance and perpetuation of this music. He's among the top few.

LOREN SCHOENBERG: As the years have gone by, we're next-door neighbors and I got to know him on that level. We share a wall between our two apartments. I got to really realize what BILLY TAYLOR'S life is really like. It's a real 24-hours a day, 7-days a week, 52-weeks a year commitment to jazz music that he has. Most people probably project their own experience, in terms of the work place or even their own musical careers or academic careers, on to someone like BILLY TAYLOR. But they don't really have a handle on what this man does.

NANCY WILSON: I think BILLY'S value to National Public Radio and to Jazz Alive has been invaluable. One of the saddest things in my life was to hear that BILLY'S not going to be doing the show. He's one of the smartest people, who can illuminate what the music is about, aside from playing it, explaining to people what he's doing and letting them in on what the music is about.

REVEREND DALE LIND: He's made an immense contribution to music; an historian, educator, top musician and a very caring person. I have the greatest respect and affection for him. I don't know anybody who has a bad thing to say about him. He's very intelligent. He doesn't brag about this or that. He's a very great, solid person.

FRANK WESS: We played together a lot over the years (more than sixty-five years!) We made a lot of records together. BILLY'S been invaluable – he's done a whole lot of things. He's first class! We did the David Frost Show for three years. I've been down to the Kennedy Center a numbers of times with BILLY. I'm going to be playing New Years Eve (2002) at the Kennedy Center with BILLY.

GEORGE WEIN: By working at the Kennedy Center, the Metropolitan Museum of Art, CBS television and touring throughout the country, he presented Jazz in a way that made every musician, whose living comes from the playing of this great music, get treated with more respect. For example, when I started my career, everybody asked my family: "When is George going to get a legitimate job"? Now my family looks at me with pride. I feel a great, great affinity to BILLY TAYLOR.

BILLY continued recuperating at a fast pace. He played several professional engagements prior to the turn of the year including the "BILLY TAYLOR AND FRIENDS" gig at the Kennedy Center on New Year's Eve. BILLY and the author met for several hours during the 30th conference anniversary of the International Association for Jazz Educator's meeting in Toronto, Canada during the week of January 6, 2003. BILLY exclaimed: "I feel 100%!" He had totally recuperated from the stroke that took away his activities during 2002!

In June 2003, BILLY TAYLOR received honorary doctorates from The University of Michigan and George Washington University.

Actors Ossie Davis and Ruby Dee have been longtime fans and friends of BILLY TAYLOR. Ossie Davis penned the following in his respect and admiration for BILLY:

DR. BILLY TAYLOR*

I use words like BILLY uses music, so listen quick,
your ears will be right back, filled to the brim with
jazz. Whoever told you the purpose of this trip is to
drive somebody crazy, stuff like that, is lying. But
maybe you'd better let me take your hand.

Jazz is a hunter, looking for a kill, something not
only beautiful, but perfect; a one way ticket to out-
of-your-mind, and back.

But don't try to catch it, that's BILLY'S job,
Willie The Lion-tamer. Listen. . . He's trying to tell
the whole world something big.

Some great jazzmasters make their passage screaming
for elbow room, off by themselves, a solitary zoomer
ecstasy bound. You stand, and watch, but duck if they
get too close – they wear dark glasses, seldom shake
your hand, hang out the sign that says "Do Not
Disturb" Give them their privacy, love them at a distance.

But BILLY, no! His music comes with open arms to meet
you. You be a jazzman too, if you don't watch it!
Especially your feet, they can't stay home. BILLY
ain't no kind of preacher . . . he don't take up acollection,
- but he ought to.

I love it so when BILLY TAYLOR takes off for heaven,
burning bright bridges behind him as he goes, I hear
me say: Good God, the man is crazy . . . how will he ever
recover from THAT chord? But somehow, by the skin of
the teeth on the keyboard he always finds safe harbor
in the keynote. And he is just as surprised as you
and me.

And when the set is done, the vamp is over, the joint
is closed and all of us, still grinning at what we
heard, spill out into the streets, still sanctified by
BILLY'S black beatitudes, we find ourselves walking
taller and talking louder on our way back home. We

cannibalize the moment with our bragging, adding as
much of BILLY to memory's collection as we had to
leave behind on the dancing floor. The garbage is
still on the curb, hate, defeat, racism and
unemployment, still live at the same address, but
BILLY has made us kings, so we don't notice; but that
ain't BILLY'S fault.

Like I told you, I deal in words. So let me answer all
your questions this way:

Two fireflies, and a hummingbird, in Flagrante
Delicto- that's jazz- (it's better if they're black,
like BILLY TAYLOR)- vamping outside in the vestibule,
till God gets ready. "A thing of beauty is a joy
forever" . . . BILLY taught us that one long before John
Keats . . . and when "forever" is over, there is jazz,
down in the piano's red-light district, where Doctor
BILLY TAYLOR keeps his mistress; but not under lock and
key- the bar above his keyboard is always open, and
all he ever pours is spotless jazz, So listen, listen
to something sweet and liquid lazy in his language,
talking in tongues, like he was the Holy Ghost: that's
jazz- or BILLY playing- take your pick. (I didn't know
that BILLY was also good for rheumatism till I saw
Mama dancing!)

Me? I can't play nothing. All I want, when jazz is
like a monkey on my back, is forgiveness for my sins.
And BILLY gives me all of that, plus car fare- and
keys to the Black Man's kingdom. Quicksilver marries
gold in BILLY'S parlor, he lets me watch, and he
doesn't charge a dime.

He takes these one-way trips into astonishment, because
he has to . . . on a never ending search for absolute
perfection. That's what drives him and all the rest of
jazz. Something the Almighty hasn't even finished
writing. I told you I ain't no musician, but I know
the truth when I hear it. Sometimes, when I'm by
myself, when I close my eyes and really listen deep, I
hear it, all the great jazzmasters, past and present –
one great big heavenly band, from sessions immemorial,

jamming around the throne! I can't quite make it out
what God, Himself, is playing, or even what key He's
in, but I ain't tone deaf. An BILLY TAYLOR – our very
own, DOCTOR BILLY TAYLOR – is right there in the middle
winking at me! My prayer is, that I will still be
standing right there with him and the other heroes,
when they find whatever it is that jazz is looking
for. And I won't need no heaven after that.

Ssh, here he comes now . . . hold on to my hand, and also
to your ears, they'll never believe what they're about
to hear!

*copyright Ossie Davis – used with permission

Jazz, students of jazz and music appreciators everywhere recognize the
tremendous contribution of BILLY TAYLOR. Although the future is unpredictable,
it is certain that BILLY TAYLOR will be sitting at the keyboard, standing behind a
lectern, speaking into a microphone and appearing on a TV screen as long as he's
ambulatory.

NOTES

I   HOW IT STARTED

1.   International Musician. "Dr. Billy Taylor Bringing Jazz To The People". pgs.14-15. September 2000.

2.   Gitler, Ira. SWING TO BOP. pgs. 100,101

3.   Gitler, Ira. Ibid, pgs. 111,112

4.   Lee, William F. III MY STORY: A TAIL'S TALE. Unpublished autobiography. Pgs 31-34

II   NEW YORK

1.   Shaw, Arnold. THE STREET THAT NEVER SLEPT. pg. 170

2.   Shaw, Arnold. 52nd STREET: THE STREET OF JAZZ. pg 172.

3.   Gitler, Ira. SWING TO BOP. pg. 101.

4.   Gitler, Ira. Ibid, pgs. 141,142

5.   Shipton, Alyn. GROOVIN' HIGH: THE LIFE OF DIZZY GILLESPIE. pg.119

6.   Shipton, Alyn. Ibid, pg. 120

7.   Gitler, Op. cit., pgs. 110.111

8.   Shipton, Alyn. GROOVIN' HIGH: THE LIFE OF DIZZY GILLESPIE. pg. 122

9.   Gitler, Op. cit., pgs. 108,109

10. Shipton, Op. cit., pgs. 120,121

11. Shipton, Op. cit., pg. 159

12. Shaw, Op. cit., pg. 172

13. Gitler, Op. cit., pg. 103

14. Shaw, Op. cit., pg. 172
15. Shaw, Op. cit., pg. 176
16. Taylor, Billy. JAZZ PIANO: A JAZZ HISTORY. pg. 122
17. Taylor, Billy. Ibid, pg. 17
18. Shaw, Op. cit., pg. 172
19. Miller, Dick. THE DICK MILLER SHOW (radio/interview).
20. Shipton, Op. cit., pg. 234.
21. Gitler, Op. cit., pgs. 103, 104, 108, 110

III   52nd STREET

1. Shapiro, Nat and Hentoff, Nat. HEAR ME TALKIN' TO YA. pgs. 360, 361
2. Gitler, Ira. SWING TO BOP. pg. 142
3. Shapiro and Hentoff, Op. cit., pg. 367
4. Gitler, Ira. Ibid, pg. 123
5. Gitler, Ira. Op. cit., pgs. 304, 305
6. Shaw, Arnold. 52nd STREET: THE STREET OF JAZZ. pg. 255
7. Shapiro and Hentoff, Op. cit., pg. 362
8. Shapiro and Hentoff, Op. cit., pg. 363
9. Shaw, Op. cit., pg. 260
10. Shaw, Op. cit., pg. 294
11. Gitler, Op. cit., pg. 304
12. Shapiro and Hentoff, Op. cit., pg. 378
13. Shapiro and Hentoff, Op. cit., pg. 367

IV   THE BILLY TAYLOR TRIO

1. Shaw, Arnold. 52nd STREET: THE STREET OF JAZZ. pgs. 221, 222
2. Shaw, Arnold. Ibid., pg. 329
3. Priestly, Brian. MINGUS: A CRITICAL BIOGRAPHY. pg. 45
4. Stokes, W. Royal. LIVING THE JAZZ LIFE. pg. 86

V   BROADCASTING – THE JAZZMOBILE – THE DAVID FROST SHOW

1. Primack, Bret, "DR. T AT 75"
2. Shaw, Arnold. 52nd STREET: THE STREET OF JAZZ. pgs. 156, 157

3. Shaw, Arnold. Ibid, pgs. 168, 169

4. Shaw, Op cit., pg. 155

5. Primack, Op. cit.

6. Primck, Op. cit.

7. Pettinger. Peter. BILL EVANS: HOW MY HEART SINGS. pg. 68

8. Primack, Op cit.

9. Nanry, Charles. THE JAZZ TEXT. pg. 173

10. Taylor, Billy. JAZZ PIANO: A JAZZ HISTORY. pg. 206

11. Taylor, Ibid. pg. 208

12. Porter, Lewis. JOHN COLTRANE: HIS LIFE AND MUSIC. pg. 288

13. Hajdu, David. LUSH LIFE: A BIOGRAPHY OF BILLY STRAYHORN. pg. 258

14. Primack, Op. cit.

VI DR. TAYLOR! – NATIONAL PUBLIC RADIO – MEDIA RECOGNITION, AWARDS

1. Chilton, John. JAZZ. pg. 159

2. Gourse, Leslie. THE BILLIE HOLIDAY COMPANION. pg. 183

3. Wilmer, Valerie. AS SERIOUS AS YOUR LIFE: THE STORY OF THE NEW JAZZ. pgs. 218, 219

VII CBS SUNDAY MORNING – AUTHOR – MORE MEDIA RECOGNITION, AWARDS

1. Stokes, W. Royal. LIVING THE JAZZ LIFE. pgs. 86,87

2. Lees, Gene. OSCAR PETERSON: THE WILL TO SWING. Pg.250

3. Primack, DR. T AT 75

VIII EDUCATION – THE KENNEDY CENTER - IAJE

1. Stokes, W. Royal, LIVING THE JAZZ LIFE. pg. 87

2. Primack, DR. T AT 75

3. Primack, Op. cit.

BILLY TAYLOR TRIO-QUARTET-QUINTET BASS PLAYERS AND DRUMMERS

BASS

Aaron Bell, Bob Cranshaw, George Duvivier, Victor Gaskin, Henry Grimes, Al Hall, Chip Jackson, John Levy, Earl May, Christian McBride, Charles Mingus, Larry Ridley, Ted Sturgis, John Simmons, Ben Tucker, Tommy Williams, Doug Watkins

DRUMS

Dave Bailey, Denzil Best, Percy Brice, Curtis Boyd, Sid Bulkin, Jimmy Crawford, Marquis Foster, Joe Harris, Kenny Dennis, Winard Harper, Albert "Tottie" Heath, Jo Jones, Steve Johns, Kelly Marin, Ray Mosca, Buford Oliver, Walter Perkins, Charlie Smith, Marvin "Smitty" Smith, Grady Tate, Ed Thigpen, Bobby Thomas, Freddie Waits, Shadow Wilson

THE MUSIC OF BILLY TAYLOR

A BIENTOT

AIN'T THAT A KICK IN THE HEAD

ALL ALONE

ALL EARS

AMUSING BUT CONFUSING

ANTOINETTE

AT LA CARROUSEL

B.T.'S D.T.'S

BABY, YOU'RE THE ONE FOR ME

BACK HOME

BACK TO MY DREAM   (ninth movement from the suite STEP INTO MY DREAM)

BALI BOUNCE

BALLADE (from FOR RACHEL)

BARBADOS BEAUTY   (third movement from the suite STEP INTO MY DREAM)

B.T.'S BASIC BE-BOP INSTUCTION (book)

BASIE SWING

BIG HORN BREAKDOWN

BILLY'S (BIDDY'S) BEAT

BILLY AND DAVE (first movement from the suite STEP INTO MY DREAM)

BILLY'S TINKLE (LOOKIN' UP)

BILLY TAYLOR SKETCHES FOR JAZZ TRIO (book)

BIRDWATCHER

BIT OF BEDLAM

BLUE CLOUD

BLUE MAX   (instrumental version of I THINK OF YOU)

BLUE SHUTTERS

BOOGIE WOOGIE BILLY

BOOGIE WOOGIE PIANO SOLOS & HOW TO (book)

BOOK, THE   (from Lion and the Jewel)

BORDER TOWN   (with M.S. Kesler)

BOURBON SONG, THE

BRIGHT STAR IN THE EAST

BUG, THE

BURST #1   (commercial)

BYE Y'ALL

C.A.G.

CAMAGUEY

CAN YOU DIG IT   (TV theme)

CAN YOU GET CLOTHES CLEAN?   (commercial)

CAN YOU TELL BY LOOKING AT ME

CANDIDO   (aka CANDIDO MAMBO)

CAPRICIOUS   (Dick Dallas, lyricist)

CELEBRATE   (fifth movement of JOYFUL NOISE SUITE)

COLD POWER LOVES THE THINGS YOU LOVE (commercial)

COLD POWER IT LOVES THE THINGS YOU LOVE (commercial)

COLD POWER #2   (aka COLGATE #2 - commercial)

COLD POWER # 1   (aka) COLGATE #1 - commercial)

COLD POWER #3   (aka COLGATE #3 – commercial)

COMBO ARRANGING; HOW TO ARRANGE   (book)

CONVERSATIONS   (three movement work; for orchestra and jazz trio)

COOL AND CARESSING   (Pitman, lyricist)

COUNTING SONG   (from LION AND THE JEWEL)

CU-BLU

CUBAN CAPER

CUBAN CUTIE   (with E. SMITH)

DADDY-O

DAVE AND BILLY   (eighth movement, from STEP INTO MY DREAM)

DAY DREAMING

DECLIVITY

DID YOU DREAM TOO?

DIFFERENT BELLS

DIXIELAND PIANO SOLOS AND HOW TO PLAY THEM   (book)

DOCKWILER'S GROOVE

DON'T GO DOWN SOUTH   (THEME AND VARIATIONS – MAIN THEME)

DON'T LOOK BACK

DON'T WORRY ABOUT IT

DOUBLE DUTY

DR. GROOVE

DUANE   (first movement, from SUITE FOR JAZZ PIANO AND ORCHESTRA)

EARL MAY

EARLY MORNING BLUES

EARLY MORNING MAMBO

EASY WALKER

EVER SO EASY

EVOLUTIONARY RAG, THE

FEELING FRISKY

FIESTA IN TUCSON   (three movement SUITE FOR JAZZ BAND)

FLAME OF OUR LOVE, THE

FOR ART TATUM   (for two pianos)

FOR RACHEL   (SUITE FOR SEVEN MOMENTS FOR SIX INSTRUMENTS)

FOR UNDINE

FOR YOU

FOUR EYES

FREE AND OOZY

FREEDOM   (with B. TUCKER)

FRIENDS OF LANGSTON HUGHES   (TV show themes)

GO TELL IT ON THE MOUNTAIN   (from CHRISTMAS ALBUM)

GOOD GROOVE

GOTTA FIND A CHICK THAT'S WORKIN'

HANDLE WITH CARE   (aka MUFFLE GUFFLE or HARD TO HANDLE)

HE AIN'T JUST BOOTED

HERE TODAY, GONE TOMORROW LOVE   (lyricist, C. NORWOOD)

HEY PRETTY BABY

HIS NAME WAS MARTIN   (second movement from PEACEFUL WARRIOR)

HISTORY AND DEVELOPMENT OF JAZZ PIANO   (book)

HOMAGE   (three movement piece for STRING QUARTET AND JAZZ TRIO)

HOPE AND HOSTILITY   (fifth movement from STEP INTO MY DREAM)

HOW TO ARRANGE FOR JAZZ COMBOS   (book)

HOW TO PLAY RAGTIME PIANO   (with R. KAIL)

I AM FAMOUS   (from LION AND THE JEWEL)

I DON'T ASK QUESTIONS

I LOVE TO LOOK AT YOU

I LOVE TO MAMBO

I SIGH   (with C. SMITH)

I THINK OF YOU

I TOLD MYSELF

I WANNA BE HERE

I WISH I KNEW HOW IT WOULD FEEL TO BE FREE   (lyricist, DICK DALLAS)

I WISH I LED HIS KIND OF LIFE   (from LION AND THE JEWEL)

IF YOU REALLY ARE CONCERNED THEN SHOW IT   (third part of PEACEFUL
    WARRIOR)

I'M A LOVER

I'M GOING TO THE CITY

I'M GONNA GET MYSELF TOGETHER RIGHT NOW   (from film MORNING FOR
    JIMMY)

I'M IN LOVE WITH YOU   (aka J AND J DANCE)

I'M REALLY GOING TO CHANGE YOUR MIND

IMPROMPTU   (in two movements; for ORCHESTRA AND JAZZ TRIO)

INCIDENTAL MUSIC FOR DAVID FROST

INSIDE   (ADAGIO from IMPROMPTU)

INTERLUDE

IN THE END   (lyricist, L. BOBROV)

IS THIS THE BLUES?   (second movement from FOR RACHEL)

IT HAPPENS ALL THE TIME

IT'S A GRAND NIGHT FOR SWINGING

IT'S A MATTER OF PRIDE   (first movement from PEACEFUL WARRIOR)

IT'S A RICH LIFE   (from LION AND THE JEWEL)

IT'S ALL RIGHT

IT'S BEEN FIVE FULL MONTHS   (from LION AND THE JEWEL)

IT'S DIZ

IT'S SPRING   (lyricist CLYDE OTIS)

I WANNA BE HERE

J AND J DANCE   (aka I'M IN LOVE WITH YOU)

JAZZMOBILE MUSIC

JOY TO THE WORLD   (from CHRISTMAS ALBUM)

JUST CLOSE YOUR EYES

JUST THE THOUGHT OF YOU

KIM'S SONG   (fourth movement from STEP INTO MY DREAM)

LA COTE D'IVOIRE   (third movement from SUITE FOR JAZZ PIANO AND ORCHESTRA)

LET US MAKE A JOYFUL NOISE   (first movement from MAKE A JOYFUL NOISE SUITE)

LION AND THE JEWEL, THE   (show score for off Broadway)

LITTLE BIRD   (from LION AND THE JEWEL)

LITTLE SOUTH SIDE SOUL, A

LIVE IT UP

LIVE ONE, A

LONDON HOUSE, THE   (with C. SMITH)

LONELY TROUBADOUR   (lyricist C. OTIS)

LONG TOM (TOM VAGUELY)

LOOKIN' UP (BILLY'S TINKLE)

LOVING HANDS   (from LION AND THE JEWEL)

MA MAMBO

MAD MONK, THE

MAKE A JOYFUL NOISE   (aka LET US MAKE A JOYFUL NOISE)

MAMBO AZUL

MAMBO PIANO SOLOS   (book)

MAMBOCITA

MAMBOMANIA

MARY'S DANCE

MATAMATA MAMBO

MERRY CHRISTMAS   (from CHRISTMS ALBUM)

MIDNIGHT PIANO

MISTY MORNING BLUES

MO TE'NI – TOLANI; CHANT

MODERN JAZZ PIANO SOLOS   (book)

MOOD FOR MENDES

MOVIN' THE GROOVE

MR. B. BOPS

MY HEART SINGS

MY MOODS

NAMELESS   (IF YOU REALLY ARE CONCERNED THEN SHOW IT)

NEWARK LOVES YOU   (lyricist LOU CARTER)

NIGHT COMING TENDERLY

NO PARKING

O.K. BILLY

OLD MAN MAMBO

OLD MAN WON, THE   (from LION AND THE JEWEL)

OLD SAMBA

OLD WINE NEW BOTTLE (from LION AND THE JEWEL)

ON THIS LEAN, MEAN STREET   (second movement from STEP INTO MY
   DREAM)

ONCE OVER LIGHTLY

1:15, THE

ONE FOR FUN

ONE FOR THE WOOFER

ONE WAY

OOPS!

PAN AMERICAN CLIPPER

PARADE OF THE PUPPETS

PARAPHRASE

PEACEFUL WARRIOR   (three movement piece for ORCHESTRA, MIXED CHORUS AND JAZZ TRIO)

PICTURE THIS (SOLACE)

PRAYER   (fourth movement of JOYFUL NOISE SUITE)

RACHEL

RADIOACTIVITY

RAGTIME PIANO SOLOS   (book)

RAT THEME   (aka ARKADIA BLUES)

RATS/CATS   (for CTW SESAME STREET)

RAY'S TUNE ,   (lyricist R. RIVERA)

REJOICE   (third movement of JOYFUL NOISE SUITE)

RIGHT HERE, RIGHT NOW   (with B. TUCKER, lyricist BOB DOROUGH)

RISE UP SHEPHERD AND FOLLOW

ROOSTOLOGY   (with BONNEMERE)

SAMBA POLKA, THE   (with E.SMITH, lyricist TAYLOR, SMITH)

SAMBA POLKA, THE   (for organ)

SAME OLD SEVEN   (fourth movement from FOR RACHEL)

SCOTTICISM

SIS

SKETCH   (first movement from FOR RACHEL)

SKETCHES AND SOLOS   (book)

SO YOU THINK YOU'RE CUTE

SOCIETY STRUT

SOLACE (PICTURE THIS)

SOMETHING ALWAYS HAPPENS   (lyricist C. BULLARD)

SOMEWHERE SOON

SOUL SISTER

SOUNDS IN THE NIGHT

SPHINX, THE   (with BONNEMERE

SPIRITUAL   (second movement of JOYFUL NOISE SUITE)

STABLE DOWN THE ROAD, A   (from CHRISTMAS ALBUM, lyricist BOBROV)

STEP INTO MY DREAM   (suite in ten movements)

STRIDING DOWN THE CHAMPS-ELYSEES

SUITE FOR JAZZ PIANO AND ORCHESTRA   (three part work)

TELL ME WHY

THAT'S FOR SURE!

THEODORA

THIEF   (lyricist C. OTIS)

THINK COLD POWER   (commercial)

TILL WE MEET AGAIN

TIRORO

TITORO

TODAY IS OURS

TOM, VAGUELY (LONG TOM)

TOO LITTLE AND TOO LATE   (lyricist PARNES)

TOUCH OF TAYLOR   (book)

TUNE FOR HOWARD TO IMPROVISE UPON, A

TUNE FOR TEX

TWINKLE TOE

TWO NOTES

TWO SHADES OF BLUE   (seventh movement from STEP INTO MY DREAM)

UNCERTAIN

UNCLE BOB   (sixth movement from STEP INTO MY DREAM)

UNE SALLE DE BAL VIDE (EMPTY BALLROOM)

VEL – NEW HOT JOIN AFTER DINNERE MIN   (commercial)

WALKING IN THE LIGHT   (sixth movement of JOYFUL NOISE SUITE)

WAND'RING STRANGER   (from LION AND THE JEWEL)

WE NEED PEACE AND WE NEED LOVE

WELL IT'S BEEN SO LONG (second movement from SUITE FOR JAZZ PIANO AND ORCHESTRA)

WEXFORD CAROL (from CHRISTMAS ALBUM)

WHAT WILL YOU DO IN THE END? (lyricist BOBROW)

WHAT'S THE WORLD COMIN' TO? (from MORNING FOR JIMMY, MOVIE)

WHEN ILUJINLE JOINS THE WORLD (from LION AND THE JEWEL)

WHEN WE ARE WED (from LION AND THE JEWEL)

WHEN YOU SMILE

WHERE'VE YOU BEEN?

WHY DID I DO IT?

WHY REGRET

WITH OSSIE AND RUBY (theme for TV show)

YOU CAN GET IT ALL TOGETHER

YOU GOTTA WALK TALL

YOU TEMPT ME (instrumental)

YOU TEMPT ME (vocal version, with CLIFF OWENS, lyricist OTIS)

YOU'RE ALL THAT MATTERS

YOU'RE MINE

DISCOGRAPHY

1944
New York City
BILLY TAYLOR TRIO
Al Hall, bass; Jimmy Crawford, drums; Billy Taylor; piano
Mad Monk, Solace, Night and Day, Alexander's Ragtime Band
BILLY TAYLOR TRIO: SAVOY XP8 095, MG 9035

1945
March 19
New York City
BILLY TAYLOR WITH COZY COLE
Cozy Cole, drums; Tiny Grimes, guitar; Don Byas, saxophone; Billy Taylor, bass;
BILLY TAYLOR, piano; June Hawkins, vocals
Hallelujah, Stompin' At The Savoy, Dat's Love, Through The Night
COZY COLE: CLASSICS 8651

1945
April
New York City
BILLY TAYOR WITH COZY COLE
Cozy Cole, drums; Tiny Grimes, guitar; Don Byas, saxophone, Sid Weiss, bass,
BILLY TAYLOR, piano; June Hawkins, vocals
Night Wind, Why Regret, Strictly Drums,
COZY COLE: CLASSICS 895

1945
June 27
New York City
BILLY TAYOR WITH WALTER "FOOTS" THOMAS ALL STARS

Walter "Foots" Thomas, tenor saxophone; Hilton Jefferson, alto saxophone, Milt Hinton, bass; Adolphus "Doc" Cheatham, trumpet Buddy Saffer, baritone saxophone, BILLY TAYLOR, piano, and others
Black Maria's Blues, Bird Brain, Dee-Tees, Back Talk
WALTER "FOOTS" THOMAS ALL STARS: PRESTIGE 7584

1945
New York City
SID CATLETT AND HIS ALL-STARS
Dick Vance, trumpet; Tyree Glenn, trombone; Hilton Jefferson, alto saxophone; Coleman Hawkins, tenor saxophone; Johnny Simmons, bass; Sid Catlett, drums; Matthew Merredith, vocals; BILLY TAYLOR, piano
Just A Riff, Before Long, What's Happenin', Mop De Mop Mop
SID CATLETT AND HIS ALL-STARS: SUPER DISC 1022-1023

1946
July 24
New York City
BUCK CLAYTON'S BIG EIGHT
Buck Clayton, trumpet; Dickie Wells, Trummy Young, trombones; George Johnson, alto saxophone; Brick Fleagle, guitar; Al McKibbon, bass; Jimmy Crawford, drums; BILLLY TAYLOR, piano
Saratoga Special, Sentimental Summer, Harlem Cradle Song, My Good Man Sam, I Want A Little Girl
BUCK CLAYTON'S BIG EIGHT: HRS 1027, 1028, 1029, HALO LP 50229

1946
October 18
Paris, France
DON BYAS AND HIS ORCHESTRA
Peanuts Holland, trumpet; Tyree Glenn, trombone; Robert Rostaing, clarinet; Don Byas, tenor saxophone; Ted Sturgis, bass; Buford Oliver, drums; Billy Taylor, piano
Gloria, Mohawk Special
DON BYAS AND HIS ORCHESTRA: SWING 232, 235

1946
October 27
Geneva, Switzerland
DON REDMAN ORCHESTRA
Featuring: Tyree Glenn, trombone and vibes; Don Byas, tenor saxophone: Peter Clark, clarinet: Peanuts Holland, trumpet; Billy Taylor, piano

My Melancholy Baby, Limehouse Blues, Laura, Carry Me Blues, I Got Rhythm, Alexander's Ragtime Band, Tea For Two, These Foolish Things, Stompin' At The Savoy
DON REDMAN ORCHESTRA: GENEVA 1946 (TCB 02112)

1946
December 4
Paris, France
DON BYAS QUARTET
I'm Beginning To See The Light, Rosetta, Ain't Misbehavin', Body And Soul, Blue And Sentimental
Don Byas, tenor saxophone; Jean Bouchety, bass; Buford Oliver, drums, Billy Taylor, piano
DON BYAS QUARTET: SWING 241, 247, 267; CLASSICS 1009

1946
December 4
Paris, France
BILLY TAYLOR TRIO
Ted Sturgis, bass; Buford Oliver, drums; Billy Taylor, piano
The Very Thought Of You, Stridin' Down Champs-Elysees
BILLY TAYLOR TRIO: SWING 234

1947
January 13
Paris, France
DON BYAS AND HIS ORCHESTRA
Peanuts Holland, trumpet; Tyree Glenn, trombone; Robert Rostaing, clarinet; Don Byas, tenor saxophone; Jean-Jacques Tilche, guitar; Jean Bouchety, bass; Oliver Buford, drums; Billy Taylor, piano
*Please Don't Talk About Me When I'm Gone, Mad Monk, I Can't Get Started, I Surrender, Dear, Lover, Come Back To Me
*full band
**Walking Around, How High The Moon, Red Cross, Laura, Cement Mixer, Dynamo
** Without Tyree Glenn, trombone and Robert Rostaing, clarinet
DON BYAS AND HIS ORCHESTRA (RE-BOPPERS): BLUE STAR 27, 28, 29

1947
June
New York City
BILLY TAYLOR QUARTET
John Collins, guitar; John Levy, bass; Denzil Best, drums; Billy Taylor, piano
Well Taylored, I Don't Ask Questions, So You Think You're Cute?, Twinkle Toes
BILLY TAYLOR QUARTET: H.R.S. 1038-1039

1947
September 26
New York City
BILLY TAYLOR QUARTET
Herman Mitchell, guitar; John Levy bass; Denzil Best, drums, Billy Taylor, piano
Mr. B. Bops, Restricted, Down The Champs Elysees, Mitch's Pitch
BILLY TAYLOR QUARTET: H.R.S. 1048-1049

1949
November 20
New York City
BILLY TAYLOR QUINTET
John Hardee, tenor saxophone; Milt Page, organ; John Simmons, bass; Joe Harris, drums; Billy Taylor, piano
Take The A Train, Misty Blues, The Bug, Prelude To A Kiss
BILLY TAYLOR QUINTET: SAVOY XP8113

1950
August 17
New York City
STAN GETZ and HIS ORCHESTRA
Stan Fishelson, Al Porcino, Idrees Sulieman, trumpets; Johnny Mandel, bass trumpet; Don Lanphere, Zoot Sims, Stan Getz, tenor saxophones; Gerry Mulligan, baritone saxophone; Tommy Potter, bass: Roy Haynes, drums; Sarah Vaughan, vocals; Billy Taylor, piano
Four Brothers, Early Autumn, My Gentleman Friend
STAN GETZ and HIS ORCHESTRA: CHARLIE PARKER CP-503

1950
August 25
New York City
COLEMAN HAWKINS and HIS QUARTET

Coleman Hawkins, tenor saxophone; John Collins, guitar; Percy Heath, bass; Art
Blakey, drums; Billy Taylor, piano
You've Got Me Crying Again, Can Anyone Explain?, I Cross My Fingers, I'll Know
COLEMAN HAWKINS and HIS QUARTET: ROOST 517, 519

1951
New York City
BILLY TAYLOR TRIO
Earl May, bass; Ed Thigpen, drums; Billy Taylor, piano
Wrap Your Troubles In Dreams, God Groove, Thou Swell, Somebody Loves Me,
PIANO PANORAMA: ATLANTIC 113

1951
February 20
New York City
BILLY TAYLOR QUARTET
John Collins, guitar; Al Hall, bass; Shadow Wilson, drums; Billy Taylor, piano
Good Groove, Wrap Your Troubles In Dreams, What Is There To Say?, Thou Swell,
Willow Weep For Me, The Very Thought Of You, Somebody Loves Me, If I Had You
BILLY TAYLOR QUARTET: ATLANTIC 676; LP 113

1951
May 25
New York City
BILLY TAYLOR TRIO
Aaron Bell, bass; Kelly Marin, drums; Billy Taylor, piano
All Ears, Darn That Dream, My Heart Stood Still, Double Duty
BILLY TAYLOR TRIO: BRUNSWICK 65025-65032

1951
September 29
New York City
MILES DAVIS
Miles Davis, trumpet; Eddie "Lockjaw" Davis, tenor saxophone; Big Nick Nicholas,
tenor saxophone, Charles Mingus, bass; Art Blakey, drums, Billy Taylor, piano
The Squirrel, Move, Lady Bird
MILES DAVIS: THE COMPLETE BIRDLAND RECORDINGS, DEFINITIVE
RECORDS DRCD 11165

1951
New York City
BILLY TAYLOR
Joe Holiday, tenor saxophone; Jordan Fordin, alto saxophone; Earl May, bass;
Charlie Smith, congas; Billy Taylor, piano, organ
Besame Mucho, I Wouldn't Want To Walk Without You, Fiesta
MAMBO JAZZ: PRESTIGE 177 OJC-17861

1951
November 1
New York City
BILLY TAYLOR QUINTET
Zoot Sims, tenor saxophone/maracas; Mundell Lowe, guitar; Earl May, bass; Jo
Jones, drums; Frank Conlon, congas; Billy Taylor, piano
Cuban Caper, Cu-Blue, Squeeze Me, Feeling Frisky
BILLY TAYLOR QUINTET: ROOST 409

1952
April 18
New York City
BILLY TAYLOR BAND
Taft Jordan, trumpet; George Matthews, trombone; Doc Clifford, George James,
alto saxophones; George Berg, Stan Getz, tenor saxophones; Bill Doggett, organ;
Earl May, bass; Charlie Smith, drums; Billy Taylor, piano
Alone, To Be Or Not To Bop, Lonesome And Blue, Paradise
BILLY TAYLOR BAND: unissued

1952
May 2
New York City
BILLY TAYLOR SEXTET
Chuck Wayne, guitar; Earl May, bass; Charlie Smith, drums; Frank Conlon, Manny
Quando bongos, conga; Billy Taylor, piano
Cuban Nightingale, Titoro, Makin' Whoopee, Moonlight Saving Time
BILLY TAYLOR SEXTET: ROOST 409

1952
July 11
New York City
BILLY TAYLOR QUARTET
Chuck Wayne, guitar; George Duvivier, bass; Sid Sulkin, drums; Billy Taylor, piano

Three Little Words, Oscar Rides Again*
*add Oscar Pettiford, 'cello
BILLY TAYLOR QUARTET: BRUNSWICK 80215

1952
Autumn
Storyville Club, Boston
BILLY TAYLOR TRIO
Charlie Mingus, bass; Marquis Foster, drums; Billy Taylor, piano
Lady Bird, I'm Beginning To See The Light, All The Things You Are, Laura, What Is
This Thing Called Love
JAZZ AT STORYVILLE: ROOST 406

1952
November 18
New York City
BILLY TAYLOR TRIO
Earl May, bass; Charlie Smith, drums; Billy Taylor, piano
They Can't Take That Away From Me, All Too Soon, Accent On Youth, Give Me
The Simple Life
BILLY TAYLOR TRIO: PRESTIGE 139

1952
December 10
New York City
BILLY TAYLOR TRIO
Earl May, bass; Charlie Smith, drums; Billy Taylor, piano
Little Girl Blue, The Man With A Horn, Let's Get Away From It All, Lover
BILLY TAYLOR TRIO, Vol. 2: PRESTIGE 139

1953
May 7
New York City
BILLY TAYLOR SEXTET
Earl May, bass; Charlie Smith, drums; Jose Manguel, Ubal Nieto, Chico Guerro,
bongos and conga; Billy Taylor, piano
I Love To Mambo, Candido, Early Morning Mambo, Mambo Azul
CROSS SECTION: PRESTIGE 7071, ORIGINAL JAZZ CLASSICS 1730

1953
November 2
New York City
BILLY TAYLOR TRIO
Earl May, bass; Charlie Smith, drums; Billy Taylor, piano
Cool And Caressing, Who Can I Turn To?, My One And Only Love, Tenderly, I've
Got The Whole World, Bird Watcher, BT's DT's, Hey Look
BILLY TAYLOR TRIO, Volume 2: PRESTIGE 7016

1953
December 29
New York City
BILLY TAYLOR TRIO
Earl May, bass; Charlie Smith, drums; Billy Taylor, piano
That's All, The Little Things, Nice Work If You Can Get It, The Surrey With The
Fringe On Top
BILLY TAYLOR TRIO, Vol. 1: PRESTIGE 7016, 24154

1953-1954
New York City
ERNIE ROYAL and HIS PRINCES
Ernie Royal, trumpet; Sidney Gross, George Barnes, guitar, Oscar Pettiford, bass;
Osie Johnson, drums; Billy Taylor, piano
Flowin', Fascinating Rhythm, Stompin' At The Savoy, Stardust, Taking A Chance
On Love, Handful Of Stars, It's A Grand Night For Swinging, What Is There To Say
ERNIE ROYAL and HIS PRINCES: URANIA UJLP 1203

1954
July 30
New York City
BILLY TAYLOR TRIO
Earl May, bass; Charlie Smith, drums; Billy Taylor, piano
Time For Tex, Moonlight In Vermont, I'll Be Around, Biddy's Beat, Eddie's Tune,
Mood For Mendez, Goodbye, Lullaby Of Birdland
CROSS SECTION: PRESTIGE 7071, ORIGINAL JAZZ CLASSICS 1730

1954
September 7
New York City
BILLY TAYLOR QUARTET
Earl May, bass; Charlie Smith; drums; Candido Camero, conga; Billy Taylor, piano

Dectivity, A Live One, Mambo Inn, Bit Of Bedlam, Hearing Bells, Love For Sale
THE BILLY TAYLOR TRIO WITH CANDIDO: PRESTIGE 7071, ORIGINAL JAZZ
CLASSICS 015

1954
November 6
New York City
COLEMAN HAWKINS BAND
Emmett Berry, trumpet; Eddie Bert, trombone; Coleman Hawkins, tenor saxophone;
Milt Hinton, bass; Jo Jones, drums; Billy Taylor, piano
Lullaby Of Birdland, Get Happy, Out Of Nowhere, Blue Lou, Stompin' At The Savoy,
Just You Just Me, If I Had You
COLEMAN HAWKINS BAND: JAZZTONE J1002

1954
November 6
New York City
COLEMAN HAWKINS QUARTET
Coleman Hawkins, tenor saxophone; Milt Hinton, bass; Jo Jones, drums; Billy
Taylor, piano
If I Had You, Ain't Misbehavin', Cheek To Cheek, Undecided, Honeysuckle Rose
COLEMAN HAWKINS QUARTET: JAZZTONE J1002,

1954
December 17
New York City
BILLY TAYLOR TRIO
Earl May, bass; Percy Brice, drums; Billy Taylor, piano
A Foggy Day, I'll Remember April, Sweet Georgia Brown, Theodora, How High The
Moon
BILLY TAYLOR TRIO IN CONCERT AT TOWN HALL: PRESTIGE 709

1955
March 15
New York City
BARBARA LEA
Johnny Windhurst, trumpet; Jimmy Shirley, guitar; Earl May, bass; Percy Brice,
drums, Billy Taylor, piano
Love Is Here To Stay, Love Me, As Long As I Live, Come Rain Or Come Shine
BARBARA LEA: A WOMAN IN LOVE: RIVERSIDE RLP 2518

1955
April 10
New York City
BILLY TAYLOR TRIO
Earl May, bass; Percy Brice, drums; Billy Taylor, piano
Early Bird, A Bientot, Memories Of Spring, Ever So Easy, Day Dreaming, Radio
Activity, Purple Mood, Long Tom, A Grand Night For Swingin', Blue Clouds, Live It
Up, Daddy-O
A TOUCH OF TAYLOR: PRESTIGE 7001

1956
January 1 and 2
New York City
BILLY TAYLOR TRIO
Earl May, bass; Percy Brice, drums; Billy Taylor, piano
But Not For Me, All The Things You Are, Cheek To Cheek, Between The Devil And
The Deep Blue Sea, I Only Have Eyes For You, It's Too Late Now, More Than You
Know, Satin Doll, Then I'll Be Tired Of You, You Don't Know What Love Is
BILLY TAYLOR TRIO: ABC-PARAMOUNT 1171

1956
January 22
Chicago, Illinois
BILLY TAYLOR TRIO
Earl May, bass; Percy Brice, drums; Billy Taylor, piano
Gone With The Wind, I Cover The Waterfront, It Might As Well Be Spring, Our
Love Is Here To Stay, The London House, Midnight Piano, Stella By Starlight
BILLY TAYLOR AT THE LONDON HOUSE: ABC-PARAMOUNT 1176

1956
March
New York City
BILLY TAYLOR TRIO
George Duvivier, bass; Percy Brice, drums; Billy Taylor, piano
Indiana
EVERGREENS: ABC-PARAMOUNT 115

1956
November
New York City
BILLY TAYLOR QUARTET

Ira Sullivan, trumpet, alto and tenor saxophones; Earl May, bass; Ed Thigpen, drums; Billy Taylor, piano
Imagination, In A Mellowtone, Leslie's Gauge, Stollin', So In Love, They Can't Take That Away From Me, You Don't Know What Love Is
BILLY TAYLOR PRESENTS IRA SULLIVAN: ABC-PARAMOUNT 162

1957
January 8
New York City
QUINCY JONES ORCHESTRA with BILLY TAYLOR
Ernie Royal, trumpet; Don Elliott, trumpet/mellophone/vibes/bongos; Jimmy Cleveland, trombone; Jimmy Buffington, French horn; Don Butterfield, tuba; Tony Ortega, tenor saxophone; Charlie Fowlkes, baritone saxophone; Al Casamenti, guitar; Earl May, bass; Ed Thigpen, drums; Billy Taylor, piano; Quincy Jones, arranger/producer.
I've Grown Accustomed To Her Face

January 22
Jay McAllister replaced Don Butterfield, tuba
With A Little Bit Of Luck, Wouldn't It Be Loverly?, On The Street Where You Live

February 5
Gerry Mulligan replaced Charlie Fowlkes, baritone saxophone
Show Me, The Rain In Spain, I Could Have Danced All Night, Get Me To The Church On Time
MY FAIR LADY LOVES JAZZ: ABC-PARAMOUNT 177, GRP 11412, IMPULSE 141

1957
March 7, April 10
New York City
MUNDELL LOWE
Mundell Lowe, guitar; Gene Quill, alto saxophone; Les Grange, bass; Ed Thigpen, drums; Billy Taylor, piano
It's A Grand Night For Swingin', Easy To Love, Crazy Rhythm, Blues Before Freud, Love Me Or Leave Me, You Turned The Tables On Me
A GRAND NIGHT FOR SWINGING: RIVERSIDE 238/ojc-1940

1957
October 25
New York City
BILLY TAYLOR TRIO
Earl May, bass; Ed Thigpen, drums; Billy Taylor, piano

Small Hotel, The More I See You, There Will Never Be Another You, Sounds In The Night, Southside, Will You Still Be Mine, Round Midnight, I Never Get Enough Of You
THE NEW BILLY TAYLOR TRIO: ABC-PARAMOUNT 1231

1957
October 28
New York City
BILLY TAYLOR TRIO
Earl May, bass; Ed Thigpen, drums; Billy Taylor, piano
Can You Tell?, You Make Me Feel So Young, I Get A Kick Out Of You, Earl May
THE BILLY TAYLOR TOUCH: ATLANTIC 1277

1957
November 17
Chicago, Illinois
BILLY TAYLOR and HIS ORCHESTRA
Willie Cook, Clark Terry, trumpets; Britt Woodman, tuba; Johnny Hodges, alto saxophone; Paul Gonsalves, tenor saxophone; Harry Carney, baritone saxophone; Earl May, bass; Ed Thigpen, drums; Billy Taylor, piano
Buddy's Beat, Theodora, Mood For Mendez, Daddy-O, Cue-Blue, Day Dreaming, Can You Tell?, Tune For Tex
BILLY TAYLOR and HIS ORCHESTRA: ARGO 650

1957
December 16, 17
New York City
BILLY TAYLOR TRIO
Earl May, bass; Ed Thigpen, drums; Billy Taylor, piano
Round Midnight, I Never Get Enough Of You
BILLY TAYLOR TRIO: ABC-PARAMOUNT RECORDS

1959
June 24
New York City
BILLY TAYLOR TRIO
Earl May, bass; Kenny Dennis, drums; Billy Taylor, piano
Summertime, One For You, That's For Sure, A Little Southside Soul, Blue Moon, Poinciana, At Long Last Love, When Lights Are Low
ONE FOR FUN: ATLANTIC 1329

1959
July 20
New York City
BILLY TAYLOR AND FLUTES
Phil Bodner, Herbie Mann, Frank Wess, Jerome Richardson, flutes; Tom Williams, bass; Dave Bailey, drums, Chino Pozo, conga; Billy Taylor, piano
The Song Is Ended, Back Home, One For The Woofer, Kool Bongos, Blues Shutters*
*Bill Slapin replaced Jerome Richardson
BILLY TAYLOR WITH FOUR FLUTES: RIVERSIDE RLP 306, ORIGINAL JAZZ CLASSICS 1830

1959
July 24
New York City
BILLY TAYLOR AND FLUTES
Jerry Sanfino, Bill Slapin, Jerome Richardson, Herbie Mann, flutes; Tom Williams, bass; Al Heath, drums; Billy Taylor, piano
St. Thomas, Oh Lady Be Good, How About You?, No Parking*
*Seldon Powell replaced Herbie Mann
TAYLOR MADE FLUTE: RIVERSIDE RLP 306, ORIGINAL JAZZ CLASSICS 1830

1960
February 4
New York City
BILLY TAYLOR TRIO
Henry Grimes, bass; Ray Mosca, drums; Billy Taylor, piano
Le Petite Mambo, Jordu, Just The Thought Of You, Soul Sister, Moanin', S'Wonderful, Warm Blue Stream, Biddy's Best, Cue-Blue
UPTOWN: RIVERSIDE 319, ORIGINAL JAZZ CLASSICS 1901

1960
March 26
New York City
BILLY TAYLOR TRIO
Henry Grimes, bass; Ray Mosca, drums; Billy Taylor, piano
Warming Up, Easy Like, That's What It Is, Coffee Break, Native Dancer, Afterthoughts, Easy Walker, Lonesome Lover, Don't Bug Me, You Know What I Mean, Uncle Fuzzy, No Aftertaste
WARMING UP: RIVERSIDE 339

1961
January 3
New York City
BILLY TAYLOR TRIO
Doug Watkins, bass; Ray Mosca, drums; Billy Taylor, piano
You Tempt Me, Did You Dream Too?, You're All That Matters, Interlude, You're
Mine You, My Heart Sings, I Sigh, Here Today Gone Tomorrow Love, All Alone
INTERLUDE: MOODSVILLE 16

1961
New York City
JIMMIE JONES ORCHESTRA WITH BILLY TAYLOR
Clark Terry, fluegelhorn; Jimmy Cleveland, trombone; Julius Watkins, French horn;
Jay McAllister, tuba; Phil Woods, alto saxophone; Frank Wess, tenor saxophone;
Jerome Richardson, baritone saxophone; Les Spann, guitar, George Duvivier, bass;
Dale Johnson, drums; Billy Taylor, piano; Jimmie Jones, arranger/conductor
Something Big, I'm Seeing Rainbows, Ordinary People, The Cocoa Bean Song,
What's Wrong With Me?, Nothing More To Look Forward To, Another Time,
Another Place, Happy Is The Cricket, The Sun Is Beginning To Crow
JIMMIE JONES ORCHESTRA WITH BILLY TAYLOR: MERCURY 20654

1962
New York City
BILLY TAYLOR QUARTET
Jim Hall, guitar; Bob Cranshaw, bass; Walter Perkins, drums; Billy Taylor, piano
Don't Go South, Empty Ballroom, Impromptu, Muffle Cuffle, Paraphrase, At The
Carrousel, Capricious, Free And Easy
BILLY TAYLOR QUARTET: MERCURY 20722

1962
May
New York City
BILLY TAYLOR QUARTET
Jim Hall, guitar; Bob Cranshaw, bass; Walter Perkins, drums; Billy Taylor, piano
Paraphrase, At La Carousel, Don't Go Down South
IMPROMPTU: MERCURY SR-60722

1963

New York City

OLIVER NELSON ORCHESTRA WITH BILLY TAYLOR

John Bello, Snooky Young, Joe Newman, Thad Jones, Ernie Royal, Doc Severinsen, Clark Terry, trumpets; Wayne Andre, Britt Woodman, Quentin Jackson, Tony Studd, Urbie Green, trombones; Phil Woods, Jerome Richardson, Romeo Penque, Stan Webb, Danny Bank, saxophones; Ben Tucker, bass; Grady Tate, drums; Billy Taylor, piano; Oliver Nelson, arranger/conductor

That's Where It Is, Lot Of Livin' To Do, Right Here, Right Now, I Believe In You, Easy Walker, Afterthoughts, Stolen Moments, Give Me The Simple Life, Something Always Happens, Soul Sister, Freedom, I Wish I Knew

RIGHT HERE, RIGHT NOW – BILLY TAYLOR: CAPITOL 2039

1964

October 12-14

New York City

BILLY TAYLOR AND HIS ORCHESTRA

Orchestra members included Joe Newman, Barry Galbraith, Tony Studd, Phil Woods, Urbie Green, Snooky Young and Clark Terry. Arrangements by Oliver Nelson.

From The Heart, It's A Grand Night For Swinging, You Tempt Me (and others)

MIDNIGHT PIANO: CAPITOL ST- 2302

1965

New York City

BILLY TAYLOR TRIO

Sweet Georgia Brown, Theodora, Foggy Day, How High The Moon, I'll Remember April

BILLY TAYLOR TRIO AT TOWN HALL

1966

July 1

Newport, Rhode Island

GERRY MULLIGAN

Rudy Braff, trumpet; Bud Freeman, tenor saxophone; Gerry Mulligan, baritone saxophone; Benny Moten, bass; Osie Johnson, drums; Billy Taylor, piano

Rose Room

GERRY MULLIGAN: NIPPON COLUMBIA COMPACT DISC 33c38-7682

1967
New York City
BILLY TAYLOR TRIO
Ben Tucker, bass, Grady Tate, drums, Billy Taylor, piano
I Wish I Knew How It Would Feel To Be Free, Pensativa, Morning, TNT, Hard To
Find, Lonesome Lover, Cag
I WISH I KNEW HOW IT WOULD FEEL TO BE FREE: TOWER ST-5111

1969
April 1
New York City
BILLY TAYLOR TRIO
Ben Tucker, bass; Grady Tate, drums; Billy Taylor, piano
La Petite Mambo, Theodora, Paraphrase, Don't Go Down South, Brother, Where
Are You
TODAY: PRESTIGE 7662 (later released on PAUSA 7096 as A SLEEPIN' BEE

1970
New York City
BILLY TAYLOR ORCHESTRA
Dick Hurwitz, Jimmy Owens, trumpet-flugelhorn; Morty Bullman, trombone, George
Berg, Frank Wess, Al Gibbons, saxophone-clarinet; Barry Galbraith, guitar; Bob
Cranshaw, electric bass; Bobby Thomas, drums; Marty Grupp, percussion; Billy
Taylor, piano-leader.
By George, O.K. Billy, Somewhere Soon, Tell Me Why, Dirty Ole Man, If You Are
Concerned Then Show It, Break-A-Way, After Love Emptiness
OK BILLY!: BELL RECORDS 6049

1977
New York City
BILLY TAYLOR TRIO
Suite For Jazz Piano and Orchestra, Ivoire, Echoes of Ellington
JAZZ ALIVE: MONMOUTH-EVERGREEN 7089

1977
December 2-3
New York City
BILLY TAYLOR TRIO
Victor Gaskin, bass; Grady Tate, drums; Billy Taylor, piano
Misty, Night In Tunisia, My Heart Sings, Naima, Birdwatcher, Lush Life, I Wish I
Knew How It Would Feel To be Free
LIVE AT STORYVILLE: WEST 54 8008

1978
BILLY TAYLOR TRIO
BILLY TAYLOR TRIO IN LIVE PERFORMANCE

1980
December
New York City
BILLY TAYLOR QUARTET (with Joe Kennedy)
Where've You Been?, Night Coming, Tenderly, Ray's Tune, Antoinette, I'm In Love
With You, All Alone, I Think Of You, Capricious
WHERE'VE YOU BEEN?: CONCORD JAZZ 4145

1981
June 24
New York City
BILLY TAYLOR TRIO WITH JOE KENNEDY
Victor Gaskin, bass; Curtis Boyd, drums; Joe Kennedy, violin; Billy Taylor, piano
Take The A Train, Let Us Make A Joyful Noise
YOU TEMPT ME: TAYLOR-MADE 1004

1986
New York City
BILLY TAYLOR TRIO
Victor Gaskin, bass; Curtis Boyd, drums, Billy Taylor, piano
Take the A Train, Tom, Vaguely, You Tempt Me, Let Us Make A Joyful Noise/
Spiritual, Rejoice, Prayer, Celebrate, Walking in the Light
LET US MAKE A JOYFUL NOISE: BETCO RECORDS A-440

1988
June 13-14
Leningrad, Soviet Union
BILLY TAYLOR TRIO
Victor Gaskin, bass; Bobby Thomas, drums; Billy Taylor, piano
Pensativa, Morning, Secret Love, My Romance
WHITE NIGHTS and JAZZ IN LENINGRAD: TAYLOR-MADE 1001

1988
August 1-2
New York City
BILLY TAYLOR (solo)
All The Things You Are, Bit Of Bedlam, Old Folks, More Thank You Know, Gone
With The Wind
SOLO: TAYLOR-MADE 1002

1989
April 5-6
New York City
BILLY TAYLOR and THE JAZZMOBILE ALL-STARS
Ted Dunbar, guitar; Frank Wess, soprano and tenor saxophones; Jimmy Owens,
trumpet; Victor Gaskin, bass; Bobby Thomas, drums; Billy Taylor, piano
Nine Billy Taylor tunes, Ceora
THE JAZZMOBILE ALL-STARS: TAYLOR-MADE 1003

1990
New York City
BILLY TAYLOR and RAMSEY LEWIS
Lucky So And So, Jitterbug Waltz, Django, Cookin At The Continental, Somewhere
Soon, We Meet Again, Quiet Now, Soul Sister, Waltz For Debby, Nigerian
Marketplace,
WE MEET AGAIN: Columbia 44941

1991
February
New York City
BILLY TAYLOR QUARTET
Fred Tillis, soprano and tenor saxophones; Victor Gaskin, bass; Bobby Thomas,
drums; Billy Taylor, piano
The Holidays, Confirmation, When Lights Are Low, It Don't Mean A Thing, Harlem
Blues
AMONG FRIENDS: HARRISON DIGITAL PRODUCTIONS

1992
New York City
BILLY TAYLOR TRIO WITH GERRY MULLIGAN
Gerry Mulligan, baritone saxophone, Victor Gaskin, bass; Bobby Thomas, drums;
Billy Taylor, piano

I'll Remember April, 'Round Midnight, Line For Lyons, Cubano Chant, Lush Life, Who Can I Turn To?, Laurentide Waltz, You're Mine, Just The Thought Of You, Rico Apollo
DR. T: GRP 9692

1993
New York City
BILLY TAYLOR TRIO with FRIENDS
Stanley Turrentine, tenor saxophone; Grady Tate, vocals; Christian McBride, bass; Marvin "Smitty" Smith, drums; Ray Mantilla, conga; Billy Taylor, piano
Ten compositions by Billy Taylor
IT'S A MATTER OF PRIDE: GRP 9753

1994
October 10-11
New York City
BILLY TAYLOR TRIO with the TURTLE ISLAND STRING QUARTET
Chip Jackson, bass; Steve Johns; drums; Billy Taylor, piano
Step Into My Dream (10 parts)
HOMAGE: GRP 9806

1996
August 6-8
New York City
BILLY TAYLOR TRIO
Chip Jackson, bass; Steve Johns, drums; Billy Taylor, piano
Lover Come Back To Me, I Wish I Knew How It Would Feel To Be Free, Wouldn't It Be Loverly, Caravan, Body And Soul, One For The Woofer, Ballade, Up Jumped Spring, Interlude, Arcadia Blues
MUSIC KEEPS US YOUNG: ARKADIA 71601

1996
August 6-8
New York City
BILLY TAYLOR (solo)
Wrap Your Troubles In Dreams, Joy Spring, Tea For Two, In A Sentimental Mood, Laura, Easy Like, Night And Day, Can You Tell By Looking At Me?, Early Bird, My Heart Stood Still
TEN FINGERS – ONE VOICE: ARKADIA 71602

2001
New York City
BILLY TAYLOR TRIO
Chip Jackson, bass; Winard Harper, drums; Billy Taylor, piano
Local Color/Can You Dig It?, Reclamation, Gracias Chucko, Etude, Conversion, Spoken, In Loving Memory, Like A Heartbeat, Invention/Looking For Another Theme, Transformation, A Duke-ish Blues
URBAN GRIOT: SOUNDPOST RECORDS-SP 3035-2

2002
New York City
BILLY TAYLOR TRIO
Chip Jackson, bass; Winard Harper, drums; Billy Taylor, piano
Impromptu, Body and Soul, Conversion, Titoro, Cote d'Ivoire (Third Movement from Suite for Jazz Piano and Orchestra)
BILLY TAYLOR TRIO LIVE AT IAJE: SOUNDPOST RECORDS-SP 5090-2

BIBLIOGRAPHY

Berendt, Joachim E. THE JAZZ BOOK. London: Granada Publishing Ltd., 1983

Berliner, Paul F. THINKING IN JAZZ. Chicago: The University of Chicago Press, 1994

Carr, Ian; Fairweather, Digby; Priestley, Brian. JAZZ: THE ROUGH GUIDE. London, England: Rough Guide Ltd., 1995

Catalano, Nick. CLIFFORD BROWN: THE LIFE AND ART OF THE LEGENDARY JAZZ TRUMPETER. New York: Oxford University Press, 2000

Cattell, Jaques (compiler). ASCAP BIOGRAPHICAL DICTIONARY (Fourth Edition). New York: R.R. Bowker Company, 1980

Chambers, Jack. MILESTONES 1: THE MUSIC AND TIMES OF MILES DAVIS TO 1960.

New York: Beech Tree Books, William Morrow, 1987

Chilton, John. BILLIE'S BLUES. London, England: Quartet Books Ltd., 1975

Chilton, John. JAZZ. London: Teach Yourself Books, 1979

Clarke, Donald. THE RISE AND FALL OF POPULAR MUSIC. New York: St. Martin's Griffin, 1995

Crow, Bill. FROM BIRDLAND TO BROADWAY. New York: Oxford University Press, 1992

DeVeaux, Scott. THE BIRTH OF BEBOP. Berkeley, California: University of California Press, 1997.

Erlewine, Michael (Ed.). ALL MUSIC GUIDE TO JAZZ. San Francisco: Miller Freeman Books, 1996

Erlich, Lillian. WHAT JAZZ IS ALL ABOUT. New York: Julian Messner, 1975

Feather, Leonard and Gitler, Ira. THE BIOGRAPHICAL ENCYCLOPEDIA OF JAZZ. New York: Oxford University Press, 1999

Feather, Leonard and Gitler, Ira. THE ENCYCLOPEDIA OF JAZZ IN THE SEVENTIES. New York: Horizon Press, 1976

Feather, Leonard. THE ENCYCLOPEDIA OF JAZZ IN THE SIXTIES. New York: Bonanza Books, 1966

Feather, Leonard. THE NEW EDITION OF THE ENCYCLOPEDIA OF JAZZ. New York: Bonanza Books, 1955

Folley-Cooper, Marquette. SEEING JAZZ. San Francisco: Chronicle Books, 1997

George, Don: SWEET MAN. New York: G.P. Putnam's Sons, 1981

Gillenson, Lewis W. (Ed.). ESQUIRE'S WORLD OF JAZZ. New York: Esquire, Inc., 1962

Gitler, Ira. SWING TO BOP. New York: Oxford University Press, 1986

Gottlieb, William P. THE GOLDEN AGE OF JAZZ. San Francisco: Pomegranate Art books, 1995

Gourse, Leslie. THE BILLIE HOLIDAY COMPANION. New York: Schirmer Books, 1997

Hajdu, David. LUSH LIFE: A BIOGRAPHY OF BILLY STRAYHORN. New York: North Point Press, 1996.

Hentoff, Nat. THE JAZZ LIFE. New York: Da Capo Press, 1978

Hitchcock, H. Wiley and Sadie, Stanley (Ed.). THE NEW GROVE DICTIONARY OF AMERICAN MUSIC. London: Macmillan Press Limited, 1986

Hodeir, Andre. TOWARD JAZZ. New York: Grove Press Inc., 1962

Jepsen, Jorgen Grunnet. JAZZ RECORDS, 1942-1962. Denmark: Copylit, 1964

Keepnews, Orrin and Grauer, Jr., Bill. A PICTORIAL HISTORY OF JAZZ. New York: Bonanza Books, 1981

Kernfeld, Barry (Ed.). THE NEW GROVE DICTIONARY OF JAZZ. London, England: Macmillan Press Limited, 1988

Kinkle, Roger D. THE COMPLETE ENCYCLOPEDIA OF POPULAR MUSIC AND JAZZ, 1900-1950. New Rochelle, New York: Arlington House Publishers, 1974

Klinkowitz, Jerome. LISTEN: GERRY MULLIGAN. New York: Schirmer Books, 1991

Lee, Bill. PEOPLE IN JAZZ: JAZZ KEYBOARD IMPROVISORS of the 19th and 20th CENTURIES. Hialeah, Florida: Columbia Pictures Publications, 1984

Lees, Gene. OSCAR PETERSON: THE WILL TO SWING. Rocklin, California: Prima Publishing & Communications, 1990

Leonard, Neil. JAZZ, MYTH AND RELIGION. New York: Oxford University Press, 1987

Lester, James. TOO MARVELOUS FOR WORDS: THE LIFE AND GENIUS OF ART TATUM. New York: Oxford University Press, 1994

Levinson, Peter J. TRUMPET BLUES: THE LIFE OF HARRY JAMES. New York: Oxford University Press, 1999

Lyons, Len. THE GREAT JAZZ PIANISTS: SPEAKING OF THEIR LIVES AND MUSIC, New York: Quill, 1983.

Lyons, Len and Perlo, Don. JAZZ PORTRAITS: THE LIVES AND MUSIC OF THE JAZZ MASTERS. New York: Quill-William Morrow Publishers, 1989

Lyttelton, Humphrey. THE BEST OF JAZZ 2: ENTER THE GIANTS. London, England: Robson Books Ltd, 1981

Mancuso, Chuck. POPULAR MUSIC AND THE UNDERGROUND. Dubuque, Iowa:

Kendall/Hunt Publishing Company, 1996

Nanry, Charles. THE JAZZ TEXT. New York: D. Van Nostrand Co., 1979

Owens, Thomas. BEBOP: THE MUSIC AND THE PLAYERS. New York: Oxford University Press, 1998

Pettinger, Peter. BILL EVANS: HOW MY HEART SINGS. New Haven, Ct: Yale University Press, 1998

Porter, Lewis. JOHN COLTRANE: HIS LIFE AND MUSIC. Ann Arbor, Michigan: University of Michigan Press, 1999

Priestley, Brian. MINGUS: A CRITICAL BIOGRAPHY. New York: Da Capo Press, 1982

Randel, Don Michael (Ed.). THE HARVARD BIOGRAPHICAL DICTIONARY OF MUSIC. Cambridge, Mass.: The Belknap Press, 1996

Shadwick, Keith (Ed.) GRAMOPHONE JAZZ. Great Britain: Gramophone Publications Ltd.,1997

Shapiro, Harry. WAITING FOR THE MAN: THE STORY OF DRUGS AND POPULAR MUSIC. New York: William Morrow and Co., 1988

Shapiro, Nat and Hentoff, Nat. HEAR ME TALKIN' TO YA. Toronto, Ontario, Canada: General Publishing Co. Ltd, 1955

Shaw, Arnold. 52nd STREET: THE STREET OF JAZZ. New York: Da Capo Press, 1977

Shaw, Arnold. THE STREET THAT NEVER SLEPT. New York: COWARD, MCCANN & GEOGHEGAN, INC., 1971

Shipton, Alyn. GROOVIN' HIGH: THE LIFE OF DIZZY GILLESPIE. New York: Oxford University Press, 1999

Sidran, Ben. TALKING JAZZ: AN ORAL HISTORY. New York: Da Capo Press, 1995

Stearns, Marshall W. THE STORY OF JAZZ. New York: Oxford University Press, 1956

Stokes, W. Royal. LIVING THE JAZZ LIFE. New York: Oxford University Press, 2000

Stokes, W. Royal. THE JAZZ SCENE. New YORK: Oxford University Press, 1991

Taylor, Billy. JAZZ PIANO: A JAZZ HISTORY. Dubuque, Iowa: Wm C. Brown Co., 1982

Ulanov, Barry. HANDBOOK OF JAZZ. New York: The Viking Press, 1960

Wilmer, Valerie. AS SERIOUS AS YOUR LIFE: THE STORY OF THE NEW JAZZ. London: Pluto Press, 1977

Woodward, Woody. JAZZ AMERICANA. Los Angeles: Trend Book, 1956

Wynn, Ron (Ed.). ALL MUSIC GUIDE TO JAZZ. San Francisco California: Miller Freeman Books, 1994

Yanow, Scott. BEBOP. San Francisco: Miller Freeman Books, 2000

PERIODICALS

Alleyne, Sonia. IMPROVS ON A FEMININE SCALE. Black Elegrance, June-July, 1992

Anon. Billboard Magazine, May 18, 1985

Anon. BILLY TAYLOR, TRINITY MUSICIANS JAZZ UP MUSICFEST VI TONIGHT. The Trinitorian (Trinity University), Feb. 21, 1986

Anon. Chicago Tribune, Mar. 11, 1990

Anon. COOKIN' IN THE ATTIC. Pittsburgh's Complete Entertainment Guide, Aug. 19, 1972

Anon. TOP PIANIST BILLY TAYLOR DEFINES JAZZ, SHOWS ITS ROLE IN CONTEMPORARY MUSIC. Down Beat, Mar. 7, 1956

Anon. Down Beat (record review), Dec. 31, 1952

Anon. HOW BILLY TAYLOR HELPS TEENAGERS BEAT THE BLUES. Parent Magazine, Jan. 1974

Anon. INTO THE OLD BASKET. Cue Magazine, Sept. 23, 29, 1974

Anon. JAZZ MAN – BILLY TAYLOR – PIANIST, AUTHOR, TEACHER. Pisces Magazine, April 1974

Anon. JAMMING IN RYE: JAZZ GREATS JOIN FORCES FOR TV TAPING. Lifestyle Magazine, Oct. 29, 1985

Anon. Jazz Times, Nov. 1985

Anon. Jazz Times, Jan. 1989

Anon. Jazz Times, Dec. 1989

Anon. JAZZ GREAT BILLY TAYLOR NAMED ADVISOR TO KENNEDY CENTER. American Weekly, Mar. 18, 1994

Anon. JAZZ MAN AS FORUM DELEGATE. Daily News, Hungarian News Agency, MTI, Budapest, Thursday, Oct. 26, 1985

Anon. JAZZ IS ALIVE AND WELL IN NEW YORK. April 21, 1973

Anon. New Times, April, 1991

Anon. New York Times, Mar, 9, 1986

Anon, Newsweek Magazine, April 26, 1971

Anon. TAYLOR JAZZES THINGS UP. San Antonio Light, Wed. Feb. 19, 1986

Anon. The Honolulu Advertiser, Thursday, April 26, 1990

Anon. Variety Magazine, Nov., 1989

Anon. YOU MADE ME LOVE YOU. Variety, Wed. Nov. 6, 1985'

Bailey, Peter. BILLY TAYLOR KEEPS JAZZ JUMPING. Black Stars, Sept. 1973

Barrett, Jr., John. FEATURED ARTIST – BILLY TAYLOR. Jazz Improv. Vol. 3, Number 4, 2002

Barrett, Jr., John. NINETY PERCENT OF GENIUS IS HARD WORK; THE BILLY TAYLOR STORY. Jazz Improv. Volume 3, 2002

Bernotas, Bob. Jazz Player, Aug-Sept., 1996

Blum, Joe. Jazz Times, April 1983

Bradley, Jeff. BILLY TAYLOR PLAYS JAZZ PIANO BETTER THAN EVER AT POP'S CONCERT. Denver Post, 1993

Butler, Jim. Variety Magazine, Oct 1, 1992

Campbell, Barbara. HOW MR. TAYLOR BROKE THE ICE WITH MR. FROST. ASCAP Today, Sept. 1971, Vol. 5, #2

Caputo, Salvatore. TAYLOR-MADE, A CHAMPION OF JAZZ. Phoenix Gazette, Nov. 10, 1995

Cordle, Owen. DR. T (review of album). Down Beat, March, 1993

Dyer, Ted. JAZZMOBILE: TWENTY YEARS OF PROGRESS. Harlem Week, Aug. 8-19, 1984

Faria, Mannie. TAYLOR TRIO DAZZLES JAZZ LOVERS. News-Times, Sat., Mar., 1982

Feather, Leonard. TAYLOR TAKES JAZZ CONCERT ON ROAD TOUR TO SPREAD WORD. Indianapolis Star, Mar. 18, 1989

Francis, Jack. MEET THE DISC JOCKEY. SESAC Music, Christmas, 1960, Vol, 18, nos. 10-12

Franckling, Ken. BILLY TAYLOR'S 50 YEARS IN JAZZ. Jazz Times, Mar. 1993, Vol. 23, #2

Gahr, David. O.K. BILLY. Time Magazine, Aug. 6, 1972

Greim, Lisa. JAZZ PIANIST BILLY TAYLOR STILL LEARNING. Greeley tribune, Sept. 21, 1989.

Gutterman, Scott. Essence Magazine, No. 9, Jan., 1989

Guzman, Pablo. Daily News, Mar. 18, 1990

Henderson, Alex. DR. BILLY TAYLOR: A TAYLOR MADE JAZZMOBILE INNOVATOR. The Jazz Link, Nov. 1989, Vol. 11, Issue 18

Holden, Stephen, HONORING BILLY TAYLOR'S LIFE IN MUSIC: FIFTY YEARS AS PIANIST AND COMPOSER, TEACHER, AND HISTORIAN. New York Times, Sat., July 2, 1994

International Musician. BILLY TAYLOR: BRINGING JAZZ TO THE PEOPLE. September, 2000

Keepnews, Peter. JAZZ BLUE NOTES. Billboard Magazine, Sept. 21, 1985

Lange, Art. FOURTH ANNUAL JAZZ TIMES CONVENTION. Down Beat, Jan. 1986

Lawrence, Robert P. L A WAS ALWAYS KEY TO JAZZ. San Diego Union, Nov. 22, 1981

Lee, Amy. TELLING TONES. Christian Science Monitor, Thurs., July 14, 1964

Lenzine, Catherine Sell. SWING, BEBOP, and JAZZ AS PART OF THE CURRICULUM. The Instrumentalist, February 1997

Leseer, Johnthan. THE DOCTOR IS IN; JAZZ LEGEND BILLY TAYLOR COMES TO VAIL CELEBRATING 50 YEARS IN MUSIC. Vail Trail's Daily Options, July 22, 1994

Lesner, Sam. Chicago Daily News, Dec. 3, 1955

Levenson, Jeff. JAZZ BLUE NOTES. Billboard Magazine, May 28, 1994

Lyons, Ken. PIANO PANORAMA: INSIGHT INTO THE IVORIES. Down Beat, Mar. 10, 1977

McDonough, John. BILLY TAYLOR: THE PLAYER'S ADVOCATE. Down Beat, Feb. 1991

Matthews, Paul. BILLY TAYLOR INTERVIEW. Cadence Magazaine, Jan., 1996

Middleton, Joe. JAZZ LEGEND MAKES LOCAL APPEARANCE. Gallery of Sound Gazette, May 1994

Mitchel, Par Banks. THE CHEMISTRY WORKS; RAMSEY LEWS AND BILLY TAYLOR TOGETHER. Century, Daily Times, Oct., 1990

Montomery, M. JUST JAZZ. Black Variety, Feb. 22, 1972

Morganstern, Dan. TAYLOR-MADE FROSTINGS. Down Beat, Mar. 4, 1971

Nemeyer, Eric. TELL YOUR OWN STORY – AN INTERVIEW WITH BILLY TAYLOR. Jazz Improv. Volume 3, Number 4, 2002

Owens, Jimmy. BILLY TAYLOR: AMERICAN JAZZ MASTER. Winter, 1991 Vol. XXIII, No.2. Jazz Educators Journal

Primack, Brent. DR. T AT 75. Jazz Times, Oct., 1996

Renninger,. Christian. DR. BILLY TAYLOR, FEDERAL FUJNDING (FOR JAZZ) HAS BEEN GOOD, BUT I THINK IT CAN GET BETTER. Radio Free Jazz, Oct. 1975

Ribowsky, Mark. BILLY TAYLOR – THE FORCE WHO KEEPS JAZZ ALIVE. Sepia Magazine, Dec. 1977

Roberts, Jim. BILLY TAYLOR: PRIMARILY PIANO. Down Beat, Mar. 1985

Roberts, Jim. DR. BILLY TAYLOR'S ART OF JAZZ. Valley Advocate, July 24, 1985

Smith, Arnold Jay. BILLY TAYLOR AND DAVE BAILEY. Down Beat, Dec. 1, 1977

Sudhalter. Richard. DOES THE JAZZ OF THE PAST HAVE A FUTURE? New York Times, Sunday, July 16, 1989

Sutherland, Sam and Peter Keepnews. JAZZ BLUE NOTES. Billboard Magazine, Oct. 26, 1985

Sutherland, Sam and Peter Keepnews. JAZZ BLUE NOTES. Billboard Magazine, Nov. 9, 1985

Taylor, Billy. AN ART TATUM RECOLLECTION AND ANALYST. Keyboard Magazine, Oct. 1981

Taylor, Billy. IS JAZZ AMERICA'S CLASSICAL MUSIC? Ovation Magazine, July 1982

Taylor, Billy. JAZZ, AMERICA'S MUSIC: WE'RE WASTING A NATIONAL RESOURCE. Billboard Magazine, Feb. 1, 1986

Taylor, Billy JAZZMOBILE: TWENTY YEARS OF PROGRESS. Harlem Week, Aug.8-19, 1984

Taylor, Billy. A MESSAGE FROM DR. BILLY TAYLOR. Jazz Education Journal, Mary/June, 2002

Taylor, Billy. Richmond News Leader, April, 1989

Taylor, Billy. A TRIBUTE TO ART TATUM. Toledo (Ohio) Magazine, June 30, 1985

Winter, Stanley. BILLY TAYLOR TALKS JAZZ. The Campus Connection – University of Massachusetts, July 6, 1983

Womble, Candace. MULTI-TALENTED BILLY TAYLOR. Encore Magazine, Aug., 1973

RADIO INTERVIEW

Miller, Dick "INTERVIEW WITH BILLY TAYLOR". WMUB (radio), Miami University of Ohio, Aug. 27, 1989

INDEX

A

A TRIBUTE TO ART TATUM 128
a walking encyclopedia 30, 128
A. T. and T 104
Aaron Bell 43, 44, 129, 224
Aaron Copland 61, 104
ABC Paramount 50, 57
activist 99, 130, 142, 188
Adams Russell 132
Adolph Sandole 113
Adolpus Doc Cheatham 20
Africa 129, 133, 191
African American Arts Alliance 173
Afro-American 24, 74, 162
AFRO-CUBAN 188
AGAC 96
Ahmad Jamal 73, 99
Aint Misbehavin 2, 55, 222, 228
Al Brehm 112
Al Casamenti 59, 230
Al Cohn 113
Al Cohn-Zoot Sims 67
Al Gibbons 19, 23, 32, 35, 41, 42, 43, 59,
       64, 67, 88, 95, 112, 179, 223, 224,
       230, 232, 235
Al Haig 35, 41
Al Hall 19, 32, 43, 224
Al Heath 64, 232
Al Jarreau 118
Al McKibbon 23, 112
Al Porcino 42, 223
Al Sears 64

Alan and Marilyn Bergman 193
Alan Arkin 142
Alan Dawson 179
Alan Pepper 82
Albany 82
Alex Henderson 143
Alex Kallao 66
Alvino Rey 51
ALYN SHIPTON 17, 18, 29
Ambassador of Jazz 136, 197
ambulatory 206
American Council for the Arts 171, 172
American Film Institute 142
American Jazz Master 147
American music 24, 108, 146, 158, 162,
       166, 177, 202
American Music Center 104
American Music Workshop in Jazz 129
American Weekly 174, 243
America's classical music 90, 94, 103, 123,
       190
Amy Duncan 139
Amy Lee 77
Amy Marshal 180
AN ART TATUM RECOLLECTION
       AND ANALYST 117, 245
Anaheim 182
Andre Previn 147
Andrew White 11
Andy Kirk 43, 44
Andy Razaf 11
Anita ODay 66

Anitras Dance 8
Ann Black 167
Anne Dhu McLucas 125
Anne Meara 102
Antoinette Bacon Taylor 1
Apollo Theater 29, 42, 140, 186
Appalachian State University 182
Arabesque 41, 145
Argentina 63
Arkadia Records 187
Army Chorus 146
Arnett Cobb 41, 66
Arnold Jay Smith 111
ARNOLD SHAW 35, 48, 68, 69
ARNOLD SMITH 112
arranger 59, 63, 67, 72, 74, 77, 86, 102,
    106, 125, 142, 145, 230, 233, 234
Art Blakey 29, 41, 42, 44, 64, 107, 113,
    165, 224
Art Blakeys Jazz Messengers 71
Art Farmer 170
Art Lange 133
Art Pepper 74
ART TATUM 117, 128, 245, 246
Art Tatum 2, 3, 5, 8, 13, 16, 17, 19, 21,
    23, 29, 30, 31, 32, 33, 38, 65, 78,
    117, 128, 138, 140, 160, 165, 167,
    174, 177, 180, 188, 202
Arthur Mitchell 139
Artie Shaw 27, 28, 32, 49, 113, 132
Artie Shaw Grammercy 5 27, 32
Arts American Jazz Master 147
Arts American Jazz Masters Awards 199
arts in education 171, 172
Arturo Sandoval 197
ASCAP 85, 96, 98, 158, 194, 196, 240,
    244
athletics 3, 4
Atlanta 124, 134, 144
Atlanta Symphony 124, 134
Audubon Ballroom 42, 45
Augustana College 70
author 57, 67, 97, 102, 105, 106, 122, 125,
    142, 145, 188, 203
Avery Fisher Hall 190

B

B.S. Pully 48
Bach 2, 41, 122, 134
Bachelor of Science 9
Back To The Rose Garden 142
Ballantine beer 81
Baltimore 29, 191, 198
Barbara Campbell 98
BARBARA LEA 55, 228
Bard College 190
Barnes and Noble 200
Barney Josephson 46
Barney Kessel 117
Barry Galbraith 75, 90, 95, 234, 235
Barry Harris 71, 192
Bartok 189
Basin St. West 100
Bay Chamber Concert 192
BBC 145
bebop 5, 6, 9, 10, 12, 13, 15, 17, 18, 28,
    31, 33, 34, 39, 41, 43, 48, 51, 119,
    163, 177, 189
Beethoven 7, 189
Belgium 84, 102
Ben Tucker 39, 64, 70, 74, 75, 77, 85, 92,
    234, 235
Ben Vereen 102
Ben Webster 12, 13, 14, 15, 16, 18, 19, 32,
    34, 37, 38, 61, 64, 169, 181
Benny Carter 43, 55, 132
Benny Golson 170
Benny Goodman 49, 66
Benny Green 170
Benny Harris 5, 18
Benny Moton 84
Berklee College of Music 116, 147, 170,
    179
Beryl Booker 23, 38
Bessie Smith 89
Bette Midler 88
Betty Carter 174, 179, 184, 191, 193
Betty Carter's Jazz Ahead 174, 184
Beverly Sills 94
Beyond Category 174

Big Nick Nicholas 44, 224
Big Sid Catlett 13
Bill Barron 74, 107
Bill Bolcom 30
Bill Cosby 108
Bill Evans 61, 109, 158, 183, 194
Bill Evans Trio 79
Bill Slapin 64, 232
Billboard Magazine 127, 130, 131, 133,
    142, 177, 243, 244, 245
Billie Daniels 113
Billie Holiday 18, 19, 20, 33, 38, 100
Billy Daniels 18
Billy Eckstein 28, 39
Billy Hart 11
Billy Hicks 19
Billy Kyle 2, 31, 69
Billy Strayhorn 86, 170, 187, 188
BILLY TAYLOR 1, 2, 3, 5, 6, 7, 9, 10, 12,
    13, 14, 15, 16, 17, 18, 19, 20, 21, 22,
    23, 24, 25, 26, 27, 28, 29, 33, 34, 35,
    36, 37, 38, 39, 40, 41, 42, 43, 44, 45,
    46, 48, 49, 50, 51, 52, 53, 54, 55, 56,
    57, 58, 59, 60, 61, 62, 63, 64, 65, 94,
    96, 97, 98, 99, 100, 101, 102, 103,
    104, 105, 106, 107, 108, 109, 111,
    112, 113, 114, 115, 116, 117, 118,
    119, 120, 121, 122, 123, 124, 125,
    126, 127, 129, 130, 132, 133, 134,
    135, 136, 137, 138, 139, 140, 141,
    142, 143, 144, 146, 157, 158, 159,
    160, 161, 162, 163, 164, 165, 166,
    167, 169, 170, 173, 174, 175, 176,
    177, 178, 179, 181, 182, 183, 185,
    186, 188, 189, 190, 191, 194, 195,
    196, 197, 198, 200, 201, 202, 203,
    204, 205, 206, 210, 211, 222, 223,
    224, 225, 226, 227, 228, 229, 230,
    231, 232, 233, 234, 235, 236, 237,
    238, 239, 243, 244, 245, 246
BILLY TAYLOR 11, 14, 20, 185, 201,
    221, 222, 223, 224, 225, 226, 227,
    228, 229, 230, 231, 232, 233, 234,
    235, 236, 237, 238, 239, 246

BILLY TAYLOR THE FORCE WHO
    KEEPS JAZZ ALIVE 113, 245
BILLY TAYLOR and DAVE BAILEY:
    MAGNETIZING THE ARTS 111
BILLY TAYLOR AND FRIENDS 203
BILLY TAYLOR DAY 164
BILLY TAYLOR HUMANITARIAN
    AWARD 201
BILLY TAYLOR JAZZ SHOW 68
BILLY TAYLOR KEEPS JAZZ JUMP-
    ING 103
BILLY TAYLOR PLAYS JAZZ PIANO
    BETTER THAN EVER AT POPS
    CONCERT
    PS CONCERT 170
BILLY TAYLOR Productions 114
BILLY TAYLOR TALKS JAZZ 125
BILLY TAYLOR TRIO 51, 54, 60, 122,
    142, 173
BILLY TAYLOR: PRIMARILY PIANO
    127
BILLY TAYLOR: THE PLAYERS
    ADVOCATE 163
BILLY TAYLORS 50 YEARS IN JAZZ
    169
Billy White 3, 5
Bing Crosby 92
Birdland 26, 29, 32, 41, 42, 44, 47, 48, 49,
    50, 51, 52, 53, 54, 60, 62, 71, 76, 94,
    96, 113, 227, 228
Birth of the Cool 26
birthday party 197
Bix Beiderbeck 146
Black Communications Corporation 99,
    114
Black Elegance 168
Black History Month 108
Black Stars 103, 243
Black Variety 98, 245
Black Visions 88: Lady Legions In Jazz
    135
Blue Note 29, 178, 188
Blues Alley 116
BMI 96
BNai Brith 141

Bob Bernotas 186
Bob Cranshaw 73, 88, 90, 95, 113, 233, 235
Bob James 139
Bob Taylor 2
Bob Wyatt 27
Bobby Short 65
Bobby Thomas 39, 88, 95, 113, 114, 135, 139, 140, 141, 162, 164, 167, 180, 195, 235, 236, 237
Bobby Timmons 66
Bobby Watson 170
Body and Soul 17, 25, 185, 239
Boettcher Hall 170
Boone, North Carolina 182
Bop City 26
Bossa nova 97
BOSTON 50
Boston 7, 29, 51, 52, 65, 96, 97, 100, 105, 117, 179, 226
Boston's National Center for Afro-American Artists 105
Bottom Line 82
Bradley University 73
BRAVO 120
Bravo 133, 178, 184
BRIAN PRIESTLEY 51
Brick Feagle 23
Bridge Festival Orchestra 142
Bright Moments Concert Series 129
Britt Woodman 60, 74, 231, 234
Bronx 76, 81, 112
Brooke Astor 142
Brooke Shields 142
Brooklyn Academy of Music 113
Brooklyn College 123
Bud Freeman 84, 234
Bud Powell 5, 15, 18, 22, 23, 27, 29, 31, 32, 34, 51, 52, 58, 62, 142
Budapest 130, 159, 243
Budapest Convention Centre 130
Budapest Opera House 130
Budd Johnson 16
Buddy Collette 51
Buddy De Franco 36

Buddy Rich 36, 132
Buddy Saffer 20
Buddy Tate 58
Buford Oliver 25, 222
Butch Warren 11
Butler, Pennsylvania 56

C

C.W. Post College 92
Café Carlyle 65
Café Society 27, 46
Cambridge 97, 242
Campbell Soup 80
Campus Connection 246
Canada 80, 84, 203, 242
Canada Dry 80
Candace Womble 102
Candido 53, 54, 70, 226, 227
Candido Camero 54, 227
Cannonball 61
Cannonball Adderly 79
Capitol 50
Captain Kangaroo Show 56, 80, 93
Carl Allen 170
Carl Perkins 74
Carleton College 138
Carlton College 136, 147
Carmen McRae 73, 79, 101
Carnegie Hall 10, 41, 57, 147, 177
Carol Conover 145
Carter Johnson 11
Cass Tech High School 71
Catherine Sell Lenzini 189
Catherine Whitmore 164
Catskills 66
Caverns in D.C. 80
CBS 19, 51, 80, 93, 115, 118, 119, 121, 122, 127, 128, 131, 137, 138, 139, 147, 157, 162, 163, 164, 165, 177, 178, 181, 182, 188, 193, 194, 199, 200, 201, 203, 209
CBS Masterworks 157
CBS SUNDAY MORNING 115

CBS SUNDAY MORNING 51, 119, 121, 122, 131, 137, 138, 147, 162, 164, 165, 177, 178, 181, 188, 199, 201
Cecil Taylor 104
Cedar Rapids, Iowa 70
Cedar Walton 64, 113
Central Avenue Breakdown 118
Central Manhattan Symphony Orchestra 50
Century Club of the Virginia State College Alumni Association sociation 97, 139
channel 47 84, 93
Chano Pozo 70
Charles Kuralt 121, 125, 137, 139, 163, 164, 170, 181
Charles Mingus 44, 45, 50, 51, 52, 63, 64, 65, 71, 76, 224
Charles Osgood 137, 181, 197
Charles Rangel 142
Charlie Barnet 25
Charlie Bourgouiso 96
Charlie Byrd 137
Charlie Christian 6, 9, 16
Charlie Drayton 12, 16, 169
Charlie Fowlkes 59, 230
Charlie Mingus 50, 174, 226
Charlie Parker 5, 17, 18, 19, 29, 41, 42, 47, 68, 71, 113, 119, 144, 158, 165
Charlie Richards 112
Charlie Rouse 11, 18
Charlie Shavers 14, 46
Charlie Smith 46, 48, 49, 51, 52, 53, 54, 62, 65, 67, 70, 201, 225, 226, 227
Charlie Ventura 37
Chemical Bank 98
Cherokee 14
Chicago 14, 37, 41, 45, 56, 57, 58, 60, 69, 73, 94, 99, 100, 113, 115, 118, 132, 144, 159, 171, 229, 231, 240, 243, 245
Chicago Conservatory of Music 113
Chicago Daily News 57, 245
Chicago Jazz Festival 115

Chicago School of Music 41
Chicago Tribune 159
Chick Corea 109, 113, 132, 157, 183
Chick Webb 3
Chico Guerro 53, 226
China 144, 145
Chinese 69, 146
Chino Pozo 64, 232
Chip Jackson 170, 178, 179, 180, 185, 188, 191, 200, 201, 238, 239
Chocolate Williams 55
Chopin 54, 128
Chow Mein Lane 69
Chris Columbus 37
Chris Connor 75
Chris White 83, 107
Christian McBride 169, 170, 238
Christian Renninger 108
Christian Science Monitor 77, 244
Christopher Kirby 180
Chu Berry 19, 36
Chucho Valdez 188
Chuck Israels 123
Chuck Mangione 179, 189
Chuck Wayne 49, 50, 225
Cicely Tyson 142
Civic Center of Madison, Wisconsin 180
Civil Rights movement 87
Clarence Profit 5, 7, 8, 16, 52, 117
Clark College 106, 137, 147
Clark Terry 60, 72, 74, 75, 76, 162, 231, 233, 234
Claude Hopkins 2
Claude Williams 144
Cleo Laine 193
Cleo Lane 197
Cleveland 69, 72
Clifford Jordan 41
Clint Eastwood 147
Clyde Hart 5, 30, 32, 35, 36
Coca Cola 81
Coca-Cola 80, 98
Cold Blood 77
Cold Power 91

Coleman Hawkins 6, 14, 15, 16, 18, 20, 33, 35, 36, 38, 42, 50, 54, 55, 71, 73, 89, 168, 200, 224, 228
Collective Black Artists 92
Colorado Music Festival 178
Colorado Symphony 170
Columbia 8, 27, 43, 132, 143, 166, 237, 241
Columbia Records 92, 166
COMPLETE ENTERTAINMENT GUIDE 101
composer 11, 62, 63, 67, 77, 86, 102, 103, 104, 106, 125, 130, 135, 136, 142, 145, 147, 158, 162, 163, 165, 170, 177, 183, 185, 188, 194
Concerto for Clarinet 28
conductor 11, 59, 63, 72, 74, 87, 89, 93, 113, 135, 142, 145, 233, 234
Congressman John Conyers 143
Connecticut 41, 45, 74, 122
Cooper Gibson 3
Cootie Williams 18, 34, 58, 146
Copenhagen 24
Corporate America 172
correspondent 121, 147, 163
Cosmopolitan School of Music 73
Count Basie 3, 19, 43, 45, 58, 107, 179
Count Basie Orchestra 179
Cozy Cole 20, 27, 32, 49, 165
Creative Award 141
Creative Music Artist Management and Publicity 200
Creed Taylor 58
Crusaders 118
Cue Magazine 105, 243
Cuesta Colleges 164
Curtis Boyd 112, 113, 120, 133, 236
Curtis Fuller 64
Cutis Amy 112
Cy Coleman 66, 67, 75, 91, 136
Cyrus Chestnut 174, 197

D

Daily News 158, 243, 244
Daily News of the Hungarian News Agency 130
Dakar Senegal 128
Dale Johnson 72, 233
Dan Morganstern 95
Danny Bank 74, 234
Daphne Arnstein 79, 100
Darius Milhaud 159
Dave Bailey 64, 94, 112, 166, 232
Dave Brubeck 52, 121, 127
David Amram 189
David Bailey 70, 79, 87, 106, 143
David Baker 99, 108, 133, 143, 160, 166, 189
David C. Knapp 135
David Darling 144
David Frost 26, 73, 87, 88, 89, 90, 91, 92, 93, 94, 95, 97, 98, 102, 105, 113, 117, 127, 139, 162, 203
David Frost Show 91, 98, 113
David Frost Television Show 87, 93
David Gahr 101
David Murray 170
David Parsons 180
Davy 70
Debussy 7, 41, 134
Dee Dee Bridgewater 197
Del Shield 91
Denver Post 170, 244
Denzil Best 26, 37, 38, 47, 223
Department of Health, Education and Welfare 53
Department of Health, Education, and Welfare 81
DePaul University 171
Derrick Sampson 14
Desert Inn 66
Detroit 18, 69, 71, 108, 136, 144
Detroit, Michigan 136
Detroit Symphony Orchestra 108
Dexter Gordon 191
Dial M For Music 80

Diana Schuur 179
Dick Cavet Show Band 88
Dick Cavett 97
Dick Clark 163
Dick Gregory 142
Dick Hurwitz 88, 95, 113, 235
Dick Hyman 40
Dick Miller 82, 137, 144
Dick Miller Show 82, 137, 144
Dick Vance 20
Dickie Wells 23, 58
DIGITAL PRODUCTIONS 162, 237
Dinah Washington 58, 71, 95
disc jockey 6, 56, 61, 65, 68, 71, 73, 75,
　　86, 92, 99, 126, 183
Disney World 117
Dizzy Gillespie 15, 18, 19, 32, 34, 35, 41,
　　42, 47, 56, 70, 79, 83, 84, 92, 101,
　　107, 113, 119, 136, 143, 165
Dizzys Diamonds 188
Django Reinhard 6, 9, 12, 22, 65, 94, 97,
　　114, 176
Django Reinhart 94
DME 107, 114
Doc Cheatham 143
Doc Clifford 48, 225
Doc Severinsen 74, 234
Doc Severinson 61
Doc West 34
Doctor, Doctor, Doctor, Doctor 201
Doctor of Arts 161
Doctor of Fine Arts 135, 175
Doctor of Humane Letters 138, 166
Doctor of Music 107, 116, 135, 165, 176
Doctor of Music Education 107
doctoral dissertation 107
Dodo Marmarosa 36
DOES THE JAZZ OF THE PAST HAVE
　　A FUTURE 141, 245
Doggett 48, 225
Don Butterfield 59, 230
Don Byas 14, 15, 16, 20, 23, 24, 25, 26,
　　33, 34, 35, 37, 222
Don Elliott 59, 230

Don Ellis 136
Don Lanphere 42, 223
Don Redman 23, 24, 26, 32, 113, 140
Don Redman Band 24, 32
Don Shirley 57
Donald Byrd 71, 84, 99, 170, 195
Donald Lambert 8, 21
Dorothy Donegan 44, 71, 174
Doug Watkins 67, 71, 233
Douglas Fairbanks, Jr. 142
Down Beat 27, 47, 51, 52, 53, 59, 65, 95,
　　102, 109, 111, 116, 127, 133, 163,
　　165, 167, 243, 244, 245
Down Beat Magazine 29
Downbeat 15, 18, 33, 35, 47, 48, 53, 65,
　　102
Downbeat Club 18, 67
Dr. Ada Harrington Belton 173
DR. BILLY TAYLOR: A TAYLOR
　　MADE JAZZMOBILE INNOVA-
　　TOR 82, 99, 113, 116, 134, 143
DR. BILLY TAYLOR'S ART OF JAZZ
　　129
Dr. Kenneth Clarke 100
Dr. Roland Wiggins 107
DR. T AT 75: A TAYLOR-MADE
　　TRIBUTE 188
drugs 33, 46, 168
Duane 56, 65
Duane Music 56
Dudley Moore 147
Duke Ellington 3, 4, 10, 11, 44, 60, 61, 70,
　　76, 79, 89, 91, 96, 101, 107, 113,
　　139, 142, 143, 158, 171, 183, 202
Dunbar High School 3, 4, 6
Durham, N.C. 124
Durham, North Carolina 75
DuSable High School 73

E

Earl Bostic 63
Earl Hines 2, 5, 16, 18, 30, 31, 37, 146
Earl May 42, 44, 45, 46, 47, 48, 49, 51,
　　52, 53, 54, 55, 56, 57, 58, 59, 60, 61,

62, 63, 65, 224, 225, 226, 227, 228, 229, 230, 231
Earl Warren 58
Earle Theater 29
East Coast Jazz 119
Ed Bradley 142
Ed Howard 11
Ed Thigpen 42, 58, 59, 60, 61, 71, 224, 230, 231
Ed Wilcox 43
Ed Williams 91
Eddie Barefield 50
Eddie Bert 54, 228
Eddie Daniels 28, 63
Eddie Gomez 63
Eddie Harris 73, 89
Eddie Heywood 44
Eddie Lockjaw Davis 44, 224
Eddie Safranski 61
Eddie South 19, 20, 21, 28, 44, 50, 54, 55, 61, 62, 63, 73, 89, 106, 159, 178, 180, 224, 227, 228
Eddie Vinson 55
Eddy South 144
Edgar Sampson 7
Edsel Hall 108
Education Research Center at New York 171
educator 39, 64, 87, 109, 111, 120, 125, 127, 130, 133, 139, 141, 162, 163, 166, 171, 174, 177, 183, 185, 186, 187, 195, 202, 203
Ego Less 168
Egypt 146
Eighth Army Band 58
Eisenhower Auditorium 161
electronic music 77, 78
Eli Fountaine II 112
Elizabeth Koeppen 180
Ella Fitzgerald 49, 108, 110, 121, 196
Ellington 5, 11, 13, 45, 51, 60, 61, 111, 140, 142, 143, 179, 235
Ellis Larkins 19, 31
Elmira Streets 2, 4
Embers 52, 67

Emergency School Aid Act 81
Emmett Berry 54, 60, 228
Emmy 121, 127, 145, 164
Encore 102, 246
England 48, 73, 84, 89, 129, 145, 179, 240, 241
Eric Nemeyer 192
Ernie Royal 54, 59, 74, 227, 230, 234
Erroll Garner 16, 18, 22, 34, 37, 39, 49, 52, 63, 94, 109, 147, 184
Esquire 47, 241
Esquire Magazine 29
Essence Magazine 136, 244
Ethical Cultural Society 195
Eubie Blake 140, 166
Eudora Welty 94
Eugene, Oregon 119, 125
Europe 10, 23, 24, 25, 26, 27, 31, 32, 48, 50, 55, 113, 134, 144, 160
Evanston, Illinois 73
Evelyn Cunningham 100
Executive Director 79, 198
Exploring 80, 93

F

F. Lee Bailey 100
Fairfield University 92, 102
Fairmont Street NW 3
Famous Door 33, 47
Fat Tuesdays 124
Father Norman J. OConnor 86
Fats Navarro 9
Fats Waller 2, 3, 11, 16, 23, 29, 30, 102, 103, 128, 146
FEDERAL FUNDING (FOR JAZZ) HAS BEEN GOOD, BUT I THINK IT CAN GET BETTER!
   K IT CAN GET BETTER! 108
Festival In The Sun 158
Festival Productions 121
Fine Arts Center 162, 197
Florida Department of Education 171
Florida Memorial College 189
Flugelhorn 60, 61, 72, 76, 235
Foots Thomas 19

FOR THE LOVE OF JAZZ 126
Ford 114, 139, 178
Ford Park Amphitheater 178
Fran Richard 104, 196
France 25, 84, 102
Francis L. Lawrence 175
Frank Conion 44
Frank Conlon 49, 225
Frank Foster 116, 170, 195
Frank Sinatra 50
Frank Strozier 73, 113
Frank Tate 11
Frank Wess 4, 18, 64, 72, 88, 89, 90, 95,
      113, 140, 170, 195, 198, 199, 232,
      233, 235, 237
Frankie Fairfax 43
Fred Brown 143
Fred Budda 179
Fred Tillis 162, 237
Freddie Waits 139
Freddy Hubbard 86, 170
Fredonia State University College 164
Free Jazz 120
Front Street 169
Full Recovery 199

G

Gail Gilbert 180
Gallery of Sound Gazette 173, 245
Galveston, Texas 111
Gary Bartz 179
Gary Burton 179
Gary Giddings 132
Gene Ammons 45
Gene Quill 59, 230
Gene Ramey 58
Genuis 67, 106, 166
gentle warrior 168
Geoff Keezer 191
George Barnes 54, 227
George Berg 48, 88, 95, 225, 235
George Bush 166
George Duvivier 50, 57, 72, 225, 229, 233
George Gershwin 159
George James 48, 225

George Johnson 23
George Matthews 48, 225
George Peabody Medal 177
George Russell 61, 62, 99
George Shearing 24, 49, 50, 60, 67, 109,
      120, 132, 138, 143
George Simon 106, 143
George Venuti 144
George Wallington 17, 34, 67
George Washington University 201, 203
George Wein 51, 52, 76, 85, 93, 96, 121,
      143, 147, 177
George Wellington 27
Georgie Auld 41, 43, 47
Germany 25, 58, 102, 145, 172
Gerry Mulligan 41, 42, 47, 59, 64, 66, 84,
      91, 100, 132, 136, 147, 167, 223,
      230, 234, 237
Gigi Gryce 91, 136
Gil Goldstein 11
Gil Melle 58
Gilbert Chase 102
Gilbert Seldes 62
Glen Yarborough 101
Goldie Hawn 142
Gordon Grinnell 143
Goree Island 129
Grady Tate 39, 71, 74, 75, 76, 77, 85, 92,
      169, 170, 234, 235, 238
Grammy 147
Grand Prix du Disque 38
grandmother 2, 4
Grants Tomb 141
Great American Jazz Piano Competition
      138
GREAT AMERICAN MUSIC HALL
      113
Greeley Tribune 142
Greenville, North Carolina 1
Greg Fried 135
Grinnel College 56
griot 191
Grover Washington, Jr. 144
GRP Records 170, 179
GRP/Impulse 147

H

Hal Doc West 22

Hamiet Bluiett 170

Hampton Hawes 67, 119

Handel 134

Hank Crawford 195

Hank Jones 22, 31, 32, 34, 49, 170, 195

Hank Mobley 71

Harcourt Tynes 132

Harlem 5, 8, 23, 27, 30, 71, 77, 78, 79, 81,
    93, 95, 97, 98, 100, 101, 106, 111,
    126, 139, 162, 237, 244, 246

Harlem Commmunity Council 81

Harlem Cultural Council 79, 100, 101, 112

Harlem Week 126, 244, 246

Harlem YMCA 106

Harold Francis 2, 17

Harold Land 112

Harold Mabern 73

Harold Wheeler 87

Harry Adams Allen 11

Harry Belafonte 77

Harry Carney 60, 231

Harry Connick, Jr. 142

Harry James Orchestra 132

HARYOUACT (Harlem Youth in Action)
    111

HAVANA FESTIVAL 188

Hawk 5, 6, 14, 15, 16, 31, 38

Hazel Scott 69

Head Start 80

Helen Forrest 132

Helen Merrill 113

Henry Grant 3, 4, 7

Henry Grimes 66, 67, 232

Henry Street 79

Herb Harris 11

Herb Pomeroy 179

Herb Wong 133

Herbie Hancock 109, 183

Herbie Jones 64

Herbie Mann 64, 75, 91, 107, 136, 232

Herbst Theater 168, 169

Herman Chittison 43

Herman Mitchell 26, 38, 223

Herman Rheinschagen 51

HICKORY HOUSE 68

Hickory House 33, 46, 47, 52, 64, 65

High School for Performing Arts in
    Philadelphia 169

Hilton Jefferson 20

Hilversum 25

Holland 25, 84, 102, 145, 170

Honeysuckle Rose 3, 55, 228

Honi Coles 142

HONORING BILLY TAYLOR'S LIFE IN
    MUSIC 177

Horace Silver 64, 71, 86, 179, 186

Horton Plaza Sports Deck 143

hospital 196, 197

Hot Club of France 25

Hot Lips Page 19, 31, 68

Hotel Northampton 197

Houston Person 191

Houston, Texas 164

HOW BILLY TAYLOR HELPS TEEN-
    AGERS BEAT THE BLUES 104

Howard Alden 143

Howard Cooper 169

Howard McGhee 41, 47

Howard Theater 4, 29

Howard University 3, 9, 10, 26, 92, 114

Hubert Laws 88, 90, 91, 113, 136, 179

Hungarian Jazz Society 131

Hungary 130, 131

Hunter College 76, 93

Hybrid Voicings 186, 187

I

I Got Rhythm 16, 24, 222

IAJE 74, 86, 120, 164, 181, 187, 193, 194,
    195, 196, 197, 199, 200, 202, 239

Idrees Sulieman 42, 223

Ike Quebec 15, 16

Illinois Jacquet 38, 43, 45, 91, 136

IMPROVS ON A FEMININE SCALE
    168, 243

Impulse 50, 147

India 122, 146, 190

Indiana University 189

Indianapolis 86, 114, 139, 244
Indianapolis Symphony 114
Indians 146
Indigo Blues 141
Ink Spots 17
International Association for Jazz
    Education 136, 166, 196, 198, 200
International Critics Award 53, 165
INTO THE OLD BASKET 105, 243
Ira Gitler 139
Ira Sabin 120, 123
Ira Sullivan 11, 58, 76, 230
Irving Alexander 18
IS JAZZ AMERICA'S CLASSICAL
    MUSIC 245
IS JAZZ AMERICA'S CLASSICAL
    MUSIC? 123
Isaac Stern 158

J

J.J. Johnson 53, 64, 119, 195
Jack the Bear (Parker) 16
Jackie Davis 63
Jackie Paris 14
Jackie Robinson Foundation 44, 94, 129
Jacksonville, Florida 19, 138, 139, 166
Jaime Martinez 180
James Brown 100
James Carter 174
James H. Harding, Jr 135
James Jordan 143
James Mack 118
James Moody 71, 107
James P. Johnson 21, 103
JAMMING IN RYE 132, 243
Japan 66, 84, 144, 172
Jay Hoggard 11
Jay McAllister 72, 230, 233
Jazz A Metaphor for American Culture
    182
Jazz Alive 114, 118, 125, 173, 188, 202
Jazz Ambassadors Program 174, 184
Jazz at Home Club of America 98
Jazz At Noon 143

Jazz At The Philharmonic 45
Jazz Blue Notes 130, 131, 133
JAZZ COUNTERPOINT 120
Jazz Counterpoint 132, 133
Jazz Education Journal 198, 246
Jazz For Life 133
JAZZ GREAT BILLY TAYLOR NAMED
    ADVISOR TO KENNEDY
    CENTER
    TER 174
Jazz History 162
JAZZ IMPROV 192
Jazz In July 115, 116, 130, 141, 162, 198,
    199
Jazz in July 84, 125, 129
JAZZ IS ALIVE AND WELL IN NEW
    YORK 102, 243
Jazz Legacy 188
JAZZ LEGEND MAKES LOCAL
    APPEARANCE 173, 245
JAZZ MAN AS FORUM DELEGATE
    130, 243
Jazz Panel 98
JAZZ PIANIST BILLY TAYLOR STILL
    LEARNING 142
JAZZ PIANO 107, 119, 120, 127, 145,
    170, 201, 242, 244
Jazz Piano 103, 111, 114, 121, 122, 138,
    141, 147, 170, 235, 239
JAZZ PLAYER 186
Jazz Times 52, 120, 123, 130, 132, 133,
    139, 144, 158, 159, 169, 243, 244,
    245
Jazz Times Convention 123, 132, 133
Jazz Times Conventions 159
JAZZMAN BILLY TAYLOR: PIANIST
    AUTHOR, TEACHER 105
Jazzmobile 79, 80, 81, 82, 83, 84, 85, 86,
    88, 93, 94, 96, 97, 100, 101, 104,
    105, 111, 112, 115, 116, 126, 127,
    133, 136, 139, 141, 147, 176, 177,
    178, 187, 190
JAZZMOBILE: TWENTY YEARS OF
    PROGRESS 126
Jean Bouchety 25, 222

Jean-Jacques Tilche 25, 222
Jeff Bradley 170
Jeff Levenson 142, 177
Jelly Roll Morton 30, 77, 118, 141
Jerome Richardson 64, 72, 74, 75, 232,
    233, 234
Jerrold Ross 171
Jerry Sanfino 64, 232
Jerry Stiller 102
Jess Stacy 69
Jet Magazine 68
Jeter Pillard Orchestra 45
Jim Anderson 176
Jim Butler 167
Jim Hall 72, 233
Jim Pepper 179
Jim Roberts 127, 129
Jimmie Lunceford 3, 19, 50
Jimmy Blanton 9, 14
Jimmy Buffington 59, 230
Jimmy Butts 15
Jimmy Cleveland 59, 61, 230, 233
Jimmy Cobb 11
Jimmy Crawford 14, 19, 23, 32
Jimmy Heath 64, 89, 106, 167, 195
Jimmy Jones 37, 38
Jimmy Lunceford 60
Jimmy Mundy 43
Jimmy Nottingham 76
Jimmy Owens 63, 95, 99, 106, 113, 139,
    140, 167, 179, 195, 235, 237
Jimmy Rosencrantz 20
Jimmy Rushing 61
Jimmy Ryans 69
Jimmy Shirley 55, 228
Jo Jones 5, 13, 15, 19, 33, 44, 45, 54, 55,
    66, 78, 180, 225, 228
Joanne Brackeen 191
Joe Blum 123
Joe Glaser 70
Joe Graves 132
Joe Harris 29, 40, 41, 223
Joe Holiday 46, 225
JOE KENNEDY 120, 236
Joe Kennedy 84, 116, 236

Joe Marsala 33
Joe Middleton 173
Joe Newman 74, 75, 84, 234
Joe Pass 147
Joe Sullivan 85
Joe Venuti 66
Joe Wilder 91
Joe Williams 73, 113, 132
Joel Sminoff 159
Joel Smirnoff 180
Joey Bushkin 69
John Bello 74, 234
John Blake 144
John Clayton 170
John Collins 22, 26, 37, 42, 43, 223, 224
John Coltrane 29, 76, 85, 86, 102, 144
John Denver 77
John Garcia Gensel 143
John Gensel 77
John Hammond 121
John Hardee 29, 40, 223
John Hicks 170
John Hopkins University 177
John LaPorta 63, 179
John Levy 26, 37, 38, 47, 223
John Lewis 99, 195
John Lindsay 100
John Livingston Eaton 11
John Malachi 17
John McDonough 163
John S. Wilson 85
John Simmons 16, 20, 29, 40, 223
Johnnie Carson 89
Johnnie Smith 44
Johnny Carisi 87
Johnny Carson 88, 97
Johnny Carson Show Band 88
Johnny Coates, Jr 173
Johnny Griffin 191
Johnny Hartman 167
Johnny Hodges 58, 60, 64, 231
Johnny Lesco 88
Johnny Mandel 42, 223
Johnny Simmons 20
Johnny Windhurst 55, 228

Johns Hopkins University 177
JON FADDIS 141
Jon Hendricks 170
Jonathan Leseer 178
Jordan Fordin 46, 225
Jose Manguel 53, 226
Josef Zawinul 109
Joseph Papp Public Theater 167
Josephine Baker 95
Joyce Taylor Hynes 26
Juilliard 66, 90, 135, 139, 158, 159, 166,
    170, 180, 189
Juilliard Quartet 158
Juilliard School of Music 66, 135, 158,
    170
Juilliard String Quartet 166, 180
Julian Priester 113
Julius Watkins 72, 233
June Hawkins 20
Junior Mance 73, 91, 136, 192
Junior Raglin 14
JUST JAZZ 98, 245
Jutta Hipp 58
JVC Jazz Festival 177

K

Kai Winding 41, 47
Kansas City 5, 45, 118, 161
Kappa Alpha Psi 6
Katherine A. Martin 173
Keith Copeland 135
Keith Eckert 60
Keith Jarrett 109
Kelly Martin 43
Kellys Stable 26
Kellys Stables 33, 47
Ken Archer 11
Ken Franckling 169
Kennedy Center 160, 164, 166, 174, 175,
    176, 177, 182, 183, 184, 185, 186,
    187, 188, 190, 191, 192, 193, 195,
    197, 199, 201, 202, 203
Kenny Clarke 19, 23, 53, 183
Kenny Dennis 63, 231

Kenny Durham 71
Kenny Durham 83, 113
Kenny Klook Clarke 25
Kentucky Symphony 146
Kevin Eubanks 170
Kevin Hayes 121
Kevin Mahogany 197
Keyboard Magazine 117, 245
Keystone Junior College 173
Kid Ory 51, 118
KIM 56, 212, 215
Kim 65, 178
Kin Bradfrod-Betty Roche 112
Kodaly 134
Korean War 73
KPBS-FM 118
Krannert Center for the Performing Arts
    181

L

L. Mars Peony Park 132
L. Shank Shankar 144
La Conga 49
La Guardia 100
LA WAS ALWAYS KEY TO JAZZ 118
Labor Department 172
Lake Placid 116
Lalo Schifrin 63
Langston Hughes 61
Larry Coryell 179
Larry Ridley 99, 114, 143
Larry Rosen 180
Larry Wilburn 175
Las Vegas 66
Laurent DeWilde 11
Lawrence J. Wilburn 174
Lawrence Marable 117
Lear Jet 100
Lee Eliot Berk 117
Lee Konitz 41, 47, 61, 66, 181
Lee Morgan 66, 83
Lee Smith 169
Lee Young 51
Len Lyons 109

Lena Horne 77
Leningrad 236
Lennie Tristano 51, 52, 58, 66, 67
Leo Parker 11, 18
Leonard Bernstein 104, 129, 159
Leonard Bernstein Festival 129
Leonard Feather 33, 139, 143
Leonard Slatkin 183
Leontyne Price 77, 165
LeRoi Joness Black Arts 81
Les Crane 75
Les Grange 59, 230
Les McCann 113
Les Spann 72, 233
Lester (Young) 6
Lester Young 15, 16, 44, 45
Library of Congress 57, 190, 194, 195
Library of Congress Music Division 190
Lifestyles magazine 132
Lifetime Achievement Award 116, 127
Lincoln Center 30, 76, 93, 105, 141, 184
Lincoln Center Jazz Orchestra 184
Lincoln Square Neighborhood Center 102
Lionel Hampton 43, 51, 107, 139, 141,
    143, 174, 186, 199, 200
Liszt 128
Little Theater 89
Living Time Orchestra 179
Liz Rohatyn 142
Liza 8
Lloyd Hunter 45
Lloyd Reese 51
LONDON HOUSE 57, 229
London Philharmonic 118
Long Beach, California 194, 196
Long Island 49, 132, 161, 199
Long Island Sound 132
Long Island University 161
L'Oreal Hair Products 80
Los Angeles 22, 50, 117, 118, 139, 242
Los Angeles Times 139
Lou Donaldson 62, 64
Lou Mucci 63
Lou Rawls 80
LOUIS ARMSTRONG 87

LOUIS ARMSTRONG 5, 51, 89, 92, 146,
    159, 162, 174
Louis Bellson 132
Louis Lonnie Chatmon 144
Lovett Hines 169
LSU 101
Lucky Millinder 43, 50
Lucky Thompson 55
Luis Russell 55
Lullaby in Rhythm 8, 16
Lynda Bramble 190, 200

M

M. Montgomery 98
Mabel Mercer 22
MACHITO 188
Machito 49, 53
Malcolm X 45
Manchester Craftsmens Guild 171, 185
Manhattan School of Music 66, 101
Mannie Faria 122
Manny Albam 89, 164
Manny Quando 49, 225
Marc Anthony Cary 11
MARIAN MCPARTLAND 69
Marian McPartland 46, 68, 69, 120, 138
Marilyn 169, 193
Mark Morgan 189
Mark Ribowsky 113
Marky Markowitz 11
Marlo Thomas 142
Marlow Morris 8, 21
Marquis Foster 50, 52, 226
Marsalas Chicagoans 69
Marshall Brown 63
Marshall Hawkins 11
Marshall, Massachusetts 100
Marshall Royal 117
Martial Solal 69
Martin Luther King 135, 182
Marty Grupp 89, 95, 235
Marvin Smitty Smith 169, 238
MARY LOU WILLIAMS 48

MARY LOU WILLIAMS 19, 29, 30, 32, 65, 66, 67, 174, 184, 188
Maryland 191
Mastbaum High School 66
Mat Mathews 44
Mathew Rodarte 180
Matthew Merredith 20
Maurice Abravenel 94
Max Gordon 121
Max Roach 15, 17, 34, 37, 64, 74, 107, 119, 137, 141, 168, 195
Maynard Ferguson's Band 120
McCoy Tyner 109
MEET THE COMPOSER 104
Mel Lewis 107, 113, 179
Mel Powell 27, 69
MEL TORME 87
Mel Torme 28, 132
Melba Moore 102
Melotones Compact Big Band 142
MENC 80, 87, 93
Mercer Ellington 53, 55
Mercer Kennedy 11
Mercury 50
Merv Griffin 97
Metropolitan Museum of Art 127, 134, 138, 164, 181, 185, 186, 203
Mia McSwain 181
Miami University 82, 144, 246
Miami University of Ohio 82, 246
Michael Abene 140
Michel Legrand 171
Microphone 76, 110, 206
Middle East 122
Mike Douglas 89
Mike Wofford 112
Mild Stroke 196, 198, 200
Miles Davis 26, 41, 42, 45, 51, 119, 141, 165, 194, 195, 224
Milt Buckner 13
Milt Hinton 20, 54, 55, 96, 99, 228
Milt Jackson 29, 53, 84, 167, 195
Milt Page 29, 40, 223
Milwaukee 144

Mingus Epitaph Orchestra 179
Minnesota 136, 138
Mintons 5, 12, 15, 18, 33, 38, 55
Miskole Jazz Festival 131
Mississippi Sheiks 144
Modern Jazz Quartet 26, 94, 119
Monte Kay 26, 41
Monty Alexander 192
Morris Levy 48
Morty Bullman 88, 95, 113, 235
Mozart 2, 54, 122, 189
Mt. Vernon 198, 199
Muhal Richard Abrams 143
Mulgrew Miller 191
MULTI-TALENTED BILLY TAYLOR 102
Mundell Lowe 44, 59, 61, 225, 230
Murray Horowitz 175
Music Center Conservatory 64
Music Director 44, 61, 87, 93, 99, 114
Music Educators National Conference 80, 87, 93
Musicians Union 81

N

NAJE 74, 120, 132
Nancy Clarke 143
Nancy Hanks 94
Nancy Wilson 117, 174, 197
Nashville, Tennessee 74
Nat Adderley 61
Nat Adderly 179
Nat Hentoff 52
Nat Jones 191
Nat King Cole 50, 52, 121
Nat Phipps 91, 135
National Academy of Jazz 131
National Academy of Recording Arts and Sciences 76
National Council for the Arts 94, 111
National Council On The Arts 114
National Council on the Arts 100, 101, 102, 133, 165
National Educational Television 61

NATIONAL ENDOWMENT FOR THE
    ARTS 136, 166
National Endowment For The Arts 147
National Endowment for the Arts 86, 98,
    99, 100, 130, 163, 171, 172, 198
National Endowment Music Program 99
NATIONAL JAZZ SERVICE 87
National Jazz Service Organization 143
National Medal of Arts 166
NATIONAL PUBLIC RADIO 94, 109
National Public Radio 114, 125, 127, 138,
    144, 173, 174, 185, 202
National Symphony Orchestra 183
NBC 61, 62, 65, 72
Neil Courtney 169
Nellie Lutcher 50
Nelson Rockefeller 100
Nestle Corporation 127
New England 129
New England Conservatory of Music 179
New Jersey Symphony Orchestra 104
New Orleans 37, 43, 80, 81, 118
New Star Award 53
New Times 164, 243
New York 5, 7, 8, 9, 10, 11, 12, 13, 15, 17,
    19, 20, 21, 22, 23, 26, 27, 29, 31, 32,
    34, 37, 38, 39, 40, 42, 43, 44, 45, 49,
    50, 51, 52, 53, 54, 55, 56, 58, 59, 60,
    61, 64, 65, 66, 67, 68, 70, 71, 72, 73,
    75, 76, 77, 78, 79, 80, 81, 82, 83, 85,
    88, 91, 92, 93, 94, 95, 96, 97, 100,
    101, 102, 103, 104, 105, 110, 111,
    112, 113, 114, 115, 116, 118, 120,
    121, 123, 125, 132, 133, 135, 136,
    140, 141, 142, 143, 147, 158, 161,
    162, 163, 164, 165, 167, 169, 170,
    171, 177, 179, 183, 185, 186, 187,
    188, 190, 191, 193, 194, 195, 198,
    200, 201, 223, 224, 225, 226, 227,
    228, 229, 230, 231, 232, 233, 234,
    235, 236, 237, 238, 239, 240, 241,
    242, 243, 244, 245
New York Amsterdam News 15
New York City 7, 11, 12, 19, 20, 23, 26,
    29, 31, 32, 37, 38, 40, 42, 43, 44, 45,
    49, 50, 52, 53, 54, 55, 56, 58, 59, 60,
    61, 64, 65, 94, 95, 96, 101, 102, 110,
    116, 120, 125, 133, 135, 136, 140,
    141, 143, 162, 167, 169, 170, 185,
    187, 190, 191, 200, 223, 224, 225,
    226, 227, 228, 229, 230, 231, 232,
    233, 234, 235, 236, 237, 238, 239
New York Community Trust 158
New York Philharmonic 103
New York Press 169
New York Repertory Company 104, 114
New York State Commission on Cultural
    Research 100
New York State Council on the Arts 81,
    97
New York Times 135, 141
New York University 50
Newark, New Jersey 84, 90, 135
Newport 62, 96, 234
Newport Jazz Festival 76, 85, 93
Newport Youth Band 62
News-Times 122, 244
Nina Simone 77, 78, 165
Nixon 99, 114
Norma Shepherd 2, 12
Norman Lear 142
North Carolina A & T University 2
North Carolina Central 124
North Carolina Central University 124
North Carolina College 75
North Texas State Teachers College 9
Northwestern University 73
Nova Scotia 60
NPR 121, 145, 174, 178, 197

O

Okay, BILLY 98
Oklahoma 5, 41, 43
Olatunji African Culture 85
Old Mt. Morris Park 199
Oliver Buford 25, 222
OLIVER NELSON 234
Oliver Nelson 74, 76, 111, 234
Olympics 116, 119

Onyx 15, 16, 17, 18, 32, 33, 34, 38, 46, 47, 113
Opera 130, 131
Orchestra Hall 158
Oscar Brown 112
Oscar Peterson 22, 49, 52, 63, 66, 132, 138, 140, 158
Oscar Pettiford 15, 16, 34, 41, 47, 50, 54, 55, 66, 159, 180, 226, 227
Osie Johnson 11, 54, 61, 84, 227, 234
Ossie Davis 203, 206
Otto (Toby) Hardwicke 11
Ovation Magazine 123, 245
Owen Cordle 167

P

Pablo Guzman 158
Pakistan 139, 146
Palo Alto 168, 169
Par Banks Mitchel 161
Paramount Center 164
Parent Magazine 104, 243
Paris, France 24, 222
Pat Metheny 144
Patrice Rushen 109
Patricia Kenny 180
Paul Anthony 110
Paul Bley 109
Paul Chambers 71
Paul Gonsalves 60, 231
Paul Horn 112
Paul West 79, 82, 83
Paul Whiteman 66
PBS 80, 93, 99, 113, 114, 132
Peabody 121, 127, 145, 177
Peabody Award 121
Peaceful Warrior 124, 134
Peanuts Holland 23, 24, 25, 221, 222
Peekskill, NY 164
PEGGY LEE 87
Peggy Lee 50, 137
Penn State 161
Pennsylvania 41, 63, 64, 66, 91, 169, 176, 190

Pennsylvania State University 190
Pepsi Jazz Corner 68
Percy Brice 55, 56, 57, 228, 229
Percy Heath 42, 53, 224
Personality Magazine 126
Pete Brown 46
Peter Bailey 103
Peter Clark 24, 221
Peter Duchin 143
Peter J. Liacouras 176
Peter Keepnews 130, 131, 133, 245
Petersburg Alumni Chapter of Kappa Alpha Phi 92
Petersburg, Virginia 6, 19
Ph.D. 43, 101, 107, 108
Phil Bodner 64, 232
Phil Donahue 142
Phil Moore 37
Phil Woods 72, 74, 75, 132, 233, 234
Philadelphia 10, 19, 29, 63, 64, 66, 169, 176, 198
Philadelphia Orchestra 170
Philip Booth 193
Phoebe Jacobs 96
Phoenix Gazette 183, 244
Piano Spectacular 138
PISCES 105
Pittsburgh 41, 101, 171, 181, 185, 243
plaques 92
Platters 95
Playback Magazine 194
Popkins 68
Prelude 28, 40, 68, 223
President Gerald Ford 139
President Richard Nixon 94, 104
Prestige 46, 50, 52, 53, 54
Pret Primack 188
Princeton Club 123
Prophets of Jazz 67

Q

Quentin Jackson 74, 234
Quincy Jones 59, 75, 91, 121, 136, 173, 230

R

R. Craig Sautter 171
Rachael Robinson 124
Rachel Robinson 128
Radio Free Jazz 108, 160, 245
Radio Stockholm 145
Ragtime 19, 24, 78, 222
Rainbow Grill 96
Rainbow Room 96
Rainbow Sundae 80, 93
Raleigh, North Carolina 1
Ralph Pena 112
Ralph Watkins 39
Ralph Watkins Basin Street 70
Ram Ramirez 106
RAMSEY LEWIS 64, 118, 157, 161, 237
Ramsey Lewis 109, 117, 120, 132, 142,
    157, 161, 164, 167, 193
Raul Julia 139
Ray Brown 41, 49, 132, 147, 170, 195
Ray Bryant 168, 191
Ray Charles 91, 136
Ray Mantilla 169, 238
Ray Mosca 66, 67, 71, 232, 233
Ray Nance 37, 86
Red Allen 146
Red Blazer 143
Red Callender 51, 117
Red Norvo 20, 51
Red Saunders 37
Reggie Workman 64
Regina Carter 193, 197
Renaissance 134
Richard Bobbitt 117
Richard Davis 113
Richard M. Sudhalter 141
Richard McClanahan 12, 32, 41, 199
Richard Rogers 104, 122
Richie Beirach 141
Richmond News Leader 140, 246
Richmond, Virginia 64
Ritchie Cole 143
Riverside 45, 50, 59, 141
RKO 29

Rob Swope 11
Robert Battle 181
Robert Mann 180
Robert P. Lawrence 118
Robert Rostaing 23, 25, 222
Rockefeller Center 96
Rockefeller Center Luncheon Club 96
Rockland Palace 42
Rocklin Center for The Arts 135
Rockport, Maine 192
Roland Hanna 75, 91, 136
Roland Wiggins 108
Romeo Penque 74, 234
Ron Carter 170
Ron Holloway 11
Ron Wynn 157
Roosevelt Hotel 123
Roosevelt University 73
Roost 26, 42, 44, 47, 50, 52, 53
Rotterdam 101
Round Midnight 35, 59, 61, 167, 168,
    231, 238
Roxy Theater 40
Roy Ayers 112
Roy Eldridge 5, 13, 14, 17, 19, 36, 41, 46,
    47
Roy Hargrove 170
Roy Haynes 42, 179, 223
Royal Theater 29
Ruby Braff 143
Ruby Dee 203
Rudy Braff 84, 234
Russell Malone 193
Russia 96, 144, 145
Rutgers University 175, 177

S

Sacramento 182
Salt Lake City 162
Salvatore Caputo 183
SALZA MEETS JAZZ 125
Sam Sutherland 131, 133
SAMMY DAVIS, JR 87
Sammy Kay 18

Sammy Price 27
Samuel Sacks award 158
San Antonio Light 134, 243
San Antonio, Texas 134
San Diego Union 118, 244
San Francisco 66, 113, 168, 177, 240, 241, 242
San Francisco Jazz Festival 177
Sarah Vaughan 42, 56, 84, 132, 223
Sarasota Jazz Society 177
SAT 171
Saturday Review 29, 47
Savannah, Georgia 99, 114
Savoy Ballroom 58
saxophone 1, 3, 4, 5, 11, 15, 16, 18, 19, 20, 23, 24, 25, 29, 40, 42, 44, 46, 54, 55, 58, 59, 60, 167, 168, 169, 222, 223, 224, 225, 228, 230, 231, 233, 234, 235, 237, 238
Scandinavia 24
Schenectady 82
Schomburg Institute for Research in Black Culture 142
School for New Learning 171
School of Education 108, 116
School of Media 107
Scott Gutterman 136
Scott Joplin 30, 77, 103
Scott Simon 166
Sepia Magazine 113
Sesac 50
SESAC MUSIC 67
Sesame Street 80, 93
Seven Lively Arts 20, 32
Shad Collins 5
Shadow Wilson 43, 224
Shanghi 135
Shelly Manne 35, 46
Shelton Powell 88
Shepard of the Night Flock 139, 143
Sherry Bronfman 142
Shirley Horn 11
Shorty Rogers 20, 60
Shubert Theater 142
Sid Bulkin 50

Sid Catlett 5, 12, 19, 20, 21, 32, 33, 35, 36, 38, 47, 169, 180
Sid Weiss 20
Sidney Gross 54, 227
Sierra Club 162
Sissy Spacek 142
Skeets Tolbert 19
Slam Stewart 22, 27, 32, 34, 49, 113, 159, 180
Slide Hampton 84, 86, 107, 170
Slim Gaillard 41
Snooky Young 74, 75, 234
Sonia Alleyne 168
Sonny Greer 13
Sonny Rollins 66, 73, 79, 170
Sonny Stitt 45, 63
Soundpost Music 56
South America 136, 146, 160
South Street Seaports Summer Pier 169
Southeast Asia 122
Southeast Utah 162
Soviet Union 136, 142, 160, 236
Soviets 146
St. Johns University 135, 147
St. Louis 45, 194
St. Peters Church 139, 143, 166
St. Petersburg Times 193
Stan Fishelson 42, 223
Stan Getz 35, 42, 48, 62, 165, 179, 191, 223, 225
Stan Webb 74, 234
Stanford 168, 169, 178
Stanford University 178
Stanley Cowell 191
Stanley Turrentine 169, 170, 179, 238
Stanley Winter 125
State Department 124, 146
Stephan Harris 193
Stephanie 11, 195
Stephanie Nakasian 11
Stephen Henderson 8
Stephen Holden 177
Steve Johns 170, 178, 179, 180, 181, 185, 188, 238
Steve Martin 142

Steve Reich 104
Stevie Wonder 110
Stockhausen 77
STORYVILLE 50, 112, 226, 235
Storyville Club 51, 52, 226
Stuart Sankey 112
Stuff Smith 19, 20, 26, 37, 38, 68, 144, 159, 178, 179, 180
Suite for Jazz Piano and Orchestra 122
Sweden 102, 145
swing 5, 6, 8, 12, 17, 22, 31, 39, 59, 63, 98, 119, 125, 143, 167
SWING, BEBOP, and JAZZ AS PART OF THE CURRICULUM 189, 244
Swing Street 169
Switzerland 24, 102
Symphony Sid All-Stars 53

T

Tad Dameron 27
Taft Jordan 48, 225
Tanglewood 87, 115
Tanglewood Symposium 87
TAVERN ON THE GREEN 140
TAYLOR JAZZES THINGS UP 134
Taylor Made Jazz 188
TAYLOR TRIO DAZZLES JAZZ LOVERS 122, 244
TAYLOR-MADE, A CHAMPION OF JAZZ 183, 244
TAYLOR-MADE FROSTINGS 95, 245
Tchaikovsky 128
teacher 2, 3, 6, 7, 19, 89, 110, 112, 122, 142, 144, 145, 162, 170, 171, 178, 181, 186, 188, 190, 199
Ted Dunbar 140, 237
Ted Dyer 126
Ted Sturgis 23, 25, 222
Teddy Bunns Washboard Serenaders 7
Teddy Reig 40
Teddy Wilson 2, 8, 17, 19, 31, 43, 44, 133, 199
Temple University 176, 177
Tennessee State University 74

Terry Gibbs 41, 47, 48, 113
Thad Jones 74, 107, 113, 179, 234
Thad Jones-Mel Lewis Band 107
THAT WAS THE WEEK THAT WAS 73
The Beetle 8
The Campus Connection 125
THE CHEMISTRY WORKS RAMSEY LEWIS 161
The Color Of the Performing Arts 139
The Composer 52, 166
The Deuces 33, 34, 46, 47
THE DOCTOR IS IN JAZZ LEGEND BILLY TAYLOR COMES TO VAIL CELEBRATING 50 YEARS IN MUSIC 178
The Duke Ellington School for the Performing Arts 171
The Electric Company 80, 93
THE GHOSTS OF MISSISSIPPI 107
The Ham and Eggery 62
THE HONOLULU ADVERTISER 160
The Instrumentalist 189, 244
The Jazz Link 143, 244
The Jazzmobile 81, 105
THE JAZZMOBILE ALL-STARS 84, 140, 237
THE NIGHT IN HARLEM 201
The Shout 2
The Subject Is Jazz 61, 62, 65, 181
THE TRINITORIAN 134
The University of Delaware 190
The University of Florida 190
The Voice of America 68
Thelonious Monk 5, 8, 15, 31, 32, 66, 85, 174
Theme and Variation for Jazz Trio and Symphony Orchestrastra 183
Theodora (Teddi) Castion 22, 32
Thomas Chapin 179
Three Deuces 12, 22, 32, 33, 34, 35
Three Dueces 14, 15, 18, 19
Three O'clock High 42
Tijuana Club 198
Tim Owens 110
Time Magazine 101, 244

Times Square 49
Tiny Bradshaw 43
Tiny Grimes 13, 20, 55
Tiny Parham 37
Tito Puente Scholarship Fund 158
Toby Walker 2, 17
Toledo Magazine 128
Tom Tilghman 21, 30
Tom Williams 64, 232
Tommy Dorsey 36
Tommy Flanagan 133, 191, 192
Tondelayo 18
Tonight Show 170
Tony Brown 80, 93, 99, 110, 114
Tony Browns Journal 80, 93
Tony Ortega 59, 230
Tony Scott 61, 181
Tony Studd 74, 75, 234
Tootie Heath 66
Toronto 69, 203, 242
Toshiko 58, 61, 85
Toshiko Akiyoshi 58, 61
TOWN HALL 55, 83, 228, 234
Town Hall 20, 26, 55
treasure 122, 190
Trinity University 243
Trio of the Year 68
Trummy Young 23
tuberculosis 9, 10, 11, 38
Turtle Island String Quartet 125, 147, 178, 179, 180
TV 61, 62, 65, 72, 84, 87, 89, 90, 91, 93, 95, 97, 102, 105, 113, 121, 130, 132, 133, 139, 163, 181, 184, 187, 206, 243
TV screen 206
TWILIGHT 102
Tyree Glenn 20, 23, 24, 25, 222

U

U.S. Department of Education 81
Ubal Nieto 53, 226
UMass 125, 129, 130, 187, 197, 199
Uncle Tom 141

Undine Moore 6
Union of Composers of the Soviet Union 142
Universal Jazz Coalition 94
University of Arizona 158
University of Central Florida 124
University of Illinois 173, 176, 177, 181
University of Massachusetts 84, 101, 103, 107, 108, 114, 125, 129, 135, 136, 141, 147, 162, 186, 188, 197, 198, 246
University of Michigan 130, 133, 191, 201, 203, 242
University of Michigan at Flint 201
University of New Hampshire 146
University of North Florida 166
University of North Texas 9
University of Pittsburgh 181
Urbie Green 74, 75, 234
US Army 45, 73
US Forum delegation 130
US HOUSE APPROPRIATIONS SUBCOMMITTEE 171
US Marine Corps 112
USA 25, 52, 120

V

Vail Trails Daily Options 178, 245
Valley Advocate 129, 245
Variety 132, 138, 143, 243, 244
Variety Magazine 143, 167
Vic Firth 179
Victor Gaskin 39, 112, 120, 133, 135, 139, 140, 141, 162, 164, 167, 180, 195, 235, 236, 237
Village Gate 125
Village Vanguard 121, 193
Vince Giraldi 122
Virgil Thompson 104
voracious reader 173

W

Wainwright House 132
Walter Anderson 99

Walter Foots Thomas 20, 49
Walter Foots Thomas All Stars 20
Walter Page 45
Walter Pages Blue Devils 45
Walter Perkins 73, 233
Warne Marsh 61, 74, 181
Washington, D.C. 1, 2, 3, 4, 5, 10, 11, 12,
    26, 27, 29, 57, 103, 142, 144, 164,
    171, 179, 186, 193, 197
Wayne Andre 74, 234
WBAC-TV 94
WCFL 99
Weekender 161
Wells 27, 40
Wells Music Bar 27
Wes Montgomery 136, 184
Wesleyan College 74
West Africa 128
West Coast 50, 97, 118, 119
West Coast Jazz 119
West Indies 7
West Nyack, New York 135
West Side Broadcast Center 163
Westchester 132, 189
Western Connecticut State College 122
Western European 162
WETA 183
WGOK 99, 114
Wharton Center 191, 192
What To Listen For In Jazz 184
Wheaton High School 26
White House 104, 114, 139, 142, 146, 165
White House State Dinner 104, 114
White Rose 34
White Rose bar 13
Whitney Balliett 143
Willard Jenkins 143
Wild Bill Davis 75
Will Marion Cook 11
Willard Jenkins 143
William Edward Taylor 1, 25
WILLIAM F. LEE III 9
William L. Blake 176
Willie Cook 60, 231

Willie The Lion 2, 21, 27, 61
Willie The Lion Smith 2, 21, 61, 85, 89
Willie Thomas 73
Willis Conover 68
Willis Jackson 66
Wilson Community College 73
Winard Harper 191, 200, 239
WLIB 61, 65, 67, 68, 71, 73, 75, 77, 85,
    91, 92, 95, 110, 127, 181
WLIU 199
Wm C. Brown Co 107, 119, 147, 242
Wm C. Brown Co. 107, 147, 242
WMUB 82, 144, 246
WNEW 73, 75, 78, 92
Wole Soyinka 146
Wolf Trap 80
Women in Jazz Festival 174
Women in Jazz Festival 184
Women in Jazz Series 71
Woody Herman 16, 43, 120, 174, 179
Woody Herman Band 179
World War II 9, 24
Worlds Fair 112
WRVR 102
Wurlitzer electric piano 81
Wymon Kelly 113
Wynton Marsalis 163, 196, 202

X

Xavier University 43

Y

Yale 53, 56, 80, 102, 242
Yale Fellow 102
Yeah Man Club 7
Young Audiences 164
Yusef Lateef 108, 130, 141
YWCA 100

Z

Zeitlin 158
Zoot 20, 35, 42, 44, 58, 223, 225

www.ingramcontent.com/pod-product-compliance
Lightning Source LLC
LaVergne TN
LVHW051457080426
835509LV00017B/1793